MW01105651

This book is published with financial support from the
Chinese Fund for Humanities and Social Sciences (本书获中华社会科学基金资助)

On Social Interests and Conflict:
A Socialist Analysis of
Contemporary China

Wang Weiguang

Translated by Huang Yusheng & Lin Wanping

CHINA SOCIAL SCIENCES PRESS

Paths International Ltd

Contents

Part 3   The Pratice of the Interests Theory

Part 1

THE HISTORY OF INTERESTS

Chapter One

History and Interests

Interests are important social phenomena in human social life and the idea of interests is the reflection of the phenomena in people's minds. Theories and viewpoints about interests constitute an important category in the treasure house of human thought. Therefore, to study interests, it is necessary to look back the history of people's understanding of interests.

I. The Reasonable Speculations of Ancient Theology about the Role of Desire in Ancient Times

"All nations once believed that God governed their history. "[1] In the minds of ancient people, the dominant view of history was of divine nature, which attributes everything to gods, and they believed that gods were the promoter of history and controller of the fate of human society. The formation of this view of history is due to the historical conditions. Under the extremely low level of productive forces, people hardly had any ability of theoretical thinking. Dominated by the powerful forces of nature and bound by the shackles of clan kinship, they couldn't understand natural and social phenomena, so they tried to explain the powerful unknown forces that controlled their fate with supernatural and transcending historical points of view. Just as absurdity often contains reasonable elements, this ancient thinking also contains the embryo of correct understanding. The 18th century Italian thinker Giambattista Vico believes

---

[1] Paul Lafargue, *The Economic Determinism of Karl Marx*, *Studies in the moral, philosophical and Religious Ideas* (Chinese Translation) . SDX Sanlian Book Store, 1963, p. 9.

that the history of the nations all started from myth and fables, which in turn constitute the most ancient history of them. Why are myths and fables the "real and reliable history" of ancient time? The answer is: in the eyes of ancient people, "all things necessary or useful to the human race were deities. "[1] The reason myths are history is because they reflect the social reality of ancient time. The gods for ancient Greeks, for instance, as many as more than thirty thousand, "were related to as many needs of physical, moral, economic or civil life of the earliest times. "[2] For example, the god of agriculture is related to agricultural activities of the Greeks; the god of time reflects the needs of people for the calculation of the seasons and hours in agricultural activities; Dionysus embodied the ancient need for wine, and so on. Ancient peoples' views on gods reflected indirectly their pursuits and objects of worship in real life and their ideas.

In social life, the most familiar emotion of ancient people was their desire, and the most important issues they faced were to make a living and to reproduce, so their strongest desires were appetites for food and sex. Therefore, the "passionate state" stimulated by food or sex are often the most eulogized themes in ancient myths, especially their "love" state aroused by libido, and their desire for "love" are worshiped as god of love. All nations have their own myths singing the passion of "love" and have their religious histories of reproductive totem worship. "Love" is the common feature of origin myths, and also a fulcrum of divine view of history, therefore god of love was worshiped by most nations.

The well-known Greek poet Hesiod sings:

"Verily at the first Chaos came to be, but next wide-bosomed Earth, the ever-sure foundations of all the deathless ones who hold the peaks of snowy Olympus, and dim Tartarus in the depth of the wide-pathed Earth, and Eros (Love), fairest among the deathless gods, who unnerves the limbs and overcomes the mind and wise counsels of all gods and all men within them. "

"Love" is the symbol of beautiful and happy life and the driving force for the development of human society. Love myths with their legendary charm reflect the conjecture of the ancient people—who were unconsciously aware of the role of desires-about the mystery of society and history. Food and sex

---

[1] Giambattista, Vico, *New Science* (Chinese translation), People's Literature Publishing House, 1986, p. 8.

[2] *Ibid.*, p. 96.

arouses desire, passion boils down to sex, and love becomes the driving force of life; this is a rational core of the ancient people's views of history. It can be said that following the guide of needs of the most basic human desires for food and sex is the embryonic form of the "outlook on need" and "outlook on righteousness and benefit" of ancient philosophy.

II. The Democritus' "Necessity" and the "Benefit" of Ancient Chinese Thinkers

With the emergence of private ownership, ordinary people, who hadn't got rid of the shackles of nature forces yet, were slaved by a new alien social force. The suffering laborers, who could not understand the sources of lifelong hardship, and found no way to get out of it, had to resttheir hopes in life on gods. On the other hand, the ruling class also needed this spiritual opium to lull people's will, thus a theoretical form of divine view of history came into being.

Many philosophers of ancient Greek and Rome took ideas as the leverage fulcrum of historical changes. They believe that harmony is the order of the world. The idealist philosopher Plato believes that ideas are real, reliable and primary, suggesting the establishment of a "harmonious" Republic. The Stoic school and the neo-Platonism in ancient Rome believe that gods are origins of all things and social life of man is dominated by fate. The Chinese idealist philosophers who were contemporaries of the ancient Greek philosophers attribute the driving forces of historical development to Heaven, believing that "Heaven disposes." Confucius regards Heaven as the supreme sovereign of nature, society and even human life, "It is only Heaven that is grand!"[1] "Does Heaven speak? The four seasons pursue their courses, and all things are continually being produced."[2]

However, man cannot live without food, clothing or shelter, this is a fact that any person with normal thinking cannot deny. Facingthe realities of life, some brave theory explorers began to realize the true meaning of the mystery of human society. Although Eros (god of love) was the symbol of happy life in the eyes of ancient Greeks, a beautiful life could

---

[1] *The Analects of Confucius*, Chapter Taibo (论语・泰伯).

[2] *The Analects of Confucius*, Chapter Yang huo (论语・阳货).

not do without material guarantee. Fire was the decisive material factor for human life entering into civilized world, so ancient Greek philosopher Heraclitus, the father of dialectics, believes that the ultimate cause of society is fire, who says that "This world, which is the same for all, no one of gods or men has made. But it always was and will be: an ever-living fire." He also believes that "War is the father of all things," genuinely recognized the role played by social conflicts in the historical development of human society. Protagoras, the founder of the ancient Greek Sophism, puts forward the proposition of "Man is the measure of all things," which definitely gets rid of theological view of history. The character in Plato's *Republic*, Thrasymachus, says when refuting Socrates: "In all states there is the same principle of justice, which is the interest of the government; and as the government must be supposed to have power, the only reasonable conclusion is that everywhere there is one principle of justice, which is the interest of the stronger."[1] These words reveal the importance of interests. Democritus, a well-known ancient Greek philosopher who developed the atomistic theory of matter, when explored the origin of society and state, clearly states: "need" plays a decisive role, and "imitation" makes people's need satisfied, and it is driven by imitation and needs that a society is organized. Democritus is one of the earliest thinkers in the history who had discussed needs and interests. The well-known Roman philosopher Epicurus opposes the doctrine of theological goal. Refuting the Stoic submissive moral teachings, he directly attributes the motive of life to the pursuit of the greatest happiness-pleasure, putting human's desires on an important position.

Many thinkers in ancient Greece and Rome began to regard material factors, man and man's needs, interests and passions as the driving forces of history, which is a great start for man to understand his own history, although these ideas are only speculations lacking scientific theoretical arguments.

Similar ideological exploration also existed in Chinese history. Ji Liang, a philosopher in the Spring and Autumn period declares: "People are the masters of gods,"[2] affirming that people are the repose of gods and people are important. Mozi advocates "universal love, mutual benefit," paying attention to the social effects of behavior and takes interests as the basic

[1] Plato, *The Republic* (Chinese Translation), Commercial Press, 1957, p. 25.
[2] *Zuozhuan*, "Sixth Year of King of Huan" (左传，桓公六年).

content of social life. Later Mohists inherited Mozi's idea of benefit, with particular emphasis on utility. They believes that "righteousness" cannot be separated from "benefit," "righteousness is benefit,"[1] and there is no such thing as "righteousness" without "benefit," and they take utility as the standard of all social behaviors. Xunzi, a Philosopher in the Warring States period says: "Now it is the inborn nature of man that when hungry he desires something to eat, that when cold he want warm clothing, that when weary he desires rest—such are qualities inherent in his nature. " "Now man's nature is such that he is born with a love of profit. "[2] He explicitly argues that food, warmth and rest are righteous desires of man. Han Fei further developed Xunzi's idea. He believes that everyone has a motive of self-interests, that all morals, feelings and behaviors of man are for his personal gains, so are the relations between the king and his ministers, between father and son and between masters and workmen. Interests are regarded by him as the motive of all behaviors of man.

Many thinkers after the Spring and Autumn period in Chinese feudal societyalso attached great importance to material interests. Wang Chong, A materialist in the Han Dynasty boldly attacked Confucius' idealist concepts of "benevolence and righteousness. " He says that "Confucius' seeking of official career was not for the Way, but for food only," and he points out that Confucius was hypercritical when advocating righteousness without benefit. He believes that "When their granaries are full, people know what are decorums; When they have enough of food and clothing, they know what is honor," advocating "discarding honesty and retaining food,"[3] and putting man's basic necessities first.

Wang Anshi, a social reformist in the Northern Song Dynasty, holds that when contacting external objects man's emotional desires are aroused, and the proper expression of desire is goodness. The famous thinkers of the Southern Song dynasty Chen Liang and Ye Shi vigorously advocated utilitarianism. Ye Shi believes that virtue and morality cannot be divorced from utility; otherwise, they are nothing but empty words. "The benevolent seeks for righteousness not benefit,

---

① *Mozi*, "The Canon (1)" (墨子·经上).

② *Xunzi*, "Man's Nature Is Evil" (荀子·性恶).

③ *Lun Heng*, "Questioning Confucius" (论衡·问孔).

for the Way not credit—this words seemly melodious but actually inaccurate. "① Li Zhi, a philosopher and fighter against feudal ethics in the late Ming Dynasty, vigorously advocates personal egoism, stressing the importance of material life and putting the basic necessities such as food and clothing above other things. He said: "Clothing and food are the ethics, no other ethics except them. "② In short, many of the ancient Chinese and foreign thinkers to different degrees had recognized the historical role played by interests.

III. Conflicts of Interests Are Behind All Class Struggles

Since the end of the 5th century, Western Europe entered the religiously dominated Dark Ages, during which religion dominated everything and was the spiritual pillar of the feudal system. The theological concept of history was established in this context. Augustine, a great theologian and philosopher in this period declared that God was the creator of social order. Italian Catholic philosopher and theologian Thomas Aquinas believes that God is the first cause of world history, the first mover and the highest purpose. At that time, religion confined the development of all scientific understandings. The thousand-year long dark feudal rule did not end people's scientific exploration. The Renaissance ignited a raging fire in the dark. The thinkers of the Renaissance turned their view of history from God to human beings, and eulogized the strength of man and his desires, and opposed asceticism. They evaluated history with man as the measure and evaluated society with humanity, establishing bourgeois humanistic conception of history. Under this theoretical premise, many Western bourgeois thinkers did some valuable exploration of the historical role of interests. Baruch Spinoza Spinoza, the materialist philosopher of Netherlands in the 17th century contends that, men deceive each other and are a state of hostility with each other in order to preserve their own being. He views egoist needs as the cause of social conflicts. The 17th century British materialist Hobbes holds that,   " each of us lives independently of everyone else, acting only in his or her own, "③ and his

---

① Xixuejiyan, vol. 23 (习学记言·卷二十三).

② *On burning Books (Fanshu)*, Answering Deng Shizu (焚书·答邓石阻).

③ Thomas Hobbes, *Leviathan* in *Translations of Selected Western Famous Works of Ethics* (《西方伦理学名著选译》), vol. 1, Commercial Press, 1964, p. 667.

well-known saying is "Man is a wolf to man." He believes that our animal nature is "self-love" and "self-interest," without regard for others, and this produces the state of war and conflict between men. He views self-interest as leverage of historical turbulences and changes, and attributes the cause of social upheavals to human physical desires.

Why do men kill each other for self-interests like wolves? What is the source of this sin? Some thinkers clearly attribute the source of evil to private ownership. French Enlightenment thinker Rousseau was the first trying to look into the origin of private ownership from the invention of the progress of means of production and technique of farming, he said: "Metallurgy and agriculture were the two arts which produced this great revolution." This gives us a clue to make an in-depth exploration of the formation of the interests from the material conditions of production.

In his book *The System of Nature*, Baron D' Holbach, an 18th century French enlightenment thinker, redefines the role of passions: "Passions are the true counterpoise to passions; then, let him not seek to destroy them, but let him endeavour to direct them; let him balance those which are prejudicial, by those which are useful to society."[①] He associates love with interests and believes that interests are benefits driving people to love or hate something. "Whenever and wherever, only our benefits, our interests... drive us to love or hate something."[②] "For his own interests man must love others, because others are necessary for his own happiness."[③] "To love others... is to incorporate our own interests with the interests of our companions, in order to work for the common interests... virtue is nothing more than the interests of the people composing a society."[④] He links love to interests, and believes that interests are the motives of love and hate.

There was no clear understanding of interests in ancient and medieval philosophy. It is not until the Renaissance that the bourgeoisie raised the issue of interests, which became the central topic of the philosophy of the bourgeoisie, who discussed this issue from the perspective of humanism.

---

① Paul-Henri Thiry, barond' Holbach, *The System of Nature*, vol. 1 (Chinese Translation), Commercial Press, 1964, p. 307.

② Paul-Henri Thiry, barond' Holbach, *Social System*, 1822. Paris edition (Chinese translastion), vol. 1, p. 112.

③ *Ibid*, p. 76.

④ *Ibid* , p. 77.

Humanism uses humanity to oppose divinity, directly explains the issue of interests from the needs of and utility to man, and utility is seen as the synonym of interests. The theory of interests culminated in the French Enlightenment theories and Hegelian philosophy. But the bourgeois theorists often confuse needs with utility, which in fact are two different things. Interests are the expression of needs and utility in certain social relations, which can only be scientifically explained from social relations, instead of humanism.

IV. Interests Constitute the Only Driving Force

The first thinker who recognized the role of social and historical role played by interests isGiambattista Vico, whose great contribution to the view of history is that, starting from the idealistic view of history, he realized class struggle plays a significant role in social development and is the main driving force of history. And he further recognized that the reason why class struggle is a historical necessity is that this struggle takes contradictions of interests as its realistic basis. He believes. " The aristocratic commonwealths keep the wealth within the order of the nobility, for wealth adds to the power of this order"[1]; and religion and laws are nothing but "arms of the nobility to preserve their private interests and rule the plebs. "[2] With these arms, the aristocracy would be able to trap the plebs in the shackles of over taxation. The plebs for their own interests fought against the aristocrats. The aristocrats occupied too much land, putting the plebs in the hunger and humiliation state; and the plebs made tireless efforts to fight for their property rights. Therefore, behind every class struggle, there is a conflict of interests. Vico points out that, for example, the reason the Roman nobility constantly resisted the agrarian laws of the Gracchi, was that they didn' t wish to enrich the plebs. It is clear that, class struggle and legal struggle are nothing more than a continuation of the economic conflict of interests, because the people ultimately concerns only about material wealth and private interests; people pay attention to legal and political issues only when they involve in

[1] Giambattista Vico, *New Sciences* (Chinese translation), People's Literature Publishing House, 1986, p. 117.

[2] Arshipipa, "Economy in Vico's System" in Giorgio Tagliacozzo, ed. *Vico: Past and present.* vol. 1, Renwen Publishing House (人文出版社), 1981. p. 148.

their own private interests. Here Vico notes that economic contradictions constitute the premise of class struggle.

A famous scholar of the early 18th century, Bernard Mandeville set forth the view of teleological egoism, and called the law of "private vice, public benefits" as the "invisible hand." He believes that people's pursuit of well-being, comfort, luxury and enjoyment of life, are all generated from natural desires. They do everything for their own sake, never really taking into account of the interests of others. Man's various so-called "immoral behaviors" out of egoist motivation to the whole society or the public interests is, in fact, not only harmless but beneficial. The pursuit of a life of luxury, for example, will bring benefit to the society, because needs and desires for extravagant life will stimulate people's diligence and enthusiasm for work, which is the law of the "invisible hand" at work.

The philosopher who really put the issue of interests to the most important position in society is Claude Adrien Helvétius, an 18th-century French materialists. He believes that interests constitute the only factor that works universally in social life, and they are the basis of social life, the only and universally working driving forces of social development as well as the root of social contradictions. All intricacies of social phenomena can be explained with interests. In his view, the most vital defect of theological concept of history is that it does not recognize the role of interests in man's life.

Helvetius attempted to "explain the social and intellectual development of man by his material needs. "[1] He regarded interests as the driving force of the most basic activity of mankind—material production activities. He believes that the primary interest of man is to eat to satisfy his hunger and to wear clothes to keep himself warm. It is the pursuit of such interests that drives people to unite to fight against nature and get materials for survival. Man "in order to get clothing.... and to feed himself and his family, in short, in order to enjoy the pleasure associated with the satisfaction of physical needs, craftsmen and farmers think, imagine and work. "[2] To avoid starvation and to look for food, people invent and improve tools. Helvetius takes the needs of material interests as the purpose

---

[1]   G. V. Plehanov, *The Development of the Monist View of Hitory* (Chinese translation), SDX Sanlian Book Store, 1961, p. 12

[2]   *French Philosophy in the 18th Century* (十八世纪法国哲学), Commercial Press, 1963, p. 496

and intrinsic motive for labor. He believes that the whole of sciences and culture is a product of these needs, the only motivation for man's activity. He also attributes the artistic creation and scientific invention to interests. Helvetius stressed the decisive role of the "interests" for spirit, and believes that interests determine all aspects of social life, including people's thoughts, feelings, morals, politics, culture, arts and so on. He attributes political, ideological and moral disagreements to differences in interests. He believes that material interests play a decisive role in people's spiritual life, because interests dominate all our judgments. [1] "Men are not cruel and perfidious, but carried away by their own interest."[2] Man consults only his own interests. Differences of opinions come from differences of interests. He asserts that only by this way can we understand the striking differences of views, because these differences completely lie in the differences of their interests. [3]He said that interests constitute "an all-powerful sorcerer, who changes shape of any object in the eyes of all beings."[4] He believes that at any time, any place, and either morally or in understanding, self-interest dominates the judgment of an individual, and public interests dominate the judgment of a nation. Of these views Plehanov commented: "In no less degree did his views threaten the view, so widely held in the eighteenth century, that the world is governed by *public opinion*. We have already seen that, according to Helvetius, men's opinions are dictated by their interests; we have also seen that the latter do not depend on the human will."[5] But Helvetius ultimately believes that the world is governed by the opinion of geniuses. Helvetius looks into the origin of human society from realistic interests. He believes that public interests are formed because of the needs of men's struggle against the hostile forces of nature, which prompted people to unite and help each other. "In order to feed themselves and

---

① *French Philosophy in the 18ᵗʰ Century* (十八世纪法国哲学), Commercial Press, 1963, p. 457.

② Claude-Andrien Helvetius, *De l'esprit*, vol. 1, 1822, p. 117.

③ *French Philosophy in the 18ᵗʰ Century* (十八世纪法国哲学), Commercial Press, 1963, p. 458.

④ *Ibid*, p. 460.

⑤ G. V. Plehanov, *Essays on the History of Materialism* (唯物主义史论丛), (Chinese translation) SDX Book Store, 1961, pp. 102—103.

reduce their own fear of the lions and tigers, they unite with others. "①
He divided interests into self-interests and public interests, and holds that
public interests underlie the formation of human society. In his view,
political facilities such as state and laws are produced based on the
interests of the people, and will change with the change of people's
interests. He said that, to make a living, people must do farming. For
this, the harvest must belong to the farmers. So the citizens make
agreements and laws. After the law is formulated, there must be some
people designated to enforce them, these people are the first officials. ②He
further explained the cause of contradictions and conflicts between different
groups, classes and strata with interests. In his opinion, different social
groups or strata have their different interests and conflicts between them are
nothing but conflicts of interests. The uprising of the poor, the reform of
the state, the domestic and foreign policies of the rulers and foreign wars,
etc., are all related to interests. Interests are the causes of contradictions
and struggles of different social classes and groups, as well as the causes
of all historical events, small or big. He realized that, there are conflicts
of interests between different levels of citizen groups, which he called
classes. He also believes that there are struggles between egoist interests
(private interests) and public interests, struggles constituting the
foundation of people's "moral" or "immoral" behaviors.

In short, Helvetius' doctrine of interests is the most creative part of his
social view of history. Proceeding from man's physical sensibility, he
reveals man's instinct of "self-love," which he believes is the underlying
basis of people's behavior, because man with feelings naturally pursues
things that make him happy, so he logically concluded that man's all
activities are built on the basis of self interests. ③So, "interest is the sole
motive of human action. "④ He maintains that "if the physical universe be
subject to the laws of motion, the moral universe is equally so to those of
interest. "⑤ Helvetius clearly recognized the social law that interests

---

① G. V. Plehanov, *Essays on the History of Materialism* (唯物主义史论丛),
(Chinese translation) SDX Book Store, 1961, pp. p. 496.

② *Ibid*, p. 471.

③ *New Caxton Encyclopedia*, vol. 9, Caxton Pub. Co. Ltd, 1977, p. 2987.

④ *French Philosophy in the 18th Century* (十八世纪法国哲学), Commercial Press,
1963, p. 537.

⑤ *Ibid*, p. 460

govern people's social life. His axiom, "The waters never remount to their source, nor man against the rapid current of his interest,"① indicates that the law of interest is regarded by him as an irresistible objective law.

Plekhanov spoke highly of Helvetius' bold exploration of social mystery. He said that Helvetius "made an attempt of the highest interest, still not assessed at its true value, to explain the social and intellectual development of man by *his material needs.* This attempt ended, and for many reasons could not but end, in failure. But it remained a testament, as it were, for those thinkers of the following century who might wish to continue the work of the French materialists. "② What then, does Helvetius' "testament" tell us? It tells us that interests are the driving forces of all acts, including mental acts of individuals and classes, the sources of wars, conflicts, disputes, and basis of social life. We must look for the answer of the mystery of history from the perspective of interests. But because Helvetius' theory of interests is based on the sensualism of intuitive materialism, he believes that man's nature is to "pursue pleasure and avoid pain" and "self-love. " He explains the importance of interests and look for the driving forces of social development from the abstract nature of man and man's physical needs. He believes that social development must depend on the expansion of people's physical needs, but he failed to recognize social nature of man's needs as well as the essence of economic relations of interests, which leads to the ultimate failure of his attempt. For example, he believes that man's needs are identical in terms of quality, the differences lie only in quantity. So the expansion of needs relies on the increase of population, therefore, the proliferation of the population becomes the direct cause of social development. He deduced man's needs from man's physical sensibility and then the real cause of social development, i. e. , the proliferation of population, and based on this established his view of history. According to historical materialism, needs first of all are social, rather than physical. Social mode of production plays a restrictive role on the needs of man; Man's material needs are the material cause for man engaging in production activities and the first premise of the survival of human society, but these needs are restricted by social mode of production. Helvetius'

---

① Claude-Andrien Helvetius, *A Treatise on Man* (Russian Edition), 1938, p. 355.

② G. V. Plehanov, *The Development of the Monist View of Hitory* (Chinese translation), SDX Sanlian Bookstore, 1961, p. 12

viewpoints of needs and interests remain largely in the scope of subjective will, and his ignorance of the restraining role of material means of production ultimately lead to the failure of his idealism.

After Helvetius, British classical economistAdam Smith, starting from man's natural inclinations towards self-interest, established the doctrines of division of labor and exchange and thus developed his economic theory, which brings out the issue of interests. He believes that man is selfish in nature, and man's motive in economic activities is dominated by "self-interests." Self-interests, on which the theories of division of labor and exchange are based, lead to the differences and contradictions of interests. He said: "This division of labor is. . . a certain propensity in human nature which has in view no such extensive utility; the propensity to truck, barter, and exchange one thing for another. "[1] This understanding, inspiring people to analyze the issue of interests from economic relations, provides a revelation for later scholars to correct Helvetius' defects. Starting from the theory of "self-interests", Smith demonstrated that man's motive of diligence and avarice of passion guide him to the production of the necessities of life, so as to provide the conditions for human reproduction, which explains the motivation of man's engagement in social production. In analyzing the relationship between self and public interests of society, both Adam Smith and his contemporary Jean Charles Léonard de Sismondi tried to demonstrate the contradictions and identity of self and public interests. Smith found that in exchange relationship, it is possible to meet the self-interests of both sides; likewise, self and public interests can be consistent. Sismondi believes that Smith's conclusion is based on two ideas: first, each knows his own interest better than an ignorant or a careless government ever can, and second, the sum of the interests of each equals the interests of all. Sismondi holds that the identity of self and general interests cannot explain all social phenomena in a civilized society except the areas of production and exchange. Then what's the reason? He believes that the reason lies in the contradictions between private and general interests in the unequal distribution of property among men and the resulting unequal strength of the contracting parties. He argues that, when everyone's interests are constrained by the interests of other members of the society,

---

① Adam Smith, *An Inquiry into the Nature and Causes of the Wealth of Nations* (Chinese translation), Commercial Press, 1979, pp. 14—16.

they will, in fact, demonstrate as general interests; but when everyone tries to achieve the purpose of increasing his own property for his own interests by means of damaging the interests of others, it is not resisted by the same moral strength, so it benefits the powerful who plunders and forces the weak to concede. The distribution system in a civilized society is realized by the violence of the strong and the retreat of the weak to survive, so contradictions between private and the general interests in a society are always resolved by the forcible seizure of the rich and the sacrifice of the poor. Therefore, the private interests of the rich in a civilized society is of forcible gains, and individual interests often lead him to the pursuit of violations of the interests of the overwhelming majority of people, even in the final analysis, the violation of the interests of all mankind.

British utilitarian Jeremy Bentham further developed the view of Helvetius and others, establishing a bourgeois utilitarian system of thought. He advocated private interests, although he recognized the identity of private and public interests. He insists that public interests are just the sum of individual interests, and it is the private interests that really exist.

" Individual interests must be subordinate to the interests of society... But what does that mean? Isn't it that everyone, like others, constitutes a part of the society? The social interests personified by you is just a kind of abstract, it is nothing but the sum of individual interests... if it is recognized that it is a good thing to sacrifice one person's happiness for the increase of happiness of others, then isn' t it better to sacrifice the happiness of the second person, the third, even the countless number of people? ... Personal interest is the sole practical interest. "①

In fact, since the 18th century the bourgeois thinkers have formed a set of relatively systematic theories of interests, which justify man's material desires and the historical role of material interests. This is undoubtedly a heavy blow to the idealist as well as theologian views of history. The interest theories of the bourgeois thinkers emphasize the individual self-interests and prettify the mercenary nature of bourgeoisie, reflecting the essence of the interests and needs of the bourgeoisie of the 18th century. Due to historical and class limitations, these theories ultimately fall into the morass of idealism.

---

① *The Rationale of Punishment and Reward*, vol. 2, 1826 (Paris edition), pp. 229—230.

V. Man's Desires Are the Leverage of the Development of History

The three well-known utopian socialists, Robert Owen, Saint-Simon and Fourier, and historians of the French Restoration period, including Thierry, (Jacques-Nicolas) Augustin, Adolphe Thiers, François Mignet and others, stepped forward on the basis of Helvetius, nearly drawing the correct conclusion of historical materialism about the dynamic role of interests. Fourier believes that man's passions constitute the basis of social development. He declared that the law of social movements is the law of passion gravity, and the contradiction between man's passions and material wealth promotes the development of society. The standard for measuring good or bad of a society is to see whether it meets the requirements of passions of its people. Although Fourier didn't clearly interpret passions as the material interests of historical materialism, he made a speculation about the social and historical role of man's needs and interests.

The 19th century utopian socialists also tried to analyze the roots of social development from production and economic reasons. They believe that the basis of historical development of human society is private ownership, which is the root of all evils, and that the development of production is the fundamental cause of social development. They argue that the motives of human activities are passions and needs. And from this they stepped further to interests, maintaining that contradictions of social interests cause class struggle, which constitutes the driving force of the development of human society. The reason they exceed Helvetius is that when analyzing the formation of human passions, needs and interests, they tried to explain the development of people's material life and activities, therefore touched the real cause of class struggle and the great historical role of it. Engels points out, "The whole previous view of history was based on the conception that the ultimate causes of all historical changes are to be looked for in the changing ideas of human beings, and that of all historical changes political changes are the most important and dominate the whole of history. But the question was not asked as to whence the ideas come into men's minds and what the driving causes of the political changes are. Only upon the newer school of French, and partly also of English, historians had the conviction forced itself that, since the Middle Ages at least, the driving force in European history was the struggle of the developing bourgeoisie with the feudal aristocracy for social and political domination. "① These historians asked: If the class struggle of the mass is the driving force of historical development, then, what prompts them to rise to struggle? Or what's the purpose of their struggle? Their answer is material interests. According to Thierry, man's interests produce needs and needs in turn stimulate them to act and to create causes and history. "Both sides of the war are for these real interests. "② The masses act on their own interests, and interests are the driving forces and sources. Mignet stated that, changes involve interests, interests form political parties, and political parties bring about struggles. Class struggle is but an aspect of interests.

What is the basis of interests? According to them, property relationsembody interests and economic benefits will result in class struggles, which determine a nation's political system. The property relations discussed by the 19th century French utopian socialists and the French Restoration period historians belong to the field of legal rights relations. These relations were thought must first be established by certain legal right system, and behind the property relations there should be some more fundamental things. However, they eventually attempted to use the innate desire of the strong to conquer the weak to explain property relations, thus again back to the old abstract theory of human nature.

VI. Selfish Desires Are the Direct Driving Forces of History

Hegel, the representative of German classical philosophy, fully demonstrated the historical role of interests from the perspective of dialectical idealism. According to Hegel, the spirit of liberty is a historical and substantial force, whereas the desires and enthusiasm generated by selfishness are the driving forces of phenomenon. He said: "The first glance at History convinces us that the actions of men proceed from their needs, their passions, their characters and talents; and impresses us with the belief that such needs, passions and interests are the sole springs

---

① *Selected Works of Marx and Engels*, vol. 3, People's Publishing House, 1995, p. 334.

② *Selected Works of Plekhanov*, vol. 2 SDX Sanlian Bookstore, 1961, p. 737.

of action. . . " ① He does not believe the empty words such as love, righteousness, virtue, sentiment. "Nothing great in the world has been accomplished without passion. " "Passions, private aims, the satisfaction of selfish desires, are the most effective springs of action. " " These natural impulses have a more direct influence over man than the artificial and tedious discipline that tends to order and self-restraint, law and morality. " ② To Hegel, the individual is a special existence, his power of activity comes from his will, and the will of the individual is associated with his selfish desires. Self-interested desire can inspire man's passion and impulse. He believes that "Passion, it is true, is not quite the suitable word for what I wish to express. I mean here nothing more than the human activity as resulting from private interests—special, or if you will, self seeking designs. " ③ Obviously, private interests, or the enthusiasm out of selfish desire is the direct force for people to engage in activities. Hegel believes that, egoism and impulse, of course, are acts of evil, but evil has been the lever of historical development. Engels said, "With Hegel, evil is the form in which the motive force of historical development presents itself. . . it is precisely the wicked passions of man—greed and lust for power—which, since the emergence of class antagonisms, serve as levers of historical development. " ④ Hegel takes selfish desires as the direct cause of the development of history. Selfish, evil desires are actually private interests. Hegel believes that it is interests and needs that prompt people to work, and work is the basis to meet human needs and to maintain the basis of the historical development. He believes that, if needs are just subjective link, labor and labor tools are more realistic. It is labor man carried out with certain instruments that constitute the basis of meeting human needs and maintaining historical development. According to Marx and Engels, Hegel's view on needs, self-interest and labor are obviously close to the viewpoint of historical materialism.

Marx believes that "Passion is the essential power of man energetically

---

① Geog Wihelm Hegel, *Philosophy of History* (Chinese translation), 1963, pp. 58—59.

② *Ibid*, p. 59

③ Geog Wihelm Hegel, *Philosophy of History* (Chinese translation), 1963, p. 62

④ *Selected Works of Marx and Engels*, vol. 3, People's Publishing House, 1995, p. 237.

bent on its object. "① Hegel also expounded the dynamic role of evil desires in the course of history. Engels affirmed it by saying that "From its first day to this, sheer greed was the driving spirit of civilization; wealth... was its one and final aim. "② It can be seen that passions, enthusiasm and aims stimulated by certain material interests are indispensable driving forces for historical changes. If man loses his interest of and has no concern on external things or desire of pursuit, he will lose vitality of rejuvenation and the society will loses its momentum of progress.

---

① *Collected Works of Marx and Engels*, vol. 42, People's Publishing House, 1979, p. 169.

② *Selected Works of Marx and Engels*, vol. 4, People's Publishing House, 1995, p. 177.

Chapter Two

Marxism and the Issue of Interests

Interest is an issue not only of practical importance in real life, but also of theoretic significance in philosophy. For Marx and Engels, it is the issue of material interests in realities that prompted them to focus on studying economic relations and ultimately created historical materialism, on the basis of which, they correctly expounded the nature, characteristics and historical role of interests and came to the following conclusions, among others: pursuing interests is the drive of all social activities of human beings; interest disputes constitute the material source of class struggle; interest conflict serves as a driving force of social development; interest is the basis of and determinant of ideas, and it determines and dominates political power and political activities; material relations of production underlie social basis and essence of interests. Marx and Engels scientifically defined the category of interests and set up the Marxist theory of interests. To fully understand interests, it is necessary to look back its theoretic evolution in classic Marxist works and review the Marxist theory of interests.

I. The Formation of Historical Materialism and Marxist Theory of Interests

Interests can been discussed from the angle of either historical materialism or historical idealism. This indicates that, the key lies not in whether the historical role of interests is recognized or not, but in under what premise it is recognized. In studying the material interest motivation of human activities, achievements in psychological and biological researches should be assimilated to help our understanding; but it is not enough to expound passions, desires and interests simply from the angle of biological and physiological sensationalism and regard it as perceptual, abstract and ever-lasting biological category. It is Marx and Engels who have discovered the essence and historical role of interests and revealed the real driving force of history; before them, neither the old contemplative materialism nor dialectical idealism could properly deal with the issue or give a scientific answer to it.

When he was young, Karl Marx has been a Young Hegelian, philosophically leaning towards Hegelian idealism. In the year 1842—43 after graduating from university, Marx took part in real social struggles and encountered the issue of material interests as editor of *RheinischeZeitung*. In "Preface to a Contribution to the Critique of *Political Economy*" written in 1859, Marx says that the reason for his turning from studying jurisprudence to studying economic issues is to express his opinion on the issue of "material interests". "I studied jurisprudence. . . as editor of the *RheinischeZeitung*, I first found myself in the embarrassing position of having to discuss what is known as material interests. "① Therefore he questioned his philosophic belief and expressed his different opinion on material interests. In Hegelian philosophy, state is the manifestation of absolute idea and Kingdom of Prussia is the supreme manifestation of absolute idea. Young Marx demonstrated on the basis Hegel's dialectics that Kingdom of Prussia was not the perfect manifestation of absolute idea; instead, it needed further development and transformation. However, real life in the time of *RheinischeZeitung*, especially the stark reality of material interests, greatly shook Marx's belief in the Hegelian philosophy and put him into a state of theoretical confusion and ideological bewilderment, which urged Marx to make a critical reflection on his previous philosophic ideas and to probe into new theoretical issues. It is this encounter with and study of material interests that led Marx to the way of exploring historical materialism and consequently gave birth to the historical materialistic theory of interests.

In his first article published on *RheinischeZeitung* in April 1842, Marx had already taken note of the material interests behind social estates. He noticed that, each member of the provincial parliament stood for a class and interests functioned behind them. What representatives of the princely and urban estates defended were private interests and only representatives of the peasant estate defended for the common interests of the peasants and

---

① *Selected Works of Marx and Engels*, vol. 2, People's Publishing House, 1995, p. 31.

for the benefit and aspiration of the oppressed. ①

In the "Debates on the Law on Thefts of Wood", Marx further associated opposite and different social groups with the opposition and differences in their material interests and therefore found the role of material interests in social life. In order to defend the interests of the exploiters, the German feudal ruling class at the time declared those who picked up dead branches guilty of stealing wood. Marx firmly stood behind the poor by denouncing privilege of the ruler and calling for keeping such right of the people. Marx went beyond the spiritual field to discuss the issue of material interests. He noticed the decisive role of economic interests of wood occupants on the state, laws and the legislators. He believed that the state and laws were used to protect private interests of the exploiting class and that it was the princely and landlord estates who controlled the state and laws. Marx wrote: "interest is keen-sighted." "a world full of dangers, precisely because it is the world not of a single interest but of many interests. "②

In the late period of his work in *RheinischeZeitung*, Marx had a deeper understanding of the decisive role of objective circumstances that are independent of man's will, and he further associate such circumstances with interests of the exploiting class. He wrote: "In investigating a situation concerning *the state* one is all too easily tempted to overlook the objective nature of the circumstances and to explain everything by the will of the persons concerned. However, there are circumstanceswhich determine the actions of private persons and individual authorities, and which are as independent of them as the method of breathing." There was "the effect" in "circumstances where at first glance only individuals seem to be acting. "③ Of course, Marx had not yet clearly stated that such circumstances are precisely economic relations.

It was the issues concerning material interests that drove Marx to study economic relations, which further led him to clarify the category of relations of production and finally set up a theoretical system of historical materialism, through which, the issue of the nature and historical role of interests were settled, and real driving force of historical development was

---

① *Collected Works of Marx and Engels*, vol. 1, People's Publishing House, 1956, pp. 35—96.

② *Ibid*, pp. 164—165.

③ Ibid. , p. 216.

found.

Similarly, it is the issue of material interests that prompted young Engels to turn to materialism and communism. In November 1842, after investigating the British social and economic situation in Manchester, Engels discovered the dominant role of economic interests in social life and came to the conclusion that the fundamental cause of class contradictions is material interests. During the period, the issue of material interests was a focus of Engels' theoretical research, which helped him to explore historical materialism with Marx and consequently formulated the Marxist theory of interests.

Interests are readily understandable forpeople, even children, with slight life experience. As a matter of fact, no one can bypass interests in doing anything in his life. Lenin said that interests "are the most sensitive nerve of public life. "[1] People usually associate interests with necessities of life, such as money, commodities, property, and so on. But they know neither the reason why these things are manifestation of interests, nor the formation and nature of interests; although they know that interests are closely related to everyone's life, they don't know the historical role of interests. Even many thinkers who put interests in the first place of social life cannot thoroughly explain the essence, origin, nature, structure, mechanism of realization, operation laws and historical role and other things of interests.

Before the emergence of the Marxist philosophy, the realm of social history had exclusively been the hereditary realm of idealism. It is anti-scientificnature is obvious: Ituses man's thought, motivation and will, in other words, notions, "absolute idea" and abstract humanity to explain the development of history and social phenomena. Although a few insightful materialists proposed some valuable ideas, they had only touched upon the general and superficial phenomenon of history, and many absurd and self-contradictory elements mixed with their correct opinions. About this, Engels wrote: "in the realm of history the old materialism becomes untrue to itself because it takes the ideal driving forces which operate there as ultimate causes, instead of investigating what is behind them, what are the driving forces of these driving forces. "[2] Through summarizing the

---

[1] *Collected Works of Lenin*, vol. 16, People's Publishing House, 1988, p. 136.

[2] *Selected Works of Marx and Engels*, vol. 4. People's Publishing House, 1995, p. 248.

genius arguments put forward by his predecessors in exploring the mystery of human society, Marx for the first time solved the problem of the relation between social being and social consciousness, an issue of fundamental significance to the philosophical conception of human history, and thus found the material foundation for understanding the society—ensemble of relations of production. On this basis, he constructed the theoretic edifice of historical materialism, with which he correctly explained the real driving forces for the development of history. Since production and reproduction of material means are the foundation and precondition of social being, then, for what purpose do people produce? Since the contradictory movements of productive forces and relations of production and that of superstructure and economic basis are the basic lawsgoverning the historical development of human society, what, then are the motives for people to defend or change the relations of production and superstructure that don't correspond to the development of productive forces and to make social reform or even social revolution? Since in class societies, class struggles are the direct driving forces of social development, what, then, is the cause of confrontation and/or connection between various classes and of wars with or without bloodshed? "... the old idealist conception of history, which was not yet dislodged knew nothing of class struggles based upon economic interests, knew nothing of economic interests; production and all economic relations appeared in it only as incidental, subordinate elements in the ' history of civilization. ' "① To answer the questions above, we must study the driving forces of people's historical activities—material interests. Interest is the objective driving force that sets man into conscious action to transform the objective world so as to meet their own needs of existence and development, and it is an important category inMarxist historical materialism.

II. Scientific Arguments of Marx and Engels on the Category of Interests

Marx and Engels discussed material interests in many of their

---

① *Selected Works of Marx and Engels*, vol. 3. People's Publishing House, 1995, p. 365.

works. They used the term " materielleinteressen " in German, an equivalent to the English phrase "material interests," which appeared many times in their works along with the term " interests " . They discussed the category of interests scientifically on the basis of historical materialism in their works such as *The Holy Family*, *Manifesto to the Communist Party*, *Preface to a Contribution to the Critique of PoliticalEconomy*, *The German Ideology*, *Capital*, *Economic Manuscripts* (*1857—1858*) , *Theories of Surplus Value*, *Anti-Duhring*, *The Origin of the Family*, *Private Ownership and the State.*

First, in *The Holy Family*, by analyzing the capitalist relations of production, Marx and Engels developed in a concrete way their cognition of interests in the capitalist society, believing that private interests are the manifestation of social relations under private ownership, on the basis of which they further made a generalized understanding of interest as a category, stating: "just as the ancient state had slavery as its natural basis, the modern state has as its natural basis civil society and the man of civil society, i. e. , the independent man linked with other men only by the ties of private interest and unconscious natural necessity, the slave of labor for gain and of his own as well as other men's selfish need. "[1] Here, civil society refers to the economic basis of a society, i. e. ensemble of economic relations in the society; man of civil society refers to man living in given economic relations. According to Marx and Engels, the basis of a capitalist state is its economic basis of the society—i. e. ensemble of economic relations—and men living in a given economic relations. Marx and Engels further explained that, men living in a given economic relations means men who linked with each other by the ties of private interests and historical necessity independent of man's will. Therefore, relation of private interests in the capitalist society is the manifestation of its social economic relations.

Second, in the chapter "Capital" *of Economic Manuscripts* (*1857— 1858*) , Marx discussed the interest relations through relations between individuals and explained the category of interests on the basis of economic relations by demonstrating that general relations of commodity exchange contain interest contradiction. Firstly, he analyzed the contradiction between individual interests and that between personally and common

---

[1] *Collected Works of Marx and Engels*, vol. 2, People's Publishing House, 1957, p. 145.

interests contained in general relations of commodity exchange. In the market place, both parties of the exchange care for their personal interests and what they try to realize are their own self-seeking interests. Although an individual's personal interests are contradictory to that of others, the whole process of exchange is meant to realize common interests. For instance, if party A needs bread and party B needs clothes, party A exchanges money with clothes to buy bread and party B exchanges money with bread to buy clothes, then both parties meet their personal interests through exchanges, thereby they realize their common interests. Marx wrote: "the common interest which appears as the motive of the act as a whole is recognized as a fact by both sides; but, as such, it is not the motive, but rather proceeds, as it were, behind the back of these self-reflected particular interests, behind the back of one individual's interest in opposition to that of the other." "The common interest exists only in the duality, many-sidedness, and autonomous development of the exchanges between self-seeking interests. The general interest is precisely the generality of self-seeking interests."[1] Interest in essence embodies social economic relations of exchange.

Third, in *Capital and Theories of Surplus Value*, Marx and Engels scientifically confirmed the category of interests from the angle of social relations of production and strictly distinguished the connotation of interest from that of utility. In Capital, they explained the nature of interest by analyzing the duality of commodity, i. e. a unity of opposite between use value and exchange value contained in a commodity. They argued that, use value is the usefulness of a commodity, i. e. the natural utility contained in the commodity itself; on the other hand, exchange value refers to the labor time socially necessary embodied in the commodity, which reflects the relation of product exchange between people. Such relation of exchange is the interest relation arising among people due to the distribution of products. Interest and utility are scientifically differentiated in that utility is linked to use value and interest to exchange value. In this way they actually revealed the nature of interest as manifestation of social economic relations.

Fourth, in *Capital*, *Theories of Surplus Value and Economic Manuscripts* (*1857—1858*), through analyzing interest contradiction and interest

---

[1]   *Collected Works of Marx and Engels*, vol. 46a, People's Publishing House, 1979, pp. 196—197.

structure in the capitalist society, Marx and Engels pointed out that interest contradiction in the capitalist society manifests itself in a concentrated way as class contradiction. They concluded that, in the process of production, circulation, distribution and consumption and in the conducts of exchange in capitalist society, interest contradiction between the two sides of exchange unfolds into three layers. The first layer is the contradiction between the proletariat and the bourgeoisie, which is manifested in the exploiting of surplus value of the proletarians by the bourgeois. The second layer is the contradiction within the proletarians in that dissension on interests often takes place among laborers themselves because of competition of employment and wages. The third layer is the contradiction within the bourgeois in that intensive competition for more profits often takes place among the capitalists, groups of capitalists, and capitalist countries. The three layers of interest contradictions constitute a complicated interest structure, in which class contradiction between the proletariat and the bourgeoisie is the most central one. According to them, after seizing power, the bourgeoisie would inevitably set its interests as common interests of the state; once contradiction between the proletariat and the bourgeoisie becomes sharp enough and threatens the basic system of the capitalist society, the capitalists would unite to defend their common interests.

Fifth, in *Manifesto to the Communist Party*, Marx and Engels pointed out that, the proletariat had no private interest of its own and its class interest is nothing but the common interest of all mankind—aiming to ultimately liberate all people and on the basis of productivity development realize the communist society for the common interests of all by abolishing the bourgeois private ownership and interest contradiction brought about by commodity exchange. They emphasized that the communists are against the tendency of pursuing momentary interests of the working class while neglecting the long-term interests; at the same time they were also against the tendency of gabbing glorious ideal of communism without any action to fight for momentary interests of the working class. "The Communists fight for the attainment of the immediate aims, for the enforcement of the momentary interests of the working class; but in the movement of the present, they also represent and take care of the future of that movement. "[1]

---

[1] *Selected Works of Marx and Engels*, vol. 1, People's Publishing House, 1995, p. 306.

Sixth, in *Capital*, *The German Ideology*, *Anti-Duhring*, *The Origin of the Family*, *Private ownership and the State* Marx and Engels used historical materialism and its methodology to expound the process of development between individual interests and common interests. According to them, at very beginning in the primitive communes of the primitive society, there weresome common interests and also individual interests that were contradictory to the common interests, thereby it was necessary to set up institutions as deputies of common interests to protect the common interests. With the increase of interest conflicts, such institutions got more and more imperative, functional and independent. Since position of the institutions could only be assumed by individuals, such institutions consequently evolved into authoritiesexercising political control over the society, and public servants became master of the society and then ruling class and state came into being. Different forms of state in history were nothing but various development forms of common interests. [1] In *The German Ideology*, Marx and Engels asserted that: "throughout history the 'general interest' is created by individuals who are defined as 'private persons'". [2] In the circumstances of private ownership, personal interests developed into common interests and indeed class interests. "Personal interests always develop, against the will of individuals, into class interests, into common interests that acquire independent existence in relation to the individuals, and in their independence assume the form of general interests, as such they come into contradiction with the actual individuals." [3] Once common interests come into existence independently as class interests, "the personal behavior of the individual is bound to be objectified, estranged, and at the same time exists as a power independent of him and without him, created by intercourse, and is transformed into social relations, into a series of powers which determine and subordinate the individual..." [4] Class interests determine individuals' behavior. Once common interests come into being, it will be different from personal interests so that common interests of the members of a class will contradict with their personal interests, although such contradiction is different from

---

[1] *Collected Works of Marx and Engels*, vol. 3, People's Publishing House, 1960, pp. 522—523.

[2] *Ibid*, pp. 275—276.

[3] *Ibid*, p. 273.

[4] *Ibid.*

the contradiction between different classes and can be reconciled. "This contradiction is only a seemingone because one side of it, what is called the 'general interest,' is constantly being produced by the other side, private interest, and in relation to the latter it is by no means an independent force with an independent history—so that this contradiction is in practice constantly destroyed and reproduced. "① In capitalist system, common interests are the special bourgeois interests. In *The Origin of the Family, Private ownership and the State*, they argued that, the fundamental interest of the working class is to ultimately build on the basis of productivity development a society in which both individual interests and common interests are in complete accord by abolishing capitalist private ownership and contradiction between individual interests and common interests brought about by commodity exchange. The working class has no private interest of their own, whose fundamental interest is the common interest of all people disregarding ethic differences. After the working class seizes power, there will be no confrontation between individual interests and common interests. Since in the circumstance of private ownership, common interests and individual interests are more or less in conflict, they will not merge into one until the communist society with the diminishing of state. Engels answered this question by quotingMorgan's judgment of civilization: "The time will come... The interests of society are paramount to individual interests, and the two must be brought into just and harmonious relations. "②

Seventh, in *The German Ideology*, Marx and Engels argued that division of labor results in private ownership, and thereby separation and opposition of interests and consequently the arising of state; interest is the actual relation of mutual interdependence of individuals. In this way they expounded the nature of interests and causes of interest contradiction. They wrote: "The division of labor inside a nation leads at first to the separation of industrial and commercial from agricultural labor, and hence to the separation of town and country and to the conflict of their

---

① *Collected Works of Marx and Engels*, vol. 3, People's Publishing House, 1960, p. 276.

② *Selected Works of Marx and Engels*, vol. 4, People's Publishing House, 1995, p. 179.

interests. "① They believed that division of labor further leads to the conflict between individual interests and common interests. "Further, the division of labor implies the contradiction between the interest of the separate individual or the individual family and the communal interest of all individuals who have intercourse with one another. "② "This communal interest does not exist merely in the imagination... but first of all in reality, as the mutual interdependence of the individuals among whom the labor is divided. "③ Interest is the social relation of mutual interdependence of individuals and lies in the first of it is economic relation. They further expounded the emergence of state and its nature, "and out of this very contradiction between the interest of the individual and that of the community the latter takes an independent form as the State. "④ They believed that, the actual basis for the emergence and existence of the State is the link in division of labor and the relation of interests and class generated thereupon; and that the State is nothing but an illusory community, a tool of class ruling in essence. "Every class which is struggling for mastery, even when its domination, as is the case with the proletariat, postulates the abolition of the old form of society in its entirety and of domination itself, must first conquer for itself political power in order to represent its interest in turn as the general interest, which in the first moment it is forced to do. "⑤

Eighth, in the above mentioned works, when discussing the issue of interests, Marx and Engels clearly stated the decisive role of material interests and distinguished the natural side fromthe social side of interest, providing us with a scientific method of research in understanding interests. In *The German Ideology*, they stated that in antiquity, people were held together by material relations and interests. They further stated: "these theoretical ideas of the bourgeoisie had as their basis material interests and a will that was conditioned and determined by the material relations of production. "⑥

---

① *Selected Works of Marx and Engels*, vol. 1, People's Publishing House, 1995, p. 68.

② *Ibid*, p. 84.

③ *Ibid.*

④ Ibid. , p. 68.

⑤ *Ibid* , pp. 84—85.

⑥ *Collected Works of Marx and Engels*, vol. 3, People's Publishing House, 1960, p. 213.

They clear noted the driving role of material interests in the development of production, believing that in class society, "the interests of the ruling class became the driving factor of production."[1] They also articulated the opinion in these works that interest is the manifestation of desires and needs of individuals in relations between them; and that since in the circumstance of private ownership, interest becomes private bounded and self-seeking, what we shall abolish is such private interests instead interest in general.

III. Main Points of the Marxist Theory of Interests

In order to clarify the nature of interest and define the term scientifically, Marx and Engels didmuch groundbreaking work in this field. The Marxist theory of interests contains the following major points: (1) Interest pursuing is the driving force of all human social activities. Marx stated:

"everything for which man struggles is a matter of his interest."[2] (2) Interest is the foundation and determinant of ideas; interest drives production and life. "The 'idea' always disgraced itself insofar as it differed from the 'interest'."[3] Interest "becomes the driving factor of production". Lenin confirmed Marx's idea, saying "interests 'moves the lives of peoples.'[4] (3) Interest dissension is the material source of class struggles. They stated that class struggles are "material interests-based" fundamental conflicts.[5] (4) Interest conflicts are forces that drive social development. Against the background of struggle between the landed aristocracy, the bourgeoisie and the proletariat in England and France, Engels concluded: "Conditions had become so simplified that one would have had to close one's eyes deliberately not to see in the light of these

---

[1] *Selected Works of Marx and Engels*, vol. 4, People's Publishing House, 1995, p. 385.

[2] *Collected Works of Marx and Engels*, vol. 1, People's Publishing House, 1956, p. 82.

[3] *Collected Works of Marx and Engels*, vol. 2, People's Publishing House, 1957, p. 103.

[4] *Collected Works of Lenin*, vol. 55, People's Publishing House, 1990, p. 75.

[5] *Selected Works of Marx and Engels*, vol. 3, People's Publishing House, 1995, p. 365.

three great classes and in the conflict of their interests the driving force of modern history—at least in the two most advanced countries. "① (5) The social essence and basis of interest is the relations of production. Marx and Engels stated: " The economic relations of a given society present themselves in the first place as interests. "② They believed that economic interests are the embodiment of relations of production, therefore, the nature and historic role of interests can be clarified only by probing into the relations of production. (6) Material interests determine political interests. They stated: "he (*Napoleon*) showed no more consideration for its essential material interests, trade and industry, whenever they conflicted with his political interests. "③ (7) Interests determine and govern political power and political activities. They believed that class struggle "first and foremost, of economic interests, to the furtherance of which political power was intended to serve merely as a means. "④ (8) Division of labor causes interest contradiction. In *The German Ideology*, Marx and Engels wrote: "The division of labor inside a nation leads at first to the separation of industrial and commercial from agricultural labor, and hence to the separation of town and country and to the conflict of their interests. "⑤   "Further, the division of labor implies the contradiction between the interests of the separate individual or the individual family and the communal interest of all individuals who have intercourse with one another. "⑥ (9) In class society, common interests are in fact special class interests. Marx said: " For each new class which puts itself in the place of one ruling before it, is compelled, merely in order to carry through its aim, to represent its interest as the common interest of all the members of society. "⑦ Such interest that was advertised as the common

---

① *Selected Works of Marx and Engels*, vol. 3, People's Publishing House, 1995, p. 250.

② *Ibid.* , p. 209.

③ *Collected Works of Marx and Engels*, vol. 2, People's Publishing House, 1957, p. 158.

④ *Selected Works of Marx and Engels*, vol. 4, People's Publishing House, 1995, p. 250.

⑤ *Ibid.* , p. 68.

⑥ *Ibid*, p. 84.

⑦ *Collected Works of Marx and Engels*, vol. 3, People's Publishing House, 1960, p. 54.

interest was indeed special class interest of the bourgeoisie.

To conclude, according toMarxist theory of interests, in any society, people's needs for material life, i. e. desire for material interests must be meet first; interest is the foundation, premise and driving factor of social development; interest is a basic category in historical materialism; while productive force is the fundamental driving force of social development, needs and interests are indeed the inner drive for the continuous development of social production; any social transformation must ultimately restructure relation of interests among people so as to improve and advance social production to meet people's needs for material interests; in class societies, interests are represented first and foremost in class interests, which serve to meet interests of the ruling class. Nowadays, since the socialist system is set up in China, there are a lot of important and urgent theoretic issues regarding interests, e. g. how to understand interest group, interest structure, interest stimulus instrument, interest contradiction and interest relation in the primary stage of socialism; how to properly deal with interest contradictions and conflicts among people in the primary stage of socialism; how to properly coordinate the relation of interests between the state, collectives and individuals and among different sides so as to fully mobilize the initiatives of various subjects of interests, give full rein to the role of interests and speed up socialist reform and modernization. All these issues need to be studied to enrich and advance Marxist theory of interests.

Part 2

THE THEORY OF INTERESTS

Chapter Three

Human Needs and the
Category of Need

Need is the premise and foundation of interest. Thereby if we are to study interest, we must study need first; if we are to understand the nature of interest, we must know the nature of need first; if we want to establish the category of interest, we must set the category of need first.

I. The Marxist Theory of Need

The Marxist theory of need is consistent with Marxist theory of interest. To understand need, it is necessary for us to review Marxist theory of need. Need is a key subject of study in classical Marxist works and Marxist theory of need is an important and basic theory for Marx in creating his theories of value of labor, surplus value and crisis.

On October 15th, 1844, when Marx was editor of *Rheinische Zeitung*, economic issues and the issues of need and interest caught his great attention. In "A Contribution to the *Critique of Hegel's Philosophy of Right*, Introduction," Marx points out when talking about the situation in Germany: "In Germany, where practical life is as spiritless as spiritual life is unpractical, no class in civil society has any need or capacity for general emancipation until it is forced by its immediatecondition, by material necessity, by its very chains."[1] Here Marx mentioned the concept of material necessity. In *Economic and Philosophic Manuscripts of 1844* written in April-August 1844, Marx discussesin details the issue of need, and touches upon suchconcepts as social need, physical need, worker's need, the need of civilization, crude need, human need,

---

[1] *Collected Works of Marx and Engels*, Vol. 1, People's Publishing House, 1956, p. 466.

selfish need, the need of companionship and natural needs. These needs can be broadly divided into the following categories: natural needs (physical needs) and social needs; human needs and animal needs; crude needs of workers and refined needs of the rich. In his completed work *the Holy Family*, Marx points out when elaborating some basic views of historical materialism: "sensory qualities and self-love, enjoyment and correctly understood personal interest are the basis of all morality."① This indicates that his theory of need is firmly founded on the basis of materialism. In *Outlines of the Critique of Political Economy* written in the 1850s, Marx further developed this theory. Firstly, he puts forward the concept of necessary need and associates it with necessary labor. Secondly, he has clarified the basic connotation of social need, saying that in the commodity society, one produces not for his direct need but mutually for the needs of others, thereby formed "a system of general social metabolism, of universal relations, of all-round needs and universal capacities."② Thirdly, he discusses the contradiction between luxury needs and necessary needs and their transformation into each other. And lastly, he puts forth the view that the totality of needs is the measurement of use value. In summary, the Marxist theory of need contains the following three major points: (1) human needs constitute the essence of human beings; (2) human needs represent social needs and give birth to social relations; and (3) production determines needs, and needspromote production.

Human needs constitute the essence of human beings. Talking about human needs, Marx points out: human needs are human inborn inner necessity. Needsare manifestations of life, and a human being with many needs, "is simultaneously the human being in need of a totality of human manifestations of life-the man in whom his own realization exists as an inner necessity, as need."③ A man as a human being is manifested in the "inner necessity" of having many human needs. As a social being with life, a man needs such necessities as food, water, clothes and house

---

① *Collected Works of Marx and Engels*, Vol. 2, People's Publishing House, 1957, pp. 165—166.

② *Collected Works of Marx and Engels*, Vol. 46a, People's Publishing House, 1979, p. 104.

③ *Collected Works of Marx and Engels*, Vol. 42, People's Publishing House, 1979, p. 129.

to sustain his life as long as he is alive; after having material means of subsistence, he still has the basic need of making intellectual activities such as learning, reading, enjoying arts. In other words, needsare manifestations of life in that any man with life has needs. It is in this sense we say that human needsconstitute the essence of human beings—needs are essential characteristics of human beings.

Human needs represent social needs and give birth to social relations. Marx believes that: "... the essence of man is no abstraction inherent in each single individual. In its reality it is the ensemble of the social relations. "① Since needsconstitute the essence of man that is the ensemble of social relations, human needs, therefore, represent social needs and give birth to social relations. Needs are social and give birth to social relations. Marx clearly points out that social relations of men are generated from and the products of human needs. "The sole bond holding them together is natural necessity, need and private interest. "② Real social links are not a product of reflection but are born out of individual needs and egoism, i. e. , a direct product produced when an individual actively seeks to realize his existence. However, needs as the most essential characteristics of human beings are isolated, static or abstract, they manifest and establish themselves in their relations to their objects, and they keep developing and enriching. Marx understandsneeds by recognizing their social nature.

Production determines needs and needspromote production; the interaction between needs and production promote social development. Marx has elucidated the nature, role and development mechanisms needs. In *The German Ideology*, Marx and Engels make a more comprehensive and systematic illustration of the Marxist theory of need. They believe that: "Life involves before everything else eating and drinking, a habitation, clothing and many other things. The first historical act is thus the production of the means to satisfy these needs, the production of material life itself. "③ This statement implies two points:

---

① *Selected Works of Marx and Engels*, Vol. 1, People's Publishing House, 1995, p. 60.

② *Collected Works of Marx and Engels*, Vol. 1, People's Publishing House, 1956, p. 439.

③ *Selected Works of Marx and Engels*, Vol. 1, People's Publishing House, 1995, p. 79.

(1) For a man to live, he must carry out production activities to meet his needs for his material life itself, which means, production determines needs of life; (2) It is human needs that promote production, that is to say, needs in a sense determine that the first historical human activity is production. Production determines needs, needs promote production and this interaction determines the material connections of men, thereby, drives the progress of human society and development of history. In Marx and Engels' view, needs and mode of production determine the material connection of men, and "this connection is ever taking on new forms," and thus creates history. [1]They argue that the needs are ever changing and society keeps "modifying its social system according to the changed needs. "[2] Production determines needs, which on the one hand constitutethe determiningfactor of social development, and on the other are determined by production and division of labor. They believes that, in the course of social development, needsconstitute a determining factor on the one hand and a determined factor on the other, the need "... depends wholly on demand, which in turn depends on the division of labor and the conditions of human culture resulting from it. "[3] They further argue that inequality in satisfying needs comes from inequality in appropriation, "differences of brain and of intellectual ability do not imply any differences whatsoever in the nature of the stomach and of physical needs,"[4] therefore "to each according to his abilities" must be changed into "to each according to his needs" . They also believe that, since human beings entered into class society due to the emergence of division of labor and private ownership, at the lower stage of productive forces, human development could only take the form in which "some persons satisfied their needs at the expense of others, and therefore some—the minority— attained the monopoly of development, while others—the majority—owing to the constant struggle to satisfy their most essential needs, were for the time being (i. e. , until the creation of new revolutionary productive

---

[1] *Collected Works of Marx and Engels*, Vol. 3, People's Publishing House, 1956, p. 34.

[2] *Ibid*, pp. 48—49.

[3] Ibid. , p. 459.

[4] *Ibid*, p. 637.

forces) excluded from any development. "[1] They discussed in this way the class nature of needs in certain stages developmentof productive forces.

II. The Nature and Characteristics of Human Needs

Needsare not unique to man as a " social animal. " Living creatures, asbiological forms of motion of matter on the earth, have their needs since their coming into being. Needs reflect the dependence of biological species upon external material, energy and information elements, a mastering of which is a necessary condition for their subsistence and development. In other words, no living creature can maintain its balance with the external environment and its subsistence without an exchange of material, energy and information through assimilation and metabolism. Living creatures manifest their lives in needs. A living creature as the subject of needs can make independent and selective responses to elements that can sustain its existence and development. Elements that can sustain the existence and development of living creatures are the objects of needs. There are some contradictions between the subjects and the objects of needs, which is manifested in the fact that, to satisfy their needs, living creatures mustget control of the objects of needs through positive activities and by solving the contradictions. As a commonness of any living organism, life and needs are consistent and identical, in that there will be no life without needs, and vice versa. The external physical environment of life is the objective material basis necessary for life.

However, as the most advanced biological species innature, man is a brand new manifestation of needs, whose needs constitute a radical leap and distinction from those of the animals in nature.

Human needs are self-evidently different from those of any other living creatures. First, animals satisfy their need son instincts to sustain their lives and ecological balance; therefore, their needs are generally passive, instinctive and subconscious. On the contrary, human needs are active and conscious, because human beings actively transform nature and draw needs from nature. Human beings satisfy their needson subjective initiative. Second, although animals are adaptive to external conditions to

---

① *Collected Works of Marx and Engels*, Vol. 3, People's Publishing House, 1956, pp. 507.

meet their needs, these adaptions are always within the limitations directly related to their lives and their physiological needs and never without, with their objects of needs always being natural things (if it is withoutthe interference of man) . On the contrary, human beings fulfill their needs with means of production and subsistence. Although the kind of labor carried out by our earliest ancestors was very primitive and simple, when they picked a stone to cut another to make it sharper tool, they have indeed smashed the shackles of animal instincts and pure physiological needs and limits of natural creatures, giving human needs broader and new content and attributes different from those of animals. And lastly, human needs are restricted not only by natural conditions but also by social conditions. While animal needs come from the external natural conditions only, human needs come from not only external natural environment but also human social environments that have considerable restrictions and influence on human needs, which are manifested mainly as follows:

Firstly, human needs produce true community of men and thus aresocial. Marx said: " Since human nature is the true community of men, by manifesting their nature men create, produce, the human community, the social entity, which is no abstract universal power opposed to the single individual, but is the essential nature of each individual, his own activity, his own life, his own spirit, his own wealth. Hence this true community does not come into being through reflection, it appears owing to the need and egoism of individuals. . . " [1] Human needs produce human community and the true community is the essential nature of man. On the contrary, animal needs can never produce any true community.

Human beings satisfy their needs through labor, which can only be done by establishing certain social relations. Men carry out labor activities in given social relations, primarily relations of production, so men's labor is of social nature. The social nature of labor, i. e. the social nature of way to satisfy their needs determine that human needs are social. Firstly, human needsare socially produced, while animal needsare determined by their biological structure and instincts. Although human needs have a physiological basis, they are largely socially produced. Human needs first

---

① *Collected Works of Marx and Engels*, Vol. 42, People's Publishing House, 1979, p. 24.

and foremost depend on the existing level of productive forces, where of the level of productive forces determines the level of human needs. In terms of needs of individuals, they are also determined bytheir economic and political statuses and their educational, social and family backgrounds as well. Human needsare the products of social labor. Secondly, the needsof individuals are inevitably part of social needs and thus become social needs. Although human needs are constituted by the needs of individuals, they must be satisfied in social forms and thus must become social needs. On the one hand, needs of individuals bear the social nature and are social needs; on the other, social needs constitutean organic ensemble of the needs of individuals and constrain the contents and level of satisfaction of them at the same time. Historically speaking, apart from the primitive society, social needs have always been the needs of the ruling classes, which were at variance with, sometimes even radically and completely opposed to the needs of individuals. Nevertheless, social needs are still the necessary forms of and necessary media for the realization of the needs of individuals.

Secondly, human needs are ever growing. A major difference between human needs and animal needs is that human needs will never remain at the same level. In contrast, animal needs will remain the same as long as there is no changes in external conditions. The infiniteness of human needs is determined by the infiniteness of the productive forces—means and capability to satisfy needs. The infinite development of productive forces creates a broad prospect for the infinite expansion of human needs. "No production without a need. But consumption reproduces the need. "① "The satisfaction of the first need (the action of satisfying, and the instrument of satisfaction which has been acquired) leads to new needs. "② While development of productive forces lays a foundation for the infinite expansion of human needs, the course of human needs expansion is essence the infinite development of social practice. Human beings satisfy their needs through production-based social practices. As an infinite and interactive process of development, the satisfaction of the first need and the action of satisfying leads to new needs, and new needs further urge

---

① *Selected Works of Marx and Engels*, Vol. 2, People's Publishing House, 1995, p. 9.

② *Selected Works of Marx and Engels*, Vol. 1, People's Publishing House, 1995, p. 79.

human beings to make new social practices, and this repeats itself in endless cycles.

Thirdly, human needs are inexhaustibly diverse. Since human beings and their production are diverse, human needs are diverse, which require them to reproduce the whole nature. In contrast, animal needs are simple. Animals only produce what they immediately need for themselves or their young. They produce one-sidedly. They produce only under the dominion of immediate physical need, while human being produce even when they are free from physical needs and only truly produce in freedom therefrom. Animals produce only themselves whilehuman beings reproduce the environment they live in. Animals' products belong immediately to their physical body while human beings freely confront their products. Since human needs are ever growing, as the result of long term deposit in the course of historical development, they will get more and more diverse and extensive. As far as material needs are concerned, natural needs that are necessary to sustain the existence of human beings gradually cast away their primitive forms and become more and more diversified. For instance, food satisfies not only the need of appeasing hunger but also the need of catering for tastes, hence their numerous varieties; clothes satisfy not only the need of covering the body and protection against cold, but also the aesthetic need with different styles and colors. Along the enriching of material needs, Human beings also have developed different varieties of intellectual needs, e. g. , needs of social intercourse, communication, aesthetic appreciation, culture, education and self-realization. The diversity of human needs is based on, at the same time promotes, the comprehensive development of production and other social practices. Marx believes that man is distinct from animals because of the infiniteness and extensiveness of his needs. [1]

Fourthly, human needs constitute a historical process and thus are historical. Just as human needs are inexhaustibly diverse and ever growing, they have also a long historical process of development. This process can be roughly divided into four stages. The first stage is the primitive society, in which social production was at a low level, objects of needs were directly gotten from nature and hence human needs were of low-level, simple and crude. The second stage includes the slavery

---

[1] *Collected Works of Marx and Engels*, Vol. 49, People's Publishing House, 1982, p. 130.

society and the feudal society, in which natural economy dominates. At this stage, social production develops a lot but social productive forces are still at a low level and products are limited; human needs are more diversified but still quite simple. The third stage is the highly commercialized society. At this stage, as products become commodities and commodity production further develops, human needs are greatly diversified, scope and objects of which largely increase and are no longer directly gotten from nature. The fourth stage is the product economy age, in which productive forces are highly developed and products overwhelmingly abundant, thus human needs are more diverse and colorful.

Fifthly, human needs are subjectively active, with objective content manifested in subjective forms. The subjective initiative of human needs lies in the fact that they are in an endless cycles of practice, need, again practice and again need, in which human beings constantly create new needs of theirown and new means to satisfy their needs. The subjective initiative of human needs lies also in the fact that they are realized by human beings as the subjects and are indispensable. Since needs must be realized through human conscious activities with their physical sense organs, therefore human needs are conscious and active in nature. For instance, needs directly associated with their physical existence, such as eating, drinking, must "begin as a consequence of the sensation of hunger or thirst transmitted through the brain, and end as a result of the sensation of satisfaction likewise transmitted through the brain. "① While animal needs are the selective and natural physiological responses to such elements as matter, energy and information they depend on, whereas human needsare subjectively active response to these elements. On the basis of such response, human needsare thus satisfied through purposely planned activities. After personally practicing and experiencing the satisfaction of needs, men will have a more profound response in their minds to their needs and produce new ones thereof, i. e. , creating new conceptual objects of needs (which possibly still do not exist yet in real world), which prompt them to new practice in order to satisfy their new needs. Animal needs give rise to at best some directed need exploration on the basis of natural physiological needs, while human needs produce

---

① *Selected Works of Marx and Engels*, Vol. 4, People's Publishing House, 1995, p. 232.

the needs of exploring and transforming the world through practice. Need for toolsare included in human needs but not in animal needs. In order to conquer nature, human beings cannot rely simply on their physical capability, so they create tools in their productive practice to extend their bodily capability. Franklin defines man as "a tool-making animal."[1]

Sixthly, human needs are practical in that theprocess of satisfying needs is a process of practice. The process of production for satisfying human needs, including the links of search, distribution and consumption, is a process of practice. It is from the perspective material production practice Marx said that labor will become prime want of man's life.

Now that we have recognized the major differences between human needs and animal needs, then the question is: "What do human needs mean?" or "What is the essence of human needs?" Some regard need as a mental state, a sense of want; others define need as a "man's dependence on external objects." These opinions stress either subjectivity or objectivity of needs. In fact, human needs are derived from, associated with yet completely distinct from animal needs.

Firstly, human needs take as their objective basis the material and intellectual conditions of life on which human beings directly rely.

As subjects with life, human beings can only exist and develop by depending on and making exchanges with materials, energy and information of the outside world, just like animals. However, as the most advanced living being—social being in the world, human beings have a more complicated relationship with nature in terms of dependence. They rely not only directly on various elements of the external world, but also on the humanized nature—social conditions of material life; not only on social conditions of material life, but also on social conditions of intellectual life. The dependence of human beings on the external world has wider scope of content and more complicated relations than which are found on animals, making the dependence of human beings on the objective world different from that of the animals. Human beings' dependence on objective environment and the relations deriving from it constitute an objectivebasis for human needs being more complicated and richer than animal needs.

Secondly, human needs are the conscious and active response of human beings to their dependence on and their relation with the material and

---

[1] *Collected Works of Marx and Engels*, Vol. 23, People's Publishing House, 1972, p. 204.

intellectual conditions of life.

One of the fundamental differences between human needs and animal needs is that human needsare active responses. Animals' responses, only to the conditions vital to their subsistence, are instinct-based. Therefore, needs of animals of the same species are identical, just as Marx put it, "a hive of bees comprises at bottom only one bee, and they all produce the same thing. "① The reason behind this phenomenon is that the bees have the same needs. On the contrary, human needsare an active response to theirconditions of material and intellectual life and are directed by conscious action of human brain, therefore are distinctive and subjective. The objective world is diverse, so are individuals and their responses to it; the subjective and objective factors determine that the content and levels of individual human needsare widely diverse, even if the circumstances are similar. Because human needs manifest themselves asthe reflection of their dependence upon the objective world, human beings have such imaginary needs as religion and fantasy, which are either the distorted reflection of their dependence on the objective world, or the outcome of their fanciful reflection on objective world, both are far beyond the reach of animal needs.

A basic characteristic of any human need is that it is an active and clear direction of the subject towardthe object. "Hunger is a natural need; it therefore needs a nature outside itself, an object outside itself, in order to satisfy itself, to be stilled. "② Just as it is true for the most fundamental physiological need, it is true for intellectual need as well, for the satisfaction of which specific objects—e. g. , such media as television and tape recorder and works of literature, art or movie—are necessary. Human needs target specifically at material or intellectual objects. This is based on human active reflection of the material and/or intellectual life. It indicates that human have certain subjective forms. Need is a contradictory relation between the subjects and the objects on which they depends, that is, the subjectshave a want, thus, a need of the objects. To address such a contradiction, the subjects of needs must be active enough to control the objects and thereby have the needs satisfied.

① *Collected Works of Marx and Engels*, Vol. 46a, People's Publishing House, 1979, p. 195.

② *Collected Works of Marx and Engels*, Vol. 42, People's Publishing House, 1979, p. 168.

Thirdly, human needs are material, realistic and objective in content but subjective in form.

Human needs take social material and intellectual conditions as their basis. The objects they depend on are all real material life conditions, means of subsistence or intellectual means of subsistence derived from them, such as food, housing, transportation facilities, television and telephone. So the actual contents of human needs are all material, realistic and objective. On the other hand, human needs manifest themselves in their subjective direction toward the objects, things that are subjective and mental in form, such as intentions, desires, so they are also active, dynamic and conscious.

Need as acategory can be defined from different angles such as physiology, biology. We will study it from the angle of historical conception. Analyzing from the angle of philosophic conception of history, we can see that human needs are in essence the manifestations of human life activity. Human needs are different from animal needs in that they social, active and dynamic, with human beings arethe subjectswhile material and intellectual life conditions essential human existence and development as the objects. Human needs reflect the direct dependence of human beings upon the social material conditions and intellectual conditions; the former include means of subsistence such as natural geographic environment, clothing, food and shelter while the later including means of intellectual subsistence derived from the material means. Human needsare material, realistic and objective in content, but subjective in form, such as mentality, desire, intention. Therefore, human needs can be defined as the humans' conscious, intentional and active reflection, direction, pursuit, absorption and satisfaction of objects of needs, therefore are the manifestations of human life activities and are represented as direct dependence of human beings on the external object of needs.

Human dependence upon external objects of need is demonstrated on their dependence upon natural and social environments, material means of subsistence, means of production and intellectual means of subsistence. Human dependence on others and on society is also a kind of human need— such as need for love, for marriage, for cohabitation, for desires, for association. Need sare therefore neither subjective product nor arbitrary imagination, but a necessary relation between the objective world and the subjective world, and necessary and objective dependence of human beings upon the objective world.

Some argue that recognizing the subjectivity in form of human needs will get us bogged down in a quagmire of historical idealism. Such an argument is not correct. Recognizing the formal subjectivity of human needs doesn't necessarily mean our recognizing human needs to be subjective products or arbitrary imagination. As direct dependence upon material and intellectual life conditions, human needs must have material, realistic and objective content and be determined and restrained by different social and historical conditions. On the other hand, recognizing only the objective basis of human needs other than their subjectivity will fail to illustrate the fundamental differences between human needs and animal needs as well as characteristic of human needs, which will consequently fall back to mechanical materialism.

III. Types and System of Needs

Founders of Marxism didn't discuss the types and system of needs systematically, but they have for many times touched upon this issue when they discussed issues of economy, philosophy and scientific socialism. In *Outlines of the Critique of Political Economy*, Marx once suggested to discuss the "system of needs. "[1] In light of Marx's discussion, we can roughly classify human needs into three major types: (1) Minimum natural physiological needs or needs of sustenance, mainly concerning means of subsistence such as clothing, food and shelter necessary to sustain a minimum level of life, direct needs that sustain the survival of man as a living being. This type of needs, however, is not rigid and purely natural, it is also "natural need historically modified at a certain level of civilization. "[2] (2) Higher level social needs that satisfies man's social life, Marx's discussion of which contains several points: firstly, "socially produced need", that is, the need generated in social production and exchange to meet the requirement of social existence of the social community other than sustaining individual's sustenance; secondly, human needs in the communist society, a truly higher level social needs extended

---

[1] *Collected Works of Marx and Engels*, Vol. 46b, People's Publishing House, 1980, p. 20.

[2] *Collected Works of Marx and Engels*, Vol. 47, People's Publishing House, 1979, p. 52.

from the general interests of the human society concerning the proportionate production in the society so as to have people therein satisfied. (3) Intellectual needs that satisfy the intellectual demands of human beings. This type of needs contains a wide range of contents, such as need for education, social intercourse, communication. In addition, Marx also, based on the historical development of needs, proposed many specific types of needs, such as necessary need and luxury need, need for money and need for human development, work becoming not only a means of life but life's prime need.

A lot of psychologists and behavioral scientists havemade systematic studies on human needs, the representative of which is American psychologist Abraham Maslow and his Hierarchy of Needs. Maslow divided human needs into seven levels: (1) The physiological need—the most fundamental and most powerful requirement for physical survival, such as for food, water, shelter, sex, sleeping and oxygen. (2) The safety need—the requirement for secured life without unexpected danger, such as for order and stability. (3) The belongingness and love need— hungering for affectionate and friendly relations with people, "for a place in his group" and senses of belonging. Also, Maslow differentiated love and sex, remarking that sex can be studied as a purely physiological need. As for love, he agreed to Carl Rogers' definition of love as "that of being deeply understood and deeply accepted. " (4) The esteem need. Maslow found that people have two categories of esteem need—self-respect and esteem from other people. Self-esteem includes such needs as desire for confidence, competence, mastery, achievement, independence and freedom. Respect from others includes such concepts as prestige, recognition, acceptance, attention, status, reputation and appreciation. (5) The cognition need—the desire to know and to understand, or in a simple term as curiosity. In Maslow's words, "We shall then postulate a desire to understand, to systematize, to organize, to analyze, to look for relations and meanings, to construct a system of values. "[1] (6) The aesthetic need—the need for beauty, such as symmetry, order and harmony. Maslow found that—in the strictest biological terms, in the same realm of discourse as the need for calcium in the diet—one needs beauty; beauty helps one to be healthier. (7) The self-actualization need—the

---

[1] Quoted from Frank G. Goble, *The Third Force: The Psychology of Abraham Maslow* (*Chinese Translation*), Shanghai Translation Publishing House, 1987, pp. 46—47.

need for growth, development and utilization of potential. Maslow described this need as "the desire to become more and more what one is, to become everything that one is capable of becoming. "① In this way, Maslow set up a pyramid of needs. Maslow stated, after the lower needs are satisfied, "At once other (and higher) needs emerge, and these, rather than physiological hungers, dominate the organism. And when these in turn are satisfied, again new (and still higher) needs emerge, and so on. This is what we mean by saying that the basic human needs are organized into a hierarchy of relative prepotency. "② Maslow also cautioned against understanding the hierarchy of needs too precisely. One must not assume that the need for security does not emerge until the need for food is entirely satisfied, or that the need for love does not emerge until the need for safety is fully satisfied.

The theory of Hierarchy of Needs to some extent generalizes the types of human needs with a focus on the close relation between needs and behavior, and found the developing law of human needs from lower to higher levels, which is suggestive for us to understand human needs. However, Maslow failed to study need as an inclusive social and historical category. Aiming at fully develop human potential—which he thought to be inherent to individuals—Maslow studied human needs mainly from the angle of ontogeny of behavior and simply interpreted needs as a psychological phenomenon, without tapping on the relations between human needs and society, or social and material foundation of needs. Weshould, based on Marxist theory, scientifically classify and study needs by treating it as a social and historical category.

Human needs are diverse and rich, and are ever growing along with the development of social civilization. They interrelated with each other and form a huge system. While human needs can be classified by different standards. In this we classify them into an inclusive socio-historical category.

1. Natural needs (direct needs) and social needs

Natural needs refer mainly to natural physiological needs, i. e. , including needs for clothing, food and shelter. In Marx's works, this type

---

① Quoted from Frank G. Goble, *The Third Force: The Psychology of Abraham Maslow* (*Chinese Translation*), Shanghai Translation Publishing House, 1987, p. 45.

② *Ibid*, p. 41—42.

of needsis sometimes called as direct needs. Social needsare needs distinctive from direct/natural physiological needs, which can be interpreted from three aspects: Firstly, human beings are social, sohuman natural physiological needs also have social nature, because human needs themselves are social needs. With the evolution of human society, natural physiological needs have gotten more social nature. In the process of transformation from uncivilized to civilized society in the primitive society, their purely natural physiological needs reduced gradually. For instance, eating became more and more social in that eating itself gradually evolved into food culture. In this sense, social needsbelong to "natural need historically modified at a certain level of civilization."[1] Secondly, human needsare socialized human needs other than specific need of any individual. Since a man exists as a social being instead of a single individual isolated from the human community, the needs of an individual are at the same time the needs of a socialized man. Thirdly, social needs are "socially produced needs", i. e. , needs produced through social production based materials provided by nature that can meet human physiological needs. For instance, on the basis of natural water, tap-water and other beverages are produced through social production, and human need for such socially produced drinking water is therefore a social need. Social needs in this sense are human needs for socially produced objects of needs. As social creatures, human beings satisfy their needs in ways different from animals' natural metabolism. Especially after entering the stage of commodity production, human beings no longer satisfied themselves with production for natural needs; instead, they produced and exchanged commodities in society to satisfy their multiple needs, through which, human needs were widely socialized. With the development of social production and social life, human needs keep changing with many new needs emerging. The change of human needs is a social process as muchas a historical process, during which, purely natural physiological human needs more and more become socialized, or social needs.

2. Individual/ particular needs and general/common needs

From the perspective of subjects, needs can be divided into individual/

---

① Collected Works of Marx and Engels, Vol. 47, People's Publishing House, 1979, p. 52.

particular needs and general/common needs. Individual/particular needs includes not only individual needs but also community needs as opposed to needs of the whole society; compared to individual needs, community needsare also a kind of general/common needs. Human beings are the manifestation as well as the subjects of needs. On the one hand, a man can exist as an individual, on the other hand he must associate with others to form a community and exist therein. In the meantime, each individual and each community are also components of thewhole human society. Therefore, from the aggregation level of their subjects, needs can be divided into individual needs, community needs and social needs in general.

Just as individuals make up communities and communities make up the whole human society, social needs are made up of needs of various individuals and communities. We can never deny the particularity of individual needs because of their social nature, for human needs are always composed of and take the form of individual needs. Likewise, the satisfaction and development of human needscan only be manifested in those of individual needs, without which, community needs and social needs would become baseless and meaningless abstract concepts, and human society would not exist or develop at all.

A community is an amalgamation of individuals that are linked by or share certain common interests. Either in primitive society or advanced modern society, there is no individual man that lives or does production in absolute isolation. Human beings must live in communities in one form or another. Community isthe organizational structure of human society. Due to their differences in cohesiveness, there form in the society various communities with different needs and different community needs. For instance, communities formed on the basis of common social and economic statuses such as class, stratum, will have their class and stratum needs; communities formed on the basis of kinship such as clans, tribes, families, will have their kinship needs; so are communities formed on the basis of professions or economic units. Communities can also be divided according to gender, age, etc. In a word, there are myriads of formal or informal communities and their needs. Among which, state is a larger and more comprehensive community based on territory. State needsoccupy an extremely important position in community needs of human society.

The needs of society as a whole are the needs of human beings as the subject of needs as a whole. Compared to individual and particular needs, needs of society are general and universal, or common needs. Individuals or communities, as components of human beings as a whole, are inevitably have their common needs. For example, physiological needs and safety need are common to any subject of needs. In modern society, education has been a common need of all members. The trend of integration of human society determines that human beings have more common needs than before. The development of science, technology and economy has speeded upthe integration trend of human society and added new content to its common needs. Once the association of free men, i. e. , communist society as envisaged by Marx comes into being, although different needs would still exist, needs of the whole society would become the supreme ones, with individual needs no longer being antagonistic to social needs.

The relation between individual needs and social needs is a relation between individual or particular needs on the side and general and universal needs on the other. Compared to community needs and social needs, individual needs are individual or particular needs; likewise, compared to social needs, community needs are individual and particular needs whereas social needs are general and universal needs. So is the need relation between a smaller community and a larger community that the smaller community belongs to. And so on. Individual and particular needs are the basis of general and universal needs, with the organic ensemble of the former constituting the latter and the latter reflecting and containing the former. Therefore, general and universal needs are higher than individual and particular needs and thus control them. A correct understanding of dialectical relations between these needs is the cognition basis for us to correctly address the relations between individual needs and that of the collective, the state and the whole society.

3. Material needs and intellectual needs

Needs, being their individual needs, community needs or social needs, from the perspective of their functions of satisfying the needs of need subjects, can be classified into two types—material needs and intellectual needs.

Material needs refer to the kind of human needs that are satisfied with the use value of material. Material here refers to not only various commodities used in our daily lives such as clothing, food, shelter and transportation, but also such matters given to us by nature as air, sun light, etc. Material needs reflect human dependence on material conditions and are indispensible for any human bodily exists as a living being. With the development of human beings, there emerged certain material that satisfy the needs of human needs not with the use value of concrete objects but of services, such as medical care and others. The reason such services can satisfy man's material needsis that, human beings as special objects have use value, whereas these services are actually a kind of special consumer goods. Both natural needs necessary for human's physical existence mentioned by Marx and physiological needs in Maslow's theory are material needs. In modern society, human needs for materials are satisfied more and more with humanized natural objects than purely natural objects.

Intellectual needs are the type of human needs for or dependence on the intellectual products derived from materials. These needs should be fulfilled through interconnections between human beings or through affection, friendship or mental state that are produced from various human activities. The higher level needs in Maslow's theory—belongingness and love, esteem, cognition, aesthetic and self-actualization—belong to this type, which is a major difference between human needs and animal needs.

Material needs and intellectual needs interact with each other. Firstly, material needs are the basis of intellectual needs. Intellectual needs will not emerge until a relative satisfaction of basic material needs. Satisfaction and development of material needs also facilitate the emergence of new intellectual needs. Although intellectual needs are relatively independent, they are generally restricted by material needs. Secondly, the satisfaction and development of intellectual needs also stimulate the development of material needs. For instance, the cognition need can provide scientific and intellectual conditions for the effective transformation of environment and for the creation of new material use value, and thus facilitate the emergence of new material needs. Moreover, material needs and intellectual needs are often mutually needed and penetrated. For instance, housing and buildings are essentially for satisfying people's need for dwelling, but with social development people take them not just asshelters to protect against wind and rain, but also as something aesthetically acceptable with certain style, thus give birth to architecture. Aesthetic need, so to speak, finds its expressions in all aspects of material needs. Furthermore, the satisfaction of material needs is instrumental to the satisfaction of intellectual needs. For instance, the intellectual needs for enjoying singing and dancing and music produce the material needs for theater, television and tape recorder and so on.

4. Economic needs and non-economic needs

Human needs, being it individual, community or social, material or intellectual, are all related directly or indirectly to social economic activities and thus gives rise to economic needs and non-economic needs. Economic needs is a type of needs for economic activity or its product, i. e. use value of an object, or value of a commodity—exchange value and use value—in market economy. Economic needs are directly associated with the process of social production and social economic activities and take economic forms. There are both connection and difference between material needs and economic needs. On the one hand, most material needs are manifested in economic needs, because objects of material needs are mostly created through economic activity and brought into consumption through certain economic relations; on the other, there are some natural materials, such as air, natural water, sunshine, which are bestowed upon us by nature that have use value but no relation to the process of social production. Needs for these natural materials are not economic needs. But sometimes some of these material needs can also be transformed into economic needs. For instance, people in modern times generally drink processed natural water, and thus drinking as a material need has become an economic need. Georgi Plekhanov remarked: "What is meant by an actual need? To our philosopher, this meant primarily a physiological need. But to satisfy their physiological needs people must produce certain articles; the process of that production must give rise to new needs, just as actual as the preceding but whose nature is no longer physiological, but economic, since such needs spring from the development of production and mutual relations entered into by people in the process of production."[1] As the social economic form of material needs, economic needs overlap with material needs and intellectual needs. For instance, people's material needs for nature-bestowed sun

---

[1] Georgi Plekhanov, "Essays on the History of Materialism", in *Selected Plekhanov Philosophical works*, vol. 2, Shanghai Joint Publishing Company, 1961, pp. 129—130.

light, air and natural water, in most cases, are not related to the social economic process, nor to any social relations, therefore are not included in economic needs. However, the needs for medical oxygen and tap-water are material needs pertaining to economic needs, or material economic needs. There are also intellectual economic needs such as needs for market-oriented cultural products.

Non-economic needs are those needs not directly associated with social productionor social economic activities, whose objects are neither economic activities nor their products. Generally speaking, most intellectual needs are non-economic needs. Political needs and military needs are special kinds of non-economic needs. In societies with commodity economy, non-economic needs can readily be transformed into economic needs. For instance, when the artists and writers compose their works, if they focus onselling their works for money instead of seeking mental delight for themselves or others, the non-economic needs becomes economic needs. An in a society of commodity economy, non-economic needs are always indirectly related to economic activities and relations. Economic needs and their satisfaction are the basis for non-economic needs, providing people who have non-economic activities with preconditions and free time. On the other hand, non-economic needs and activities are dependent on, sometimes even have, counteractive effect to economic needs and activities. Therefore it is imperative to take account of both economic needs and non-economic needs in making social development plans, so that economic development respond to human needs and thereby facilitate human development.

5. Needs for production and needsfor life

Social activities of human beings can be divided into two types, namely, activities of production and life. Production includes the production of men and production of means of subsistence. In order to sustain social production and reproduction, human beings must produce not only means of subsistence but also means of production. Activities of social life involve use and consumption of social means of subsistence. According to Marx, production includes, on the one side, the production of the means of existence (material production) and on the other side, the production of human beings themselves (the propagation of the species). By production here is meant by us the production of the means of existence. Needs for production thus refer to needs arising in human activities of material production that is necessary to the continuation of social production and reproduction. Needs for life refer mainly to needs arising from human activities of social life, including needs for material needs and intellectual needs; political needs; some economic needs; needs for individual life, community life andsocial life; needs for natural physical life and needs for social life in a broad sense, and so on. Needs for production serves as the precondition and basis of needs for life, without which, there would be no needs for life. On the other hand, needs for life constitute the purpose of needs for production. Needs for life, such as consumption, can stimulate and drive needs for production. Needs for production are consistent to economic needs in general but with a slight difference. Needs for production are not necessarily economic needs, and vice versa. In general, needs for production that get into the exchange domain will be transformed into economic needs, because most needs for production are related to social economic relations such as relations of exchange, distribution. Needs for production and needs for life are interrelated with material needs and intellectual needs but not completely identical. In fact, there are both material needs and intellectual needs in needs for production and needs for life.

6. Realistic needs and ideal needs

Realistic needs refer to the material and intellectual needs that are available in the natural and social-cultural environments people live in. Ideal needs refer to the material and intellectual needs pursued by people but are not readily available under current productive forces and natural and social-cultural environment. Realistic needs and ideal needs are divided on the basis of the availability of the needs. Whether social needs at given historical period of a society can be satisfied or not are determined by the material and intellectual life conditions, which in the final analysis, are determined by level of its productive forces. Social needs usually exceed the real level of productive forces, accordingly, human needs can be divided into two parts— "realistic needs" that can be satisfied and "ideal needs" that cannot be satisfied at given time. Since the division of realistic needs and ideal needs is based on the actual capability of a society in satisfying human needs, such a division is different from yet to some extent overlap with the divisions between material needs and intellectual needs, between economic needs and non-economic needs and between individual needs and social needs. For instance, realistic needs include, among others, both material needs and intellectual needs, both economic needs and non-economic needs, both individual (and community) needs and (general) social needs. Realistic needs and ideal needs constitute a contradiction: human needs often pursue ideal needs are beyond the bounds of realistic possibility. Turning ideal needs into realistic needs are necessary for social development and human development.

7. Necessary needs and luxury needs

Necessary needs refer to the minimum needs necessary to sustain human life and social activities, whose material objects are the necessities for sustaining these activities. Necessary needs are changing historically. Under different historical conditions, in different countries and regions, the minimum needs necessary to sustain human life and social activities vary and keep changing. Human necessary needs in the primitive society are different from that in the modern civilized society and the same holds true of people living in China and those living in the U. S. Luxury needsare, as opposed to necessary needs, are not indispensable and therefore beyond necessary. Luxury needs are relative. Luxury needsvary and keep changing in different historical conditions, different countries and different regions. For instance, cars serve as a necessary need in some countries but as a luxury need in others. Necessary needs and luxury needs are interchangeable, which means that with the development of social production, luxury needs can become necessary needs. With the development of social production, some luxuries become necessities, along with the change of their producers. Historically speaking, such a change marks social development.

Needs can be divided into other different types according to different standards. All these different types of needs form a huge system of needs through their extensive internal relationships, such as relationship between man and nature, between man and society and between individuals.

IV. Development Mechanism of Needs

Human needs keep changing and enriching throughout history, a process of constant development from lower to higher level needs. This is also the development process of mechanism for needs.

First, motives serve as the internal factor driving the development of human needs. As subjects of historical activities, man conducts all his activities consciously. That is to say, man's activities are the manifestations of his motives, which is a kind of physiological and psychological phenomenon. It can bean idea, a thought or will in man's brain generated by his material desiresthat drives him to take actions. Motives are the inner driving forces of human activities, and the underlying cause that sets man to achieve certain goals. Engels said: "As all the driving forces of the actions of any individual person must pass through his brain, and transform themselves into motives of his will in order to set him into action. "[1] In man's motives, motive of need is the underlying drive of his actions and the precondition of human production, just as Marx stated: " the ideal, internally impelling cause for production... as an internal image, as a need, as drive and as purpose. "[2] The most basic needs of life such as clothing, food and shelter and transport set man to make production and other social practice.

Second, material conditions man depends onare the precondition and basis for human needs.

Material conditions for human existence, including natural environment, humanized natural environment, material conditions made available by human labor, material conditions bestowed by nature and intellectual conditions derived from material conditions, are the objective content, preconditions and basis for human needs, without which there would be no human needs at all, not to mention their satisfaction.

Third, human practice, primarily productive activities, serves as a source of satisfying human needs.

Human needs, on the one hand underlie human motives ofaction, and on the other, get their content through human activities such as labor, production, social practices. With the development of human society and productive forces, human needs can no longer be met byonly natural materials; instead, they rely more and more on humanized material and intellectual conditions. Since human practice is the source of human

---

① *Collected Works of Marx and Engels*, Vol. 21, People's Publishing House, 1965, p. 345.

② *Selected Works of Marx and Engels*, Vol. 2, People's Publishing House, 1995, p. 9.

needs, it is reasonable to say that there will be no human needs without human practice. Human needs are satisfied through social practices, and in this process, new needs will created to conduct new practice, and so forth.

Fourth, productive forces and mode of production are the driving forces for the need development.

Human practice, when creating human needs, must be carried out in certain social form and with certain social capabilities, that is, mode of production and productive forces, which are the driving forces for satisfying human needs. Mode of production determines the content and level of human needs. Human needs differ in different historical periods, the underlying reason for which is the difference in the modes of production. Rich and high-level needs will arise only under the condition of advanced mode of production. Although emperors and kings in ancient times lived in excessive luxury, they could not imagine the needs of today. What limits their imagination and their level of needs is the mode of production and level of practice in their times. Human needs will not develop until the level of productive forces can meet them. While needs create motives for human activity, they cannot develop independently without activities to meet them. Various human needs can be satisfied only when social productive forces are capable of doing it. Level of need satisfaction is thus determined by productive forces, mode of production and level of practices. As the manifestation of man's dependence on material and intellectual conditions, needs sometimes may be mere illusion that can never be fulfilled, such as the need for making a perpetual motion machine. When a need motivating human activity cannot be met after being tested by practice, it will no longer become a motive for human action. For instance, during the "cultural revolution" period, in terms of relations of production, the lopsided emphasis on "making the communes large and collective" was not suitable for the development of China's productive forces; and in political sphere, class struggle was taken as the key link, and endless political movements were launched, so that productive forces were seriously damaged. As a result, the basic material and intellectual needs of people could not be met. Since the Third Plenary Session of the Eleventh Central Committee, the focus was shifted to economic construction. It is after reform and opening up when socialist market economy and the productive forces were fully developed that people's material and intellectual needs were met with their contents increasingly enriched and levels greatly raised.

Fifth, direct needs give birth to indirect needs, making them constantly develop and enrich.

One of the reasons for human needs getting more and more diverse and developed is that direct needs can create abundant indirect needs. Direct need and indirect need are two concepts relative to each other: the former is directly produced from the contradiction between the subject and object of the need while the latter arises in the process of satisfying the former. A need can be a direct need or an indirect need depending on social, economic and political statuses and living environment of the subjects of the need. The direct needs of the same subject are not unchangeable; rather, they can change along with the change of the subject, their satisfaction, etc. The direct needs of the same subject at one time may become indirect needs or even become needless at all at another time. The reason for direct human needs deriving abundant indirect needs is that most human needs cannot be directly satisfied by materials bestowed by nature. Nature can never fully satisfy human needs, and human beings are never satisfied with what nature bestowed. For instance, at the time when the productive forcesare relatively low, direct human needs are mostly physiological and natural such needs as for food, clothing. etc. , therefore indirect needs for production and labor emerge to meet them. In the capitalist society, the working class struggle for their right to labor, because they are aware that only after their need for labor is met can they fulfill their other needs. The connection in the process of production between social members further gives rise to needs of intercourse and exchange, etc. In the market economy, human direct needs are mostly fulfilled through money as a universal equivalent, as a result, need for money becomes a universal indirect need. In order to get money, a lot of other indirect need will further arise, and the indirect needs will give rise to further and further indirect needs. Thus human needs will actually enrich and develop in an endless way.

Sixth, luxury needs becoming necessary needs makes the level of human needs keep rising.

Human needs keep enriching and their levels keep rising. Necessary need and luxury need are also a pair of relative concepts. Necessary needs are needs that are essential to humansas bodily and social beings under certain social conditions. A Need other than necessary needs is a luxury need. The contents and levels of necessary needs vary in different historical times. In the primitive society, necessary needs were mainly natural needs, i. e. , physiological needs for sustaining human life. There was no division between necessary needs and luxury needs, because they were identical. It would be the most luxury satisfaction for primitive people tohave feast on meat in a warm shelter and maintained good health. Entering the society of private property, there disparities between rich and poor appeared, along with it the division between necessary and luxury needs and the antagonistic relations. The ruled class with lower social, economic and political statusescan only had the minimum level of needs for their survival so as to create wealth for the ruling class; only the ruling or upper classeswith higher social economic and political statuses hadluxury needs and means of satisfaction. The transformation of luxury needs into necessary needs keeps going on and even speeds up, the most distinctive of which is the transformation of luxuries into necessities. In the feudal society, the most luxury life for a Chinese farmer was "thirty mu fertile land and a strong ox, lovely wife and children in a warm house. " But nowadays, tremendous changes occurred to Chinese farmers, especially those got rich since the Third Plenary Session of the Eleventh Central Committee with their needs greatly changed. For them, high-grade consumer goods such as household appliances, clothes, modern furniture, etc. , were no longer regarded as luxuries but necessities of life. In some developed capitalist countries, such top grade goods as top grade home appliance and cars that have been regarded as luxuries now become necessities of life. The same is also true for intellectual needs. In feudal society, education was the upper class's luxury need that was unimaginable for ordinary laborers. Similarly, political and state affairs were also regarded as the privileges of the ruling class. But nowadays, getting education is already a universal need for ordinary people, and with the rising of peoples'political awareness, political participation has become an essential part of people's life. The same happen in all parts of human needs, making their level keep rising and their content enriching. With the progress of science and technology, development of productive forces and change of social system, the transformation of luxury needs into necessary needs will go on and speed up. By the time when private property is abolished, class differences disappear and productive forces are highly developed, the contradiction between luxury needs and necessary needs will eventually disappear and people in the "realm of freedom" will produce proportionately to satisfy human needs, making them more abundant and diverse. By that time although there will bedifferent needs, luxury needs and necessary needs will become identical at a higher level.

Chapter Four

Social Interests and the
Interest Category

On the basis of a discussion of human needs and the need category, we can further study social interests and the interest category, to examine the nature, characteristics and classification of social interests. A theoretic premise of studying issues concerning real social interests is to define the interest category.

I. The Constituent Elements of Interests

Before defining the interest category, we shall first of all analyze the constituent elements, which include the following five aspects:

First, needs serve as the natural basis of interests. It follows that a given interest is formed on the basis of a given need. Needs serves as the basis of interests; natural needs, physiological material needs in particular, serve as the natural basis on which interests, primarily material interests are formed. What are needs? Marx and Engels points out: "But life involves before everything else, eating and drinking, a habitation, clothing and many other things. The first historical act is thus the production of the means to satisfy these needs, the production of material life itself. "[1] Human needs reflect man's objective dependence on material and spirituallife conditions, which are demonstrated in man's conscious direction to and desires for the objects of his material and spiritual needs. In other words, needs reflect the desire of man as the subject of needs for living conditions as the objects of needs. Needs are objective in content and subjective as forms of satisfaction. Human needs are the internal motives forhuman

---

[1] *Selected Works of Marx and Engels*, Vol. 1, People's Publishing House, 1995, p. 79.

historical activities and the initial driving force for the development of social production. In this sense, human needs constitute the natural basis of interests.

Second, social relations serve as the social basis of interests. Man's social attributes determine that human needsare social nature, and the formation of interest is associated with given social relations. Social relations serve as the social basis of interests in the following three points: firstly, it is in a given social relation that human beings can engage in practice, primarily productive practice, to address the contradictions between subjects and objects of needs; secondly, economic interest in the manifestation of relevant economic relations and is determined by the latter and; thirdly, social relations between human beings restrain the relations between different subjects of interests. Contradictions between subjects and objects of needs are on the one hand resulted from the relations between man and nature, and more on the other hand, importantly are resulted from the relations between human beings themselves. Human beings exist not as isolated individuals but essentially in communities. It is the contradictions between human beings that make the contradictions between subjects and objects of needs become contradictions in real social life. Moreover, the social differences between the subjects in different social relations give rise to the distribution relations, difference and contradictions because of the objects of needs among the subjects and then their contradiction in interest relations. Various subjects in society need to satisfy their needs with certain objects, which will lead to shortage of the objects and thus the contradictions between the subjects and the objects of needs, and further the interest contradictions among human beings. It can be seen from the above discussion that social interest relations arise only on the basis of social relations.

Third, social practice serves as the objective basis of interests. To solve the contradictions between subjects and objects of needs, there must be sufficient objects, which can only be sought and created by human beings through their social practices and then be distributed and brought into the domain of social consumption to satisfy human interest needs in given social relations—which is essentially practical. Social practice thus serves as the objective means and basis of interests.

Fourth, objects of human needs serve as the real content of interests. What are interests? The interest is something that can satisfy human beings in one way or another. That is to say, the realization of interests must have their real objects of needs as the precondition, without which—even the spiritual ones—there would no interest at all. Objects of human needs in actual existence can be either something material such as material products or something spiritual such as spiritual products; it can be either the fruits of human social practice such as man-made products or substance in nature like air and sun light. Whatever their sources, objects of needs constitute the real content of interests, material content in particular.

Fifth, human desires serve as the subjective elements of interests. Given their natural basis, social basis, objective basis and real content, interests reflecthuman subjective pursuit of needs, which is manifested in interest propensity and cognition based on human desires. In this sense, human cognition of interests, being it perceptual or conceptual, is the subjective constituent elements of interests.

We have discussed five constituent elements of interests. However, elements of the interest are not the interest itself. For the interest to come into being, the five elements must be integrated, which can only be done by its social basis, that is, interest relations. Social relations constitute not only the necessary condition for creating objects of needs but also agent that links the subjects and the objects. Among the five constituent elements, social relations play the important role of linking and uniting.

II. Characteristics, Social Nature and Definition of Interest Category

Seeing from the five constituent elements, we can find that interestsh ave the following characteristics:

1. Interests have objective content and thus are objective

Although interests represent human subjective demands in forms, they are objective, and material andreal first of all, in forms. Interests are material and objective in terms content, means of formation and basis. For instance, the process in which people seek for food is a process of material production. Interests first of all manifest themselves as social material production, and thus the products of mode of material production. Human relations manifested in interests are primarily material and economic relations and secondarily ideological, political and ethical relations. In this sense, interests are objective, and whose objectivity must primarily be understood as material and physical. The objectivity of interests implies that the formation, existence, functions and laws governing them are independent of human will. All interests pursued by their subjects are objective rather than abstractive and empty. For instance, life necessities sought by subjects of interests for the subsistence and extension of their lives are material and objective; honor, status, power, fame and gain and the like are all based on material existence and therefore are objective. Interests take object as their contents, premise and basis and therefore are objective and concrete, perceivable to their subjects.

2. Interest has subjective form and thus is subjective

Interests reflect human subjective pursuit for and propensity and cognition of the objects of needs; and the realization of interests are impossible without human subjective efforts and subjective activities. Interests thus show a nature of subjectivity, which is mostly manifested in human subjective needs for interests, their physiological desires for interests, their feelings, understanding and active pursuits of interests, their pursuit of, competition and fighting for interests, their production andobtaining of interests, and their purposeful distribution and consumption of interests. The subjectivity of interests also finds its expression in the fact that, there are subjective differences of perceptions between subjects of interests; in other words, different subjects of interests have different perceptions of same objects of interests.

3. Interests are the manifestations of social relations and thus are social

Interests are primarily material and economic interests, which are the embodiment of economic relations, without which there would be no interests at all. Social relations are necessary in the formation ofinterests, so are their distribution. Therefore an important characteristic of interests is their social nature. Human needs are natural and social dual-sides. Human natural physiological needs such as breathing, drinking and eating, are barely distinguishable from that of animals. But the other sides of human social needs are social needs, which essentially distinguish human beings from animals. In fact, with the evolution and development of human society, pure natural characteristics in human needs have been diminishing, that is, become more and more different from that of animals. Take water drinking for example. Humans less and less drink water directly from nature and drinking water in general has become socialized products like tap-water, leverages, etc. Even sexual relations between male and female also have evolved from direct and physiological one in the primitive society into complicated marital relations, which involves various complex social, economic, cultural and historical factors. It should be pointed out that human needs are human social needs, which after all, have some physiological remnants. The case is different with interests, which themselves been the manifestations of social economic relations from the very beginning, so are the interest relations between human beings, which are indeed the distribution relations of social products on the basis of given productive forces, as well asdistribution relations between political powers. It is in this sense we say that interests are social.

4. Interests are objective in content and subjective in forms, thus have the dual character of being subjective and objective

The content, formation and realization of interests on the one hand are subjective, but on the other are objective because they are restricted by objective factors. The interest isthe dialectical unity of subjective and objective factors, in which, objectivity, actuality, materiality and sociality shall be taken as their primary or essence and their subjectivity as secondary or form.

In addition to the characteristics discussed above, interests also have the nature of vector-like and distinctiveness. By vector-like we mean interests have their directions and quantities depending on human needs. For instance, gain or loss of interest involves direction while great or small of interest involves quantity. By distinctiveness we mean that different subjects and objects are different. Subjects of interests, individual or group, are different from each other, so are objects of interests. Material interests are different fromspiritual interests, for instance; so are economic interest and political interest.

Needs and interests are both consistent and distinct from each other, which cannot be confused. Needs are the manifestations of human activities of life, the representation of the subjects' (human beings) demands of and satisfaction with the objects of needs, and the reflection of the direct dependence of human beings as the subjects upon the objects of needs, or material and spiritual life conditions necessary for human beings to sustain their lives. Interests, arising from needs, are human beings' propensity, cognition, pursuit, distribution and satisfaction of needs, and also the reflection of the distribution and social relations among human beings in dealing with the objects of needs. Between needs and interests, there are the following two major differences with the social relation nature of interests being the most distinctive feature: First, needs reflect human direct desires for their objects while interests manifesthuman higher level and rational propensity, concern and cognition of the objects of needs; Second, needs reflect human direct dependence upon the objects of needs while interests reflect the social relations among human beings, i. e. , the distribution of objects of needs among them. Interests are needs that can only be manifested through the intermediary of social relations, especially economic relations. While needs reflect only the relations between human beings and the objects of needs, interests reflect the relations among humans because of their dependence on the objects of needs. For needsto become interests, social relations, especially economic relations are indispensable. In any given social formation, human needsalways manifest themselves as interests in a given social relations. Interestsare the manifestations of needs in economic relations, without which, interests can hardlybe understood. For instance, food is man's most basic material need. To have it satisfied, however, he must have means of production first and then acquire it through means of social distribution. Thus, man's needs for material conditions of production and his direct demands for materials are manifested as the interest relations between human beings. It can be seen that with the intermediary of economic relations, man's direct demand for materials are manifested as interest relations between humans derived from needs. So the social nature of needs is their social economic relations.

In regard to the definition of interest, there are mainly four different views. The first view takes interest as something purely subjective, or nothing but man's subjective desires. The second view thinks interest as the unity of subject and object, with its content being objective and form being subjective. The third view believes that interest is purely objective both in content and in form, something that is physical, material and objective. The fourth view sees interest as relations, or the manifestations of material, economic and social relations; interest is nothing but social relations, first of all, material and economic relations. We believe that, interests are a kind of social relations, in which, the subjects of needs, takinga given social relation as the intermediary, social practice as the means, the results of social practice as content, subjective desires as the forms, physiological needs as the precondition, overcoming the contradiction between the subjects and the objects of needs, make certain distribution objects of needs among the subjects of them, thus to a certain degree, satisfy the subjects of needs. In other words, interests are the higher level and rational propensity, pursuit and cognition of the objects of needs, and are the manifestations of needs in economic relations, and reflect a kind of economic distribution of the objects of distribution among human beings. In essence, interests are a kind of social relations and therefore fall into the category of relations. In short, the constituent elements of interests significantly show that, social relations, especially economic relations, as a medium, are indispensable for interests to come into being. Although finding their expression in the solution of contradictions between the subjects and objects and distribution of the latter, interest, in essence, are the manifestations and reflections of certain social relations, and thus the relations among human beings. So, interests are a form of social relations with certain attributes, which is formed in the process of distributing the objects of needs among and with the purpose to satisfy the subjects of needs.

III. Classification of Interests

To study interests, it is necessary not only to make a definition but also a classification of it. Interests constitute a big and complex system composed of interests of different properties, characteristics, functions and categories. To make a clear classification of interests, a scientific method of classification is necessary so as to have a complete grasp of their internal structure. So do an objective principle of classification. Interests can be classified on the basis of different criteria. For instance, on the basis of the relation between general and particular, interests can be classified into individual/particular interests and common/general interests (universal interests); on the basis of scope of realization, interests can be classified into local interests and overall interests; on the basis of the differences between subjects, interests can be classified into individual interests, group/collective interests and overall social interests, which can be sub-divided into family interests, enterprise interests, unit interests, regional interests, stratum interests, class interests, ethnic interests, state interests, etc. , the interests of certain kind of subjects, such as the interests of farmers, working class, etc. ; on the basis of time of realization, interests can be classified into long term interests and immediate interests; on the basis of degree of importance, interests can be classified into fundamental interests and temporary interests; on the basis of state of realization, interests can be classified into future interests and vested interests; on the basis of objective content, interests can be classified into material interests and spiritual interests, economic interests and political interests, etc. ; and on the basis possibility of realization, interests can be classified into realistic interests and ideal interests.

1. Individual/particular interests and general/common interests

Interests of any individual are individual ones compared to that of the group and the whole society; interests of individual group are individual ones compared to that of the larger group and the whole society. Individual interests are certain particular interests, which are in contrast to general and common interests. It should be noted that personal interests are individual and particular interests and group interests are common interests; interests of smaller communities (such as collective interests) are individual and particular interests and that of larger communities (state interests) are common interests. And each subject of interests has dual character, which means that it embodies both individual/particular interests and common interests. Individual interests, particular interests and common interests form a complicated network of unity of opposites, which ultimately links the whole human society with common interests. Group or group interests are particular ones compared to the interests of the whole human society. General/common interests exist in individual/particular interests and the general/common interests contain individual/particular interests. For instance, the common interests of the whole human society are on the one hand based on individual and group interests, and on the other, contain the individual or particular interests.

While general/common interests are based on individual/particular interests, they are not just the sum total of the latter; rather, they have become interests of higher level. Although general/common interests are composed of the most general and fundamental parts of individual/particular interests, they represent or contain not all of the individual/particular interests, but the most imminent parts of them that can only be realized after common interests have been realized. For example, the Third Estate during French Revolution had its general/common interests of overthrowing the feudal autocracy, although there were acute interest contradictions within the class itself. It was the general/common interests that united the Third Estate to finally win the revolution. Similar stories are common in history. The cooperation between the Communist Party of China and Kuomintang based on the common interests of the Chinese nation is another good example.

2. Personal interests, group interests and overall social interests

Interests always have their subjects that are large in number in terms of types, on the differences of natures of which the classification of interests is based, such as the common natures, natures of group, class, physiology, profession, locality, culture, and so on. Based on common nature of subjects, interests can be classified into personal interests, group interests and overall social interests. Personal interests refer to the objects or targets of needs pursued by individual persons, which constitutes the main motivefor personal action and reflect the interest relation between individuals. Among personal, group and overall social interests, personal interests constitute the basis. "Throughout history the 'general interest' is created by individuals who are defined as 'private persons'."① The common basis for personal interests to be elevated into common interests is the sociality of human beings. Some bourgeois scholars believe that human beings are selfish and their relations thereof are just like that of wolves, because they see only that personal interests constitute the major motive for individual actions and personal interests always conflict to each other. What they fail to see is behind personal interests there are common interests acting as constraints. In *Capital*, when he analyzed the commodity exchange, Marx points out the unity of personal interests and common interests. In the market of commodity exchange, both parties aim to realize their own personal interests on the basis of personal needs. Party A exchanges money with his products and purchases commodities of his needs with the money from party B, and thus realizes his personal interests; through this exchange, party B can also purchase what he needs with the money to realize his own personal interests. The content in this exchange is the common interests of party A and party B,

---

① *Collected Marx and Engels Works*, vol. 3, People's Publishing House, 1960, pp. 275-276.

because it exists "behind the back of these self-reflected particular interests"[①], which is imperceptible. According to Marx, personal interests constitute a major factor that links the civil society. Therefore, on the basis of personal interests there must be common interests.

Common interests have two sub-categories: one is overall social interests and the other is group interests. Overall social interests

is the interest of the whole society as a subject of interests and is presented in two embodiments: one is the common interest of individuals and individual communities and the other is the interest realized as the human society integrated as an organic subject of interests. It is a gradual course for common interest of the whole society to have emerged and further developed, and now is more and more clearly recognized with the development of science and technology as well as the improvement of civilization. Many issues of concern to modern social scientists as well as natural scientists, such as energy, population, ecology, environment and pollution, are issues of common interest to the human society as a whole. Although these issues are far away from being settled, people around the world now recognize that they must be settled on the basis of the common interest of the whole human society.

People can form various kinds of communities through the link of their own relative common interests, e. g. , women's interest, family interest and enterprise interest. Anyway, group interests are very complicated and diversified. As a special kind of group interest, collective interest does not refer to the interest of the ensemble of average people but that of the ensemble of laborers who engage in the social economic course through the link of concrete economic relations and make their economic liquidation independently. The collectives are basic units of social production and cells of national economy. In the socialist states, the collective interests are key factors constituting state interest and of effect to personal interests, because the socialist laborers' collectives, as basic units of social production, are the most important forms organizing individual laborers in the society to have simple reproduction and expanded reproduction, to accumulate social wealth and thereby form the state interest. On the other hand, individuals can realize his personal interests with the remuneration for work and other payment got from the collectives. Therefore collective

---

① *Collected Marx and Engels Works*, vol. 46a, People's Publishing House, 1979, p. 196.

interest is a medium and link between state interest and personal interest, whose state of play is relevant to them both.

3. Class interest, national interest and state interest

As far as group interest is concerned, there are several types of group interests that are of great importance in the social life at given stages of social historical development.

Firstly, class interest. As for the term class, Lenin had an all-round definition: "Classes are large groups of people differing from each other by the place they occupy in a historically determined system of social production, by their relation (in most cases fixed and formulated in law) to the means of production, by their role in the social organization of labor, and, consequently, by the dimensions of the share of social wealth of which they dispose and the mode of acquiring it. Classes are groups of people one of which can appropriate the labor of another owing to the different places they occupy in a definite system of social economy. "① Class interest is the common interest of these social groups. It is based on the individual interests of people with different social places and manifests the essence of common interest of different individuals, groups and stratums in the class. It is in the meantime higher than individual interest and hence conditions individual interest and individual action of members in the class. Since the human society was ushered into class society with the emergence of private property, class interest has played an extremely important role in driving social development. In class societies, there are necessarily two major class interests contradictory to each other—that of the ruling class and the ruled class, of the exploiting class and the exploited class. While they have different content and forms of contradiction in different social formations, the two contradictory class interests in general determine acts of most people in any of the social formations and are source of economic and political conflict in the society, whose contradiction, conflict and solution therein drives the development of class societies.

Secondly, national interest. A nation is a stable social group of people with shared language, geographical boundary, economic and political life and psychological characters shaped in the long history of development. In such social communities, there arises national common interest. National interest has far ranging contents, among which national economic interest

① *Selected Works of Lenin*, vol. 4, People's Publishing House, 1995, p. 11.

necessary to sustain national subsistence and development is the most fundamental one. Owing to national interest, members in the nation maintained their shared cultural identity and national sentiments. Shared national interest doesn't necessarily rule out class interest and the contradiction and difference of different class interests in the same nation. In the class societies, national interest is also class interest, or at least is influenced and conditioned by class interest. National interest as a special kind of interest, is different from class interest, especially when a nation is invaded by a foreign nation, the conflicted classes may disclaim their special interest and strive for their common national interest. In multinational countries, national interest can be further classified into national interest common to all nations and national interest specific to any one nation, e. g. , national interest of the Chinese nation and nation interest of an ethnic group.

Thirdly, state interest. State divides the inhabitants in it on the basis of geographical boundaries and has public authority, designated officials and various apparatus of violence. Since the emergence of state, its public authority and apparatus of violence have been under the control of the ruling class in that social formation. " The state is a machine for maintaining the rule of one class over another. "[1] The class nature of state determines the nature of state interest, which is not for the interest of all inhabitants wherein but for the class interest of those in the ruling position, and thus is a special form of class interest. In multination states, common national interest are consistent with the state interest, while national interest of any particular nation is a kind of special interest as comparing to state interest.

State has the function of regulating relations among inhabitants, keeping social order and undertaking public affairs. It protects its state interest from being violated by others. State as an ensemble of inhabitants living together in a geographical territory has certain common interests. When a state is invaded and state interest seriously threatened, contradiction and conflict of various national interests and class interests therein will drop to a less important position, the state interest will rise to a dominant position, and people of any nation and any class will thus temporarily ignore their interest difference and unite against foreign aggression to defend their state interest. Even in these circumstances, however, we shall not forget the

---

[1] *Selected Works of Lenin*, vol. 4, People's Publishing House, 1995, p. 31.

nature of state interest. At the time when various classes and nations were fighting for state interest, their interest contradiction and conflict didn't ever disappear but simply drop to less important position. At that time, it would be impossible to ensure their interests without defending the state interest. Realizing the part of interest in state interest that satisfies the common needs of inhabitants therein is in essence ensuring interest of the ruling class. If this part of interest is not materialized, the ruling class won't be able to maintain its ruling and hence realize its class interest. Therefore, no matter what laurel does the exploiting class crown on its interest, they cannot cover its nature. Just as Marx and Engels remarked: "For each new class which puts itself in the place of one ruling before it, is compelled, merely in order to carry through its aim, to represent its interest as the common interest of all the members of society, that is, expressed in ideal form: it has to give its ideas the form of universality, and represent them as the only rational, universally valid ones. The class making a revolution appears from the very start, if only because it is opposed to a class, not as a class but as the representative of the whole of society; it appears as the whole mass of society confronting the one ruling class. It can do this because, to start with, its interest really is more connected with the common interest of all other non-ruling classes, because under the pressure of hitherto existing conditions its interest has not yet been able to develop as the particular interest of a particular class. "[1] When the new class becomes the ruling one, then state interest or social interest must become the particular interest of a particular class—the ruling class.

4. Material interest and spiritual interest

As an interest category with the material object of need as its actual content, material interest shows the relation of material allocation among subjects of interests. Material need is the most fundamental human need, the satisfaction of which is the precondition of human subsistence and development and the basis of any other historical actions of human beings. Material interest shows a relation of economic allocation and material possessing of material need by subject of interests. People strive directly for material interests by working and production; their engaging in class struggle and social revolution is also for actual material

---

[1] *Collected Marx and Engels Works*, vol. 3, People's Publishing House, 1960, p. 54.

interest. Spiritual interest is an interest category with spiritual object of need as its actual content. Along with the development of human civilization, people will seek more eagerly for spiritual interests to satisfy their ever growing actual needs.

Material interest is the basis and guarantee of spiritual interest, although for some people at a specific time, realizing their spiritual interests is important than realizing material interest.

In the Chinese history of thought, although some figures have noticed " interest " as a necessary condition for human subsistence and development, they didn't know the difference between material interest and spiritualinterest, therefore their perceptions on interest were narrow and limited. For instance, Mozi advocated a biased opinion of abolishing music, because he regarded music as something wasteful against interest due to his ignorance of the important role of spiritual interest in human life, although he affirmed the place of material interest. Sima Qian, a great Chinese historian, thought it proper for people to seek "interests", and that it is man's seeking of " interests " that drives the social development. He believed that seeking personal interests is the " human nature" of people that can be contained by nobody. However, he also limited "interest" to material interest that gives people happy life, without any consideration of spiritual interest. In the West, after the Renaissance, the bourgeoisie justified man's desire, but didn' t recognize the spiritual interest beyond the material interest. That is why the bourgeoisie philistines denounced Materialism as the seeking of extravagant material interests by putting material interest and spiritual interest in opposite. Engels bitterly satirized such philistines: " By the word materialism, the philistine understands gluttony, drunkenness, lust of the eye, lust of the flesh, arrogance, cupidity, avarice, covetousness, profit-hunting, and stock-exchange swindling — in short, all the filthy vices in which he himself indulges in private. By the word idealism he understands the belief in virtue, universal philanthropy, and in a general way a ' better world' , of which he boasts before others but in which he himself at the utmost believes only so long as he is having the blues or is going through the bankruptcy consequent upon his customary ' materialist' excesses. It is then that he sings his favorite song, what is man? — half beast, half angel. "[1]

---

[1] *Selected Marx and Engels Works*, vol. 4, People's Publishing House, 1995, pp. 232—233.

In fact, both material need and spiritual need are indispensable to any man, which means that man has not only material interests but also spiritual interests. Contents of both material and spiritual interests are determined by the level of productive forces. With the improvement of information technology, content and level of people's material interests change greatly, and their requirements for spiritual interests also become higher and more imperative. Some of the requirements are the result of defects in the capitalist society. For instance, the highly automatic capitalist production and the penetrating capitalist way of "cash payment" relations drowned the bright emotions between men in icy water and made people more and more isolated and lonely, people in such relations were eager for some psychological compensation, therefore they broadened their social intercourse for idea exchange and emotional interactions. Some requirements of spiritual interests are the logical result of development in modern society. For instance, the highly developed modern production posed higher requirements on people's knowledge and skills, making such spiritual interests as learning science and technology, training and education more and more stressing, to accommodate them, life-long education becomes more and more popular in developed capitalist societies. With the development of material interests in both content and level, people have higher requirement for cultural achievements as well. Some futurists believe that among the five major categories of work in the future, two are related to the realization of human spiritual interests: one being creative work such as science and art, one being colorful social activities arranged for leisure time, e. g. , organizing traveling, physical activities and entertainments and recreations.

To conclude, both material and spiritual interests are necessary to human beings, and it is ridiculous to put them in contradiction and bias people's seeking material interests as scourges and source of social disorder.

5. Economic interest and political interest

Both material and spiritual interests can be realized only through various economic and non-economic activities carried out in given social relations. Hence, in real social lives, they also appear as economic interest and non-economic interest, such as political interest.

To get material interests, one has to create objects' use value by engaging in social economic activities on the basis of given economic relations, and further create objects' value by introducing their use value into the domain of distribution, circulation, exchange and consumption through economic relations, so that there arises economic needs and thus generates economic interests. When referring to economic interests, we mean the possessing and consuming of economic relations, economic activities and the products produced wherein, or the satisfaction of needs for income (most generally wages, profit, bonus and etc), which is the manifestation of social interests in the form of social economic relations. Economic interests can be further classified into many sub-classes, e. g. , consumptive interest, monetary interest and income interest. With regard to the relation between material interest, spiritual interest and economic interest and political interest, they are different but with some overlapping. Most material interests are in the form of social economic relations, hence overlap with economic interests. However, there are still many material interests that are not economic ones, and on the other hand some spiritual interests can also be economic ones. At the time when social material consumables are not in great abundance, material consumption is the economic interests of most people. In human societies at the stage of commercial economy, the universal equivalence can only be money, hence monetary interest is the most general form of economic interests that can realize people's material interests and at the same time can also serve as an important medium of realizing spiritual interests. The realization of certain economic interests can not only satisfy people's material needs, but also their spiritual needs and thus realize their spiritual interests. For instance, preference of economic activities and success in business often give people great mental pleasure, serving to satisfy people's higher spiritual needs such as self-actualization in given fields; the satisfaction of needs of certain economic relations can only indirectly assure man's material interests but not the satisfaction of material interests.

Counterpart of economic interest is non-economic interest, mostly spiritual interest. Non-economic interest is the interest of satisfying people's non-economic need through non-economic activities.

Among non-economic interests, the most important one is political interest. To realize economic interests through economic activities preconditions by specific economic relations, there must be relevant assurance from the political superstructure that involves political activities, therefore there arises political need. People's political needs are satisfied through political activities and the filtering of certain political relations—political interests. Therefore political interest is the manifestation of political relations, although it is basically determined by economic interests. In class society, main content of politics lies in the fact that some large groups of influence realizing their interests (mainly material and economic interests) by achieving their political and further their economic goals through state power and various apparatuses of power. Political interests are the manifestation of economic interests. Also, political interests can be further classified into many sub-classes, such as interests of political parties, of rights and of revolution. Different political interests exist not only in different classes, but also in the same class.

As for the relation between economic interest and political interest, a basic fact is that economic interest is the basis. Firstly, economic interest is the source of political interest. It is economic interest that prompts some groups to defend or change social relations and social structure, to maintain or change power, and in this way political interest arises. It is economic interest that results in different political activities, which further determine political ideas and ideologies. Secondly, change of political interest is determined by changes in economic interest. If economic interests of different people or groups change, their political interests will also change. Change in economic relations will result in the change of political interests being sought. Change of political interests can be either qualitatively or quantitatively. Qualitative change is resulted from the solving of diametrically opposed economic interest contradiction; quantitative change is the turning over of power from one stratum or group to the other inside the same class. Thirdly, the ultimate purpose of seeking political interest is to realize economic interest. "In the struggle between landed property and the bourgeoisie, no less than in the struggle between the bourgeoisie and the proletariat, it was a question, first and foremost, of economic interests, to the furtherance of which political power was intended to serve merely as a means."[1] Therefore economic interest is the source and final destination of political interest.

However, once political interest arises, it will be independent of economic interest, which is manifested in the following:

Firstly, political interest is sometimes disconnected with economic interest. Although political interest is generally and ultimately consistent

---

[1]   *Selected Marx and Engels Works*, vol. 4, People's Publishing House, 1995, p. 250.

with economic interest, sometimes, due to the limitation of subjective and objective conditions on people's perception and seeking of political and economic interest, political interest may disconnect with economic interest, that is to say, people may seek a political interest that doesn't conform to their economic interests and take it as the goal of their action. There are three reasons for that to happen: firstly, people didn't know what economic interests they are to seek, what they seek is the political goal publicized by some political organizations, for which they don't know the economic purpose and economic interests embodied therein; secondly, although people seek some economic interests in a conscious way, they don't know that the political program and political goal publicized by some political parties or political leaders cannot realize, or at least cannot fully realize their economic interests; thirdly, for some leading individuals and the political groups organized by them, they could relinquish their personal economic interests for the sake of the long term economic interests of the majorities, and thus for them, political interest is disconnected with personal economic interest. Therefore, people's political activities and political front cannot always precisely reflect the existed social economic interests.

Secondly, political interest may react on economic interest. Politics is the manifestation of economy. As a means and instrument for the realization of economic interest, politics serves economy and assures the realization of economic interest. Reaction of political interest on economic interest is of two folds. On the one hand, realization of political interest is the precondition of realizing economic interest. In order to get some economic interests, it is necessary first of all to realize relevant political interests, among which the most significant one is to seize and consolidate state power. It is possible only to realize economic interests after the realization of political interests. On the other hand, political interests can serve to consolidate vested economic interests. Vest interests can be consolidated either by political activities such as political struggle and political propaganda or by diverging focus of others from changing the economic relation and the existed system in the way of concealing economic interests with political deceiving.

Thirdly, various specific political interests can mutually reinforce or undermine with each other. Although political interests are based on economic interests, each single political interest can be reinforced or undermined due to the reinforcement or undermining of one more political interest. For instance, strength and stability of state power can further strengthen other political interests of the state power holder.

Due to the importance of political interests to economic interests, they are extremely important to the political parties and politicians who strive for their class interests. Seeking state power is the supreme manifestation of seeking political interests. That is why classes with economic dominance would do their best to consolidate their political position.

Long-term interest and immediate interest; overall interest and partial interest; future interest and vested interest; fundamental interest and temporary interest; actual interest and ideal interest

On the basis of the scope of interests, we can divide them into the above mentioned pairs of interests.

Long-term interest is the interest that impacts on the existence and development of certain human needs in the future and can be realized in the long run. Immediate interest, or short-term interest, is the interest of immediate need that can be realized shortly. Long-term interest and immediate interest are comparative and interchangeable. For instance, some long-term interests may become short-term interests if compared to longer-term interests; some short-term interests may become long term interest if compared to shorter-term interests.

As far as the relation between long-term interest and immediate interest is concerned, the latter is the basis of the former, without which people's immediate needs cannot be satisfied and their subsistence not assured, not to mention the satisfaction of long-term interests that are relevant to their future development. On the other hand, long-term interest is more fundamental and essential than immediate interest. Focusing on immediate interests without caring for the long-term interests will terminate the course of development and thus immediate interests will ultimately get lost. Generally speaking, immediate interests are the major motives that prompt mass actions, since the average people often decide their interest goal on the basis of immediate needs. Since long-term interests are often not in the horizons of the average people, for them long-term interests have no relation to immediate ones and even in conflict, therefore some people, through their blindfold acts, jeopardize the long-term interests that are essential to the future survival and development of human beings with their immediate interests. In this sense, as an important part of improving people's awareness of their acts, they shall be encouraged to improve their horizons with any means possible, so that they can recognize the importance of long-term interests and thus associate them with their immediate interests, or even be ready to temporarily relinquish their immediate interests for the sake of the long-term interests. Of course, when seeking the long-term interests, we shall not forget people's immediate interests and shall try to satisfy them; otherwise the pursuit of long-term interests will lose driving force and become a meaningless dream. Comrade Mao Zedong comments on Chinese agricultural co-operative movement that, "if, we had nothing new to offer the farmers and could not help them to raise their productivity, increase their income and attain collective prosperity, the poor ones would no longer trust us and would believe that there was no point in following the Party. Since they were poor usual after land distribution, how could they still follow us?" This remarks points out the importance of immediate interests.

The overall interest, or interest of the whole, refers to the common interest of a group, a state, a nation, a class, a stratum, an enterprise, a party and or a group. Partial interest refers to a certain part of interest in the overall interest. The overall interest is made up of partial interests but not as the result of a simple adding of them. The overall interest serves to direct, limit and influence partial interests, and on the other hand the realization of partial interests serves as a precondition of realizing the overall interest. While partial interests shall subordinate to the overall interest, to realize the overall interest must take account of the partial interests. Sometimes in order to realize or save the overall interest, certain partial interests can be temporarily relinquished or sacrificed.

Future interest is the long-standing and fundamental interest to be strived for. Vested interest is the interest that has been attained temporarily or in a short term but may get lost or be relinquished. The future interest serves to guide vested interest. It is not proper to be limited to vested interest and relinquish the long-standing and fundamental interest, to give up struggle and strive, or even do something harmful for long-term and fundamental interest against the progress of history with an aim of preserve vested interest.

Fundamental interest is the long-term and overall interest that reflects needs of the majorities. Temporary interest is the super-facial, immediate and individual interest that sometimes only reflects needs of the minorities or the unreasonable needs. The fundamental interest serves to guide, limit and dominate the temporary interest and the latter subordinate to it.

Generally speaking, human interests can be divided into two parts: one can be taken as actual interest that can be offered under the current productive force by subjective and objective conditions in a given time; the other can be regarded as ideal interest that cannot be offered under the current productive force by subjective and objective conditions in a given time but can be satisfied after certain time of development. Actual interests are existed interests provided by the society under existed productive force and subjective and objective conditions to people to satisfy their material and spiritual needs. Basically, judging whether the interest in a given society at a given historical period is actual or not shall be based on the judgment of whether the interest provided by the society can satisfy people's material and spiritual need or not, and ultimately on the state of productive force at that time. Ideal interests are in fact interest goals reachable in the future through struggle and effort, which share to a certain degree characters of long-term interest and future interest.

Chapter Five

Interest Subject and Interest Object

As a relational category, interest is the dialectic unity of its subject and object. In this chapter, we will discuss the subject and object of interests, their characteristics and the relations between them.

I. The Structure and Characteristics of the Subject of Interests

The subject of interests, derived from the subject of needs, refers to humans (individuals or groups) who engages in productive or any other social activities in given social relations to directly or indirectly satisfy hisown social needs, or in other words, a subject of interests is a pursuer, bearer, producer, realizer, consumer and owner of interests. Interest relations and contradictions of different forms, as well as their contents and natures, will inevitably find their expressions in the relationsand contradictions between subjects of interests as the conscious, active and subjective components of social interest movement. Different subjects of interests can be roughly divided into two categories, namely, interest individuals and interest groups. Interest individuals refer tosubjects of interests existing as isolated individuals; interest groups refer to aggregates of individual subjects.

1. The characteristics of the subject of interests
The subject of interests has the following six major characteristics:
(1) Naturalness. Man as the subject of interests is not super-natural being outside nature, but rather a product and a special part of nature. Man is the product of the long-term developmentof the material world, thebody of which is the physical form composed of complicated elements, and the activities of which is the outcome of their long-term response to the elements. The physiological, psychological and mental

activities and social practical activities of the subject in interest pursuit, such as desires, inclination, etc. , all have their natural material basis. Therefore naturalness is the first natural characteristic of the subject of interests, and the carrier, premise, condition, content and basis of its other characteristics.

(2) Practicality. Practicality is the fundamental characteristic of the subject of interests. The reason man becomes the subject of interests is that he doesn't passively pursue interests to satisfy his needs or sustain his subsistence and development by relying only on the conditions and materials provided by nature; on the contrary, he actively changes the natural and social environment through his social practice in pursuing material interests for that. As the subject of interests, man changes and perfects himself in the process of changing the external world. That is to say, the subject of interests is not only a pursuer and consumer, but more importantly, a producer and creator of interests. Man constantly perfects himself in the course of satisfying his most fundamental material interest needs through his productive practice, and his political and spiritual interest needs through his political and spiritual practice. Practice is a basic form of activities of man as the subject of interests, and the most important and concentrated manifestation of his interest pursuit. The practicality of the subject of interests finds its expressions in the fact that, on the one hand, human needs must be created through social practice; on the other, the process of man's seeking, attaining and consuming interests is also a process of practice.

(3) Sociality. Man is a social being and the sum total of social relations. Since the subject of interests is man, he is also a social subject, namely, social being and totality of social relations. In fact, since interest itself is the manifestation of social relations, the subject of interests is naturally social as well. Without sociality, there will be no subject of interests at all. In a class society, the sociality of the subject of interests has a class nature, so isthe subject of interests.

(4) Consciousness. Since man has consciousness, the subject of interests also has consciousness. The consciousness of the subject of interestsfinds its expression in forms of sentiments, desires, will, purposes, ideas, subjective demands, inclination, etc. , which manifest themselves as his subjective demands, desires, purposes, inclination and cognition of interests. On the other hand, however, the subjective manifestation of the subject of needs take objective needs as its target and

actual content. The expression, direction, purpose and inclination of the subject in seeking, attaining and consuming interestsare precisely the manifestation of this consciousness.

(5) Activeness. Since man is self-conscious, purposeful and practical, as the subject of interests, he is active in his thinking and actions, i. e. , he has subjective initiative. By activeness we mean that, the subject satisfies his needs by actively, instead of passively, seeking, attaining, creating and consuming interests. The difference between animal needs and human needs is that animal needsarecompletely natural, physiological and passive while human needsare self-conscious, active and creative. In pursuing and obtaining interests, the subject of needs is intentional, active, selective and creative and free of will. In other words, he shows a subjective initiative.

(6) Collectivity. The sociality of the subject of interests determines its collectivity. By collectivity we mean that the subject of interests usually seeks interests in a collective or organized way. No individual subject of interests can independently realize the seeking, attaining and distribution of interests. Althoughthe motive or action may be individual, the whole process of pursuit can only be carried out collectively, other than individually, in and through given social relations.

2. Classification of subjects of interests

Subjects of interests can be divided into six levels of individual, household, collective, group, state and human society, which can be categorized into two broad categories of interest individuals and interest groups, with interest individuals belonging to the former and the rest to the latter.

Individuals constitute themost basic elements of the subject of interests. Under private ownership, individuals are subjects of private interests and there are antagonistic contradictions between opposing classes. Under socialist system, although individuals are the subjects of their own interests and the basis forthe contradictions between opposing classes have been basically eliminated, there are still interest contradictions and conflicts.

The household assubject of interests is at a higher level than individuals. In the society of natural economy, households are the most basic economic units and groups; accordingly, household interest relations are the most basic interest relations. In such a society, a household is not only a consumer unit, but also a unit that engages in production and other activities. Since a household is the subject of economic interests and consumer interests, the interests of a household thus have a direct influence on the interests of its members. In asociety of market economy, although its economic role is less important, household is still an important subject of social interests. In addition, a household involves in some special interest relations arising from its needs in social life, such as marriage and heritance.

A collective refers to an organization consisted of individuals with shared interests; it is, on the one hand, the representative of its member's individual interests; on the other, the subject of common interests of the organization. In the society of market economy, enterprises are economic collectives with a relatively independent status and the most significant collectives of interests. It has higher interest demands than an individual and a household subject of interests. In a market economy, there are interest competitions among enterprises. Collective interests are links and intermediary between individual interests and state interests.

A group is an interest entity higher than a collective and lower than a state. It has concentrated interests and is well-organized. Examples of interest group include tribes and tribal confederations in primitive society, classes and strata and political interest groups in a class society, and group company in economic life, etc. A group is a more concentrated and more cohesive interest entity with stronger interest orientation and well-organized structure.

State is the representative and subject of the common interests of a society. In the society of private ownership, a state represents essentially the interests of the ruling classes; a socialist state is the representative of the common interests of all its citizens. Sate interests, immediate or long-term, represent individual interests and collective interests on the one hand, and the overall interests of all members in the society on the other. This kind of statusalso leads to the existence of contradictions between state interests and individual and collective interests. The state is the representative of common interests of the ruling class, but state interests cannot be equatedwith the common interests of the whole society.

By society we mean the human society as a whole. It is the subject of the common interests of the human society. Although different interest individuals and interest groups all have their own particular interests, such as national interests, state interests in a broad sense and individual interests in a narrower sense, all member of the human society havetheir common interests. For example, disease prevention and control is a common interest concerning the health of all human beings. Overall social interests are interests at the highest level of the whole human society with the whole society as the subject representative and subject of them. The part of common interests of the individuals, households, collectives and states are all organically integrated in the common interests of the whole society. On the other hand, the common interests of the whole human society are generally expressed in the demands of truly representative international organizations. For instance, the issue of global environmental protection relevant to the survival and development of the whole of humanity is expressed in the common program of international environmental organizations.

3. Relation between subjects of Interests

Various subjects of interests are socially related in given social relations. We can vertically and horizontally analyze the relations and contradictions between these subjects, especially interest groups. Since interests constitutea system of multiple levels, areas, functions and types, various social subjects of interests are vertically and horizontally linked. Theirmutual interaction, influence and restraints form a complex networkof relations, in which, the vertical relations include those between individuals, groups and the whole of humanity and the horizontal oneinclude relations among individuals and among groups.

First, the vertical relationsbetween subjects of interests.

The vertical relations between subjects of interests are relations between individuals, groups andthe whole of humanity. Individuals are the subjects of individual interests and each individual has his own individual interests. Groups are the subjects of the common interests of aggregates, whose forms include households, enterprises, work units, regions, groups, strata, classes, nations and states. A household is not only a consumer unit, but also a unit that engages in production and other activities. Since a household is the subject of economic interests and consumer interests, the interests of a household thus have a direct influence on the interests of its members. In addition, a household involves in some special interest relations arising from its needs in social life, such as marriage and heritance. In the society of market economy, enterprise interests are links and intermediary between individual interests and state interests. Different social groups, strata, classes, ethnic groups, nations, etc. , all have their own common interests, such as the common interests of the intellectuals, the farmers, the working class. In social economic life, social economic unitsare economic entities with a relatively independent social status, elementary cells of social economic life and the most significant interest entities, whose interests are higher than individual and household interests. As the part of group interests at the highest level, state interests constitute a very special kind of group interests. In terms of state interests in a class society, first of all, they are the concentrated expressions of interests of the ruling classes, and secondly, some of the common interests of the interest groups within its territory. The relations of these three kinds of subject of interests, i. e. , individuals, collectives and the state are very important, which vertical speaking, is a unity of the opposites.

Second, the horizontal relations between subjects of interests.

Due to various social and historical reasons, there are some social differences, primarily economic differences between different individuals and differentgroups (states, nations, classes, strata, regions, enterprises, sectors, organizations and families), which form the horizontal relations between subjects of interests. For instance, in a class society, there are fundamentally antagonistic contradictions of class interests between the ruling and the ruled classes. In a socialist society, there are also differences and relations of economic interests between members with different work positions and professions (such as cadres, ordinary laborers, farmers, military men, teachers, artists, athletes, doctors, nurses, service workers, shop assistants and others) due to their differences in income, economic status and social identity; so are differences and relations between ethnic groups, classes, strata and groups, even regions and work unit, given their different conditions of economic development. Within the ranks of the working people, there are also the differences and relations of economic interests among the working class, farmers, and intellectuals, as well as among different enterprises, sectors, work units, etc. , due to differences in economic conditions, environments, returns and the like.

II. Object of interests, Its Connotations and Classifications

Above we have discussed the subjects of interests; next we will analyze the object of interests and the relations between the subject and the object.

1. The object of interests

In the broadest philosophical sense, the subject refers to man engaging in social cognition and practice, while the object refers to person or thing to which man's social cognition and practice directed, or the world the subject's practice directed to. In a word, subjects are men and objects arethesubject's cognition and practice directed to. It is, however, one-sided to simply equate men with the subjects and the natural world with the object. In a strict sense, only men who engage in social practice and relevant cognitive activities can be regarded as the subjects. In other words, only a man having his object of cognition and practice is a subject, who, at the same time, shall be a social, practical, historical and thinking man. Accordingly, a subject of interests is entity that engages in interest pursuit and satisfaction while an object of interests is the thing that the subjects pursue and get satisfaction from. Strictly speaking, interest is a relational category other than asubstantial category. Relation in philosophical sense is first of all material and economic relations, and likewise, interest relations are in the first place material and economic ones. Interest relations imply the following three: firstly, relations between subjects and objects of interests, i. e. , the relations between the subject and object of interests as subjects and objects; secondly, relations between subjects of interests, i. e. , the relations of interest distribution between subjects of interests, which, in fact, are a kind of social relations between different subjects of interests; and thirdly, relations between objects of interests, i. e. , relations between different objects of interests, such as that between material and spiritual interests, between economic and political interests.

As far as therelations between the subject and object of interests is concerned, the subject of interests is a pursuer, bearers, producers, realizers, consumers and owners of interests, i. e. , men with interest needs, which can be either individual or group of individuals; objects of interestsare what the subjects of interests cognize, seek after, need and create, or direct to; or, what the subjects pursue and get satisfaction from.

1. Connotations of the object of interests

The object of interests has the following meanings:

(1) An object of interest is first of all what the subject of interests directs to, needs, desires, pursue and consume. The object of interests is relative to the subject of interests, without the latter, the former will not exist at all; interest itself indeed embodies the relations between the subject and the object. Take an enterprise for example. An enterprise itself is a subject of interests, with its objects being what the enterprise seeks after: profit is the manifestation of its interest, its products is its actual content. No object of interests can exist independent of subject of interests; they are relative to, dependent on each other and mutually preconditioned: they are objections to each other, in which the subject is the active side.

(2) The object of interests is objective and extensive in scope and content. They include both material objects such as an enterprise's productive interests, and spiritual objects such as cultural interests needed by people; both humanized natural objects transformed by human beings and completely natural objectsunchanged; both political objects and economic objects, and so on.

(3) The objects of interests can be either material and substantive carriers or non-material yet concrete and objective content. For instance, food, as a material interest sought after by men, has its actual material content; while some non-material or spiritual interests, such as political interests, are not empty or abstract at all, but rather have their concrete and objective, though intangible, content.

2. Classification of object of interests

Since the object of interests is material, concrete, objective and relational, it can be classified accordingly into the following types: (1) Material objects, including both material interests with purely natural content such as air, land and minerals, and material interests with humanized natural content such as food, house and clothes. (2) Economic objects, with economic interestsas their actual contents such as profit sought after by enterprises. (3) Intellectual objects, with psychological, emotional and cultural needs as their actual content, such as music, songs. (4) Political objects, with rights, political power and other as their content; (5) extensive social objects, with social activities as content such as social activities, social intercourse as well as gatherings, family, clan or group activities. (6) Collective or group objects containing class interests and state interests, and so on; (7) Comprehensive and relational objects, which have intangible yet extensive content and reflect certain relations, such as long-term interests, local interests, etc. Objects of interests oftenmanifest themselves in corresponding ways, such as material interests vis-à-vis spiritual interests, economic interests vis-a-vis political interests, individual interests vis-a-vis group interests, long-term interests vis-a-vis immediate interests, overall interests vis-a-vislocal interests, private interests vis-a-vis collective interests, individual interests vis-a-vis state interests and class interests, etc.

III. Relation between the Subject and Object of Interests

The subject and object of interests is a pair of relational categories, which means that they are mutual dependent and mutual conditioned. Without the existence of objects and the satisfaction the subjects get from them, the subjects would be meaningless, vice versa. Therefore they are the object to each other, which means that, the subjects of interests, under certain conditions, strive to understand, change, pursue, use, possess, consume and get satisfaction from the objects of interests, a process of social activities of absorbing, assimilating and getting satisfaction from the subjects. This relation is multi-dimensional: desire and be desired; need and be needed; satisfy and besatisfied; use and be used; understand and be understood; change and bechanged; build, rebuild, create and built, rebuilt, created. In this process, first of all, the subject of interests have direct material desires for the objects of interests, the precondition of which is the subject's needing and using and getting satisfaction from the objects, on this basis, the subjects' interest inclination towards the cognition of objects will be generated, which, will in turn set the subjects into action for further desires, needs, satisfaction, use and creation.

Generally speaking, in the relations between the subjects and objects of interests, the subjects are active and the objects are passive, but the former will have a counteraction towards the former, and the former is the basis, condition and purpose of the latter.

The relations between the subjects and objects of interests are both material and spiritual with the material needs, satisfaction, utility and recreationbeing the basis, premise and condition, on which the spiritual relations between them are formed. Spiritual relations between them refer to the subjects' pursuit of and satisfaction with the spiritual objects. For example, by listening to music, a subject of interests gets satisfaction from the object of interest of music. In the process of the objects' satisfying the material and spiritual needs of the subjects, the subjects' will naturally make value assessment of the objects, i. e. , to what degree the objects can satisfy their needs, or how much is the use of the objects to the subjects. On the other hand, the subject will make value assessment of itself, to see how much he will experience the significance of self-existence, or whether his self-value can be realized.

Chapter Six

Interest Individuals and
Interest groups

The subjects of interests can be divided into two broad categories, namely interest individuals and interest groups. In this chapter we will discuss them and their characteristics.

I. Interest Individualsand Its Characteristics

An interest individual refers to the subject of interests that exists as an independent individual with real human being as an interest pursuer, bearer and consumer. Besides characteristics of naturalness, practicality, sociality, consciousness, activeness and collectivity that are common to all subjects of interests, an interest individual has its own characteristics, including individuality, uniqueness, concreteness, distinctness and dependence.

(1) Individuality. Since an interest individual is the subject of interests existing in the form of separate individuals, individuality thus serves as the first characteristics of n interest individual, by which we mean that the subject of interests exists independently as the smallest unit of subject of interests in the form of concrete individuals that cannot be further divided.

(2) Uniqueness. Since interest individuals exist in the form of separate individuals, each individual is apparently unique, with characteristics different from any other interest individuals. Independently existing, each interest individual has its specific features that are unique, which gives birth to diversity of interest individuals that in turn determines the uniqueness of each individual. The uniqueness of interest individuals further determines that each has its own particular interest needs, pursuit, tendency and values. Even in the same clan of the same tribe in the primitive society, different individuals have their different interest demands. The uniqueness of interest individuals means interest particularity.

(3) Concreteness. The individuality and particularity of interest individuals further determine its concreteness. Anything individual and particular must be concrete. As the interest individuals are actual, living and diverse human beings, they are naturally concrete individuals with concrete interest demands.

(4) Distinctness. Individuality, particularity and concreteness of interest individuals determine that interest individuals differ from each other. That is to say, different interest individuals have different interest needs and pursuit; even for a similar interest need, their ways of fulfillment are different. The distinctness of interest individuals involves both the qualitativeand the quantitative aspects. Qualitative difference refers to the differences or even antagonism between interest individuals. For example, the interest differences between slave-owners and slaves are fundamentally antagonistic and irreconcilable, so they are qualitative differences. Quantitative differences refer to the differences of interest demands between interest individuals on the basis of fundamental identity of interests. For example, the income gap betweenthe people in a socialist countryin terms of distribution is the quantitative difference. We should realize the both identity and the differences between interest individuals, and distinguish their qualitative differences from their quantitative differences.

(5) Dependence. Men are social beings that cannot be independent of society. Every human being is necessarily dependent on others and the society, so is every interest individual or interest group. No individual laborer can fulfill his interests without the labor of others and the society. In addition, the dependence of an interest individual is without doubt includes his dependence on the objects of needs, such as clothing, food, shelter and other material conditions.

II. The Interest Group and its Characteristics

Individuals can only realize their interests through certain social connections. Interest individuals form different aggregates, or individual groups, on the basis of common interests. An interest group is stronger in pursuing and safeguarding the interests of its members, therefore is more competitive and powerful than individuals in interest conflicts or rivals. Individuals usually take part in interest competition and realize their individual interests by joining interest groups. Insociology, a group is usually consisted of well-organized and relatively steady collection of human beings, which is different from interest group, while a loosely organized one with low stabilityare regarded as an aggregate. Groups can besociologically divided into different types. From the perspective of organization, there are informal groups and formal groups, the former referring to the well-organized collection of human beings, such as societies, social organizations, while the latterto temporary or short-lived and loosely organized one, such as fishing or Qigong association, etc. From the perspective of size, status and scope, they can be divided into high level groups, middle level groups, lowerlevel groups and grassroots groups. High level groups include nationwide, regional even international groups, such as the UN, the European Community, national level associations. Middle level groups are organizations in a region within a province or region, such as youth leagues, trade unions, women's federations, etc. in a province. Lower level groupsusually refer to cross-area groups, such as factories and enterprises. Grassroots groups refer to small groups within a small or neighborhood scope, such as professional associations in a district. From the perspective of direct causes, groups can be divided into kinship groups, clan groups, geographical groups, hobby groups, etc, such as tribes, families, artist association, stamp collection association. From the perspective of social function, they can be divided into productive groups, service groups, intellectual groups, political groups, etc. From the perspective of social nature, they can be divided into classes, strata, political parties, political groups, social organizations, etc.

The interest groups we discussed here aresimilar to yet somewhat differences from sociological groups. The latter covers a larger and wider scope, while the interest group we discussed here are smaller in scope. In fact, every group has its common interests, but interest ties of aninterest groupare stronger and stricter in definition. Firstly, an interest group must have common interests as its basis; secondly, members of aninterest group are more closely and steadily bonded; and thirdly, an interest group is relatively well-organized. Therefore aninterest grouprefers to acollection of human beings formedwith similar interest demands, relatively similar interest attitudes on the basis of certain social relations. Different interest groups have different or even contradictory and antagonistic interest demands.

An interest group usually has the following characteristics:

(1) Extensiveness. Compared with a class, an interest group is much looser in definition, which refers to social interest community formed on the basis of common interests. Any social group with common interests can be called an interest group. With common interests and strong interest identification as its basis and mark, an interest group is not necessarily of class nature, which is different from a class or a stratum. In a broad sense, any collection of individuals with certain common interests can be regarded as an interest group. For instance, interest group can be either a larger one such as a state, a nation, a class ora stratum, or a smaller one such as a political party, an organization, an association or a gang. In the narrow sense, an interest group mainly refers to a group that are formed on the basis of relatively steady common interests such asa class, a political party in the class societies, etc. Since a class or a stratum can be further divided, so in a narrower sense, in class societies, interest groups refer to social groups that are included in but smaller than and subordinate to a class and a strata, or the kind of social groupsthat are smaller than and different from a class or a stratum but at the same time associated with them.

(2) Historical nature. An interest group is a historical category that has different contents under different historical conditions. The earliest interest groups in human society are groups of primitives formed the basis of kinship and common territory, such as clans, tribes, tribe confederations. With the development of social division of labor and private property, the society is consequently divided into different classes and further different strata as the most stable interest groups in the class society, and smaller groups can be subdivided in a social stratum. In a socialist country where the exploiting classesas a whole no longer exist, the form and content of interest groups have also changed accordingly.

(3) Intersection. Interest groups are mutually crossed, overlapped or inclusive. By intersection, we mean members in a society have double or even many positions in interest groups, and thus interest groups are mutually crossed, overlapped and inclusive in terms of their member composition and interest tendencies. For a given interest group, its members must have shared interests; for any individual, he can simultaneously be member or participant of several interest groups and have different social roles. The intersection shows the tendency of mutual integration and proximity between interest groups. For instance, larger and more stable interest groups with common interest demands are formed

between different classes, strata and interest groups through some horizontal social links, such as families, nations and various economic entities (such as enterprise, consortiums, guild), which overlap with class, strata or smaller groups. At present, the most populous intersected interest group in Chinese society is the farmers working in the township enterprises. In addition, there are also group of entrepreneurs that are composed of intellectuals and managerial personnel; groups of worker intellectuals and famer intellectuals composed of workers, farmers and intellectuals; groups composed of farmers who work in commercial, industrial and service sectors. Interests of different interest groups are not absolutely opposed to noridentical with each other, but rather identical yet different in a temporary and partial manner. Such identity and differences blurthe boundaries between the original social groups to form new intersectional interest groups, fully demonstrating the intermingle features of interest groups.

(4) Collectivity. Any interest group is a group of interest individuals formed on the basis of common interests, thus is internally cohesive with their common interests. In this sense, collectivity is a distinctive character of all interest groups.

(5) Identity. An interest group is a group of interest individuals joining together on the basis of common interests, in which all interest individuals are identical and common in their interest pursuit and demands. For instance, all members in the same class have their common class interests, so are citizens in a nation and members in a family.

(6) Diversity. Diversity means that interest groups are different in type because of their differences in interests. Pursuing interests is the eternal motivation behind human activities, which gives rise to various interest relations. The differences in conditions, interest relations and interest demands bring about the diverse content and complicated structure of interests, hence the diversity of interest groups. For instance, in terms of mode of labor, there are mental laborers and manual laborers; in terms of social division of labor, there are different interest groups of workers, farmers, intellectuals, civil servants, self-employed, etc. ; in terms of position in the economic system, there laborers and of non-laborers, exploiters and the exploited; in terms of locality, culture and language, there are different interest groups of ethnicity. The diversity of the interest groups fully shows the complexity of social group structure.

(7) Multiplicity. In a society, the diversity of interest groups

determines that the structure of interest groups must be multiple, which is an important content of a diversified social structure. The multiplicity of interest groups manifests itself in two aspects, one is the structure between different interest groups and the other is the structure within the same group. On the basis of material and economic interests, interest groups can be divided intothe working class, the farmers, the intellectuals, and so on; on the basis of political interests, they can be divided into political parties, etc. ; and so on so forth. All this different interest groups are interconnected or contradictory to each other, forming a complicated and multiple social interest group structure.

(8) Contradiction. In a society, there are complicated relationships of contradictions within the complicated structure composed of different interest groups. On the one hand, there are interest contradictions between different interest groupswith different interest demands; on the other, there are interest differences and contradictions among members within the same interest group. Contradictions among different interest groups with basically identical interests are non-antagonistic and reconcilable; but in a class society, contradictions among interest groups of fundamentally opposed interest demands are antagonistic and thus irreconcilable.

In present-day Chinese society, although the interests of different interest groups among the people are fundamentally identical, there are still certain differences, which will inevitably lead to contradictions and conflicts. In the period of reform, contradictions between interest groups tend to intensify, because the disparity in interest distribution among groups will generate economic, political and ideological conflicts. Contradictions between different interest groups among the people are largely resulted from and dominated by contradictions of economic interests. The contradictions, being those between the working class and the farmers, between the Party and government officials on the one side and the masses on the other, or between private enterprise owners and other social groups, are all economically rooted. These contradictions fully demonstrate the instability of China's social group structure at the present stage.

In today's China, in addition to the influence and subversion of external anti-socialist forces in economic, political, ideological and cultural fields, there are still residue of the old society in this fields, leading to the existence not only contradictions between ourselves and the enemy in a certain scope, but also occasional antagonistic contradictions among the people. For example, there are the contradiction of exploiting and the exploited phenomenon between private owners and their employees, although they are non-intrinsic and non-dominant and are few in quantity and secondary in nature in the entire system of contradictions among the people, so is not an essential characteristic. But these contradictions, if not properly handled, can develop into antagonistic contradictions. With the development of socialism from lower to higher stages, antagonistic contradictions among the people will gradually reduce.

III. Special Interest Groups

The special interest group refers to the well-organized interest groupswith fundamentally identical interest demands and attitude. There are distinctively different or even opposed interest demands among different special interest groups. This kind of interest group has its functions in a society. In other words, special interest groups are social organizations with strong and distinctive interest demands, which are better organized and more cohesive and therefore are more competitive than ordinary interest groups. Individuals are the most elementary cells of the subjects of interests; once an interest group composed of individuals with common interest demands comes into being, it thus becomes a subject of interests in name and in fact.

The special interest group we discussed here is different from the interest group in the West in connotation. In Western political science, interest group is a concept with specific connotation. In the early 1950s, David B. Truman, a well-known professor of political science made a clear definition of the "interest group". In *The Governmental Process: Political Interests and Public Opinion*, he says: "Interest group refers to any group that, on the basis of one of more shared attitudes, makes certain claims upon other groups in the society."[1] In the 1960s, Robert Alan Dahl, a professor of political science at Yale University said in his *Democracy in the United States: Promise and Performance*that in the broadest sense, any group of people that act together to strive or defend for shared interestsis an

---

[1]   David B. Truman, *The Governmental Process: Political Interests and Public Opinion*, Alfred A. Knopf, 1951 pp. 33 and 37.

interest group. ①Professor Carol S. Greenwald of Brooklyn College of the City University of New York said in *Group Power: Lobbying and public policy* that an interest group is "a combination of individuals who seek to pursue shared interests through a set of agreed upon activities. "② Professor D. George Kousoulas of Harvard University in his book *On Government and Politics: an Introduction to Political Science* termed interest group as an aggregate of interacting individuals pursuing the realization of shared interests. ③ProfessorGraham K. Wilson of University of Essex said that an interest group "is an organization which seeks or demands to represent people or organizations which share one or more common interests or ideals. "④ It is a noticeable social phenomenon in the Western society that, a lot of interest groups will involve in the political gaming when act or amendment is discussing in the legislature, or a decision or statement is made, or a draft bill is proposed by the government. This is particularly true in the United States, where many such groups with great influence and various mannersare very active in the political arena. Some politicians and theorists call this as "interest group politics" . On the basis of it, some Western scholars put forth the theories about interest group and political power, asserting that political interest groups that interact with each other exist more or less in all industrial societies, and within the ruling class in the society, there are at least two opposing political interest groups: one is the group that is in power that wants to maintain the existing power structure and the state quo, the other is the group that is excluded from the power structure and thus want to change it. Although they have noted the existence and social role of the interest groups, the Western bourgeois theorists didn' t catch the fundamental source of the interest groups and their key characteristics. According to them, the interest groups arise on the basis of political instead of the economic reason, and their key characteristic is political power and status other than

① Robert A. Dahl, *Democracy in the United States: Promise and Performance*, 4th ed. Houghton Mifflin Co. Boston, 1981, P. 235.

② Carol S. Greenwal, *Group Power: Lobbying and public policy*, Praeger Publishers, New York, 1977, p15.

③ D George Kousoulas, *On Government and Politics: an Introduction to Political Science*, 3rd. ed. , Duxbury Press, North Scituate, Mass. , 1975, p. 92.

④ Graham k Wilson, *Interest Groups in the United States*, Oxford University Press, 1981, p. 4.

economic features. Although the political purpose of the interest groups and character of political power cannot be denied, they can only be properly understood from their economic source and nature. A type of ownership of the means of production is the manifestation of the interests of relevant classes and social groups. Although interest groups are based on interest differences, the very rootof them is the economic relations dominated by ownership of the means of production. An interest group is first of all an economic group backed by economic interest groups; economic interests are always behind any political interest group, and any political group is without doubt under the control of and works for relevant economic interest groups. In a class society, economic interests are in a concentrated manner manifested in political interests and further in the class interests. So an interest group will fully represent the interests of its members and thus are well-organized and highly utilitarian, which is conducive for social members to express their interest demands. It is an important social organization in that they actively take part in state economic and political life and decisionmaking to strive for their own interests.

As a historical category, the interest group has different historical contents under different historical conditions. The earliest interest groups appeared in the human society were primitive groups, such as clans, tribes, tribe confederations. With the development of social labor division and private property, the society was divided into classes and further into strata and smaller interest groups. Class and stratum are the most stable interest groups in class societies. And the cross relations between smaller interest groups with shared interest demands give birth to some relatively stable hyper-interest groups, including families, nations, various economic entities (enterprise groups, financial groups and group companies, etc.), states and international organizations (such as the European Union) . Therefore it is necessary to fully understand the objectivity, diversity and complexity of interest groups.

IV. The Theory of Interest Group and Its Significance

Marxist theory of interests is an important part of the Marxist historical materialism. It is necessary to construct Marxist theory of interest group by scientifically analyzing it based on Marxist theory of interests under the guidance of historical materialism.

Marxist theory of class is consistent with Marxist theory of interest group, and the latter is a necessary complement to the former. Marxist theory of class, class struggle and proletariat was constructed on the basis of the Marxist historical materialist standpoint, ideas and methods by examining the society of private ownership and by expounding the origin and extinction of class, criteria of class division, class relations as well as class struggle and its complicated tendency. Marxist theory of class is the guidance for us to understand the phenomena in class societies. Marxist theory of interest group, based on basic standpoint of historical materialism, proceeding from the relationship between economy and interests, makes scientific analysis of interest groups, including classes in class societies, and propose the basic principles and measures. From the economic relations and interest relations, including class relations, it can be seen that the theory of class is in accordance with the theory of interest group. This is because, in a class society, class groups and interest groups overlap. The theory of interest group covers and is also a complement to the theory of class. But the two are different in that the latter is applicable only to the analysis of class in the class societies while the former to all societies, including class societies, because interest relations exist in any society where there are human beings. Even in a class society, the theory of interest group can be a complement to the analysis of social members, and this is particularly true and relevant with a transitional social formation as the primary stage of socialism.

Along with the changes in Chinese economic, interest and social structures since reform and opening up, it is evident that the subjects of interests have become more diverse, the interest relations more complex and interest conflicts more outstanding. In terms of group structure, a society is consisted of various social interest groups that are dynamically interconnect and interact to each other. During this process that will bring about changes of interest relations, interest contradictions of myriad variety are bound to emerge. Analyzing the structure of social members with themethods of theory of interest group on the basis of social reality can not only enrich and develop Marxist historical materialism in theory, but in practice can help us to have a scientific understanding of and properly handle contradictions among different interest groups of the people, and to better building socialism with Chinese characteristics.

First, it is conducive for us to adhering to and developing Marxist theories of social structure and classes and method of class analysis.

Marxist theory of social structure is its theory of social class structure. The core category of it is class, sometimes referred to as stratum, estate, or order. In *Manifesto of the Communist Party*, Marx wrote: "With the dissolution of the primeval groups, society begins to be differentiated into separate and finally antagonistic classes. "[1] In *Poverty of Philosophy*, Marx pointed out: "The very moment civilization begins, production begins to be founded on the antagonism of orders, estates, classes, and finally on the antagonism of accumulated labor and actual labor. "[2] Starting from analyzing class differences among social members on the basis of the materialist conception of history, Marx and Engels divided members in society into different classes, strata and interest groups, drawing a clear-cut picture of social structure in class societies and therefore for the first time placing the analysis of social structure on the basis of reality. According to the Marxist theory of social structure and class, the criteria of dividing different groups in the social structure should be focused on their economic relations. This is a principle for us to materialistically analyze social structure in a scientific and orderly way.

Marx and Engels had not witnessed the victory of proletarian revolutions, so they couldn't expound the specific social structure of the predicted socialist society. But when researching the social formation and development of the future society on the basis of analyzing social contradictions in capitalist societies, they made somepredictions of fundamental significance about the structure of the future society. For instance, Marx remarked that in the first phase of the communist society, due to the limitations of production, the principle of distribution to each according to his work would dominate in the distribution of personal consumables. "Accordingly, the individual producer receives back from society—after the deductions have been made— exactly what he gives to it. " "Right can never be higher than the economic structure of society and its cultural development conditioned thereby. "[3] Marx further pointed out that the antithesis between mental and physical labor would vanished only in a higher stage of the communist society. This insightful predictions made by Marx and Engels can further serve as our theoretical guidance to

---

① *Selected Marx and Engels Works*, vol. 1, People's Publishing House, 1995, p. 272.

② *Collected Marx and Engels Works*, vol. 4, People's Publishing House, 1958, p. 104.

③ *Selected Marx and Engels Works*, vol. 3, People's Publishing House, 1995, pp. 304—305

investigate the social structure and to study and handle contradictions among various interest groups at the primary stage of socialism in current China.

The Marxist philosophy, as the essence of the underlying trend of the times anda scientific system that is open and ever developing, will advance along with the development of times. In China today, although the exploiting class as a whole has been eliminated, there are still class struggles and class differences. Under these circumstances, the social structure of China has already witnessed qualitative changes in terms of classes, strata and their forms of existence and connotation. The fundamental changes in the ownership relation as the major content of relations of production have resulted in corresponding changes in economic and political interests of members in each class and stratum. At present, in the Chinese social structure, besides the two major classes of workers and farmers, there emerged some interest groups of no class nature. The development of these classes, strata and interest groups along with their complicated relations make the Chinese social structure become more diverse. Under the premise of fundamental identity of interests, there are also some differences among them, which often trigger conflicts. Therefore, it is significant and necessary, on the one hand, to thoroughly analyze the complicated social structure under the guidance of the Marxist theory, on the other, to comprehensively analyze different interest groups and their contradictions from various angles. Under the new historical conditions at the primary stage of socialism, applying basic principles of philosophy, sociology, economics and other disciplines to analyze different interest groups and their contradictions in China will surely enrich and develop Marxist theory of social structure.

Method of class analysis is an integral part of Marxist theory of social structure and class. Investigating different interest groups among people in the primary stage of socialist China will complement to the Marxist method of class analysis. As we know, the complete theory of class and social structure as well as the method of class analysis in the treasure house of Marxist theories is the basic approach for us to study and analyze the social structure of class societies. However, in this treasure house, there is no specific conclusion about how to investigate and analyze the social structure in a socialist society. The establishment of socialist system in China and the historical process of reform and opening up, the great progress of scientific and technological revolution and the ever developing of the market economy in China, allurge us to have a profound analysis of the country's social structure. Under the new conditions, we shall, besides adopting the method of class analysis in relevant fields, further develop new methods of interest group analysis as an important way to grasp the social structure in the primary stage of socialism. Advocating method of interest group analysis doesn't necessarily mean denying the Marxist method of class analysis, or replacing it with the Western approaches in this respect, because the method of class analysis is still a basic means in our analysis. The method of interest group analysis means to examine the interest orientations, interest relations and attitudes in social life of the social members in given relations of production, which are made on the basis of historical materialism by taking people's positions and roles as the basic yardsticks. When adopting this method to do the analysis, we focus first of all on economic factors. The relations among various interest groups at the primary stage of socialism in China are non-antagonistic relations on the basis fundamental identity of interests. Therefore, it will certainly enrich Marxist class analysis adhering to Marxist class analysis to some extent while applying the method of interest group analysis to have an overall and macro grasp of China's social structure.

Second, it is conducive to enriching and complementing to Comrade Mao Zedong's theory of contradictions among the people.

Since the founding of New China, especially the completing of socialist transformation in 1956, the exploiting class as a whole, including the landlord class and bourgeoisie, had basically been eliminated, and class and class struggle exist only within certain limits, and principal contradiction in China had changed fundamentally. In September 1956, the Eighth National Congress of the CPC made a correct analysis of the class structure and class contradictions in China after the completion of socialist transformations, which state that the principal domestic contradiction is the that between people's rapidly growing economic and cultural needs and the state that the existing economic and cultural development could not adequately satisfy them. The major task for the Party and people of the country is to solve this contradiction and transform China from a backward agricultural country into an advanced industrial country as soon as possible. [1]At this historical juncture, Comrade Mao Zedong published the great work *On the Correct Handling of Contradictions among*

---

[1] *The Resolution of the 8th National Congress of the CPC on Political Report.*

the People in 1957. In the article, he creatively expounded the contradictions in the socialist society, especially contradictions among the people, and for the first time in the history of Marxism put forward the theory of correct handling these contradictions. According to Mao Zedong, in the socialist system, although there are still class enemies, they are not many in number; what dominate are contradictions among the people; while the contradictions between the enemies and ourselves must be addressed in dictatorial means, contradictions among the people must be solved in democratic approaches, that is, the unity-criticism-unity method. It has been proved in the practice of socialist construction and reform that this important thought proposed by Mao Zedong is correct and can still serve as a powerful ideological weapon for us in the new times to further develop socialism. However, due to various reasons, before the Third Plenary Session of the Eleventh Central Committee of the CPC, these important ideas were not implemented. At the same time, the theory itself is still imperfect due to the limitations of objective conditions and subjective cognition. And Comrade Mao Zedong himself latter in practice gradually deviated to a large extent from this correct theory

After the Third Plenary Session of the Eleventh Central Committee of CPC, the Marxist ideological line of seeking truth from facts was restored, and it was clarified that the principal contradiction in the primary stage of socialism was the one between the ever-growing material and cultural needs of the people and the low level of social production instead of class struggle, and that an important theme of the current social and political life is to correctly handle contradictions among the people. Nowadays, at the new situation of socialist reform and opening up, especially in developing toward socialist market economy, the interest structure of our society has changed dramatically: the content and manifestations of contradictions among the people show some new characters; many economic and interest relations need adjusting, and many new contradictions and new interest groups have emerged in addition to the new ones. Specifically speaking, contradictions among the people at the current stage of China prominently manifest themselves as the contradictions among different interest groups, which are extensive in all sectors, economic sector in particular. In the context of current complex social interest relations, a deep analysis of contradictions among different interest groups will surely enrich Comrade Mao Zedong's theory of correct handling of contradictions among the people.

Third, examining different interest groups at the primary stage of socialism can lay basis for handling interest contradictions among different interest groups.

With the development of socialist market economy, then interest structure of China's society has witnessed profound changes. Firstly, the subject of interests has changed from single to become diverse. Secondly, the patterns of interest distribution become more diverse. Mode of interest distribution has changed with multi-channel distribution channels for different interest groups having formed. At present, diversified interest distribution ways have come into being in China, in which, distribution according to factors of production are encouraged, and the principle of distribution each according to his work is also manifested through different measures, so that different forms of distribution co-exist. Thirdly, interest relations become more complex. Among various interest contradictions, there are contradictions between overall interests of the state, the collective and the individuals; contradictions between economic interests, political interests and material interests; and contradictions between different groups, including workers, farmers, the intellectuals, Party and government officials, etc. Therefore, under these new situations, the analysis of social structure by using the theory of interest group and method of group analysis enable us to study more deeply the interest differences and contradictions among different interest groups, so as to find the clues, realistic foundations and correct methods to reconcile and handle them.

Since the productive forces at the primary stage of socialism are relatively backward, it is inevitable that imbalance exist between interest relations among different groups. Although some contradictions have been eased with the unfolding of China's modernization and reform, some new contradictions among groups have emerged that need coordinating. For instance, interests gained from some non-productive sectors are far higher than that from productive sectors, which greatly dampened the enthusiasm of production of the massesand results in contradictions and conflicts among different groups. If we overlook or ignore these contradictions, the progress of our reform and socialist construction will certainly be affected. At present, fundamental interests of different interest groups are basically identical, which make it possible for us to analyze, coordinate and satisfy their different interest demands in fair and reasonable ways under the principle of the partial interests subordinating to overall interests. To be specific, we can ease the contradictions among groups by making policies conducive to the development of all groups on the basis of analyzing their different interest demands.

Fourth, enhancing study of contradictions among different interest groups at the present stage is imperative to maintain social stability and promote the all-round development of the socialist economy and society.

At the primary stage of socialism, although contradictions among different interest groups are the ones on the basis of fundamental identity of interests, there are still interest differences and contradictions brought about by the old social division of labor and occupation and class difference. So, ensuring the harmonious development of different groups will be of great significance to the maintaining of social stability. Without enhanced study of contradictions among different interest groups and relevant measures, these contradictions may intensify, even result in the anti-social or law-breading acts of some groups, which will be harmful toour social stability and development. Historical experience has proved that keeping social stability is essential to the development of a country. Social stability constitutes the foundation and precondition of development, without which, socialist market economy cannot be established. At present, contradictions among interest groupsare prominent due to differences of ideas, the restructuring of systems and the adjustment of interests. Thecareful analysis and correct handling of them will be of great significance to the social stability and development of socialist market economy. Under the conditions of market economy in particular, it is necessary to develop a complete system of theory of interest groups to analyze the generation, evolution, operation mechanism and coordinating system of them, and apply it to guide our practices in analyzing and coordinating economic and interest relations.

The theory of interest groups is a scientific theoretical system established on the bases of historical materialism, class theory and class analysis and can be used to make comprehensive analysis of the interest groups in our society. Its analyses include the following aspects, among others: the material, economic and social conditions under which different interest groups exist; their economic, cultural and social relations; the differences and channels of incomes and economic interests of different interest groups; the state quo, structure, development and interest orientation of different interest groups; the classification of the interest groups and criteria by which they are divided; the positions and roles of interest groups in the political relations, their political interests and power exercise; the positions, roles and functions of the interest groups in the government and the society; the cultural expressions, social psychological state, cultural characters and cultural behaviors of different interest groups; the ways of life and habits of different interest groups.

V. Economic Analysis, Class Analysis and Interest Analysis

As a scientific conception of history of the proletariat, historical materialism provides us not only with the basic way to understand the universal law of social development in our social practice, but also the basic analytical methods for us to observe, analyze and explain social phenomena. So it is the ideological weapon that guides us to understand and handle complex social problems. Economic analysis, class analysis and interest analysis are basic methods used in historical materialism to analyze social phenomena.

Lenin said that it is "obliged to seek for the roots of social phenomena in production relations (and) obliged to reduce them to the *interests* of definite classes. "[1] Economy constitutes the prerequisite to the existence and development of all societies, and economic relations are the bases of the existence and development of social relations. In social life, economic relations inevitably demonstrate themselves as or find their expression in interest relations. In class societies, economic relations find their expression mainly in relations and interests of classes. Therefore, to understand social phenomena and structure of social members, it is important to make analysis from economic foundation of social existence, and the analysis of interest relations is imperative. In a class society, the economic and class analyses of social phenomena will inevitably lead to correct method of understanding, that is, class analysis. The three analyses are both consistent and different.

Stratification is an important sociological method of analyzing social structure, which, although different from the economic, class and interest analyses of historical materialism, has a degree of consistency and connections with them, so it can also be applied, under the guidance of

---

[1] *Collected Works of Lenin*, vol. 1, People's Publishing House, 1984, p. 464

historical materialism, to analyze social structure.

1. Understanding social phenomena must take economic analysis as the starting point

Historical materialism believes that it is man's social being that determines his social consciousness. Therefore, the ultimate cause of social development is material and economic factors, so are all social phenomena. Historical idealism, on the contrary, insists that social existence is determined by social consciousness, so the ultimate cause of social development is spiritual power, and all social phenomena are inevitably explained from this point of view. Explaining social and historical phenomena based on the material and economic factors fundamentally distinguish historical materialism from historical idealism.

To reveal the general law of social development based on the characteristics of social history and to analyze complex social phenomena, the structure of social members and the classes, strata and interest groups and their relations, we should, on the one hand, understand the roles of ideological motives of social members and their relations; on the other, we should not stop here, but to find the material and economic reasons behind these motives.

Marx provided us with a good example of economic analysis. Marx of 1835—1841 was a firm revolutionary democrat politically, but largely a Hegelian idealist philosophically. During 1842—1843, after graduated from school to the society and came into contact with material interests, Marx turned from his philosophical and political criticism of society to the study of economics, shifting his focus to the material and economic relations in the then so-called "civil society," especially the analysis of economic structure of capitalism and the criticism of its political economy. Through economic analysis of social phenomena, Marx recognized the social significance of labor practice and found that, the production of material goods is the foundation of the existence and development of society, and productivity is the ultimate cause of social development, and relations of production is the most basic economic relations of social life. Proceeding from this, he revealed that mode of production of material life conditions the general process of social economic, political and intellectual life. He therefore scientifically resolved the fundamental problem of relations between social existence and social consciousness, thus established historical materialism. It is clear that economic analysis is the basic method used by Marx in creating the theory of historical materialism.

Given the fact that all material and economic factors are the bases of all social life and the decisive forces promoting social development, and all social problems are rooted in the most profound economic facts, and all social phenomena are ultimately conditioned and affected by certain economic reasons. So, to understand social problems, we must start from the analysis of economic issues, so does the analysis of structure of social members and the understanding of classes, strata and interest groups and their relations.

In making economic analysis, we must first of all adhere to the criterion of productive forces, which ultimately determine the social and historical development. Progress of human society, in the final analysis, is the result of the development of productive forces. This is a fundamental view of historical materialism, and also the basic starting point from which we understand and explain social and historical phenomena. In expounding Marxist historical materialism, Lenin pointed out: "... only the reduction of social relations to production relations and of the latter to the level of the productive forces, provided a firm basis for the conception that the development of formations of society is a process of natural history. "[1] Later on, he explicitly mentioned that the development of productive forces is the "supreme criterion in judging social progress. "[2] In the period of democratic revolution, Comrade Mao Zedong pointed out that, the criterion for testing the good or bad and big or small of the policies and role of all parties is to see whether they favor the development of productive forces. The report to the Thirteenth National Congress of the CPC Central Committee clearly put forward the concept of "the criterion of productive forces," and specifically states: "We should take it as the fundamental criterion and the starting point of all our work whether it is favorable toward promoting the growth of the productive forces. " Comrade Deng Xiaoping clearly put forth the "three favorables," that is, whether it promotes the growth of the productive forces in a socialist society, increases the overall strength of the socialist state and raises the people's living standards, and at the same time, he pointed out that, the "three favorables," in the final analysis, can be boiled down to whether it is favorable toward the

---

[1] *Selected Works of Lenin*, vol. 1, People's Publishing House, 1995, pp. 8—9

[2] *Collected Works of Lenin*, *vol. 16*, People's Publishing House, 1988, p. 209

development of the productive forces. The criterion of productive forces, in fact, is to take whether it is favorable to the growth of the productive forces as the fundamental criterion for measuring social advancement and all our work and as the fundamental method of understand and explain social and historical issues. Taking the development of productive forces as the criterion in understanding social issues means that, it is the fundamental criterion for judging whether the relations of production, superstructure and specific institutions of a social formation meet the requirements; the chief criterion for determining the nature of a society, for measuring the stage of social development and for judging social progress; the supreme criterion for making distinction between good and bad and between success and failure of lines, principles, policies and measures of a political party; the basic criterion for judging between right and wrong of a person, a class, a political party. It is without doubt that, we must use this criterion in a scientific, comprehensive and proper way, and combine it with the balancing the relations between overall benefit and partial benefit, long-term benefit and short-term benefit, material benefit and intellectual benefits, and so on. And we must use it in a consistent way when taking it respectively as the fundamental, supreme, chief and basic criterion, to prevent from replacing other specific criteria with it. In practice, we cannot use it everywhere in an absolute, simplistic and vulgar manner. It is just a general principle and criterion for us to understand structure of social members, and understand classes, strata and interest groups and their relations.

In making economic analysis, we must adhere to the principles that material relations determine political and ideological relations, and economic relations determine non-economic relations, thus explain political and ideological relations on the basis of material and economic relations. In the process of social production, men establish relations not only with nature, but also among themselves. Marx said: "They produce only by working together in a specified manner and reciprocally exchanging their activities. In order to produce, they enter into definite connections and relations to one another, and only within these social connections and relations does their influence upon nature operate, i. e. , does production take place. "[1] The social relations established among people in the

---

[1]   *Selected Works of Marx and Engels*, vol. 1, People's Publishing House, 1995, p. 344

process of production are the relations of production, i. e. , economic relations, which essentially are material relations. Relations of production consist of three dimensions: ownership relations, status of people in social production and their relations and the distribution relations of labor products, which exist throughout all the four links of production, exchange, distribution and consumption. Of these, ownership relations are the primary part and direct criterion for judging the nature and level of development of a society. In human social life, the relations of production of a society, that is, material and economic relations are the primary ones that determine all other social relations, including ethical, family, political and ideological relation, and determine also the superstructure and specific form of a society. Therefore, it is also an important way to analyze social phenomena starting from the relations of production on the basis of the productive forces.

To analyze the structure of social members and the changes of social classes, strata and interest groups from the point view of material and economic relations means that, we should take the nature and situation of relations of production as the criterion for measuring whether the superstructure corresponds to the economic base, as well as a direct indicator for determining the formation and stage of development of a society; take relations of production as the basis for analyzing the law of all changes of social relations; take the forms and amount of possession of means of production, the position and role of people in production and the forms of distribution of products as important criteria for judging a person, a social group and a political party in the structure of society, as well as their class nature, political attitudes, social behavior and ideological thinking.

In doing so, we should see to it that "economic factors" are not vulgarized as "the only decisive type of factors" and the economic analysis as the only means of analysis. Ideological relations are relatively independent to material relations and the former have a certain degree of counteraction to the latter, as are the relationships between political relations and economic relations, social consciousness and social existence, superstructure and economic base, relations of production and productive forces. Social life is extremely complex, so are factors affecting it. If we analyze society and structure of social members only from the angle of economic factors by denying the role of other social factors, we will fail to correctly explain the complex social and historical phenomena, structure of social members and social classes, strata and interest groups and their relations and changes.

2. Class analysis is the expansion of economic analysis

Class analysis refers to the application of Marxist theory of class and class struggle to analyze social and historical phenomena, structure of social members, as well as classes, strata and interest groups and their relations. This approach is the necessary expansion of the method of economic analysis, and application of dialectic method in social sector, which is a scientific method used by the proletariat and its party in analyzing social structure, classes, strata and interest groups.

The emergence of class is the result of development of productive forces, and private ownership is economic cause of society being divided into classes. And the class identification must be based on such basic economic criteria as people's possession of the means of production, position and role in the relations of production and distribution methods of getting products. Class struggle comes from confrontation and conflict in socio-economic relations. Using the method of economic analysis in the study of social and historical phenomena, one necessarily will come the following correct conclusions: class struggle exists in class societies; people can be divided into different classes; the social nature of human beings are mainly reflected in their class attributes; every kind of thinking without exception is stamped with the brand of class; and class struggle is the basic line and direct driving force of class societies. Faced with the complicated class relations in class societies and constant change of class struggle, "Marxism has provided the guidance—i. e. , the theory of the class struggle—for the discovery of the laws governing this seeming maze and chaos. "[1] The theory of class struggle is the fundamental method of analyzing historical phenomena of class societies and analyzing structure of social members.

To correct grasp and use the scientific method of class analysis, we must uphold materialist dialectics and oppose subjectivism and metaphysics.

First, we must insist on seeking truth from facts in class analysis. In class societies, the phenomenon of classes, although existing everywhere, is not the only or all-embracing one; although class relations are the basic

---

[1]   *Selected Works of Lenin*, vol. 2, People's Publishing House, 1995, p. 426

relations between man and man, it does not mean that all social relations fall under the category of class relations; and class struggle, although being important, is not the only form of social practice. That is to say, we should, on the one hand, recognize the universality and importance of the method of class analysis, but on the other, must not go to extreme in applying it. We must maintain the "objectivity of observation", proceed from reality and seeking truth from facts, so that to recognize the objective class structures, class relations and class struggle as what they are, and not to turn a blind eye to the simple reality of the existence of class and class struggle. At the same time we can never ignore facts by arbitrarily categorizing the structure, relations or phenomena of non-class nature into class one.

Second, we must maintain an all-sided way and try to avoid one-sidedness. Class phenomena in society are extremely complicated and diverse. And class struggle finds its expression not only in economic struggle, but also in political and ideological struggle; not only in economic sector, but also in ideological, political, cultural and other sectors. Therefore, in applying the method of class analysis, we must grasp "the entire totality of the manifoldrelations of this thing to others,"[1] to maintain an all-sided way and avoid one-sidedness. That means that, we should both analyze class struggle in economic sector and not neglect class struggle in political, ideological, cultural and other sectors; analyze both the economic status and political attitudes of all social groups; analyze both the economic status, political attitudes and ideological tendency of each class and its relations with other classes, its social environmental changes and development, etc. In short, we should understand the complicated class relations and class struggle in a comprehensive, dialectical and development way, instead of in an isolated, static and one-sided way.

Third, we must, in making class analysis, to the principle of concrete analysis of concrete conditions, the living soul of Marxism. Class and class struggle will be different in forms and characters depending on time, place and conditions. Class structures, class fronts, class enemies, class friends, classes as reliable forces, as well as the expression and features of class struggle will be different with the differences of formations of society, the differences of development stages

---

[1] *Selected Works of Lenin*, vol. 2, People's Publishing House, 1995, p. 411.

of the same formation of society, the differences of countries at the same stage of the same formation of society, and even the differences of localities, ethnic groups and time span within the same country of the same stage of the same formation of society. This requires that we should grasp the change and special law of class struggle in different time, place and conditions. Take China for example. At the present primary stage of socialism, the exploiting class as a class has been eliminated, and class struggle is no longer the principal contradiction in our society and exists only within certain limits, so its targets, scope, scale and methods are different from those in the revolutionary war years. We are bound to make serious mistakes if we fail to keep to the living soul of Marxism of concrete analysis of concrete conditions, and maintain the out-dated attitude of the revolutionary wartime in viewing and handling the classes, strata and interest groups in the primary stage of socialism and the class struggle within certain limits. In the specific circumstances of today, we can neither make the mistake of magnifying class struggle by regarding it as the principal contradiction and taking it as the central task, nor can we neglect or deny the existence of class struggle in certain limits.

In short, the method of class analysis is a scientific and exact method, so we must, by applying material dialectics, make concrete, historical, realistic and all-round analysis of the existence of classes, class relations and class struggle. The indiscriminate application of this method with rigid thinking is opposite to the principle of class analysis of historical materialism.

3. The special significance of interest analysis

Lenin pointed out that "if you do not show the interests of which classes and which particular interests are dominant at the moment in determining the nature of the various parties and their politics, you are not really applying Marxism and have, *in fact*, rejected the theory of the class struggle. "[1] Interests dominate people's social and historical activities, and certain economic relations are necessarily reflected in certain interests—this is an important principle of historical materialism. To analyzing the complex economic, political, cultural, ideological and other social life and their relationships based on principle of interest is an

---

[1] *Collected Works of Lenin*, vol. 15, People's Publishing House, 1988, p. 375

important method to see through the mysteries of social history and to analyze social structure, classes, strata and interest groups and their relations.

Interest is an important category of historical materialism in observing society and history. By interest analysis, we mean that, according to the principle of interest, to unveil the interest motives underlying people's social activities and the relations of production on which the interest relations are reflected, and then proceeding from it, to explain various social relations and social and historical phenomena. In the methodological framework of historical materialism, economic analysis, class analysis and interest analysis are consistent and complementary to each other rather than mutually exclusive or opposed. Whether it is economic analysis, class analysis, or interest analysis, they are all built on the basis of the basic principle of historical materialism of "productive forces and the relations of production is the premise of whole society. " Economic analysis advocates analyzing social and historical phenomena from the perspective of material production and their relations, while the method of class analysis is the concrete use of economic analysis in observing social life and social phenomena, and method of interest analysis is the further manifestation of economic analysis. In a class society, the method of interest analysis, although being consistent with the method of class analysis, has its own special significance by taking the interest relations, contradictions and conflicts as basic clues.

First, the method of interest analysis is more specific than the methods of economic analysis and class analysis. The former focuses on analyzing the root causes of social history from the angle of macroeconomics, while the later stresses on dividing classes and analyzing the basic clues of class struggle from the perspective of economic relations in class societies. In contrast, the method of interest analysis makes specific study on social problems by investigating human relations. In a class society, the relations of production manifest themselves as certain class relations, which in turn manifest themselves as class interests. Method of interest analysis is to analyze the social phenomena from more direct and specific interest relations.

Second, interest analysis can be taken as a supplement to class analysis. In a class society, neither all social phenomena fall into class struggle, nor all social relations belong to class relations. Therefore, method of interest analysis can be used in non-class struggle areas. In class societies, there are interest differences not only between classes, but also between different strata and interest groups within the same class, so interest analysis can be used in dividing strata and interest groups within the same class. In a non-class society, although class relations and class struggle do not exist, a degree of interest differences and contradictions do exist. For instance, there are interest contradictions and relations between tribes in the primitive society. In these circumstances, analysis method has a universal significance.

Lastly, the method of interest analysis has its special significance in the primary stage of socialism. In this stage, the exploiting class as a whole was eliminated, and class struggle and antagonistic class contradictions exist only in certain limits. Under the condition that class contradictions and class struggle no longer takes the dominant role, how should we understand the changes of relations between classes, social strata and interests, as well as the relations of contradiction among the people? To answer these questions, the method of interest analysis has its special methodological significance.

The key to doing interest analysis is to use it to scientifically divide the interest groups, and then to further examine the statuses and roles of these groups in the interest relations and their contradictions, so as to grasp the objective laws governing their development. An interest group refers to a group of people with similar interest demands and attitudes toward their common interests based on certain social relations. Different interest groups have different, even contradictory interest demands. An individual needs to gain his interests through certain social relations. An interest group is far more powerful than individuals in pursuing and maintaining the interests of its members, so individuals tend to engage in interest struggle and realize their interests by joining in interest groups. The contradictions among different interest groups are the theme of interest contradictions in the society. Analyzing the social and historical phenomena by interest analysis requires the analysis of the positions, roles, attitudes of the interest groups and methods to solve their contradictions. Examining social and historical phenomena by using the method of interest analysis by no means imply that we deny the basic methods of economic analysis or class analysis; on the contrary, we should, under the guidance of the scientific outlook of historical materialism, make a good combination of these three methods in observing, analyzing and explaining classes, strata and interest groups and their relations.

VI. Criteria for Interest Group Division and the Division of Interest groups

The key to interest analysis and scientific division of interest groups lies in its criteria. Interest groups with interest differences exist in every society in human history so far. What are the criteria for interest group division then? As discussed above, it is economic relation, and primarily material relations of production that determines interest relations. Therefore as a basic principle, interest groups should be divided on the basis of economic relations, especially material relations of production.

First, dividing the interest groups based on their ownership of means of production. In the primary stage of socialism, the Marxist theory of identifying classes by ownership of means of production is still of methodological significance. The differences of status and role of people in the relations of means of production in the primary stage of socialism determine their economic interest groups. In the ownership relationship with the public sector remaining dominant and diverse sectors of the economy developing side by side, great differences exist between different sectors: within the public ownership, there are the differences of state-owned economy and collective economy; within the same economic sector there is the separation between the ownership and management of the enterprises; between the enterprises in the same sector of ownership, there is the differences of degree of independence; and there are also different forms of realization of ownership in the same sector of ownership. All these differences determine that, the social members, who are inevitably integrated with one of the sectors of ownership, will necessarily fall into different interest groups with different interests, and that different production units constitute different relatively independent economic interest groups. So it is a premise to analyze the interest groups starting from the relationship of ownership.

Second, dividing interest groups on the basis of distribution and other relationships in the primary stage of socialism. In this stage, the differences of interests are prominently reflected in distribution: different forms of distribution and different forms of interest realization also determine the existence of different interest groups with certain differences in economic aspect. In the primary stage of socialism the distribution pattern in which distribution according to work is the main form that coexists with other forms of distribution determines the differences of distribution between interest groups. For example, the group that earns their income in accordance with the principle of distribution according to work are different from groups realizing their income according to other forms, such as capital, management, factors of production; even within the same distribution form there are differences of interests. This determines the existence of different interest groups. In addition, relations between people in the production, exchange, consumption and other links also contribute to the existence of different interest groups. For example, in the process of production, there are groups of managerial personnel, technical personnel, salespersons, and so on; in the process of exchange, there are also commodity producers, sellers, buyers and so on.

Third, under the precondition of dividing interest groups on the basis of economic relationships, we can also divide interest groups from the point of view of broader social relations. For example, by differences of division of social labor, we can divide them into urban residents, rural residents; manual laborers, mental laborers (intellectuals), etc. The similar occupations can also bring about similar economic and political interests, and thus form corresponding interest groups, such groups of teachers, lawyers. Likewise, the differences in division of labor, occupation, income, wealth, etc. , will also cause the differences in social status and between groups, such as high income group, middle income group, lower income group, disadvantaged group.

In short, in dividing interest groups, we must insist on the criteria of ownerships, possession of products, roles, status of the individuals in social and economic relations, in addition to other social factors. These criteria show that different interest groups have their different demands, interests and contradictions.

Besides the basic criterion of economic relations, interest groups can be further divided and distinguished by other criteria. In this book, our focus is the division of interest groups by the criteria of economic relations from the perspective of historical materialism.

From the perspective of stability, we can interest groups can be divided into super stable, stable, relative stable and unstable groups. In class societies, super stable interest groups can be further divided into three tiers of family, group (such as class, stratum and ethnic group) and state. Super stable interest groups in the early ages of human society were primitive groups formed on the basis of kinship and territory, such as nation, tribe and tribe confederation. With the development of social division of labor and private ownership, class society emerged and along with itfamilies, classes and states. The family is the most basic and also super stable unit among social interest groups. In the society of natural economy, the family is the elementary unit of maintaining production and reproduction of man and material means, the bearer of social economic interests, the interests of which directly influence personal interests of its members. In the course of emergence and development of families, class gradually formed. Class can be further divided into different strata. Both class and stratum are super stable interest groups in class societies. A stratum can be subdivided into different interest groups, among which, there are also myriad aggregates in a cross way on basis of social, economic, political and cultural relations, including nations, ethnic groups, families, kinships, social organizations, political parties and political groups, international organizations such as EU, UN and ASEAN, regional and trans-regional organizations and administrative divisions such as provinces, cities, counties, villages, villagers' groups. All these are stable interest groups. The state is a stable interest group formed with ethnic groups or nation within a certain territory. Relative stable interest groups refer to groups formed under specific historical and geographical conditions that are relatively stable yet unstable to some extent. For instance, under the fierce competition of the market economy, such economic entities as companies, factories, enterprises, financial groups and banks are relatively unstable. Changeable or unstable interest groups are groups formed for temporary common interests, which are short-lived, loose and inconstant without organizations or leadership nor strict regulations, example including such associations as alumni association, friendship association and association of townsmen; trade unions formed on the basis professions, or groups based on cultural needs, such as cultural associations, clubs, art groups, etc. Unstable interest groups refer to interest groups that are temporary, transient, loose or simple.

In terms of size and number of members, interest groups can be divided into super large, very large, large, medium, small ones and micro ones. State and nation belong to super large groups, class and stratum belongvery large ones, which can be subdivided into different large interest groups (such as teachers group). Medium interest groups include regional associations, etc. And below them there are also small interest groups and micro interest groups such as families.

In terms of territory or administrative division, interest groups can be divided into international organizations such as UN, countries such as China, the U. S. , Japan; administrative divisions within a country, such as the provinces, cities, autonomous regions, counties, towns and villages in China.

In terms of types of interests, interest groups can be divided as follows: interest groupsbased on some material and economic interests, such as enterprise; on political interests such as political parties; on cultural interests such as schools of art style, cultural bodies and academic organizations; on specific social interests, such as friendship and other associations; on interestsnations, ethnic groups, clans.

In terms of connotation, interest groups can be divided into the groups in the broad sense and the groups in the narrow sense. Interest groups in the narrow sense refer to relative stable interest groups under class and stratum formed on the basis of common interests with some interest differences. Class, stratum and interest group in terms of connotation are large, medium and small in order. In class societies, the division of class is the division in the most basic and essential way, but the class cannot include all differences among the people in their social life. In contrast, interest groupis an all-inclusive category, through which, diverse social differences among the people and their real social positions can be moreexactly manifested.

Interest groups in the broad sense refer to the collections of individuals with generally identical interest demands and relatively identical attitudes towards their common interests. Class, stratum, and the smaller one below them such as the working class, the farmers, the intellectuals, the teachers, the engineers, the writers, the artists the employees, etc. , are all belong to this category. In short, interest groups in the broad sense are more inclusive, with class and stratum being only part of it.

To sum up, in dividing interest groups, we must insist on the criteria of ownerships, possession of products, roles, status of the individuals in social and economic relations, in addition to other social factors. These criteria show that different interest groups have their different demands, interests and contradictions. The basic criterion of Interest group division indicates that the Marxist theory of class division is still of methodological relevance and consistent with the basic criterion of Interest group division. As an importance clue in analyzing social phenomena, it shall be noted that different interest groups have different interest demands, and among them there are some interest differences and interest contradictions.

Chapter Seven

Interest Contradictions and Conflicts

Social contradictions and conflicts are universal in the human society and history, the highest manifestation of which is war. The history of human civilization so far is indeed the history of social contradictions and social conflicts, or even the history of war. As far as the current international situation is concerned, the world arena itself is a domain of complicated social life full of contradictions and conflicts. While each conflict and each war is different from others in terms of social conditions, participants and form, it is, however, governed by one ultimate motive. What is the ultimate motiveor source of contradictions, conflicts, fights and wars in human social life? It is interests, material and economic interests above all, that constitute the fundamental and underlying reasons for all social contradictions and conflicts. Interest contradictions and conflicts are important phenomena in human society.

I. Interest Relations

Human social relations, in the last analysis, are interest relations, because social relations must manifest themselves in interest relations. In order to survive and develop, man has to engage in social activities to satisfy his interests for his survival, in which he inevitably will establish certain social connections with others. These connections are actually interest relations manifested as interpersonal relations. Marxism tell us, for man to satisfy his needs for life, he must first of all engage in productive activities, which actually is a process of pursuing and attaining interests. In this process, interest and economic relations will certain established, which are manifested as material and economic relations. Lenin said that we are "obliged to seek for the roots of social phenomena in production relations, obliged to reduce them to the *interestsof definite classes. "*① Material and economic relations are the most basic human social relations with relations of production as the primary one of them. From different angles, social interest relations can be divided into material interest relations, non-material and intellectual interest relations; economic interest relations, non-economic and political interest relations. The most important interest relations between individuals, groups, nations, classes and countries are material, economic and life interest relations. That means that, the interest relations emerge in the process of production and distribution, or in the process of production of materials and means of living, are the most important ones. In other words, production and economic relationsare in the last analysis manifested themselves as material and economic interest relations. Interest relations we discussed here refer mainly to material and economic interest relations, which take the dominant role in all interest relations.

To understand social relations, we must beginwith interest relations, which in turn need tobe started with the understanding of production and economic relations. Interest relations are the source of origin, development and change of all social relations, which in turn are the manifestations of relevant interest relations, which, ultimately determined by production and economic relations. Economic relations determine interest relations and all other social relations, such as political relations, cultural relations. For example, the major production relations under the condition of the socialist market economy, such as ownership and distribution relations, determine the complex interest relations, which in turn determine the complex interpersonal social relations. A basic way of understanding social phenomena is to understand social relations on the basis of understanding interest relations, which in turn are based on the understanding of relations of production.

In class societies, major interest relations among the people are of class nature, which manifest themselves in a concentrated way as wide class differences, grave class contradictions, confrontations and struggles. Under the socialist system, the exploiting class as a whole has been eliminated and antagonistic class contradictions, class conflicts and class struggles will gradually reduce to a less important place and smaller scope in the social relations in the primary stage of socialism, therefore interest

---

① *Collected Worksof Lenin*, vol. 1, People's Publishing House, 1984, p. 464.

relations among the people are largely of non-class nature, and therefore are non-antagonistic. In non-class societies where the class has been eliminated, interest relations will no longer be of class nature.

Interest relations are embodied in relations between subjects, between objects, between individuals, between groups, between natures, between tendencies, etc.

All these relations form a complicated network of multi-tiers and cross subjects, in which, various interests are connected horizontally or vertically, linearly or reflectively, differentially or antagonistically.

1. Relations between subjects of interests

The subject of interests refers to that who engages in productive or any other social activities in given social relations to directly or indirectly satisfy his own social needs, or in other words, a subject of interests is a pursuer, bearer, producer, realizer, consumer and owner of interests.

Subjects of interests can be divided into broad categories of interest individuals and interest collectives, which can be further divided into five levels of individual, household, collective, state and human society that are connected both horizontally and vertically.

Individuals constitute the most basic elements of the subject of interests. Under private ownership, individuals are subjects of private interests and there are antagonistic contradictions between opposing classes. Under socialist system, although individuals are the subjects of their own interests and the basis for the contradictions between opposing classes have been basically eliminated, there are still interest contradictions and conflicts.

The household as subject of interests is at a higher level than individuals. In the society of natural economy, households are the most basic economic units and groups; accordingly, household interest relations are the most basic interest relations. In such a society, a household is not only a consumer unit, but also a unit that engages in production and other activities. Since a household is the subject of economic interests and consumer interests, the interests of a household thus have a direct influence on the interests of its members. In a society of market economy, although its economic role is less important, household is still an important subject of social interests. In addition, a household involves in some special interest relations arising from its needs in social life, such as marriage and heritance.

A collective refers to an organization consisted of individuals with shared interests; it is, on the one hand, the representative of its member's individual interests; on the other, the subject of common interests of the organization. In the society of market economy, enterprises are economic collectives with a relatively independent status and the most significant collectives of interests. It has higher interest demands than an individual and a household subject of interests. In a market economy, there are interest competitions among enterprises. Collective interests are links and intermediary between individual interests and state interests.

A state is the representative and subject of the common social interests of a country. In the society of private ownership, a state represents essentially the interests of the ruling classes; a socialist state is the pursuer, carrier and representative of the common interests of all its citizens. Sate interests, immediate or long-term, represent individual interests and collective interests on the one hand, and the overall interests of all members in the society on the other. This kind of status also leads to the existence of contradictions between state interests and individual and collective interests. The state is the representative of common interests of the ruling class, but state interests cannot be equated with the common interests of the whole society. In the international community, there are interest relations among countries. Relations of interests that of course contain the interests of the citizens and ethnic groups of the respective countries, between countries with different class nature have a certain degree of class nature; and countries of the same class nature are also have extensive relations.

State interest doesn't equal to the common interest of the whole society, which is at the highest level and organic integration of common interests of individuals, household, community (group) and state interests.

The five levels of subjects of interests give us a clear picture of the horizontal and vertical dimensions of the relations. The relations of individuals, households, collectives and the state are not only horizontally but also vertically connected, among which individuals, collectives and the state are the most important links.

As far as the two broad categories of subject of interests—individual and group—is concerned, if individuals and households are regarded as interest subjects, there are both horizontal and vertical interest relations between them. Group is a category of subject of interests with a very broad sense. Any interest community and interest aggregate, including enterprises, collectives, regions, units, ethnic groups, strata, classes, states, etc. , can be regarded as interest groups (collectives) . All these different interest groups (collectives) are connected both horizontally and vertically.

2. Relations betweeninterest organizations

The interest organization refers to the long-term interest group that is formed on the basis of certain common interests and is relatively stable and strongly cohesive and competitive, such as class, stratum, political party and enterprise. Temporary, loose or short-term groups such as arts associations, professional clubs do not belong to this type. An interest organization itself is also a subject of interests, which is at the third and fourth levels in the network of interest subjects, or at the state and collective levels. It is the type of interest group that is formed on common interests in a close and long-standing way, which has stronger forces in interest pursuit, conflicts and competitions and in safeguarding the interests of its members. Individuals tend to realize their interests and face interest conflicts and competitions. An interest organization is like a gladiator in interest conflicts. For instance, in imperialist countries, financial consortiums of monopolized capitalists are interest organizations formed by capitalists based on shared economic interests, which are much more powerful and competitive than individual capitalists in capitalist competitions. Cooperation and conflicts between interest organizations are the most basic and obvious social interest relations. Countries, ethnic groups, classes, strata and smaller interest groups and economic entities (enterprise, consortium, companies, etc.) are the most common and most stable interest organizations. Different interest organizations compete for theirown different interest objectives, leading to the complicated interest exchanges, frictions, connections, contests, conflicts, etc. , which form their mutually connected, restrained and dependent relations. For example, cooperation and struggle between classes, contradictions and unity among strata, alliance and wars among countries, horizontal joining and competition for profits between enterprises. Relations between interest organizations are the concentrated and distinct manifestations of interest relations.

3. Relation between objects of interests

Interest relations are threefold: firstly, the objective relations between the subject and object of interests in terms of cognizing and being cognized, demanding and been demanded, attaining and being attained, satisfying and being satisfied; secondly, the relations of interest distribution, that is, social relation between men, which can be said as relations between different subjects of interests; and thirdly, relations between objects of interests. While relations of subjects of interests are interpersonal relations between men as interest pursuers concerning interest distribution, relations between objects of interests are objective relations between the objects of interests pursued by men, and the relationsbetween different kinds of interests belong to the relations of objects of interests. Relations between objects of interests sometimes manifest themselves in pairs, such as material interests and intellectual interests, political interests and economic interests, personal interests and collective (state, social) interests, partial interests and overall interests, individual interests and overall interests, long-term interests and immediate interests. Besides, there are still relations among individual interests. Under socialist condition, for example, personal interests can be divided from different angles: in terms of ownership, there are personal interests of the employees in state owned enterprises, collective enterprises, privately owned enterprises and Sino-foreign joint ventures, interests of farmers under household contract system, interests of the self-employed; in terms of division of labor and possession, there are the personal interests of physical laborers, mental laborers, teachers, clerks; in terms of employment, there are the personal interests of the employed, the unemployed, the retired... Among all these personal interests as objects of interests there exist also complex relations. The same is true among subjects of interests, such as those between or among classes, strata, political parties, enterprises, states, ethnic groups, clans, families, regions, units, etc.

Relations between objects of interests and that between subjects of interests are in accord with each other, because the relations between the interest subjects are interpersonal social relations arising from their pursuit and distribution and are manifested in their understanding, altitude toward, form of distribution and degree of satisfaction of the objects of interests. The must be relevant relations of subjects behind given relations of interest objects, so to understand the latter must first of all to understand the former.

4. Relations between natures of interests

By examining the relations between the subjects and objects of interests, the objectives and content of interests pursued by the subjects, either vertically or horizontally, either two-dimensional or three dimensional, we can see that, there are always three kinds of change of unity of the opposites: partial vs. overall, long-term vs. short-term and vested and pursued. Accordingly, there are three pairs of corresponding interest relations of unity of the opposites, they are: overall interests and partial interests, long-term (fundamental) and short-term (immediate) interests and vested and pursued (ideal) interests. These three sets of dialectical interest relations intertwine with the vertical and horizontal interest relations, making them more dialectically complicated. For example, any subject of interests must face the choice of long-term interests and short-term interests; any lower level subject must face the problem of how to handle the relations between overall interestsof the higher level and its own partial interests. In the complex socioeconomic and political relations, any subject of interests must face the choice of whether cease to advance after gaining vested interests or continue to strive for higher ideal interests. Generally speaking, interest groups representing backward relations of production tend to be content with their vested interests, which will lead to serious interest conflicts with interest groups striving for higher interest goals. The three pairs of relations concerning natures of interests add some dialectical elements, making the already crisscross mechanism more complicated.

Under certain conditions of social material life, the production and economic relations give rise to interest relations, on the basis of which, relations between different subjects and objects are formed, which, in addition to the relations of dialectical unity among the objects of interests themselves, constitute the mainstay of the whole of interest relations.

II. Interest Differences

Difference is relation, without difference there be no relations at all. To examine interest relations, we first of all must examine the relationships between interest differences. Interest relations are born out of different subjects of interests with interest differences. Therefore, to understand interest relations and interest contradictions, we must first understand interest differences.

Interest contradictions and conflicts emerge and change on the basis of interest differences. Interest differences between individuals and social groups (clans, tribes, strata, classes, ethnic groups, various organizations, parties, enterprises, etc.) are the basis of social interest contradictions and conflicts. In the primitive society, each tribe hadits stable social organization, fixed territory, way of life, means of production and means of production and means of livelihood, making their interests different from other tribes. The greater the differences, the greater the possibility of interest contradictions, disputes or conflicts, with war launched by the poor tribes to plunder the rich ones, vice versa, being one of the expressions of them. It was a common practice in the world history for the barbarous tribes and backward nomadic peoples to plunderthe advanced and prosperous agricultural peoples. In class societies, for various historical, social, economic and political reasons, there are differences between among individual interests, stratum interests, class interests, ethnicinterests, state interests, which are causes of all social contradictions, including contradictions between classes, ethnic groups, and countries. In order to rob the wealth of other peoples, the old aggressive colonial empires launched unjust aggressive wars against other nations to loot their gold, trade slaves and slaughtered people. Since the Opium War, China has suffered a lot from the plundering and aggression of the Western aggressors. The Chinese people, in order to defend their national interests, waged a century long epic struggles in the defense of the nation. In order to seize more material wealth, the exploiting classes mercilessly suppressed and exploited the working people, which forced the working people time and again to rise in rebellion to defend their own interests.

While interest difference serves as the basic reasons for interest contradictions and conflicts, where do the interest differences come from?

First, differences in human natural needs and social needs are the elementary factor determining interest differences between subjects of interests. The complex and diverse factors such as living conditions determines that human natural physiological needs are different from each other. For instance, there are great differences in natural needs between man and woman, the aged and the young, the youth and the middle-aged. More importantly, the myriad forms of social life conditions determine the different needs of different classes, strata, groups, nations, countries, as well as the diversity of individuals and social needs. Differences in natural and social needs are the objective basis for interest differences. But all these differences are conditioned by social relations and all interest differences are ultimately conditioned by the different sownership relations.

Second, social division of labor is the fundamental reason for interest differences. Social labor is the basic condition for the satisfaction of human interest needs, and the division of labor is the decisive precondition for the development of social labor. It is division of labor, which made social labor divided and more specialized, that determines fundamentally the existence of interest differences. The earliest division of labor was that occur in a naturalway in the primitive clan communes, based purely on physiological differences of gender and age. The male adults were out hunting while women at home doing housework and plantings, and children helping with their mothers. Natural division of labor determines that men and women are masters in their own spheres, which further determines their differences of interests and social statuses. With the development of productive forces, three major divisions of labor took place in human history, namely, the separation of animal husbandry from agriculture, agriculture from handcraft and commerce from other industries. These divisions of labor promoted the rising of private ownership and class antagonism, causing the division of labor to develop from natural one to the old one, so that aggregate social labor was divided into antagonistic and separated individual labor. This division fixes specific individuals to specific jobs, making labor compulsory and purely profit-seeking. Individual labor determines the differences and antagonism of individual interests. With the development of production and the perfection of public ownership, the old division of labor will ultimately be replaced by the new one, which is no longer fixed, compulsory, individual or pure profit-seeking. But this division of labor still makes individual labors different from each other, which in turn will determines that there are differences in individual interests, though non-antagonistic.

Third, social differences caused by the old division of labor are the direct reason for interest differences. Besides differences among strata, classes and social groups determined by ownership of means of production, differences between urban and rural, between mental and physical labors and between workers and farmers resulted from old division of labor are direct causes for interest differences. Under socialist conditions, while class antagonism has been eliminated, there are still differences between classes and between social groups, as well as the three major differences, which determine that there interest differences. The working class and the farmers are different in terms of their combination with means of production and way of obtaining means of livelihood, which determines that the workers and farmers have their own different interest demands in daily life and culture. Urban-rural differences determine the great differences between urban and rural inhabitants in economic, political, cultural life and welfare, which also give birth to their different interest demands. Differences between physical and mental labor determines the differences of laborers in the nature and content of labor, in education, technical level, remuneration for work done, cultural life, which further determines their different interest demands.

Fourth, differences in people's possession of means of production and thereby means of subsistence constitute the decisive factor for interest differences. People's ownership of interests, in the final analysis, is conditioned by the relations of production. Their ways and amount of possession of means of production determines their ways and that of their means of subsistence and thereby their interest differences. Marx said: " The property differences within one and the same gens had transformed its unity of interest into antagonism between its members" . [1]In the primitive society, the property was publicly owned, thus in same tribe, the members ' interests were basically identical and non-antagonistic. The emergence of private ownership and the differences in the ownership of property turned identical interests into interest differences of antagonistic nature. Therefore, people's possession of means of production determines that of their means of subsistence and therebytheir interest differences. If we say that differences of possession of means of production is the major reason for interest differences, can we say that there will be no differences between people's interests in societies with publicly owned means of production? The answer is no. Public ownership of means of production determines only the non-antagonism of interest differences rather than eliminating them, because common ownership indeed realizes rather than eliminating individual property. In *Das Kapitla*, Marx wrote: " capitalist production begets, with the inexorability of a law of Nature, its own

---

① *Selected Marx and Engels Works*, vol. 1. People's Publishing House, 1995, p. 165.

negation. It is the negation of negation. This does not re-establish private ownership for the producer, but gives him individual property based on the acquisition of the capitalist era: *i. e.*, on cooperation and the possession in common of the land and of the means of production. "① While private ownership is the negation of the primitive communist ownership, socialized production of the capitalist society is the negation of the private ownership. But this negation neither re-establishes private ownership nor restores the primitive common ownership, but establishes private ownership on the basis on new common ownership. Here private ownership twofold in meaning. First is the real ownership by each individual as a member of the joint labor of means of production and the total productive forces. According to Marx, in the communist society, "a mass of instruments of production must be made subject to each individual. "② It is "the appropriation of the total productive forces through united individuals. "③ In the primitive society, human beings were subordinate to natural forces and therefore could not become their own masters. They can only become their own masters of social productive forces in the society of common ownership with highly developed productive forces. The second is that individual's possessing and mastering of means of subsistence. At the higher stage of common ownership, the productive forces are highly developed and everyone can get the social means of subsistence sufficient for the needs of his all-round development. Hence, common ownership doesn't eliminate individuality but to develop it; doesn't cancel individual needs, but to fully satisfy it; doesn't reject individual interests, but to recognize more of it. Individual interests in the society of common ownership do arise not only from the economic relations of united producers possessing means of production, but also from the distributive relation of personal consumables. Therefore, there will still be individual interests and interest differences even in the society of highly developed common ownership; it is more so in the primary stage of socialism, in which the common ownership has not fully developed and different forms of ownership co-exist. But it should be noted that in the primary stage of socialism, differences of possession of means of production is a decisive but not the

---

① *Collected Marx and Engels Works*, vol. 23, People's Publishing House, 1972, p. 832.

② *Collected Marx and Engels Works*, vol. 3, People's Publishing House, 1960, p. 76.

③ *Ibid*, p. 77.

only factor for interest differences.

From the above analysis we can see that interest differences exist in all societies. The differences lies in the fact that, in the society of private ownership, the antagonism of possession of means of production determines the class antagonism of interest difference while in a society of public ownership they are differences on the bases of interest identity. Socialism is a society transiting from incomplete and imperfect public ownership into complete one, so there are still interest differences determined by social differences brought about by the old division of labor, by different ownership relations, and by forms of distribution, including distribution to each according to his work. If not properly handled, these interest differences can be intensify into contemporary interest conflicts. Interest differences make interests different in content, strength, intensity and ways of fulfillment.

III. Interest Contradictions

Relations mean universal connections, which is basic phenomenon in the universe. Among which the most stable and primary one is the relation of unity of opposites, i. e. , relation of contradiction. It is the most stable, important and primary interest relation that determines and influences all the specific forms of interest relations.

Interest contradictions can be divided into internal and external contradictions. The former includes mainly contradictions between social production and social interests. The most basic social condition for interest realization and satisfaction is social production, and human ever increasing needs can only be satisfied through continuous production and re-production. People's needs for interests, on the other hand, act as stimulus for production development. The movement of contradiction between social production and interest needs constitute a basic thread of development of human society. Since production can only be carried out in certain relations of production and only through distribution and exchange can fruit of production enter the field of consumption to satisfy people's needs, the contradiction between social production and social interests inevitably manifests themselves as human interest relations, which will find their expressions in internal contradictions of interests, that is, the inherent contradictions of interests. Therefore, to analyze the interest contradictions, we must start with analysis of the internal contradiction of interests.

Internal contradiction of interests can be analyzed in three levels as follows.

1. Internal contradiction of the object of interests

Social interest has a dual character of subjectivity and objectivity. On the one hand, interest is subjective in that it is the dependence of human beings as subjects on objective life condition and their needs for it, and men are the subjects of interests. On the other hand, interest itself must take objective material and spiritual life conditions as its real content. Interest itself, i. e. , the object of interests, is the vehicle of interest objectivity. Interests, as objects, can be divided into different forms from perspectives of content, function or nature, such as individual interests, group (collective) interests, stratum interests, class interests, state interests, social interests and enterprise interests; fundamental interests, long-term interests, overall interests, general interests, partial interests, immediate interests, vested interests; material interests, spiritual interests, economic interests, non-economic interests, productive interests, distributive interests, exchange interests, consumptive interests, etc. And they can be further subdivided. All these different forms constitute a complicated social system of interests. We will analyze the contradictions of universal significance within the objects of interests and between them in the following.

(1) Internal interest contradictions between egoism and altruism. Interest itself contains two diametrically opposite characters—egoism and altruism. While interest is in essence for self-benefit, it by nature involves interpersonal relations, any of which is bilaterally ormutually intermingled and complementary. On the one hand, self-benefiting might cause damage to others, vice versa; on the other hand, they each other's premise of existence. In the primitive society, the contradiction between egoism and altruism was so slight that they could be regarded as identical. In the society of private ownership, the contradiction between egoism and altruism are externalized and intensified. The intrinsic contradictions of egoism and altruism of interest contains the embryo of all other contradictions of interest relations.

(2) The contradictions between individual interests and general interests and that between partial interests and overall interests. The further unfolding of the intrinsic contradiction between egoism and altruism manifests it as the contradictions between individual interests and general interests and between partial interests and overall interests, taking the form of opposites of antagonism. Any individual or partial interest has certain degree or scope of amplified egoism, whereas any general or overall interest has certain degree and scope of altruism because it represents, in addition to its own interests, interests of others. On the other hand, without individual or partial interest, there would be no general interest or overall interest. In this sense, individual interest is the foundation of general or common interest. Marx said: "... throughout history the 'general interest' is created by individuals who are defined as 'private persons'". ①The opposition of individual interest to general and common interest arose with the emergence of social division of labor and private ownership. In the primitive society, individual interest was inseparable from the collective interests of the tribe. With the emergence of social division of labor and private ownership, private interests were separated from common interests. In commodity production under the private ownership, there is the contradiction between the common interests of individual producers who are mutually dependent and self-benefiting private interests. Only with the bankruptcy of backward and weak individual producers in the course of competition among all producers, can the society get the common interests, that is, commodities of excellent quality and reasonable price in large amount and varieties. In the meantime, any individual interest is governed by general social interests, because caring only individual or partial interests will damage common or overall interests. In some cases, the opposite sides of interests will take the form of open antagonism, resulting in the sacrifice of one sidefor the other. But in some cases, if properly coordinated, they can be identical. In the society of private ownership, the identity and transformation of individual or partial interests with common or overall interests are realized through spontaneous movement of contradictions. The bourgeois common interests are spontaneously formed among the private producers in the market competition, which can only be realized as a blind force and the product of mutually fighting private interests. In the stage of as a "class in itself", the working class also spontaneously forms their common class interests. In the capitalist society, the working class is made up of individual producers

---

① *Collected Marx and Engels Works*, vol. 3, People's Publishing House, 1965, pp. 275—276.

who sell their labors, who in the competition of the labor market try to sell their own labors at a price generally unfavorable to others for the sake of private interests. After long-term practice, the working class came to consciously recognized, directly concerned about and became theoretically aware of its common class interests. After it became a class of itself, the working class consciously identified their personal interests with their common class interests.

(3) The contradiction between fundamental or long-term interests and obtained or short-term interests is another manifestation and externalization of the intrinsic interest contradiction between egoism and altruism. If bounded by egoism, obtained or immediate interests will become obstacles for the realization of fundamental or long-term interests. On the other hand, advocating only long-term or fundamental interests to the neglect of individual, immediate or obtained interests, the advocacy will be vague.

2. Contradiction between subjects of interests

Subjects of interests are the carriers, pursuers and realizers of interests, so contradictions between objects of intereststhat are different in forms, contents, function and natures will necessarily be expressed through and manifested in contradictions between subjects of interests.

The contradictory relations among subjects of interests can be examined vertically and horizontally. The three levels of the subject of interests— individuals, groups (collectives) and state constitute the contradictions of vertical dimension. First, both group (collective) interests andstate interests embody the common ground of and are for the satisfaction of individual interests that can only be realized group and state interests. On the other hand, any individual interest is apart of group (collective) and state interest, in which any social member's activity of interest pursuit is thus part and link of the whole interest pursuing activities of the group (collective) and state. Therefore, the three are dialectically identical in interests. Second, there is always contradiction between individual interestson the one side and group (collective) and state interests on the other, and between group (collective) interests and state interests. For instance, in economic activities, each laborer produces first of all for his individual interest at least, who always hopes as much as possibleto increase his own income and turns his products into means of life or means of consumption. On the contrary, group (collective) and state as representatives of overall interests, may limit, restrain even temporarily damage individual interests for the overall, long-term or fundamental interests, and taking expansion of reproduction into consideration, consider turning some of the products into reproduction or public welfare instead of means of consumption. Contradictions between individual interestsand group (collective) or state interests thus arise. If state or group (collective) interests is over-accumulated, individual interests will be infringed on, resulting in a worsen relations them. On the other hand, if individual interests expand unrestrained, it will also damage the overall and long-term interests of the group (collective) or state, which will in turn cause loss to individual interests. Similar contradictions also exit between group (collective) interests and state interests.

Under different social conditions, the vertical contradictions among subjects of interests have different manifestations. In the society of private ownership, the interest relation among individual, group (collective) and state are diametrically antagonistic. The contradiction between individual interests and state interests finds its expression in the contradiction between individual interests and the overall interests of class, in which state interests are in essence the overall interests of the exploiting class in dominant position that are completely antagonistic with the interests of individuals and the exploited classes. In a society of public ownership, contradictions among the three subjects that are fundamentally identical in interests are expressed in direct ways.

There are also horizontal interest contradictions among individuals, groups (collectives) and the state. Interest contradictions exist between individuals, between groups (collectives) and between states. In a class society, the horizontal contradictions between subjects of interests mainly find their expression as class contradictions, with interest contradictions among persons being one kind of them. Interest contradictions between states or countries may evolve into armed conflicts or even all-round wars. Due to various historical and realistic reasons, there exist also interest contradictions between socialist countries, which if not properly handled, may also lead into bloodsheds.

3. Contradictions between interest groups (collectives)

Any individual who want to realize his social interests must join a group (collective), or establish social relation with others; no one can ever realize his social interests on his own. Robinson Crusoe can only realize his interests by his relation with "Friday" as master and servant. A man separated himself from society can only fulfill his pure physiological needs or animal instincts such as eating, drinking and sleep. The contradiction between interest organizations—the most stable interest groups (classes, strata, nations, states, enterprises, financial groups, political parties, etc.) —is the most concentrated manifestation of interest contradictions, interest contradictions between individuals and between groups will inevitably find their expressions in interest contradictions among interest organizations. Therefore the key to understand interest contradiction lies in understanding interest contradiction between interest organizations.

All societies are made up of different social interest organizations, whose contradiction movements result in social transformation or even social revolution. In a society wheresome groups are contented with and aiming at safeguarding their vested interests and thus lost social vitality and initiatives but in fact its distribution mode cannot satisfy the interest demands of the major interest organizations, the interest organizations that conform to historical trend will put forth new interest demands and launch social transformation or revolution, indicating grave contradictions between social l groups, which will lead to the change of pattern of interest distribution and recombination of interest organizations. Social transformation or revolution will inevitably make some interest groups lose their unreasonable vested interests and some other groups get their due interests that they cannot get before. Therefore, different interest organizations will have different altitude, reaction and tolerance to transformation and revolution, making them either actively participate in it, or reject or even sabotage it. Social transformation and social revolution are the most important manifestations of intensified contradictions between interest organizations and also an important expression of interest dynamic.

IV. Interest Conflict

Some interest contradictions can develop into interest conflicts, the intensified state and expression of interest confrontation and antagonism.

Interest conflicts are the interest disputes and interest contests between subjects of interests because of interest differences and contradictions. Interest conflicts signify a dynamic state between the subjects of interest, in which, different subjects of interests, because of their differences in interest goals, are in conscious or unconscious antagonism that evolves from emotions to actions. An interest conflict usually manifest itself in:

first of all, the overlapping and somewhat incompatible claims of two or more interest subjects over their interest objectives; second, in the threat of one subject's interest claim or behavior to that of others; and finally in the hostile actions of one subjects against others in asserting its interest claim and denounce that of others. Interest conflicts are manifested in a concentrated way in economic, political and ideological fields. Interest conflicts between individuals are conditioned by conflicts between interest groups (collectives) and in certain conditions may develop into interest conflicts between interest groups (collectives). Analyses of interest conflicts usually focus on that between interest groups (collectives) in economic, political and ideological fields.

Modern Western political science attaches great importance to the study of conflicts. American political scientist Quincy Wright pointed out that the concept of conflict is sometimes referred to the inconsistency of motivation, wills, objectives and claims between social entities, and sometime referred to process of addressing the inconsistency. Therefore, conflict is not a static but a dynamic social process. Modern Western conflict theory divides conflicts from different perspectives: in terms of content, conflicts are divided into economic conflict, political conflict, diplomatic conflict, military conflict, cultural conflict and ideological conflict; in terms of scope and nature, conflicts are divided into local conflict, overall conflict, internal conflict, external conflict, secondary conflict and fundamental conflict; in terms of forms, they are divided into symbolic conflict of language, actual behavioral conflict, non-violent conflict and violent conflict; etc. War is the highest and typical form of violent conflict. According to the modern Western conflict theorists, conflict is mainly of five ways: (1) Making persuasion, that is, to persuade and get round the opposite side to make decision against his will. Political war, psychological war and propaganda belong to this way. (2) Making promise, which means that one party offers something favorable to the opposite sideso that the latter relinquish its interest demands with kid-glove methods. (3) posing threat, that is, indicating undesired consequences to scare the opposite side, including display of force, making ultimatum and warning. (4) Bestowing the opposite side with favor, that is, to buy off other side with favor if intimidation doesn't work. (5) Using force. According to them, human conflicts are manifested in three levels— the low level, medium level and high level, just as music is divided into low pitch, medium pitch and high pitch. Conflicts at different levels are different in intensity and means. The escalation of conflict is a process of positive feedback of the mutual interaction between the conflicting parties. Antagonistic action of one party triggers the counteraction of the other, which is fed back positively and serves as a new starting point of a next round of escalation. For example, fighting between two kids over a candy or toy may begin with scorning and cursing, then mutual threatening with mailed fist and finally scuffling. Likewise, interest conflicts between subjects of interests beginwith persuasion using language, and then show of force, threatening, and finally, the use of violence. As for the cause of conflict, some Western scholars believe that the core is "power urge", which is manifestedin personal ambition, pursuit of personal reputation and satisfaction, or taking profit from others' work, etc.

Studies of the Western political scientists on the form, means, developing stage of conflict have their reasonable part but wrong in conflict root analysis. All social, ideological and political conflicts and fighting can be attributed to conflicts of material and economic interests and thus find their root in economic sources. Interest conflicts in economic field are the origins of all other interest conflicts in the social field. Conflicts of economic interests will inevitably lead to conflict of ideological and political interests, which in return, will have counteraction on the conflicts of economic interests. In a class society, for example, classes emerged due to economic reasons, and different classes have their different interest demands and engage in class struggle first of all for their own economic interests. Struggle between the exploiting and the exploiting classes always starts from struggle in the economic field, such as for the raising of wages and improvement of work welfare, which finally evolves into the struggle for political rights and interests. All class struggles in essence are conflicts of economic interests. The interests representing the trend of economic development are always realized in their opposition to interests against the requirements of economic development. Generally speaking, social economic contradictions always find their expressions in the conflicts of economic interests between opposed interest groups. Interests of the groups that represent the requirements of the development of the productive forces conform more to the trend of social development, whereas the interests of the groups that represent the requirements of backward relations of production are against the trend of historical development, and the interests of the former are always realized in the course of interest conflicts with the latter.

Interest conflicts basically manifest themselves in antagonistic and non antagonistic forms. Antagonistic interest conflicts are conflicts incompatibility and antagonism of fundamental interests between the sides. On the contrary, non antagonistic interest conflicts are conflicts on the basis of fundamental identity of interests, so the interest conflicts come either from the fact that all subjects cannot realize their interests at the same time or their fundamental interests due to the restraint of conditions or time, or from the that the balance of interest distribution is broken between the subjects because of the subjective mistakes. But fundamentally speaking, interest conflictsare determined by social economic relations. In antagonistic conflicts, one side of the subjects of interests, sometimes together with its alliance, radically negate, act against or grab the interests of the opposite side, making it a necessary condition for the realization of its own interests. This conflict endangers not only the interests but also survival of the opposite side, and ultimately leads to readjustment and reorganization of the interest relations. In contrast, in non-antagonistic interest conflicts that don't take the realization of the interests of one side at the expense of the opposite side as its necessary conditions, conflicts can be eased or settled through the proper ways; non-antagonistic interest conflicts neither endanger the survival of other parties nor result in the radical readjustment of interest relations. The differences between antagonistic and non-antagonistic conflicts arenot absolute; on the contrary, they can mutually transformunder certain conditions. Generally speaking, conflicts between the opposingclasses are generally antagonistic, but under certain historical conditions, they can transform into non-antagonistic ones. For instance, during the period of War of Chinese People's Resistance against Japanese Aggression, interest conflicts among classes in China, to some scope and degree, transformed into non-antagonistic conflicts.

In a class society, interest conflicts are generally of class nature, but there are also some non-antagonistic ones. For instance, interest disputes among different groups with the same class or stratum are seldom of class nature. Class conflicts can be either antagonistic or non-antagonistic. The same is true of non-class conflicts.

Interest conflicts can be broadly divided into two types of conflicts between interest individuals and that between interest groups. Interest conflicts between interest individuals include that among individuals from different groups and that among individuals within the same group, andin terms of intensity, the latter usually are lower than the former; and the same is true of interest conflicts among individuals with identical fundamental interest. For example, conflicts may occur among members within the same class, but they usually much less fierce than that among members from different classes. However, fighting between individuals inside the exploiting classes can be very cruel. For instance, the law of the jungle is prevalent among in the capitalist society, within which, interest conflicts areby no means less violent than those among groups of fundamental opposition in interests.

Interest conflicts have three major manifestations: emotion conflict, conflict in language and conflict in behavior. Emotion conflict includes emotional opposition, resentment, abhorrence, animosity (such as emotional estrangement, abomination, scoff and curses, etc.) between subjects of interests, it is a latent behavioral conflict; conflict in language refers to conflicts and disputes in forms of language, such as verbal statements, written language and audio & video, etc. They are rational and intellectual conflicts derived from emotions, including paper battle, war of public opinions. Conflicts in behavior refer to physical conflicts between subjects of interests, such as fighting, sabotage, strike, demonstration, protest, violence, war. As a general law, emotion conflict comes before conflict in language behavior and serves as the trigger of the latter two; then both conflict in language and in behavior break out at once; and after conflict in behavior ends, emotion conflict will linger over, which sometimes may express itself in the form of conflict in language. Althoughemotion conflict can upgrade into conflict in language and behavior, some of them can be restrained, distracted or removed before their upgrading. Compared to conflict in behavior, emotion conflict and conflict in language are ahead in time and are provoking, concurrent andenduring. Only by recognizing laws governing interest conflicts can we observe their signs in advance, and proceeding from addressing issues of emotion, avoid conflicts in language or behavior before they break out.

Chapter Eight

Interest Incentive and
Interest Motivation

Social dynamics is an important category for us to scientifically understand the laws governing social and historical development. To understand a society, we must understand the incentive and motivation behind people's social and historical activities as well as the real motive force of social development. Social dynamics refers to forces and factors that incentivize, drive, guide and dominate the activities of human beings (individuals, groups, strata, classes, ethnic groups, countries and even the of human society), and thereby drive social and historical development and changes. Since interests arethe driving forces behind human social and historical activities, the better understanding of which is a must for us to have a deeper understanding of the society.

I. The Real Driving Forcebehind Social and Historical Development

To understand the role of interests as driving forces, we shall firstly study from the philosophical perspective the methodology of understanding the driving forces behind social and historical development to get a clear picture of them.

Historical materialism regards human beings as part of nature and, and human society as the product of nature in its long development, thus the development of human society is a " natural historical process " . However, to explore the driving forces of social and historical development, it is obviously not enough to recognize only the coherence of nature and society: we must also recognize their differences and their relations as opposites.

Firstly, the human society is a special part of nature that has its own characters and laws. While in nature what function are the spontaneous forces without the involvement of human beings and their consciousness, the course of human history is the result of human beings' conscious and purposeful activities. Therefore, society is the society of human beings, as is social history is created by the purposeful activities of human beings. Men engaging in production in given social relations are the subjects of social activities and masters of history, and in this sense, social history is the history of human conscious activities, in which each social phenomenon is the result of human activities with human marks.

Secondly, though a part of nature, humankind is a unique species. Men and animals are essentially different, because activities of lower animals in nature are purposeless, unconscious and passive, while social and historical activities carried out by human beings are conscious and purposeful. Human motivations and driving forces are diverse, "it is precisely the joint forces of these many wills operating in different directions, and of their manifold effects upon the outer world, that constitutes history. "[1] One important character distinguishing men from animals is that human activities are conscious and active, in contrast to the unconscious and passive ones of animals. Any human social activity must first pass through the medium of conscious thinking or mind.

Therefore, to examine the process of social history we must examine human activities, and to examine the driving forces of social history we must examine impetus behind human historical activities, which necessarily involve human motivations, including wills, desires, purposes, etc. , that apparently set men into actions.

The consistency of and differences between human society and nature, and that of men and animals, may easily lead us to a paradox in exploring the driving forces of social history: recognizing the human society as a course of natural history and men a species of the animals will inevitably make us attribute the ultimate driving forces of history to material factors; on the contrary, the differences between society and nature, and that between men and animals seem to have created an illusion: In nature it is the natural laws and aimless forces that work while in human society and human activities, it is such motivations as wills, aims and desires that work, which seems to lead to the conclusion of dual-impetus. So what on

---

[1]   *Selected Works of Marx and Engels*, vol. 4, People's Publishing House, 1995, p. 248.

earth is the most fundamental driving force of social and historical development?

It is because of the consistency of and differences between society and nature, and between men and animals, in exploring the driving force of historical development, we, on the one hand must consider the material source of it, but on the other, should not fall into vulgar materialism by taking specific things as the driving forces. To examine the material roots that consistent with and related to human initiative, we must avoid being deceived by illusion to believe that social history is governed by human motivations, and avoid attributing human historical activities to specific matters in a philistine and simple way. Engels said: "in the realm of history the old materialism becomes untrue to itself because it takes the ideal driving forces which operate there as ultimate causes, instead of investigating what is behind them, what are the driving forces of these driving forces."① Obviously it is absurd to attribute the ultimate causes to idealist driving forces. But the differences between historical materialism and historical idealism lies not here, but in whether it is to stop at the conclusion about thedriving forces or to further investigate things behind them. Engels further said in another occasion: "According to the materialist conception of history, the ultimately determining element in history is the production and reproduction of real life. Other than this neither Marx nor I have ever asserted. Hence if somebody twists this into saying that the economic element is the only determining one, he transforms that proposition into a meaningless, abstract, senseless phrase."② Attributing historical causes to only material factors in a simple and tag-putting way are meaningless metaphysical words that are opposed to dialectics.

On how to explore the mystery behind human historical activities, Engels pointed out insightfully: "When, therefore, it is a question of investigating the driving powers which — consciously or unconsciously, and indeed very often unconsciously — lie behind the motives of men who act in history and which constitute the real ultimate driving forces of history, then it is not a question so much of the motives of single individuals, however eminent, as of those motives which set in motion great masses,

---

① *Selected Works of Marx and Engels*, vol. 4, People's Publishing House, 1995, p. 248.

② Ibid. , pp. 695—696.

whole people, and again whole classes of the people in each people; and this, too, not merely for an instant, like the transient flaring up of a straw-fire which quickly dies down, but as a lasting action resulting in a great historical transformation. To ascertain the driving causes which here in the minds of acting masses and their leaders—to so-called great men — are reflected as conscious motives, clearly or unclearly, directly or in an ideological, even glorified, form — is the only path which can put us on the track of the laws holding sway both in history as a whole, and at particular periods and in particular lands. "① The approach is to understand the enduring acts of the great masses that cause great historical transformation behind the seemly disordered social historical phenomena, then to find out the motivations that trigger these ideological actions and finally, the ultimate driving force. In terms of social dynamics, the order in which social forces function is from ultimate driving forces to motivationsand then to historical activities and finally to social phenomena. However, people's cognition of the social forces is in reverse order: that is, from social phenomena to historical activitie sthen to motivations and finally to the ultimate driving forces. We call this approach of examining historical driving forces as reverse tracking. In terms of order, we can see that motivation is the key link or point that distinguishing materialistic from idealistic conception of history.

On how to ascertain the driving forces behind human motivations, we advocate starting from the understanding of man's particularity. Marx said that the essence of the man is the ensemble of social relations. As a social animal, man's particularity can only be grasped from social relations, first of all, relations of production. Animal behaviors are the functional manifestations of their living organisms whose biological structures determine their instincts and their behaviors: seeking for food, mating, self-defense, etc. It is clear that the motives behindanimal behaviors are intuitive reflexes of instincts arising from their response to the environment, thus are spontaneous and passive, and the individual of which represents that of the species, therefore, animal behaviorsrefer to both the behaviors of individual animal and that of the species. Men's acts are different. Human beings living on the earth for tens of thousands of years belong to the same species— " homo sapiens ", meaning

---

① *Selected Works of Marx and Engels*, vol. 4, People's Publishing House, 1995, p. 249.

"intelligent man" or "man with intelligence". Man's acts are self-conscious and any individual of it is first of all social. The sociality of man's acts can neither be simply explained from his biological structure nor hereditary gene. The program of animal acts is transmitted through hereditary gene code, which is recoded in the cells and passed through DNA. Man's social acts, in contrast, are transmitted otherwise, that is, the instrument of ideas, language or written materials. If animal's hereditary program is recoded in cells, the program that determines man's social acts is recorded in his consciousness with the brain as the vehicle. That is to say, all social acts of human beings are consciously and purposely passed on from generation to generation, which means that the motivation in form of idea is the direct motivation behind man's social acts. More intuitively speaking, man's social acts directly come from his motivation, and without consciousness there would not be human act. But man's consciousness comes from his social practice, which ultimately determines his consciousness. Here come two unavoidable questions: What is the ultimate cause that determines man's historical acts? Since every man has his own conscious acts, how can individual conscious acts pool together to form the objective driving forces independent of man's will? To answer these questions, we must find out the "driving force behind the driving forces" from something that is independent of man's consciousness but covers the subjects of acts and manifests man's initiatives.

First, labor is an elementary category in understanding the driving forces of social history and the key to solving the puzzle of history. Animal acts are determined by its physiological desires, which in turn are determined by its biological structure and the interaction between the animal's living organism and external environment. The essential difference between man and animal is man's sociality, therefore, it is man's social organism (social relations) together with his living organism, instead of his living organism alone, that determine man's social needs and further his acts. Man's social needs are the direct motives behind his acts, and his social organism (social relations) determines his social needs.

This will naturally lead to a further question: if we say that it is the social organism that determines man's consciousness and his acts, where does the social organism come from? The answer of historical materialism to this question is: labor created man and thereby "a new element which came into play with the appearance of fully-fledged man, namely, society. "① Man's labor is first of all social labor, which means that labor can only be carried out through division of labor and collaboration in certain relations of production. Labor created not only man but also social relations, and a social organism is constituted by certain social relations. From this point of view, labor created social organism, and therefore is the force that created history.

Labor created man and human society; on the other hand, labor is man's activity, so man is thus boththe object and subject of labor. It is not only the movement of objective and material force, but also conscious movement that contains active and subjective elements. It is social labor practice that is the intermediary linking the subjects and the objects and material and mental worlds. Taking labor as the fundamental force creating social history can avoid making errors of vulgar materialism or idealism. Labor is the most primary and most basic human activity that determines all other social acts and activities. Therefore, to solving the puzzle of driving force of history, it is needed first of all to examine human productive activities and the relations of production, which will inevitably involve the motivation and purpose underlying man's labor. The ascertaining of causes behind the motivation of man's labor means the finding of the fundamental motivation of historical activities of human being. In this way, it will be " recognized that the key to the understanding of the whole history of society lies in the history of the development of labor. "②

Second, history, thoughthe result of human conscious activities, has its own objective law of driving forces independent of man's will. In other words, although the driving forces of historical development are manifested in man's activities and initiatives, the development of history, on the other hand, presents itself as a force that dominates man and at the same time is independent of man's will. Hence, to reveal the driving force of social history necessarily involves the discovery of the objective law governing the driving forces independent of human will. This put people intoa quandary of cognition: since the objectivity of material production and the relations of production are intertwined with man's consciousness,

---

① *Selected Works of Marx and Engels*, vol. 4, People's Publishing House, 1995, p. 378.

② Ibid. , p. 258.

motivation and other non-material things, recognizing only the irreversible force of objective law without taking into account the initiative of man's will inevitably lead to historical fatalism; on the other hand, the denial of laws governing human activities without recognizing human initiatives will necessarily lead to voluntarism.

Historians in the past could not overcome this cognitive contradiction, whocould not but attributed the causes of history to spiritual factors. Master of idealist dialectics Hegel keenly grasped it and raised a question that was unable to be raised by old materialists: "Each makes good his own individuality, but at the same time does not come off successfully, because eachindividuality meets with the same opposition, and each is reciprocally dissipated by the others. What appears as public ordinance is thus this state of war of each against all, in which every one for himself wrests what he can, executes even-handed justice upon the individual lives of others, and establishes his own individual existence, which in its turn vanishes at the hands of others. We have here the Course of the World. "[1] That means, in the domain of social history, although people act with purpose, they seldom achieve what they wishes, because there is an objective law independent of man's will. Hegel asserted that man's motivation is absolutely not the ultimate cause of history, behind it there must be much more profound causes—the ultimate cause that governs man's act but haven't been realized yet. Unfortunately, Hegel didn' t go further in this correct direction. On the contrary, he believes that there is "worldspirit" behind man's motivation that governs history. Although each person seeks to reach his own goal, the process is nothing but the instrument for "worldspirit" to meet its goal and each man is unconsciouslyrealizing "the cunning of reason". That is to say, although every man acts purposely, the result doesn't work out right, because man has been plotted by reason—worldspirit or reason realizes its goal. Although Hegel reached a wrong conclusion, he profoundly revealed and demonstrated the dialectical relations between man's subjective initiative and the objective laws, and insightfully pointed out the objective law that the development of social history is independent of man's will. Engels lauded: "That Hegel did not solve the problem is here immaterial. His

---

[1] G. W. F. Hegel, *Phenomenology of Spirit* (Chinese version), Shanghai: The Commercial Press, 1979, p. 251.

epoch-making merit was that he propounded the problem. "①

Why the underlying trend of historical development is independent of man's will, given that history is created by man's conscious activities? Engels profoundly answered this question whendiscussing the historical joint forces. Firstly, man's motivation and his activities are restrained by social material conditions of subsistence, which determines not only man's motivation and his activities, but also the level of idea realization and success of activities. Secondly, will and activities of individuals and even classes can speed up or slow down the social historical process but cannot change the overall process and the overall tendency. The conscious activity of an individual organically joining the social course as an element or atom is but a link, element or component of the whole society, which are conditioned by the elements, processes, relations of the mechanisms of the social organism that are interactive and interconnected. Thirdly, behind man's motivation, there are objective material forces independent of man's will. Although historical activities are created by man and social relations are established by man, individuals can neither anticipate nor fully realize the result of his activitiesor the outcome of them. For instance, the inventor of steam engine didn't anticipate the great impact his invention on the society. Although every individual wants to reach his goal, it often cannot be achieved, and sometimes even gets to the opposite.

Third, needs and interests serve as the motivation of man's historical activities, primarily productive activities.

Man is a higher social animal with active consciousness and initiative, and all his acts are governed by his motivation. Needs and interests arouse his motivation and thereby his acts. It is in this sense that needs and interests cause people to make social historical activities, productive activities in particular, therefore are the incentive factors. In order to get the basic necessities of life, man has to take productive labor. Therefore man's needs for subsistence and material interests become the driving forces of his social productive activities. On the basis of satisfying his minimum needs for subsistence, man seeks for higher needs and interests, which further prompts him to make new and higher historical activities, including productive, political, military and cultural activities. Needs and

---

① *Selected Works of Marx and Engels*, vol. 3, People's Publishing House, 1995, p363.

interests are thus incentive factors for man's social historical activities.

Fourth, human social productive practice is the ultimate driving force of social and historical development.

Man's social needs and social interests are the factors that trigger, stimulate and motivate his social historical activities. That is to say, in order to live, to survive in particular, man has to satisfy his basic needs for subsistence, such as clothing, food, housing and transportation, which leads tohis most basic material practices —productive labor, to produce the material means of life. But this labor must be conductedin a given social relations instead of in isolation. These relations are relations of production and the relation between man and nature is the productive force. The unity of opposite of productive forces and relations of production constitutes the mode of social production, namely, ways people attain means of subsistence. The productive forces determine relations of production, and the contradictory movement between the productive forces and relations of production drives the development and transformation of mode of production, and the society thus is developed by this movement. So the productive forces constitute the premise, foundation and driving forces of all societies.

Itis a correct approach of understanding the driving forces of social and historical development to start from man's labor practice to ascertain the causes behind the motivation of productive labor and law governing the driving forces of historical development that is independent of man's will.

II. Manifestations of Interests as Driving Forces

The role of interests as the driving forces discussed here is in a general sense. In fact, interestsare onlyactivators that drive man to carry out historical activities. The term driving force refers to the capacity for self-generation and doing work by itself, and other things can be driven by it. The interest itself is not the driving force but a factor that activates or motivates the driving forces. It is in this sense we say that interest is an activator behind driving forces, which is manifested in four ways: incentive, promotion, guidance and domination.

1. The incentive role of interests
Interestshave the function as an incentive to makepeople carry out

various activities of interest seeking or even various social activities. The study of the role of interests must start from their function as incentive.

(1) *Man's motivations and their forms*

Man's activities are initiated from his consciousness, that is, must have the form of motivation. Studying the incentive role of interests must start from man's motivations and their forms.

In the mid—1950s, a new branch of science—behavioral science emerged, which, by adopting achievements of psychology, believes that man's behavior is determined by motivation, which in turn is generated by needs. This is to say, needs produce motivation and motivation governs behavior. A man's enthusiasm and vigor in work is determined by his motive for the work. The key reason for two persons with similar competence but different performances is that they motives behind the work are different. Only when his motive is activated can a man strive to achieve the planned objective. The stronger the motive, the more enthusiastic he is, and the more achievements he will achieve. There is a behavioral science formula for this: achievement = competence × enthusiasm (motivation) . According to behavioral science, behavior is a basic psychological process and motivation is intentional. Psychological study indicates that a man with some needs unsatisfied will be in a nervous and worried psychological state; when he comes across a reachable aim, his nervous and worried psychological state will be transformed into motivation, under the direction of which he will act to satisfy his needs and work towards it. After the aim is realized and the needs are satisfied, new needs, new motivation and new acts will emerge.

The role of motivation can be studies fromboth macro-level and micro-level. Micro-level refers to investigating the motivation of individual activities from psychological process while macro-level, from the systematic mechanism of the whole society.

Motivation is a psychological phenomenon. Once needs are sensed, they will manifest themselves in the form of motivation, including idea, thought, intention, etc. , which drive and guide people's action to meet the needs. Motivation sets people into action and determines the direction and intensity of the action. Hence, motivation is subjective, directional, incentive and purposeful. So Marx said: "As all the driving forces of the actions of any individual person must pass through his brain, and transform themselves into motives of his will in order to set him into action. "① Among various motives, economic motive is the subjective cause of man making economic activities and man's basic motive that determines other motives. With regard to this, Marx said: "the ideal, internally impelling cause for production... as an internal image, as a need, as drive and as purpose", "is the premise of production. "② Any individual engaging in productive activities is subject to his intention. The difference between man and tool, both as factors of productive forces, is that man has his purpose and is active while tool is purposeless and passive. "The internally impelling cause for production" is the working intention and purpose of the laborer, or motive that triggers his productive activities.

Man's motivation has three forms, which is also the three stage of development of consciousness: desire, interest and cognition.

Firstly, desires appear in thestage of sensation in human cognition. Sensation as a form of human cognition is the reflection of the aspects orfeatures of a matter with sense organs. For instance, sense of sight reflects color, sense of hearing reflects sound, sense of smell reflects smells, sense of taste reflects tastes and sense of touch reflects the facial features of matter, such as cold or warm, soft or hard, sharp or round. As the starting point of human cognition, sensation is the direct link between consciousness and the external world. Perception is the ensemble of senses and an overall reflection of the matter's various features based on all senses gathered. For instance, the perception of an apple is the ensemble of senses of its color, smell, taste, etc. Sensation and perception are the bases of cognition, and desires refer to man's most direct intentions, purposes, wishes, etc. , that are stimulated by his social needs, commonly known as the seven emotions defined by Confucianism—happiness, anger, sadness, fear, love, hatred and desire, and six sensory pleasures referred by Buddhism—desires for sights, for sounds, for smells, for flavors, for tactile sensations and for pleasure—directly incite man's impulse and drive him to seekfood, sex and recreation, and to do all social activities. Desires are the most direct and most intuitive motives that set man into action.

Secondly, interest. Interest (both the meaning of concern about or

---

① *Collected Works of Marx and Engels*, vol. 21, People's Publishing House, 1965, p. 345.

② *Selected Works of Marx and Engels*, vol. 2, People's Publishing House, 1995, p. 9.

attention to and the meaning of benefit) is the second form of motive, appearing in the representation stage, which is based on sensation and perception and also the reflection of senses. It is the recalland reappearance of past sensation and perception recorded and imprinted in memory. The story of " quenching thirst by thinking of plums " in the novel *Romans of Three Kingdoms*is a vivid example in this regard. Interest is the enduring and higher motive arising on the basis of desires. After being stimulated repeatedly by outside needs for a long time, the desires of man triggered out will stay in man's memory for a long time in subjective forms, so that he has persistent interest in the needs, which will continue to generate his impetus even without direct stimulation.

Thirdly, cognition. Cognition is the highest level of motive, the stage or form of rational cognition, by which man can grasp the essence, wholeness and internal relations of matter through abstract thinking. Cognition here refers to man's rational cognition of his own needs formed on the basis of desires and interests, the higher level motivation of needs manifested in abstract and theoretical forms. For instance, man's profound cognition of love can result in his more noble behaviorsin pursuing love. Likewise, man's theoretical reflection on state and class can make people to engage in class struggle and social revolutionary activities in a conscious way. Cognition can make people engage in social activities by following objective laws more consciously and purposefully.

How domotives give birth to man's impulse? Or in other words, how are man's actions activated? To answer this question, we can take productive activity as an example. Since man cannot live without food, a relation of dependence on or requirement for foodis established between the subject and the object. Food is the stimulator of man's action of impulse deriving from hunger toward food. With the development of societyand human evolution, this impulse for food seeking becomes man's interest in diet and thereby leads to his continuing productive activities, such as hunting and planting. In the long run, man's interest in food develops into his profound deeper understanding of the variety, structure and needs for food, which gives rise to theories on diet, such as bromatology, nutriology, which in turn bring about man's impulse toward higher productive activities that drives human beings to have more scientific and modernized productive activities, with a viewto satisfying their needs for food.

(2) *The fundamental role of impulses of desires and the stimulating role of social needs*

In the initiation of human acts, desires are fundamental motives, on which allhigher and rational ideological motives are based. Newton discovered the "universal gravitation", taking it as the governing force of universal nature. Jean Baptiste Joseph Fourier propounded the doctrine of "appetite gravity", trying to label it as the force governing human society. Engels spoke highly of Hegel's view on the role of "wicked desires" as the driving forces of history, "it is precisely the wicked passions of man—greed and lust for power—which, since the emergence of class antagonisms, serve as levers of historical development."① Man's desires for objects and his interests and cognition are the basic motivations of his social historical activities. And desires are the most basic motivation for human action. From a physiological point of view, "desires" are the conscious reflection determined by the physiological mechanism of the living organism. However, physiological reasons can only explain the motivations of animals' action rather than that of man's social actions. Where do man's desires come from? While associated with physiological mechanisms, man's desires are in fact impulses sparked by physiological and psychological stimuli, which in turn are sparked by his social needs.

Food, clothing, housing and transportation are man's most basic desires that drive man into productive struggle and other social practices. So we say that man's desires have greatly influence the "development of all enterprises" of life, including the development of productive forces. These basic desiresare arouse by his basic needs for subsistence. The cycle is that man's consumer needs cause his desires of life, which give rise to his motivations and further to his social activities. So the basic needs for subsistence are the material and objective stimuli behind man's desires.

However, human needs cannot be simply equated with material or spirit; rather, they should take material objects as vehicle, content, basis and premise. Human needs for subsistence take such material means of subsistence as food, clothing, housing, etc. , as vehicle and premise; so do man's cultural and intellectual needs, which take such cultural

---

① *Selected Works of Marx and Engels*, vol. 2, People's Publishing House, 1995, p. 237.

infrastructure and materials as movie theatre, library, stationery as their basic conditions, and material life as their content. On the other hand, man's needs are always conscious ones that manifest themselves in subjective forms such as desires, purposes, intentions, interests and theories. Therefore, human needs, different from instincts of animals that are determined by their physiological mechanisms, represent the dependence of the subjects on the objects of social production and serve as the stimulifor the motivations of human actions.

(3) *The transformation of the needs as stimuli into interests as incentives*

Man's needs determine his motivations, which further determine his actions. But human needs are social and essentially different from animal's physiological needs. Georgi Plekhanov said: "What is meant by an actual need? To our philosopher, this meant primarily a physiological need. But to satisfy their physiological needs people must produce certain articles; the process of that production must give rise to new needs, just as actual as the preceding but whose nature is no longer physiological, but economic, since such needs spring from the development of production and mutual relations entered into by people in the process of production. "①

Since human needs are social, man's creative production becomes the rich sources of his new needs. Being social nature, man's needs are therefore conditioned by social economic relations, first of all by the ownership of means of production—whoever owns the means of production, he owns the objects of needs. For human needs to establish relationship with their desires, the media of distribution and exchange are indispensable. But after the filtrating, infiltrating and interweaving of economic relations, human needs are no longer that of separated individuals, but social needs that are interrelated, mutually contradictory and conflicting. In this way, human needs and their relationship in given economic relations become relationships of interests. So, in social life, human needs appear in the form of interests. Interests, to some degree, are the social forms of human needsin given economic relations, reflecting on the one hand the dependence of man as the subject on the objective life conditions, and on the other the social relations between men, and the basic manifestations of economic and political relations between men as

---

① Georgi Plekhanov, "Essays on the History of Materialism", in *Selected Plekhanov Philosophical works*, vol. 2, Shanghai Joint Publishing Company, 1961, pp. 129—130.

well.

In this sense, it is more precise to say that, it is human interests, rather than needs, that give birth to man's motivationsand social actions. Material and economic interests are the most basic social interests of human beings. Material interests are the economic manifestations that reflect man's dependence on material objects, primarily material means of subsistence; social economic interests are the manifestations of economic relations that are formed when a certain amount of social outcome meet the needs of the subjects. Material interests and economic interests almost overlap, for example, the substance interests in economic relations. Philosophically speaking, material and economic interests are the most basic stimuli to man's social and historical activities.

Interests make man to conduct social activities, which is initiated by his motivations to social production, and then his social actions, primarily productive activities. Motivations aroused by interests also have three forms: interest desires, interest concerns and interest cognition. Interest desires refer to earliest subjective forms of man's desires aroused by interests, which are the most original and simple motives, such as "intentions", "wishes", "ideas", "purposes". Interest desires as the basic part of man's motivations, after being stimulated by interests, display themselves as strong wishes, which will generate impulsive wills and strong desires with concrete objectives. They are temporary, fitful, non-continuous and direct. Interest concerns emerge on the basis of interest desires. Lenin said: "Personal incentive will step up production."[1] Interest concerns are enduring willingness generated on the basis of interest desires. They are no longer directly linked with the incentive of interests, but motivations associated with the imprints or ideas of needs. They are enduring, solid, consistent and form-based. Interest concerns can have a lasting incentive role on people without directly linking with concrete substance. For instance, with enterprising spirit, some people may have great ambition for and dedicate themselves to their work or social undertakings. Interest cognition is the motivations aroused on the basis of interests, which is a category on a higher level than interest concern. Stimulated by interests, people have motivations, and carry out activities to pursue interests; if, in this process, they have an

---

[1] *Collected Works of Lenin*, vol. 42, People's Publishing House, 1990, pp. 176—177.

understanding of the relevant theories, such as the long standing interests and fundamental interests of the working class, then this understanding will have a counteraction of modifying or enhancing interest desires and interest concerns, so that people can firmly devote themselves to the activities for achieving the fundamental interests. Correct interest cognition can encourage people to relinquish their temporary personal interests to engage in social reform or social revolution conducive to social and historical progress.

(4) *The process of realization of interest incentiveand its mechanism*

The process of interest incentive is also the process of interest realization, which is manifested in a concentrated way as the incentive functions and mechanism of interests.

First, the process of interest realization.

We can divide the process of interest realization into the following stages or factors:

Firstly, interest incentive and the pursuit of interests. Physiologically speaking, external stimulus on organism will generate in it physiological behavioral reactions, so is man's social act from its initiation to its actions. But man is different from animals that receive direct stimuli in that man, on the one hand, need some direct incentives, but on the other, are subject to indirect stimuli or incentives, such as those that are spiritual, ideological or conceptual. Nevertheless, direct economic and material incentives are still the most basic ones that initiate man's acts, that is, activating his "internal motivation" by "external objects".
Stimulation is "dynamic", which means that, external objects are necessary. For instance, food can stimulate animals' foraging, and various interests can stimulate man to take social actions. Interests, as the external objects stimulating man to take action, first of all activate his motivations. By saying that interests are the driving forces of man's historical activities, we mean that interests can first of all stimulate and activate man, making him have desires, interest concerns and interest cognition, and then their long-standing pursuit of certain interest goals. Interest incentives and interest objectives are the first stage and primary factor of interest realization.

Secondly, interest seeking activities. Interest seeking activities refer to man's conscious and purposeful social activities for interests, which are driven by material desires, stimulated by interest concern and guided by interest cognition. These activities are the most basic stage and factor of interest realization, and they are consciously carried out by the subjects of interests, or the subjects of interest seeking. In this process, tools, instruments and other materials are necessary, including means of production as the primary ones in man's labor activities. Therefore, the subjects of interest seeking and possession are first of all subjects of owners of means of interest seeking. Under the condition of private ownership, laborers as the subjects of interest seeking are separated from means of life, therefore are not the subjects of it in its full sense, but rather passive tools and instruments under the manipulation of others, so they are neither the real subjects of interests, norsubjects of interest seeking and possession. The establishment of socialist public ownership enables the laborers to possess means of interest seeking and become the real subjects of it. The laborers can freely dispose their means of production according to their own interest requirements, make interest seeking activities and thereby get their interests following the principle of distribution to each according to his work.

Thirdly, interest competition. Interest stimuli make man to seek for interests and to carry out his activities of interest seeking, which give rise to interest competition. The aspects of the competition involve strength, intelligence, talents, etc. , which ultimately will advance the development of society. Competition promotes the economic and academic development as well as talent training, sports, and so on. Interest competitions exist in all human activities, which mean vying each other, self-reliance, hardworking, enterprising, initiatives, innovation, progress, etc. In short, interest competition is a basic force driving the development of human society. From the psychological point of view, interest competition can maximize people's desires, bring their energy into full play and turn their pursuit into enduring actions to pursue one after another new life goals.

Man's seeking for interests is the material source of interest competition. The differences of human economic relations, ownership and diversity in needs determine their interest differences. Differences imply contradictions, which constitute the deepest roots of social interest competitions. In the society of private ownership, the opposition of economic status and the great differences in interest possession determine that there are diametrically antagonistic interest competitions between the subjects of interests, which will ultimately develop into antagonistic interest conflicts. In class societies, interest competitions and struggles between different classes are the driving forces of social development. In a socialist country, although the economic basis for the existence of antagonistic interest contradictions no longer exists, there are still interest differences, interest contradictions and interest competitions on the basis of fundamental identity of interests because of the limitation of socialist economic conditions. Under socialist conditions, interest contradictions among the people are also incentive factors that activate people's motivations and promote them to make interest seeking activities.

Lastly, constraints on the realization of interest incentives. The choice of interest objectives and the ultimately realization of them are restrained by various factors, the most important of which is social system and institutions. Social system is the most fundamental mark, main content and the ensemble of economics, politics, laws and culture of a society; Social economic system is the totality of relations of production, in which ownership is the most important part. Institutions refer to the "concrete forms" of relations of production and superstructures set up on the basis of a given social system. Corresponding to economic system is the economic structure, the concrete economic forms of the relevant relations of production, including structure and form of social ownership, economic management system, etc. System determines institutions, which are relatively dependent and can have reaction on the system. Different systems have different institutions and the same system can also have multiple modes of institutions. Systems are more stable than institutions. Suitable institutions can maximize the superiority of a system. Under given social system, people can choose the best institution by following social laws.

Interests are the expressions of economic relations. The possession of means of production is manifested in possession of interests of the interest subjects. In other words, possession of means of production determines the possession of interests, and economic system fundamentally conditions the realization of interests. For instance, private ownership of means of production determines that the private owners of the means of production possess the majority of social interests, and further determines the quantity and quality of interests of the laborers. In a given system, the institutions adopted also has significant influence on the realization of interests incentives, in which efficiency of labor and initiative of laborers are all related to the institutions. For instance, under socialist system, the initiatives of the enterprises and individuals will be hampered if a rigid planned economy and equalitarian distribution are adopted; on the contrary, if a socialist market economy and reasonable principle and distribution systems are adopted, the initiatives of enterprises and individuals for interests will be aroused, and the development of social production will be advanced. Therefore, system and institutions are important guarantees for realizing interest incentives and the adjustment of various interest relations. Under a given social system, the choice of institutions is essential to the realization of interests and interest incentives.

Second, interest incentive structures and mechanisms.

People enter into certain social relations on the basis of relations of production to satisfy their needs for social life and social interests. Interests therefore become the direct and ultimate goals of people's activities in every aspect of social life, primarily production and reproduction. As goals, interests make man's activities, economic activities in particular, have orientation, dynamics and internal incentive. Interests can stimulate people to engage in social activities, which is the concrete expression and basic functions of interests.

Interest incentives can be divided into two broad types, namely, material and spiritual, or economic and non-economic, in which material and economic interest incentives are the most basic forms. Of course, moral and non-economic interest incentives can also have some influence under the precondition that material and economic interests are satisfied. Interest incentives include positive and negative ones. Positive incentivesrefer to offering some interests, and increasing the interests to enhance the incentives that intensify man's activities. Negative incentives refer to incentives in a negative way, such as reducing payment, revoking privilege, fining, disciplining and withdrawing honorary title. In terms of effect, the larger the quantity of interests, the greater the possibility of man's dependence on incentives and his demands for them. Therefore, although positive incentives have obvious positive effects, theircosts are also greater, and sometimes side effects will emerge. On the contrary, with less negative incentives, the possibility of man's dependence on incentive may be greater and the side effect of positive incentives may reduce. Therefore, if properly used, negative incentives can be effective with less cost. Taking positive incentives as the major instrument and necessary negative incentives as a complementary means, ideal effectscan be produced. The types and forms of incentives constitute the incentive structure, the best of which is the one that can maximize the positive effect and minimize the negative effect at least cost.

Incentive mechanism refers to relevant measures and organizations adopted under given system and structure to fully realize the social functions of interest incentives. The functional mechanism of interest incentives is objective and has its own law, which can be used to promote social progress.

Mechanisms of interest incentive differ under different social systems. In the capitalist society, the mechanism of interest incentive mainly manifests itself in the capitalist's pursuit of private profits that constitute the major driving force of the capitalist economic activities. In the socialist society, the goal of production is to satisfy people's needs, which determines that the major task of its mechanism of interest incentives is to make the laborers concern for their labor products and arouse their initiatives. The socialist system determines that labor of the working people is directly linked to the realization of their own interests, and that personal interests are identical with that of the collective and the state. Given this conditions, positive (material) incentives can be directly applied to mobilize people's initiatives. Therefore, interest incentive mechanisms in socialist societies are largely realized through material and moral incentives.

Third, improvingand giving full play to mechanism of interest incentives.

It has been proved byhistory of human beings that the constraint upon the "free action" of a social laborer—his activity of creating history— reflects the development level of the productive forces. In a macro point of view, constraint on the "free action" involves systems and institutions. For instance, in the mid-and late period of Chinese feudal society, constraint of the despotic shackles upon the laborers was an important cause for the slow development and stagnation of the productive forces. In a micro point of view, constraint on the "free action" has a relation with interest incentive mechanism. Theoretically speaking, an advanced social system can better arouse people's initiatives than a backward one; and within the same system, suitable social institutions can do better in this respect than unsuitable ones. And socialist system, with its favorable conditions, can give full rein to the function of interest incentive mechanisms, under which, an important condition is to fully make use of the potentials of socialist system, improve the interest incentive mechanisms and properly bring them into play.

In socialist countries, moral incentives play a more important role in arousing people's initiatives. In establishing the mechanisms of dynamic incentives, moral encouragement should not be overlooked. It is an inseparable part to set upand make effective use of socialist political and ideological works through methods of moral incentives to stimulate the initiatives of the socialist laborers.

Exploration is necessary for setting up interest incentive mechanisms in socialist countries, which can be done in three aspects. First, reform of distribution system and forms so as to fully implement the principle of distribution to each according to his work by combining responsibility, rights and interests. During which, legitimate unearned income should be allowed, and wages, bonus and other forms of personal income should play their incentive role. Second, implementing democratic management in labor organizations, respecting the employees and realizing extensive self-governance and economic democracy, so that the political enthusiasm of the workers can be stimulated. Third, improving the mechanism for political and ideological work, enriching workers' spare time cultural life and setting up a complete set of effective measures and mechanisms for moral encouragement, so as to improve the workers ideological and moral levels and raise their initiatives.

2. Interests as driving forces

After discussing the incentive role of interests, we can now further discuss the role of interests as driving forces. Essentially speaking, the basis of social material production is the premise and conditions for the formation of social interests, but interests are not the passive product of the development of social production; they can promote the development of social production and human society as a whole. The emergence of new interest demands marks first of all the development of social production and its driving forces. The driving role of interests in this respect is mainly manifested in its stimulating people to carry out productive and various other activities.

Interests constitute the intrinsic motivation behind people's social and historical activities, especially productive activities. History is men's history and men are the subjects of historical activities. Therefore, exploring the driving forces of historical development requires the study of the driving forces of historical activities. The well-known philosopher Bertrand Russell said: "All human activities spring from two sources:

impulse and desire. "① Disregarding the idealistic premise of Russell's philosophy, we can see that Russell pointed out an idea that, all human activities have to pass through their consciousness, that is to say, man's activities are determined and started from motivations, without which, there would be no human actions.

Human needs in essence are social ones. After the filtrating, infiltrating and interweaving of economic relations, human needs are no longer that of separated from each other, but social needs that are interrelated, mutually contradictory and conflicting. In this way, human needs and their relationships in given economic relations become relationships of interests. In real social life, human needs take the forms of interests, which are the higher forms of social needs in given economic relations. Hence, interests become the motivations and driving forces for people's social activities.

Interests are the concrete motivations behind man's historical activities in all societies. Under different social historical conditions, however, interests as the driving forces have different forms. In the primitive society, the collective interests of the primitive communities were the driving forces of social development. In the society of private ownership, interests refer mainly to private interests, "thus the interests of the ruling class became the driving factor of production," ② and private interests become the concrete driving forces of the ruling classes in historical activities. In the slavery society, seeking for maximum surplus labor of the slaves became the major driving factor of the economic development. In the capitalist society, seeking for profitsis the driving force of economic development. In societies where private interests constitute the driving force behind historical activities, the working people are only tools of the exploiting classes to realize their private interests, and the personal interests of the laborers cannot be duly met and the conscious activities of the laborers are largely restrained. In a socialist society, the laborers work for themselves, and the interests of the people become the driving forces behind their social activities and the development of socialism. In a socialist system, interests as the driving force need no longer to manifest themselves in distorted and

① Bertrand Russell, *Principles of Social Reconstruction* (Chinese Translation), Shanghai People's Publishing House, 1959, p. 3.

② *Selected Works of Marx and Engels*, vol. 4, People's Publishing House, 1995, p. 385.

indirect way through the private interests of the exploiting classes. In such a direct form, interests can release much greater vigor than in the private ownership. Under the socialist conditions, the driving role of interests has the following characteristics:

(1) In the whole system of interests, reasonable individual interests constitute the most effective factor stimulating individual initiatives due to the separation of socialist labor. (2) The socialist system makes the three driving factors—individual interests, collective interests and state interests—are consistent in direction, in spite of some contradictions among them. Socialist laborers work not only for personal interests but also for collective and state interests, which strengthen the joint forces of the three interest factors. (3) The socialist system itself can consciously coordinate the contradictory relations between the subjects of interests to minimize the internal frictions of interest competition and therefore can optimize the efficiency of the joint forces of socialist interests. (4) The overall socialist social needs and interests directly constitute the internal driving force of the development of social production. Human needs in the socialist society are the driving factors of social production. Since interests constitute the driving force of individual in historical activities, economic activities in particular, then, what is the internal driving force of the development and economic activities of the society as a whole? Marxist theory of historical joint forces indicates that all historical changes, including historical progress, are determined by the overall historical joint forces of all individuals and classes consisted of individuals. Needless to say that social production and social economic activities are composed of activities of numerous laboring individuals and communities. But the simple summation of productive and economic behaviors of each individual and each organization doesn't make the whole of the social production and social economy. Only when they become components of the productive forces and economic operation, andare organically coordinated through social economic relations, can they for mintegrated actions and movement ofthe production andsocial economy of the society as a whole. Although each individual is a conscious participant of the productive activities and economy, the behaviors of the individuals are just spare parts of them. Under these circumstances, the social production and economy become the movement of things independent of the will and behaviors of any individual or organization. As for the overall social production (economy), social needs and interests become the objectives and

motivation of social production, and therefore become the internal driving forces of social economic development. The differences of ownership of means of production in different social formations determine the differences of objectives of production and their internal motivations. The purpose of production in the socialist society is to satisfy to the maximum the ever increasing material and cultural needs of all people, so the overall social needs and interests directly manifested as purpose of the social production and the internal driving force of social economic development. Of course, they are identical with the proposition that interestsare the intrinsic motivations behind people's concrete historical activities. This is because the purpose of socialist production is to satisfy the social needs of all the people, while that of the socialist workers is to get more means of subsistence, so the two are identical. (5) At the stage of socialist market economy, human needs are diverse, or even contradictory to each other, which are manifested as market demands that have internal contradictions and competition, making the subjects of interests more diversified and interest competitions fiercer. Of course, these will ultimately become the joint forces of promoting production. (6) With the ever improving of people's intellectual and cultural needs, the role of moral encouragement also becomes more important. Under socialist conditions, work of the laborers has the nature of subjective labor, with individual interests of the laborers are identical with the overall interests of the state, therefore it is necessary to raise the laborer's awareness of working for the collective and the state. With the development of socialist material and intellectual and ethical progress, the morals of the laborers will improve as well, making the role of spiritual driving forces under given material conditions become stronger. Of course, this will take a long process.

3. The guiding role of interests

The incentive and driving role of interests will necessarily lead to their guiding role to man's ideas and actions, which is fully manifested in economic, political, cultural, ideological, educational and other sectors of social life.

(1) Connotation of the guiding role of interests

The guiding role of interests refers to the role of interests in regulating and guiding man as the subject of interests in his pursuit of various interests arising from their objective interest demands. It mainly includes:

Firstly, making the subjects of interests, based on their social ideals and goalsof life, and on interest utility principles and values, rationally understand and judge these principles and values; Secondly, making the subjects of interests, based on their understanding and evaluation with regard to the nature (positive, negative, or neutral) and levels of the principles and values above; Thirdly, making the subjects of interests achieve their interest pursuit or meet their interest demands based on the principles and values. The guiding role of interests, first of all, is objective, and it is the embodiment of the above principles and values in man's interest activities. Reasonable interest guidance can orientate the subjects to take the correct direction and actions that are in accordance with the requirements of historical trends, andcan regulate and guide them to take the advantages and keep away from the disadvantages and to seek reasonable interests and refuse unreasonable ones. Unreasonable interest guidance, on the contrary, will guide the subjects to do the opposite, even jeopardize or appropriate the interests of others.

Interest guidance is an objective phenomenon in social life. A class society is always divided into classes, strata, groups and communities based on interest differences. Therefore the society is always made up of different subjects of interests (interest groups) with different interest choices and pursuits. Even the same subject may also face different interest choices between proper and improper, between individual, collective and state interests, between economic interests and political interests, between material interests and spiritual interests, etc. Whatever the choice is, it is conditioned by the social relations that the class, the stratum, the group and the individual is in, and the restraint of class relations in a class society. Interest choices first of all are conditioned by social relations; in other words, interest guidance is in fact determined by economic, class and social relations. Under this major premise, whatever the subjects of interests choose, and however they make choices, they always stick to the principle of interest maximization, which needs to be regulated and guided. In this context, interest guidance is objectively necessary.

(2) *Content of interest guidance*

Interest guidance and its content are determined by specific economic relations, historical conditions and relationships between demand and supply.

First, guidance on instruments.

To survive and develop, man must have means of subsistence,

including food, clothing, housing and transportation, etc. For this, material production is imperative. That is the primary needs for man's subsistence andalso the basic interest needs—material economic interests, on the basis of which there further springs up the political interests and spiritual interests. Generally speaking, the pursuit of material interestsand their derivatives that are in accordance with historical conditions is reasonable, but this doesn't mean all human interest pursuits are absolutely " reasonable by nature " without the question ofinterest guidance. In fact, to satisfy interest requirements of the subjects of interests, some means must be used, which maybe proper or improper. Regulating and guiding the subjects to use proper instead of improper means needs interest guidance. The differences of means used in getting interests determine the reasonable or unreasonablenature of the interests gained. For instance, the intention to acquire wealthis justifiable. To this end, some people work hard, but some peopletry to get it bystealing or robbing. Generally speaking, the former is reasonable and the latter unjustifiable. To guarantee that the pursuits of interests of the subjects are honestly conducted under interest guidance, the guidance of means is very important. Subjects of interests must be regulated and steered, so that they achieve their goals through proper means whileimproper means are forbidden. When conditions exist, subjects of interests should be guided to realize their interests by making good use of the conditions; when conditions are unavailable, they should also be guided to create them.

Of course, means of interest gaining have their historical limitations. They have class nature in a class society. A means might be proper and reasonable under one historical condition and improper and unreasonable under another, or proper and reasonable for some classes and improper and unreasonable for other. For instance, land rent is justifiable in the eyes of the landlords but improper in that of the peasants. In a class society, it is not correct to judge the fairness of a means without considering the given historical and social relations. In short, the guidance of interest means is historical and concrete and is class nature in a class society.

Second, moral guidance of interests.

Interest contradictions manifest themselves in interest contradictions between individuals, groups (collectives) and the state (whole society) vertically and horizontally as contradictions among individuals, groups, strata, classes, ethnic groups and countries. These contradictions will inevitably reflected in people's minds and find their expressions in their altitudes and moral orientations. Even under the conditions of socialist society, some people can properly deal with the vertical and horizontal contradictions, while some people cannot. If all the people cannot properly address them, harmonious and stable development of the society is impossible. Therefore it is necessary to make full use of the role of interests in moral guidance by combining it with ideological and political works. Moral guidance of interests refers to, in addition to ideological and political works, making use of the leading position of state interests relative to collectiveand individual interests, long-term, fundamental and overall interests to short-term, immediate and partial interests, and class and national interests to individual interests, to guide the people to put state, long-term, fundamental and class interests before individual, short-term or immediate interests; and to making some advanced elements become exemplary models in this respect.

Third, the action guidance of interests.

Man's pursuit of interests gives rise to his profit-seeking actions or activities. For instance, in order to satisfy his needs for food, clothing, housing and transportation, man needs to carry out material production, or labor activities, either farming or working. The act of interest seeking is influenced by motivation which is the result of interest incentive. It is interests that drive politicians to compete for political power and artists to create artworks. In this sense, interests can guide people's behaviors, that is to say, norms of interests guide the direction and effort in people's interest seeking. Strong interest incentive can make the subjects to put great efforts in it; distinct long-term and fundamental interests can make some advanced elements strive for it by relinquishing their short-term or immediate interests. In short, interests can play a role in guiding people's actions.

Fourth, guidance in the content of interests.

Interests constitute a system composed of manifold levels that are closely linked in a progressive manner, in which material and economic interests are the foundation. Generally speaking, political and intellectual interests can only be formed and become targets of pursuit after material and economic interests have been met.

Because of the progressive relationship in which material and economic interests determine political and intellectual interests, it is imperative to guide the subjects of interests to seek political interests on the basis of economic interests and seek intellectual interests on the basis of political interests. On the other hand, it is also necessary to make use of the reaction of political and ideological interests on material and economic interests. So the subject's care for and pursuit of economic interests in proper ways should be recognized and respected and their realization should be fully guaranteed; at the same time, the subjects should be guided to seek his political interests with legitimate means and protect their rights and fulfill his obligations, and further be guided to seek their intellectual interests with legitimate means. That is, guidance on economic interests must be upgraded into political interests and further to intellectual interests. On the other hand, the subjects should also be guided to direct and guarantee their economic interests with political and intellectual interests. Only by combining the pursuits of political and intellectual interests with economic interests to let them complement and promote each other on the basis that material interests and political interests are the guarantee and intellectual interest is the guidance, can the pursuits of the subjects of interests become legitimate, proper and diverse.

(3) *Mechanismsfor realizinginterest guidance*

The mechanisms for realizing interest guidance for the subjects to achieve their interests include: First, material incentive. Material rewards are offered to those who conform to interest guidance and punishments for those who do the opposite; Second, institutional restraints. Through systems and institutions, the subjects are guided and regulated to seek reasonable interests and prevented from seeking the unreasonable interests; Third, legal guarantee. Legal means should be used to protect the subjects of interests in seeking interests in legitimate ways while guard against the opposites; Fourth, moral guidance. By moral value education and personal moral cultivation, reasonable interest pursuits should be rewarded while the unreasonable denounced.

4. The dominating role of interests

As an important force setting maninto action and a great lever of historical changes, interests, on the basis of their functions of incentive, motivation and guidance, alsohave the function of dominating, that is to say, under given social conditions and the premise of recognizing the decisive roles as a fundamental driving force of the society, interests play a dominating role in determining people's ideas and actions, in social conflicts and struggles, in political operation and activities, etc. Interests serve as the leverin great social changes and historical progress, and a powerful engine inpeople's social and historical activities.

(1) Interestsarethe direct driving motivation and purpose of people's activities intransforming nature and in production, which dominate their production and other social activities. In order to survive, people need material means of living, which is not only the ultimate goal but also the direct motivation of their production. At different stages of social development, people improve their tools and productivity for a basic reason of getting more material means of subsistence or interests from nature. Therefore, interests, material interestsmore exactly, play the role asleverin man's historical activities, productive activities in particular. And on this basis, interests further underlie other social activities of human beings, includingactivities in political, military, cultural fields.

(2) Material and economic interests serve as the foundation of all social groups and organizations, the economic sources of all social conflicts and struggles and interests dominatesocial conflicts, contradictions and struggles. The law of unity of opposites is the fundamental law governing not only nature but also human society. In any society, there are at once consistency and contradictions, unity and conflicts, alliance and struggles; and this kind of struggle and unity between the opposites is the universal law governing social development. In the process of historical development, interes tsunderlie all contradictions among the people, between nations, classes, parties and countries. People join together based on various interest relations, especially economic relations, to form social groups and organizations such as strata, classes and states, as well as various political groups and parties representing different economic interest demands, which give birth to class society. In the French Revolution, the proletariat and other working people united with the bourgeoisie to form the Third Estate; during the period of the War against Japanese Aggression in China, the Anti-Japanese National United Frontwas, in the last analysis, set up on the basis of common interests among various class and strata. On the other hand, origins of social contradictions and social struggles can be traced back to interest differences and contradictions. In class societies, all confrontations, contradictions and conflicts between classes are ultimately determined by material interests, and class struggles in fact are the fights between different economic interest groups. Social contradictions and struggles constitute the sources and driving

forces forsocial and historical development. In this sense, interest conflicts, or interests constitute the driving forcesfor historical development.

(3) Interests are the driving forces that push people to make social reform and revolution, so to some extent they dominate social changes. While relations of production reflect the relations of interests between men, superstructure also serves for the interests of certain social groups and political power serves as meansfor realizing economic interests. Power is dominated by interestsand serves interests. Power struggle in essence is the struggle for interests, and power groups thus represent relevant interest groups. Power struggle culminates in violent power contest. There is a logical relation in the process from relations of production to economic interests, then to political power and finally to violent power struggle, among which interests is the key factor. In the contradiction between the productive forces and relations of production, the former is active, dynamic and ever changing, while the latter is relatively stable and have some inertia. This is because, when a new kind of relations of production replaces the old ones, it will inevitably impair the interests of the people whose interests are represented by the old ones, and these people will desperately protect their invested interests by using the superstructure and political power. The replacement of old relations of production by the new ones is in essence the adjustment of interests, that is, the replacement of old relations of interests by new ones. Through the adjustment, thevested interests of some people are lost, but the interest demands of some others are metand their initiatives are fully mobilized. As a result, the productive forces are promoted. In class societies, the reactionary ruling class always tries to protect the outdated relations of production with their superstructure and political power to safeguard their vested interests. On the contrary, the working people and the revolutionary classes, for their own interests, will carry out political and economic struggles and social revolutions to break the old relations of production. By saying that the old relations of production restrain the development of productive forces, we mean that such relations of production jeopardize the economic interests of the classes representing the new productive forces and dampen their enthusiasm for social production. So objectively speaking, social revolution transforming old superstructure and relations of production meets the interests of classes standing for new productive forces and thus mobilize their initiatives.

In societies where productive forces generally conform to the relations of production, there are still some aspects and segments in the relations of production and the superstructure that do not conform to the development of productive forces and thus need to be adjusted and transformed, which means the adjustment and reform of social relations of interests. When some segments in the relations of production and the superstructure don't conform to the further development of the productive forces, it also means that some interest relations are imbalanced and that interest distribution among interest groups are unreasonable, with some groups getting too much while the reasonable interests ofother groups not being met and their initiatives being seriously dampened. Therefore, some segments in the relations of production and the superstructure that don't conform to the further development of the productive forces shall be transformed to mobilize the initiative of the workers to the maximum, so that social progress can be advanced. From this point of view, interests constitute the intrinsic force that drives people to change and transform the old relations of production and superstructure.

(4) Economic interests determine political activities, interests and power, and have some dominance over the political altitude, actions and power of the political groups. Making economic activities to realize people's interests under given economic relations must be guaranteed by relevant political superstructure, which gives rise to political needs that must be satisfied through political activities and political interests. To safeguard political interests, political power and political activities are indispensable. In the interaction between economy and politics, economy acts as the basisand determines politicswhile politics is subject to economy; on the other hand, politics can also reacts to economy. First, economic interestsare the sources of political activities and political power. It is economic interests that prompt some groups to maintain or change certain social relations and social structures, which result in political interests, different political activities, political thoughts and ideologies. Second, political activities, power and interestsare subject to economic interests. When change occurs to the economic interests of different people or groups, their political activities, power and interests also change accordingly. Most importantly, changes in economic relations will bring about changes in political power and interests, which can eitherbe qualitative or be quantitative. Qualitative changes comefrom the solution of completely antagonistic contradictions of economic interests, manifested in the transfer of political power from backward and decaying classes to advanced and revolutionary classes; while quantitative changes

are manifested in the regime shift from one stratum or group to another within the same class. Third, the ultimate purpose of seeking political power and political interests is to realize economic interests. " In the struggle between landed property and the bourgeoisie, no less than in the struggle between the bourgeoisie and the proletariat, it was a question, first and foremost, of economic interests, to the furtherance of which political power was intended to serve merely as a means. "① In short, economic interestsarethe source and final purpose of political interests.

(5) Interests underlie and dominate ideas. Marx said: "The 'idea' always disgraced itself insofar as it differed from the 'interest' . "② Man lives in given material and economic relations of interests, whose ideas, consciousness and subsequently theirtheoretical views are all dominated, influenced and determined by interest relations. Interests determine man's idea and views. In class societies, relations of class interests determineman's ideas and thoughts, which are all stamped with the brands of class. In analyzing man's ideas and views in a class society, his class position and class interests must be taken into account. In the current stage of socialism in China, there are still some differences between classes and between interest groups, which will inevitably find their expressions in their ideas and attitudes.

III. The Dynamic Structure of Interests

Since interests underlie the motivation of man's social activities, two important questions will come out. First, how do interests as the driving forces of individual activities transfer into the impetus that sets the collective or even the whole nation or state into action? Second, how do interests as the forces driving the subject's activities transfer into driving forces that plays a role in the objective social and historical development? To answer these two questions, detailed analysis of the dynamic structure and transfer of interests should be analyzed from both macro and micro levels and from subjective and objective aspects.

---

① *Selected Works of Marx and Engels*, vol. 4, People's Publishing House, 1995, p. 250.

② *Collected Works of Marx and Engels*, vol. 2, People's Publishing House, 1957, p. 103.

1. The dynamic structure and transfer of interests at the micro level

First, let's go to the details of therole of interests as a driving force at the micro dynamic structure of the subject's economic activities, to look into their dynamic structure and transfer.

All interests involve men as the subjects and function as a driving force through men's initiatives. We can investigate the dynamic structure and transfer of interests from three levels of individual, groups (strata, classes, ethnic groups, enterprises and various special interest groups) and state interests. The subjects of these three levels constitute a complex and interconnected dynamic structure of interests. We can go into the details of the micro structure of the role of interests as a driving force to analyze its transfer.

(1) Individual interestsare the initial cells of the dynamic structure of interests. The historical activities in any times are consisted of the social activities of numerous individuals. Men as the subjects of historical activities are the most basic elements of the whole subjects of social historical activities. Producing necessary means of living is men's first historical activity, and the interests meeting individual basic necessities of life are the initial cells of interest structure. Although there are different social formations in history, all must first of all satisfy men's needs for subsistence. The differences lie in the forms and levels of importance of individual interests. Under the conditions of private ownership, needs for both subsistence and production of the subjects are satisfied in the form of individual interests in the forms of self-interests. For instance, in the capitalist society, the individual interests of the capitalists manifest themselves as pursuit of profits. Due to the nature of the ownership, individual interests split into antagonistic interests, in which individual interests of the exploiting classes, taking the forms of forged collective or social interests, dominate, control and deprive the individual interests of the exploited classes. Under the socialist conditions, the antagonism among individual interests no longer exists, in which individual, collective and social interests are basically identical. But the satisfaction of social needsis still embodies inthe individual satisfaction of means of subsistence, which must be associated with the labor of the individuals, so individual interests remain the driving forces behind the historical activities of individuals.

(2) Collective interests are the intermediary in the dynamic structure

of interests. The cell ina living organism is a basic unit of life that can independently finish the biological and biochemical process of metabolisms and energy transmission. But, for a single cell to have normal life activities, it must organically integrate with other cells. This is true with individual interestslikecellsin the whole interest system. Since human beings are social animals, the labor of any individual is dependent on certain social relations, i. e. , social division of labor and collaboration. Individual interests are integrated with the interests of that of the whole collective through labor, which gives rise to common interests of the collective. Collective interests are consisted of and integrate individual interests into an organic whole. Independent individual interests without integrating with given collective interests cannot exist. In class societies, the collective interests manifest themselves in the form of class interests, which are the supreme common interests of the class; at the same time, individual interests are somewhat contradictory with and separated from collective interests. The organic integration of individual interests constitutes collective interests, which organically constitute the social interests. Therefore, collective interests are the medium between individual interests and social interests. Collectives are the second level subjects of historical activities and also the forces that push the whole collective into actions.

(3) State interests are at the highest level in the dynamic structure of interests. In a society with state power, the common interests of the whole society can only be legally effective when they are embodied in the form of state interests through the will of the state. In term of content, in the social stage where state still exists, social interests expected by the peopleare state interestsconsisted organically of individual interests and collective interests. In the state, the common points of interests of each collectiveconstitute the common interests of the whole society, among which, state interests dominate the direction and limits of individual and collective interests, and coordinate and balance the interest relations among individuals, relations between individuals and collectives and relations among collectives. In a class society, "the interests of the ruling class became the driving factor of production. "[1] The class interests of the ruling class appears in the form of forged common interests of the society in

---

[1] *Collected Works of Marx and Engels*, vol. 20, People's Publishing House, 1965, p. 521.

the form of state interests which act on the development of social production. Engels said that state "is on the whole only a reflection, in concentrated form, of the economic needs of the class controlling production."[1] On the one hand, the ruling class must strive hard to maintain the functioning of social production and social activities, on the other, it deceits and dominates the working class by flaunting the banner of social and state interests to satisfy its own class interests. In a class society, because of the antagonistic economic conditions, state interests, individual interest and collective interests are somewhat antagonistic and separated from each other.

Individual, collective and state interests are different in content, which, as the basic components in interest system, are interdependent yet mutually contradictory, forming a complex dynamic structure with each as driving forces playing their respective role. We can understand the social dynamics by analogy with ginseng. A ginseng can be decomposed into specific chemical elements with modern chemical methods, but the simple combination of these elements doesn't have the medical effect like ginseng. Likewise, social dynamics can also be decomposed into different forces, but the just sum total of these specific forces cannot play the role of a composite force that can only be formed by combining them organically toward the same direction. Therefore, we must study how the dynamics of interests of the individual, the collective and the state are transferred.

Individual interests serve as the most basic driving forces that directly set man into labor activities. But individuals must form relations of production to carry out the activities, through which, the driving forces of individual interests pass on to the labor collective, making collective interests the forces that drive the collective's productive activities. Likewise, the driving forces of collective interests further pass on through the social relations of production of the whole society to form state or social interests of a composite force nature that drives the development of social production.

The dynamic transfer of any social interests is certainly not in such an ideal linear and direct way. There are usually disagreements and contradictions, counteractions, conflicts and internal frictions among the

---

[1] *Collected Works of Marx and Engels*, vol. 21, People's Publishing House, 1965, p. 346.

three forces. The driving forces of individual interests might not always in complete accordance with that of collective interests, and arethe relations between collective interests and social interests. Based on their own interests, individuals and collectives hope to get maximal interests for themselves and turn more labor products into their own means of consumption, which will certainly increases resistance and internal frictions to the realization of social interests. In other words, the driving forces of collective interests consisted of individual interests may become the restraining factor or counteractive force of the driving force of state interests. Through adjustment of economic relations on the basis of this mechanism, these forces join together organically to form a composite force driving the development of society and history.

Based onthe optimization principle of the system theory, individual and collective interestsare the optimal factor for social interests to play their role as driving forces, but it can also be a factor that restrains the driving forces of social interests to their maximum. It is a basic requirement for social development and also an indicator proving the efficiency of social driving force that the individual interests, collective interests and state interests operate synchronically and coordinately toward the same direction, so that the impetus role of interests reach their optimal effect, or approach its optimal function.

For interests to play their optimal role as driving forces, the key lies in the economic and social environments. Under the conditions of private ownership, the fundamental antagonism between individual, collective and state interests intensifies the internal frictions among them and restrains them from full play as joint forces in society. The establishment of socialist public ownership put the dynamic structure and transfer of interests on the basis of identity of fundamental interest, which offers favorable conditions for the social interests as driving forces to have optimal function. This because: First, socialist public ownership canmaximize the enthusiasm of the laborers so that individual interests can fully play their role as driving forces. Satisfying the individual's needs for subsistence is a necessary precondition for the existence of any society. In the socialist society, the subsistence and development of individual laborers and their families are still their own affairs, so it is an important task for socialism to turn consumer goods into the property of individuals to re-establish their "individual ownership" on the basis of common possession of means of production. Therefore, individual interestsare the direct motivation behind individual labor, and the establishment of socialism has liberated and strengthened rather than eliminating the dynamic mechanism of individual interests. Socialism makes laborers combine with means of production, which ensures laborers to get means of subsistence with their own labor and thus creates a favorable environment for individual interests to play their role as a driving forces. Second, socialist public ownership makes the direction of the three forces of interests of the individual, the collective and the state more identical. Individual laborers in socialist society become masters of their own labor and more clearly recognize that working for the collective and state interests is at once working for individual interests, which strengthens the role ofthe three forces of interests toward the same direction. Third, socialist system itself can automatically reduce the restraining elements among the three interests and minimize internal frictions of conflicts so that the joint forces of the three forces can be optimized. However, due to some historical reasons, China is still at the primary stage of socialism, and the old economic and political systems still restrain, to some extent, the impetus of socialist interests. It is therefore imperative to reform the current socialist institutions so that the vitality of socialist interests as driving forces can be fully invigorated.

2. The dynamic structure and transfer of interests at the macro level

From the macro point of view, social driving forces constitute a system of multi-level and multi-component that can be divided into three major levels: the general driving forces ofsocial and historical development; the specific driving forces in specific domains and stages, such as the driving force of economic development; andthe driving forces for individual activities. The general driving forces of social and historical development refer to the driving forces and factors that play a fundamental and decisive role in the changes of human social and historical development at all levels, domains, stages and social formations. Specific driving forces refer to forces that drive the development of specific sectors. For example, driving forces for social economic development refer to forces and factors that drive the economic development of human society, which are the direct purpose and driving forces of production of the society as a whole. The driving forces for individual activities refer to forces that directly motivate individuals into economic, political and cultural activities, especially production.

How do interests play their role in macro dynamic structure? As discussed above, interests by nature can be classified into two major categories: material interests and spiritual interests, or economic interests and non-economic interests. Material interests and spiritual interests refer respectively to material forces and spiritual forces behind historical activities of human society. Among them, material forces determine and pass their dynamics into spiritual forces, while the latter in turn can either enhance or weaken the role of the former. Economic interests are forces behind human economic activities and non-economic forces, with the latter can either enhance or weaken the former. The transfer of forces of interests within themselves will play their role in the three levels in the macro structure. The concrete social activities of individuals can be divided into productive activities and non-productive activities, in which the former are motivated by their material interests, and drive and determine their other activities, productive activities in particular. Each individual is dominated by his own individual economic interests that are conditioned by the economic relations of the whole society. All individual economic interests, being their positive or negative to the individual, will mix up and integrate into the joint forces of history, or driving forces of economic interests that are conditioned by relations of production. Because the common economic interests of the society become the driving forces of individuals in their activities, they therefore become the driving forces behind the economic activities of the society as a whole. But the common economic interests are not the simple sumtotal but the organic integration of individual economic interests, so the direction of the common economic interests as driving forces cannot bechanged by that of any driving force of individual economic interests. In this way, the driving forces of interests are transferred from the level of individual activities into the level of social economic activities. The forces of economic interests determine that of non-economic interests and transfer into to general social interests. Through these processes, interests finally become the general driving forces of social development.

Theview that the contradiction between productive forces and relations of production is the fundamental driving force of social development is consistent with the view that interests constitute the driving forces of human social and historical activities. This is because, it is in productive activities that people realize their material interests, and people at different positions in the relations of production have different material interests, so relations of production in fact are relations of human material interests. Classes representing old and vested interests always strive hard to protect their old relations of production, so as to safeguard their interests; while classes representing new productive forces always strive to change the old relations of production and oppose the ruling classes, so as to obtain their due interests. The movement of contradictions between the productive forces and relations of production, through the dynamic transfer of interests, manifests itself as human contradictions. Among which, interests are the media, which transfer the role of forces in the contradictions between materials into the relations of contradiction between human beings, and through which further to the movement of contradictions between the productive forces and relations of production. Productive forces are the final decisive forces, which is consistent with interests as the driving forces. Interests can be interpreted as needs; needs promote production, which gives rise to new needs that drive production to develop in depth and breadth. Therefore needs and interests become the most fundamental internal forces of the developmentsocial production; the development of productive forces, and the movement of contradiction between the productive force and relations of production become the fundamental forces driving social development. In this way, the driving forces of men as the subjects of social activities are linked with the driving forces of social development as the objects.

As we have mentioned earlier, needs and interests are the forces behind men as the subjects of social and historical activities; but for them to become the driving forces of social and historical development as the object, the role of needs and interests must go through several processes of transfer after they finally transform into the movement of contradictions between the productive forces and relations of production. That is to say, interests themselves cannot directly become the fundamental and decisive driving forcesor factors of social and historical development. The reasons are as follows:

Firstly, interests cannot play their roles as driving forces independent of given relations of production. Needs and interests are needs and interests of human beings who are not abstract but are in the totality of given social relations and whose needs and interests are conditioned by these relations. In societies with exploiting classes, weavers have no sufficient clothing and farmers have no sufficient food, and people who directly take up productive labor cannot get their due means of subsistence. It is clear that it is the ownership of means of production and corresponding system of distribution that determine whether and how people's interests can be realized. Interests are the manifestations of social economic relations, and relations of production are indispensable for the promotion role of needs and interests in historical activities of human beings.

Secondly, the extent of interest realization is ultimately determined by the productive forces. From the point of view of individual behaviors in productive activities, any individual who engages in production must first of all have the motive then the action of production. In the entire process of human productive activities, the motivation as a whole is also the intrinsic motivation behind human productive activities. Therefore, needs and interestsare the starting points of human productive activities in terms of idea. On the surface, interests and needs are the ultimate driving forces behind productive activities of individuals and the society as a whole, but no production can be carried out without the condition of existing productive forces, which are the conditions and starting points of the productive activities of individuals and the whole society. Here someone may ask: Isn't it that the first person in human history who picked upa tool to labor was urged by his needs of life? The answer is yes. Because, as to any individual, his first act of labor is motivated by needs; but in terms of the entire history of human beings, the preconditions of human productive activities were the results of the long accumulated historical process of the labor of the ape in their evolving into the man, the physical production and reproduction of humankind and the combination of this physicalproduction with the natural conditions. All individual productive activities are conditioned by them. Therefore, production of human society is developed under given conditions of material production. It is the new needs that constantly create production, which in turn stimulates the progress of production. Certain social productive forces and social relations of production developed on the basis of them are the foundation and condition for the realization of needs and interests.

Third, interests can only play their role as forces driving man's historical activities through competition of needs and the movement of interest contradictions. Literally, a driving force refers to a force that can arise from within. But, neither needs nor interests can generate any driving force themselves. Interests must play their role as driving forces through interest contradiction, conflicts and competitions between human beings under certain relations of production. For instance, in socialist countries, there are certain differences of interest distribution among the people, on the basis of which, there emerge some interest contradictions and competitions. Among which, interests play their role as driving forces in that people are motivated to do more productive activities so as to gain better satisfaction of their interests. In this process, interest contradictions and competitions play their role as driving forces. During which, the medium and conditions of economic relationsare indispensable.

Lastly, men's conscious creative activities motivatedby interests will irresistibly be subject to social laws. Interests reflects the dependence of men as the subjects of needs on material and intellectual conditions as the objects of needs, manifested as man's desires for and pursuits and possession of the latter. But in real social life, people cannot always achieve their expected goals in terms of distribution and possession of their final products of labor. In other words, people's conscious pursuit of interests cannot always be fully accomplished, or even just the opposite, which indicates that there is still an objective decisive force behind human needs and interests, which is independent of men's will, that is, "productive forces and relations of exchange" .

The above analysis shows that interests are only motivations behind the activities of social members, which can transform into the driving forces of historical development under given social conditions. Social and historical process as part of the natural process independent of man's will must have its own driving force that is different from and at the same time interrelated with man's voluntary and conscious creative activities. Therefore, the movement of the contradiction between productive forces and relations of productionis the fundamental driving force of the development of society as an object, in which the productive force is the decisive factor. Interests can only play their role as driving forcesthat are subject to this fundamental driving force. Of course, by stressing the fundamental role of the contradiction between the productive forces and relations of production doesn't mean that we deny the role of motivation of interests for laborers. Since the most active factor in productive forces is the laborers, satisfying the needs and interests of the laborers to the maximum can mobilize their enthusiasm and thus facilitate the development of social productive forces. The driving factors behind the subjects of historical activities are consistent with the objective driving forces behind social development.

Interests as the subjective driving forces of man's activities are consistent with the movement of the contradiction betweenthe productive forces and relations of production as the objective driving forces of social development, and the two kind of driving forces are interchangeable. Marx and Engels have amply proved this in theory. In *Ludwig Feuerbach and the End of Classical German Philosophy*, Engels talks about three very important ideas: first, the final driving force and ultimate cause of historical development of humanity is economic factor; second, class struggle is the direct driving force of historical development; and third, needs and interests are the concrete motives behind man's social activities. He points out: " When, therefore, it is a question of investigating the driving powers which — consciously or unconsciously, and indeed very often unconsciously — lie behind the motives of men who act in history and which constitute the real ultimate driving forces of history, then it is not a question so much of the motives of single individuals, however eminent, as of those motives which set in motion great masses, whole people, and again whole classes of the people in each people. "[1] Here Engels proposed the concept of "ultimate driving force", which means the force of ultimate decisive role or ultimate cause behind the motivation of individuals or even the whole nation, the whole class that act. Then Engels takes the social and historical development of capitalism in Western Europe as an example to demonstrate that the struggle of the "three great classes" of land lord, bourgeoisie and proletariat and "the conflict of their interests" is "the driving force of modern history"[2] . And he further analyzes the economic causes of class struggle, arguing that these class struggles " first and foremost, of economic interests, to the furtherance of which political power was intended to serve merely as a means", "but how did these classes come into existence? ... the origin and development of two great classes was seen to lie clearly and palpably in purely economic causes"; "the will of the state is, on the whole, determined by the changing needs of civil society, but the supremacy of this or that class, in the last resort, by the development of the productive forces and relations of exchange. "[3] It can be seen from Engels words that class struggle is the direct driving force of historical development; class struggle is determined by economic interests

① *Selected Works of Marx and Engels*, vol. 4, People's Publishing House, 1995, p. 249.

② Ibid. , p. 250.

③ *Ibid*, pp. 250—251.

and the latter constitute the factor that sets men into historical actions; and economic interestsare further determined by the development of certain productive forces and relations of production. "Productive forces and relations of exchange" is the ultimate driving force or ultimate cause of social and historical development, and the ultimate driving force of social and historical development is purely the material and economic factors. Do material factors constitute the only driving force? In September 1890, against the prevailing philistine view onhistorical materialism that "economic factor" is "the only decisive factor," Engels put forth the concept of historical joint forces. He said: "History is made in such a way that the final result always arises from conflicts between many individual wills, of which each in turn has been made what it is by a host of particular conditions of life. Thus there are innumerable intersecting forces, an infinite series of parallelograms of forces . . . are merged into an aggregate mean, a common joint forces. "① Therefore, the finally result of historical development is the result of historical joint forces. How can we understand historical joint forces then? The answer is: historical joint forces are the overall result or totality of interactions and tendencies of social contradictions among human beings. Lenin said in summing up Marxist historical materialism that Marx had examined "the totality of opposing tendencies", revealing that condition of material forces of production is the source of all contradictions and tendencies, estimated "the total joint forces of historical development" and "indicated the way to a scientific study of history as a single process which, with all its immense variety and contradictoriness, is governed by definite laws. "② Therefore, it is clear that joint forcesare not just the sum total or unity of various social forces, but total force resulted from the interactions among various social forces. Conflicts and interactions among the people motivated by interests finally merge into the total joint forces independent of the will of any individual, but subject to the overall objective law governing historical development and social modes of production. In this way, the incentive role of interests is in complete consistence with the ultimate decisive role of material and economic factors.

---

① *Selected Works of Marx and Engels*, vol. 4, People's Publishing House, 1995, p. 697.

② *Selected Works of Lenin*, vol. 2, People's Publishing House, 1995, p. 425.

VI. The Driving Forcesbehind Human Historical Activities

Interests are the decisive forces that set man into historical actions and the great lever of historical changes. The interest theory of historical materialism is an important key solving the puzzle of history. Examining history from the basis of interests, we can see through the whole social history and all the complicated social phenomena, to find in them a clear thread, in which interests are the powerful engine that drives people into social historical activities.

First, interests are the direct motivation and ultimate goal behind man's productive activities in all times. Man needs material means of subsistence, which is the ultimate goal and direct motive of his production. At any stage of social development, the ultimate motivation of people improving tools and productivity is to get more material means of subsistence, or material interests, from nature. Therefore, interests, to be more exact, material interests, constitute the lever of human historical activities, productive activities in particular.

Second, material and economic interests are the material basis of all social groups and organizations and the economic roots of all social contradictions and struggles. The law of a unity of opposites is a basic law governingnot only thenature but also human society. So in any society, there are both agreement and contradiction, unity and opposition, alliance and struggle. In the process of historical development, interests act as the material source of the contradictory relations between men, between nations, between classes, between parties and between countries. It is on the basis of interest relations, in particular economic interests, that people shape various social groups and organizations, such as stratum, class, ethnic group, country, and forms various political groups and political parties and class society. In the French Revolution, the proletariat and other working people united with the bourgeoisie to form the Third Estate; during the period of the War against Japanese Aggression in China, the Anti-Japanese National United Frontwas, in the last analysis, set up on the basis of common interests among various class and strata. On the other side, sources of social contradictions and social struggles can be traced back to interest differences and contradictions. In class societies, all confrontations, contradictions and conflicts between classes are ultimately determined by material interests, and class struggles in fact are fights between economic interest groups. Social contradictions and struggles constitute the origins and driving forces of social and historical development. In this sense, interest conflicts, or interests constitute the driving force of historical development.

Third, interests are the driving forces that push people to make social reform and revolution. While relations of production reflect the relations of interests between men, superstructure also serves for the interests of certain social groups, and political power serves as means for realizing economic interests. Power is dominated by interests and serves interests. Power struggle in essence is the struggle of interests, and power groups thus stand for relevant interest groups. Power struggle culminates in violent power contest. There is a logical relation in the process from relations of production to economic interests, to political power and finally to violent power contest, among which interests isthe key. In the contradiction between the productive forces and relations of production, the former is active, dynamic and ever changing, while the latter is relatively stable and have some inertia. This is because, when a new kind of relations of production replaces the old ones, it will inevitably impair the interests of the people whose interests are represented by the old ones, and these people will desperately defend their invested interests by using the superstructure and political power. The replacement of old relations of production by the new ones is in essence the adjustment of interests, that is, the replacement of old relations of interests by new ones. Through the adjustment, the vested interests of some people are lost, but the interest demands of others are met and their initiatives are fully mobilized. As a result, the productive forces are promoted. In class societies, the reactionary ruling classes always try to maintain the outdated relations of production with their superstructure and political power to defend their vested interests. On the contrary, the working people and the revolutionary classes, for their own interests, will carry out political and economic struggles and social revolutions to break the old relations of production. By saying that the old relations of production restrain the development of productive forces, we mean that such relations of production jeopardize the economic interests of the classes standing for new productive forces and dampen their enthusiasm for social production. So objectively speaking, social revolution transforming old superstructure and relations of production meets the interests of the classes standing for new productive forces and thus mobilize their initiatives.

In societies where productive forces generally conform to the relations of production, there are still some aspects and segments in the relations of production and the superstructure that do not conform to the development of the productive forces that need adjustment and transformation, which means the adjustment and reform of social relations of interests. When some parts in the relations of production and the superstructure don't conform to the further development of the productive forces, it also means that some interest relations are imbalanced and that the interestdistribution among interest groups are unreasonable, with some groups getting too much while the reasonable interests ofothers not being met and their initiatives being seriously dampened. Therefore, some parts in the relations of production and the superstructure that don' t conform to the further development of the productive forces should be reformed to mobilize the initiative of the workers to the maximum, so that social progress can be advanced. From this point of view, interests constitute the intrinsic force that drives people to change and transform the old relations of production and superstructure.

Social interestsas an important category in historical materialism play decisive rolesin social development and serve as the engine in people's creatingof history. Human society is a social organism full of vitality, the underlying cause of which is people's interest pursuit and competition. Comrade Mao Zedong said: "A basic principle of Marxism-Leninism is to enable the masses to know their own interests and unite to fight for their own interests. "[1] "They should now be given new benefits, which means socialism. "[2] Socialism has opened a big world for the satisfaction of people's interests and created a better environment for interests to fully play their role as driving forces. In a socialist country, interests are still objective driving forces setting the people into historical activities, so it is imperative to properly handle the socialist interest relations and bring about intangible benefits to the people, so as to mobilize their enthusiasm for production.

---

[1]   *Selected Mao Zedong Works*, vol. 4, People's Publication House, 1991, p. 1318.

[2]   Mao Zedong, "The Debate on the Co-operative Transformation of Agriculture and the Current Class Struggle. " (October 11, 1955)

Chapter Nine

Interest System and Interest Coordination

Interest individuals and interest groups exist in any society, so does social interest system with certain interest differences and interest relations, which find their expression in the pattern of social interests. With the changes in the social, economic, political and cultural conditions, the original interest system and pattern will change accordingly, with the original balance broken and new interest system and pattern formed after the fluctuation and changes. In a sense, the changes in interest system and interest pattern mean the changes in social formation and the development of social history. For an interest system and interest pattern to keep stable and balanced, and for a society to normally develop, a relevant interest system and interest pattern meeting the needs of the social productive forces must be set up, so as to coordinate the relations among different interest subjects. In fact, certain interest system and structure essentially represent certain social system and social structure.

I. Interest System and Interest Pattern

A society is composed of individuals with their different interest demands. Individuals must rely themselves on communities and society; accordingly, the realization of their interests relies also on the realization of interests of their communities and the society. Therefore, individuals in a society will inevitably form, on the basis of common interests, interest communities in forms of families, collectives, strata, classes, ethnic groups, nations, and so on. Due to the complexity of social relations, including socio-political relations, cultural relations, historical relations, and economic relations in particular, interest differences inevitably exist between individuals and groups. The mutual dependence, restraint, influence, penetration and opposition among these diverse and complex interest communities ultimately give birth to a complex social system of multi-interest, which in turn manifests itself in a multi-interest pattern.

"Multi-interest" here refers to at least the following three aspects: First, it is multi-formed, that is, an interest system consists of various interest communities coexisting in the same social environment. Second, multi-position, that is, each interest community has its own position and its due share of interests in the community. And third, multi-share, which means that the interest communities are mutually dependent, mutually inclusive and mutually premised (although there are differences of distributions among them); in other words, there are also some common and shared interests between different interest groups. Generally speaking, under fulfilled social conditions, a multi-interest system is a system of unity in opposites and is relatively balanced and stable, and it constitutes a stabilizer of the society. This relatively stable interest system will produce a relatively stable distribution pattern. So, in the final analysis, interest pattern is the pattern of interest distribution.

The stability and balance of a certain interest system and pattern is, without doubt, conditional: First of all, it depends on the social conditions on which the multi-interest system and pattern exist; Secondly, it depends on whether the interest distribution system meets the primary interest demands of the diverse interest groups. The basic structure, composition and distribution relations of interest system and pattern in a society are determined by the social conditions of the society. For example, the productive forces and production relations of the feudal society determine the structure of its social communities such as classes, strata, which give birth to its interest system and interest pattern. Although in its historical process, interest conflicts occur frequently, leading to the partial adjustment of its interest system and interest pattern, when the system as a whole has not been fundamentally shaken or broken down, its interest system and interest pattern will basically remain stable despite various social unrests. As long as the basic social conditions including the basic contradiction between the social productive forces and relations of production, and the basic social system remain unchanged, its basic interest system and interest pattern will keep on. Take China's feudal society for example. All peasant uprisings, from the uprising of Chen Sheng and Wu Guang until the Taiping Rebellion, each one, more or less, impaired the foundation of feudalism as well as the productive forces and relations of production, and brought about some adjustment to the interest system. But the feudal foundation had not collapsed, and its interest system basically remained stable.

Under certain social carrying capacity, a specific and relatively stable interest system can restrain interest conflicts within certain limits. The social and economic conditions of capitalist society determine that, its multi-interest pattern is an interest system with the interest confrontation of the working class and the bourgeoisie as its dominant. The capitalist ownership determines that the interest distribution between the bourgeoisie and the working class are extremely favorable to capitalist class, resulting in the huge interest disparity and consequently the fundamental interest antagonism and conflicts between them. However, the tolerance of any society to interest conflict is limited, so is the carrying capacity of a relatively stable interest system and pattern. As long as the development of capitalist relations of production can fit to the development of its productive forces, and its social and economic structure has not yet developed to the culmination of interest contradictions, it will tolerate partial conflicts of interests between the two classes and take partial adjustments to its distribution system to ease the conflicts and thus maintain its relative stability for a period of time. When this kind of adjustments can no longer work, that is, the relations of production no longer correspond to the growing productive forces, the working class will no longer tolerate the interest distribution pattern in which the capitalist interest group as the dominant. This is when the conflicts of interest system of the capitalist society comes to the point of instability, social crisis, violent conflicts and outbreak of total conflict of interests. New social formation will be born from it, and come along with it, a new social system and interest distribution pattern.

II. Interest Change and Interest Balance

Interest system is an inevitable existence in any society, so are complex contradictions, conflicts and changes of interests, which will further desire relative interest balance. Interest changes or instability is an imbalanced situation caused by interest conflicts in the interest system; in contrast, interest balance is the relatively balanced or stable situation of an interest system. Recognizing and understanding the issues of interest changes and balance on the basis of socio-economic realities, minimizing and properly handling interest contradictions, and maintaining the stability and balance of our interest system: all this are favorable to our social stability and progress. The establishment of China's socialist system has provide an objective conditions for us to correctly understand the contradictions and conflicts within our interest system, to consciously adjust the interest relations and to maintain an overall stable interest pattern. At present, China is still in the primary stage of socialism. This determines that, on the one hand, the establishment of public ownership as the basic system has eliminated the fundamental antagonism between various interest groups; on the other, due to complex factors, certain degree of interest contradictions and conflicts do exist in the multi-interest system. It is especially true now in the juncture of socialist reform and opening up when the old system is transforming into the new one. Instability occurs because the old interest system, pattern and balance has been shaken, broken down or changed. In this regard, the most important thing for us is to minimize the scale and time of turbulence to achieve a smooth transition. One of the important advantages of socialist system is that it can address the issue of fair distribution of social interests as fair as possible through various policies and measures that represent the fundamental interests of all interest groups without resorting to cruel class struggle. The interest system in the primary stage of socialism is not highly unified; on the contrary, it is a system with diverse interest groups having their distinct and separate interests and demands on the basis of identical fundamental interest. They take actions to safeguard their own interests and oversee the equitable distribution of interests. The aggregation of their competing actions will often break the existing balance of interests. Despite all this, however, this kind of multi-interest is fundamentally different from that in the exploiting societies. This is because there is no fundamental interest contradiction among the interest groups in the primary stage of socialism, nor it necessarily leads to political multi-polarity advocated by bourgeois thinkers. Under the multi-interest system in this stage, the fundamental interest of all interest groups with diverse interest demands is identical. Therefore, a socialist country can make full use of the advantages of its economic and political systems to consciously and continuously reform its interest distribution system, and to timely adjust its interest relations, so as to ensure the relative stability of its multi-interest system and pattern, maintain its political stability and unity and advance social progress.

All interests fall into two categories of economic interests and political interestsThe former determines the latter and they together determine other social interests. Economic interests are determined by the economic relations. Other types of interests first and foremost are determined by political interests, which in the final analysis, is subject to economic relations. Economic relations manifest themselves as economic interests, which determine the political interests and all other interests of the society. Social relations consist of economic and non-economic relations, with political relations as one of the important aspects of non-economic relations. Economic relations determine economic interests and political interests and all other interests of the society. But on the other hand, political relations can also affect and restrain economic relations, as is political interests affect and constrain economic interests. Economic relations gain interests through direct and indirect ways. The first way to gain interests is directly from labor through certain ways of possession. In the communities in the primitive society, primitive people jointly possess crude production tools, and used them to get food directly from collective labor. In the natural economic society, individual peasants directly got basic life necessities of clothing, food, shelter and others through family labor of household economy. With the progress of history, the possibility and opportunity of getting interests through direct ways greatly reduced. The second way to gain interests is, under the premise of a certain ownership, through the medium of political superstructure, i. e. , political relations. With the development of history, complete political superstructure is established. People use it as a tool, along with political relations, to achieve political interests, and then to safeguard and gain more economic and other social interests by taking use of the counteraction of politics on economy. Any ruling class is bound to use the state apparatus to control the distribution of interests, in order to, in a maximum way, satisfy the interests of its own class. In contrary, the ruled class is always trying to change the existing pattern of interest distribution through political struggle, in order to meet its own interest needs. Political superstructure is the basic means and tools of realizing and safeguarding social interests.

In political superstructure and political relations, interests are manifested as political interests, which are derived from economic interests and reflect the positions of certain individuals and interest groups in the political relations, with political power as the pivot. To achieve their own economic interests, the individuals or groups, first of all, must gain certain political interests or hold certain power, and then through political means, such as class struggle, party struggle, to safeguard their grasp of economic interests. The core and essence of political interests is the possession of power resources, so the focus of political struggle is power. In a sense, political struggle is the struggle for power. The culmination of power struggle is violence, with armed struggle for power as its highest form. The struggle for political power in the final analysis is the highest form of interest contradictions.

The above analysis has provided us with two clear threads: interest—power—violence; interest—economy—politics. In other words, certain economic relations determine certain interests, while politics is only a means for realizing interests; certain economic interests give birth to certain political interest, the core of which is political power as the basic means of achieving interests, whereas violence is the highest form of struggle for political power.

The ups and downs of the French Revolution eloquently illustrated these two threads. Since the 18th century, the capitalist economy in the feudal society of France had significantly developed. But the Bourbons still maintained its rigid feudal hierarchy. At that time, there were three estates in France: the clergy and aristocracy were the first and second estates who occupied all political power, which was used to protect their economic privileges, while the rest 99 percent of the population, including farmers, workers, craftsmen, poor urban citizens and the emerging bourgeoisie belonged to the third estate without any political power except for the burden of feudal taxes and obligations. With the development of bourgeois economic forces, they were no longer satisfied with their political position. The demands of them conform to the common interests of the whole third estate. It was in this situation that the economic conflicts changed into political conflicts, and then the Paris uprising that opened the prelude to the French Revolution. In the first stage of the Revolution, the political power fell into the hands of those who advocated constitutional monarchy and represented the interests of the financial big bourgeois and liberal aristocrats. Since their interests were closely linked with that of the feudal forces, they had no intention to completely eliminate the feudal system. This in turn triggered the second armed uprising of the Parisian to overthrow the constitutional monarchy, and power was taken over by the

Girondists, who represented the interests of the commercial and industrial bourgeoisie, the Revolution then entered the second stage. After the interests of their class were fulfilled, the Girondists did not want, even tried to stop the revolution. As a result, the people of Paris launched the third armed uprising to overthrow the rule of the Girondists. The power was then shifted to the hands of Jacobins, bourgeois revolutionary democrats, which advanced the French Revolution into the third stage. Just before the Revolution thoroughly completed its task, the Jacobins split: its right wing represented by Georges (-Jacques) Danton want to stop the revolution while its left-wing led by Jacques René Hébert demanded to advanced revolution further. The struggle of the two factions fully showed the interest differences of the different social groups within the Third Estate. The French big bourgeoisie took the chance to launch the Thermidorian Reaction and seized power, which ended the Revolution. The world-shaking revolution, although lasted only 5 years, witnessed the fierce struggles of various political forces and staged vividly a series of "puppet show" of power, or supreme political interests, which was controlled by economic interests behind the stage and performed by political forces. Being it overthrowing a regime or system or establishing a new one, the aim is the same: to obtain or safegurad certain interests.

The vivid acts of drama of the French Revolution tells us that, whether it is the Girondists, the Jacobins, the Dantonists or the Hebertists, all represented the interests of different interest groups to struggle for their own interests and political power, aiming to satisfy their own interests by changing the old economic relations via political superstructure.

From the chaotic picture of the French Revolution, we can clearly see:

• For people to survive and develop, they must change political relations through political struggles, in order to achieve its varied and diverse interests; to achieve these interests, they must have a certain socio-economic and political system as a guarantee.

• The establishment of socio-economic and political system is related to people's interest contradictions, the essence of which is to ease these contradictions; in a class society, its establishment first of all is for the realization of economic and political interests of the ruling class.

• A reasonable social system should ensure the realization of interests of all its individuals and groups. Social systems should play the role of coordinators of interest contradictions to prevent the annihilation of interests of all sides in interest conflicts.

- Social systems are essentially interest systems, so are social institutions. In vying for their interests, every interest group is trying to establish a certain social interest system and interest distribution system that can gain and safeguard the interests of their own class or stratum.

Lenin pointed out that "People always have been the foolish victims of deception and self-deception in politics, and they always will be until they have learnt to seek out the *interests* of some class or other behind all moral, religious, political and social phrases, declarations and promises. "[1] Likewise, we cannot really understand a society and reveal its essence until we really understand the class interests represented by each socio-economic and political system. Behind all social systems are interest systems established for certain people and certain groups. Whatever beautiful words used by the representatives of the systems, the interest essence of social systems cannot be covered.

Social system is the main content and fundamental mark and the inborn and generic nature of a society, and is the totality of the economic, political, legal, cultural and other systems, which can be generally divided as economic base and superstructure. Among them, economic system falls into the category of economic base while political, cultural, educational and legal systems into superstructure. The main components of a social system are its economic and political systems. The economic system of a society is in fact the sum total of social relations of production, which constitutes the economic base of the society. Of them, the most important is the ownership of the means of production. The economic system embodies the basic nature of the economic formation of the society. The political system is the "superstructure of economic base," mainly referring to the superstructure, the core of which is the state power, or the state system, concerning the problems of who is in power and over whom the dictatorship is exercised, which marks the fundamental nature of a state. Economic and political systems mark fundamentally the basic nature and the main characters of a social formation. Accordingly, socialist economic and political systems are the fundamental characters of socialist social formation while capitalist economic and political systems are the fundamental characters of capitalist social formation. The socialist system refers mainly to the economic system with public ownership as the mainstay and the political system with people being masters of the country. A social

---

[1]   *Selected Works of Lenin*, vol. 2, People's Publishing House, 1995, p. 314.

system, once established, should remain relatively stable, so as to form a relatively stable interest system and pattern, in view to forming a rather stable social environment for the development of the productive forces. Of course, any social system is bound to go through a process of gradual improvement. Only when the relations of production can no longer suit the development of the productive forces, the revolution of social system will occur.

Social system refers also to the fundamental and basic system of the society. Social system is essentially an interest system that protects and safeguards the main subjects of interests. Human society has gone through five social formations or social systems. The primitive society was the primary stage of human society, which didn't have social, political, economic and cultural systems in the true sense. However, its simple and crude social system was also an interest system, which maintained the community interest with clan as its basic unit while individual interests were merged in community interests. After entering the class society, human society, with social relations becoming more complex and class contradictions more sharpening, more complete and complicated social, economic, political and cultural systems came into being. The social system in this stage is to protect the interests of the ruling class and its interest system. This is fully manifested in the role of state, the core of political system, "Since the State is the form in which the individuals of a ruling class assert their common interests,"① and "If the state even today, in the era of big industry and of railways, is on the whole only a reflection, in concentrated form, of the economic needs of the class controlling production, then this must have been much more so in an epoch... than we are today" . ②Therefore, in a class society, social system is a system for the satisfaction of the interest of the ruling classes, with its function of, to the maximum, maintaining and realizing the economic, political, ideological and other interests of the ruling class. This is the essence of the social interest system of all classes.

By saying that interest system is the system of satisfying the interests of the ruling class of the society, we of course do not mean that the ruled class in a class society can get no interest or guarantee at all. In the interest

---

① *Selected Works of Marx and Engels*, vol. 3, People's Publishing House, 1960, p. 70

② *Collected Works of Marx and Engels*, vol. 21, People's Publishing House, 1965, p. 346

system of any class society, the ruled class can get certain interests and interest guarantee; otherwise, the ruling class cannot get their interests, and a new interest system usually will give more interests to the ruled classes, which are not contradictory with the essence of the class society. The reason for this is that, only after their needs for keeping subsistence level of life and work of the ruled class are met, can the ruling class gain interests by appropriating the surplus labor of the ruled class. On the other side, the ruled class can only get their interests when the ruling class needs them. In the slave society, the reason the slave owners did not kill all prisoners of war was that slaves could produce surplus products and create wealth and interests for the slave owners. In capitalist society, in order to exploit the workers, capitalists give workers more freedom to sell their labor. However, the fact that the ruled class can get their interests cannot in the least change the very nature of a class society.

An interest system is not static. Its fundamental change depends on the change of the dominant mode of distribution of the society, which in turn depends on the fundamental change of relations of production determined by the productive forces. The change of the dominant mode of interest distribution implies that, the class representing the new interests will seize power to establish new interest system from the hands of the declining class representing the old interests. The qualitative change in the interest system is the substitution of social formation.

The functions of a social system, which essentially is interest system, is to ensure the maximum realization of the dominant mode of distribution, to coordinate all kinds of relations, to meet the different interest needs of different interest subjects and to ensure social stability. In a class society, the functions of social system is to protect the interests of the ruling class, to ensure the satisfaction of the common interests of all sides of the ruling class, to meet certain needs of the ruled class for the purpose of avoiding turbulence of the social system by social unrest, to coordinate the relations between various classes and to ensure social stability. How, then, does interest system achieve these functions?

First, protecting the dominant interests of the society, and protecting the interests of the ruling class in class society. The economic and political systems of a society are set up to protect the interests of the dominant social groups or classes. In primitive society, although a complete socio-economic system had not yet emerged, the traditional social systems played the function of protecting the interests of clan members. In a class society, the social system is established by the dominant class. Therefore, this system will: firstly, fix the relations of production in favor of the ruling class in form of laws and take state power as the guarantee to protect it from violation; secondly, when the social system is violated, the state power will repress the violators. In private ownership society, the rights of the private ownership of the means of production and livelihood are inviolable, and the social system is a tool to safeguard them. Young Marx witnessed a legal debate, in which the poor's gathering of fallen wood in the forests was regarded by the capitalists as theft. In analyzing the debate, Marx explicitly pointed out the essence of the interest system: "This logic, which turns the servant of the forest owner into a state authority, turns the authority of the state into a servant of the forest owner. The state structure, the purpose of the individual administrative authorities, everything must get out of hand so that everything is degraded into an instrument of the forest owners and his interest operates as the soul governing the entire mechanism. "[1]

Second, coordinating the interest relations between dominant social groups or classes so as to ensure the realization of their common interests.

There are also interest contradictions within ranks of the ruling class, which, if not handled properly, will become obstacles for the realization of the common interests the class. Take the capitalist society for example. There are financial capitalists, commercial capitalists and industrial capitalists and others in a capitalist society. In this society, the capitalists care only about their own interests or the maximum profit of their group: some want to raise tariffs, others want to reduce them; some want to raise interest rates, while others may want to lower them, and so on. Another example is the old Chinese society, where there were big bourgeoisie, medium bourgeoisie and petty-bourgeoisie, and the inevitable different interest groups and contradictions within them. Economic contradictions are bound to bring about political conflicts. The differences of interest strata and groups give birth to different political parties, which engage in various political activities to unable the development of the economic and political processes of the society to benefit their specific interests by means of controlling or influencing the country. The interest system of the society must handle such contradictions

---

[1] *Selected Works of Marx and Engels*, vol. 1, People's Publishing House, 1956, p. 160.

within the ruling class to ensure that the common interests of the ruling class are not jeopardized. Even in a socialist country, although the working class and the masses have become the ruling class, there are still contradictions among classes, strata and groups, such as interest differences and contradictions between workers and farmers, between physical and mental laborers, only that these interest contradictions are those on the basis of identity of fundamental interests instead of antagonistic ones in nature. So it is the major functions for the socialist interest system to make good coordination facing these contradictions and to safeguard the fundamental and common interests of the working class and the broad masses.

Third, easing the interest contradictions between the ruling and the ruled classes in order to safeguard the former's interests.

In a class society, in order to ensure the realization of its interests, the ruling class will suppress the interests of the ruled class. It, in its interest system, will consolidate the relations of production favoring the interests of the ruling class and safeguard its interests and even will use violent means to suppress activities threatening its interests. But due to the constant improvement of struggle capacity of the ruled working class, the ruling class often has to make certain concessions to ease the contradictions between the two classes, to indirectly maintain its own interests. In modern capitalist society, the coordination and reconciliation of contradictions between capital and labor are necessary for the ruling class to maintain social order; otherwise, modern capitalist society cannot last long, neither the realization of interest of the bourgeoisie.

Fourth, minimizing the interests of the ruled classes to maximize the interests of the ruling class.

In a class society, because the ruling class holds the means of production and state power, the social interest system established on this basis is bound to minimize the interests of the ruled class as well as maximizing the interests of its own class. This is the fundamental essence of interest system of class society. As long as the two classes of ruling and ruled classes exist, this tendency will last.

Fifth, coordinating the interest relations among classes, strata, groups and individuals, so as to maintain the normal order of the society and its healthy development.

The handling of contradictions among classes, strata, groups and individuals is of great significance to a society. Whether in a class society or non-class society, without the mechanism of handling interest contradictions, human society would come into destruction because of contention, not to mention development. Although the purpose of this handling is to safeguard the interests of the ruling class, it without doubt plays an important role in the development of human society. This is because this mechanism constitutes the conditions not only for the ruling class to satisfy its interests but also for the ruled class to achieve and develop its interests. In a non-class society, interest system is a basic guarantee for maintaining the normal operation of the society.

Interest institutions are the specific forms of interest system. To understand interest institutions, one first of all must understand social institutions.

What are social institutions then? Social institutions refer to specific forms of relations of production and superstructure set up on the basis of a social system, i. e. , the specific embodiment of a social system in a given period, also known as "specific systems" . The economic structure corresponding with certain economic system is the specific structure and forms of the economic relations. The structure of the socialist market economy is the specific economic operation system related with the socialist public ownership. And the structure corresponding with a certain political system is a political structure, referring to the specific structure and form of the political system, namely system of government, or the way the state power is exercised. Included in the political structure are the reasonable structure of state power, the leadership structure of party and state, the system of social management, the system of officials and personnel, administration system, the operation mechanism of the country's political life, and so on

The sum of a certain relations of production constitutes the economic system and the sum of the political superstructure constitutes the political system of a society. Economic system determines political system and the entire set of social systems with economic and political systems as the backbone constitute the fundamental mark and main content of a social formation. Interest system is unfolded forms and manifestation of social system. Therefore, the economic and political systems of a society represent the interest relations and forms of distribution of the society. The form and realization of interests are subject to economic system while its distribution and realization need the intermediary of the political system. The interest system of a society is the basic guarantee as well as constraints of the realization and distribution of interests. A certain social system is surely to protect, realize or strive for certain interests. By saying that a social system is essentially an interest system we mean it from the perspective of fundamental interest system. But there must be a kind of interest distribution system to guarantee and implement specific distribution and share of interests. Interest institutions are the sum total of forms of distribution, protection and realization of interests, which is established on the basis of fundamental interest system of a society. So a social system is essentially an interest system and the economic and political systems of any society are the specific forms of certain interest system. An interest system plays the role of restraint and guarantee for the interest distribution among all interest subjects and the realization of social interests. In a sense, the interest institutions are the specific forms of interest regulation and distribution, and can be said as the specific forms of interests under the premise of the fundamental interest system of the society. Interest institutions are the specific forms of interest distribution and realization, and they are determined by the economic and political systems of interests, which essentially determine the extent of realization and the distribution proportion and form of interests. In the capitalist society, for example, capitalists possess the means of production and state power while the working class possesses neither. This predetermines the basic distribution of interests in the capitalist society. The function of interest system is to make specific proportion of distribution among interest subjects through political and economic systems, as well as through certain exchange, allocation and circulation institutions or systems. For example, through incentive structures and mechanisms, the interest proportion of the each capitalist, worker and enterprise can be specifically decided. Interest system can not only determine the realization and distribution of interests but also reconcile the contradictions and conflicts of interests constantly emerging in the system, thus safeguard the smooth distribution of interests. For a socialist interest system, the most important tasks include the proper handling of interest relations between individuals, the collectives and the state, and contradictions among different interest groups within the ranks of the people and the establishment of corresponding interest system and pattern. Socialist interest system is the basic guarantee to maintain normal interest relations among interest subjects and to control the interest contradictions and conflicts within certain limits. So interest system plays the role of protection and coordination for interest realization and distribution.

III. Interest Protection and Representation

Essentially speaking, interest system and interest institutions play the important role of interest protection. A certain interest system maintains and protects the interests of certain individuals and groups.

All interest subjects and groups have their own interest representatives. In a class society, the representatives of the interest subjects of ruling class are also the representatives of the interest system and institutions of the ruling class; so are other classes, strata and groups. The various factors in political superstructure are means and instruments for the realization and coordination of various interest relations; whereas the interest representatives must use their position in political relations and use economic and political means to protect the realization of the interests of the groups represented by them and to coordinate relations with other interest groups. The relations of interest representation reflect the major social and political relations of the society. During the French Revolution for example, the adherents of constitutional monarchy represented the interests of the big financial bourgeoisie and free nobility, the Girondinists represented the interests of commercial and industrial bourgeoisie, while the Jacobins in the early stage represented the common interests of the bourgeois democrats, the petty bourgeoisie and the laboring masses. These factions occupied certain political positions and sought to meet the interest demands of the classes they represented through relevant political forces. Representatives of interests can be parties, organizations, countries, and also individuals. Individuals, parties and interest groups are closely related. Take Chinese history for example. Leaders of the peasant uprisings such as Li Zicheng, Hong Xiuquan, etc. were the representatives of the peasantry. Feudal emperors were the chief representatives of interests of the feudal landlord class. In modern world history, political parties and trade unions have developed into interest representatives. The Communist Party of China (CPC) represents the interests of the Chinese working class and the laboring masses, while Mao Zedong and other great leaders of the CPC were the representatives both of the CPC and the Chinese working class and masses. In socialist countries, the Marxist parties in power and the states are the chief representatives of people's interests, while democratic parties, trade unions, women's federations, associations of entrepreneurs, economic associations and other social organizations are representatives of different interest groups in socialist countries. On the other hand, representatives of any groups, strata and class, must subject to the chief representative of fundamental interests of socialism, that is, the governing party. Representatives should consciously represent and safeguard the interests of various social groups they represent and coordinate the various interest relations. In a society, interest representatives from different levels, sectors and parties constitute a complete structure of interest representation; while political struggle is the struggle among these representatives. Recognizing the positions and roles of interest representatives is the key to understanding the relationships among social interests

IV. Interest Mechanism and Interest Coordination

Interests are objectives sought after by all individuals and social groups and also impetus of human behaviors and activities. Differences in social, economic, political positions and as well as cultural and other factors lead to the great diversity of interests and the extremely complicated interest system. In a society of private ownership, every individual and social group attempts to achieve their own interests, making interest confrontations and conflicts inevitable. As a consequence, scramble among individuals, antagonism and even wars are frequent between social groups, which will surely damage the interests of the majority of the social members (including big social groups) to different degrees. In a society of public ownership, interest differences, contradictions or competitions will also occur, which, if not properly handled, will affect social development. Therefore, mechanism is needed to coordinate the interest relations. An interest coordinating mechanism includes but is not limited to the functions of interest system and institutions. It is a comprehensive mechanism consisted of means of economic coordination, political coordination, legal coordination, moral coordination, administrative coordination, etc .

1. Economic coordination

Interest contradictions involve mainly economic and material interest contradictions, for whose settlement, economic coordination is the primary means. Economic coordination is to coordinate the interests of all sides and to meet their interest demands by using approaches of ownership, distribution, economic policies and measures, etc. How is this means used then?

First, giving play to the role of social and economic system and institutions. Interest relations actually involve mainly relations of interest distribution in terms of means of production and means of existence among various interest groups and subjects. Every social formation will form its relations of production, economic base, economic system and institutions suitable for the development of its productive forces. As long as these systems and institutions correspond with the productive forces, they will are conducive to their development, and there can make good coordination of various interest relations among all sides in the distribution of means of production and living.

Second, making use of economic approaches and methods such as economic regulations, policies and management to properly handle interest contradictions and relations between different interest subjects. Economic system and institutions objectively determine the basic proportions of interest distribution, so that the society can maintain a relatively stable interest pattern. But on the micro level, various economic approaches need to be used to coordinate interest relations. In the market economy, for example, we need to make good use of the law of value and the rules and procedures of the market economy to adjust interest relations.

2. Political coordination

The function of economic means in coordinating interest relations are subject to restraints and influence of political coordination, because politics, as the concentrated expression of economics, reflects the fundamental interests of all classes in economic relations.

The coordinating function of the state was gradually formed with the emergence of private ownership. When human society got caught in the trap of interest conflicts, "controller" easing interest conflicts—state and political system—came into being and became an indispensable and extremely important means for maintaining social order. In ancient Greece, for example, King Theseus formulated the first constitution, which stipulated that a central administrative body was set up in Athens and the whole people (slaves not included) were divided into three classes: the aristocracy, the farmers and the craftsmen, among which, only aristocrats could take official positions. This marks the replacement of the weak clan organizations by the emerging state agencies. Under the protection of this political system, clan aristocrats still had full political and economic privileges and their interests could be fully satisfied. They exploited and suppressed both the slaves and the ordinary people, i. e. , farmers and craftsmen. The slaves who were at the bottom of the society had no economic or political status and right. So in Athenian states, interest contradictions and conflicts mainly occur among aristocratic slave owners, industrial and commercial slave-owners, and the commoners of the city-states. To get rid of economic exploitation, political oppression, rightless status and the possibility of becoming slaves, the Athenian commoners rose to struggle. Facing these contradictions, the city-states of Athens had to make a series of political reforms to ease the interest contradictions. This is the well-known Solon's Reform. This was a political reform to establish a national political system, aiming at easing the interest contradictions between industrial and commercial slave owners and aristocratic owners, and those between commoners and aristocratic slave owners, to avoid the sinking of the city-states in sharp interest contradictions and conflicts. It was through political coordination that the ancient Greek eased the contradictions between aristocratic slave owners and the commoners for the common interests of the class of slave owners. Only by doing this could the destruction of the country be avoided and the long-term and common interests of slave owners were fulfilled. We should see that, this kind of coordination was positive, or, was in accordance with the long-term interests of social development.

In ancient China, many philosophers and statesmen expressed their views on maintaining social order by means of state political coordination to avoid annihilation of the state in fruitless interest conflicts. Among which the Confucianism, the legalists and the Taoism are the three most important schools of thought. The political philosophy of Confucianism, in brief, comprises two aspects: first, "govern the country by putting propriety first,"[1] and second, "govern with the power of virtue. "[2] The first intends to coordinate interest relations among people with the rituals handed down from the Zhou dynasty to avoid interest disputes, while the second aims to maintain ruling order by ethics and moral cultivation. Confucius also advocated that rulers should make good

---

①   *The Analects of Confucius*, Chapter XianJin.

②   *The Analects of Confucius*, Chapter Weizheng.

exemplary and not strive for interests against common people, so as to " cultivates themselves and thereby bring peace and security to the people. "① The legalist advocated regulating interest relations among the people based on the law, and "To govern the country based on the law" . ②And they believed that " nothing is as effective as the law in regulating people's behaviors. "③ Taoism, on the other hand, seeing that life and growth in the universe, despite competitions, continue endlessly and orderly, advocated governance by non-interference. They held that "By handling affairs on the principle of non-action everyone will do well" . ④They hoped that their ideal society of "small country with small population" would bury people's desires for or disputes on interests into oblivion.

Engels's analysis of the emergence and role of the state is penetrating: " The state. . . is the admission that this society has involved itself in insoluble self-contradiction and is cleft into irreconcilable antagonisms which it is powerless to exorcise. But in order that these antagonisms, classes with conflicting economic interests, shall not consume themselves and society in fruitless struggle, a power, apparently standing above society, has become necessary to moderate the conflict and keep it within the bounds of 'order' ; and this power, arisen out of society, but placing itself above it and increasingly alienating itself from it, is the state. "⑤

The state is the major means and approach in a class society to coordinate interest relations.

In a modern state, the coordinating role of the state and political system not only exists but shows a trend of increasingly strengthening. In modern capitalist society, for instance, intervention of the state in all aspects of social life has greatly enhanced. The purpose of this intervention through economic and political policies is to ease the contradictions within the capitalists themselves and at the same time make some concessions to the working class to ease the interest conflicts between capital and labor. In addition, the social functions of the modern capitalist state are

---

① *The Analects of Confucius*, Chapter Xianwen.

② *The Hanfeizi*, Chapter 6

③ *The Hanfeizi*, Chapter 38

④ *Taoism*

⑤ *Selected Works of Marx and Engels*, vol. 4, People's Publishing House, 1965, p. 170.

strengthening, including the construction of necessary utilities in the sectors of water conservancy, transportation, communications, culture, education, health care, public services, social welfare, etc. , which also play a certain role in coordinating the interests relations.

In short, the most powerful tools is political system, especially means of state power, in coordinating interest relations, easing acute contradictions among interest groups, maintaining social order, advancing social development and avoiding social destruction by sharp interest conflicts. However, in a society of class antagonism, because of the fundamental opposition of interests, the interests between exploiting class and the exploited class are fundamentally antagonistic, so are interests among the interest groups themselves. Therefore, the ease and coordination of the interest conflicts is only temporary. After a period, these relations will become tense again, alongside with sharp interest conflicts. Various interest groups will struggle against each other to scramble for interests in various forms. Thus, in a society of class antagonism, interest confrontation and conflict can never be fundamentally gotten rid of.

In a given society, in accordance with its economic development, there must be a kind of dominant economic relations representing the trend of social development. The interest group taking the dominant position in economic relations will naturally rise to become the group in power and take the ruling position politically. Therefore, the essence of interest coordination conducted through political system is to meet the interests of the interest group in power. Just as Engels put it, "State is the result of the desire to keep down class conflicts. But having arisen amid these conflicts, it is as a rule the state of the most powerful economic class that by force of its economic supremacy becomes also the ruling political class and thus acquires new means of subduing and exploiting the oppressed masses. " ①

In the slave society, slave owners took the economic and political dominance with the slaves under their oppression. Accordingly, the interest contradictions between slave owners and the commoners were subject to those between slave owners and slaves. The concessions made by the slave owners were aimed to protect their slave state and meet the

---

① *Selected Works of Marx and Engels*, vol. 4, People's Publishing House, 1995, p. 172.

interests of themselves—the exploitation and oppression of the majority of the slaves and expansion of their territory, so as to coordinate their relations with the commoners and to avoid the annihilation of their interests. The same is true with the function of the political system of the capitalist society. Conflicts of interests between the interests of the capitalists, although fundamentally of antagonistic nature, are internal contradictions among the capitalist interest groups; they share the common interests of extracting more surplus value from the working class and obtaining maximum profits. Their internal interest struggle will inevitably damage their forces against the working class. So their interest contradictions can be coordinated for safeguarding these common interests. However, due to the nature of private ownership, the interest conflicts cannot be resolved essentially by coordination. The temporary ease of the conflicts and the concessions of the capitalists to the ruled classes are to maintain the ruling position of the bourgeoisie and their firm control of the society for their long-term interests. In a class society, the fundamental contradiction between the two opposing interest groups is irreconcilable, and cannot be essentially resolved by the limited concessions of the ruling class.

3. Legal coordination

The law and politics are closely related. Politics in any society cannot go without legal system, and there is no state without law. The law is essentially the translation of the will of the ruling class and its political tool for implementing political measures. The interest system of any social formation must be manifested and consolidated through certain legal forms. Therefore, legal system plays a very important role in coordinating interest relations.

The interest subjects in a society are extremely complex and diverse, including not only big ones such as classes, strata, but also small ones such as interest groups and individuals. All these subjects have their own special interests and are bound to have, in one way or another, complex interest relations, which, although deeply influenced by political coordination, cannot entirely be handled by political or state power. A diverse and multi-level interest system calls for diverse coordinating mechanisms to keep society in order and avoid unnecessary interest conflicts, to ensure the full satisfaction of interests of the ruling class. The law, as a kind of social code, and as fixed and basic rules regulating people's behaviors, not only can be used directly as a political means to coordinate the interest relations between classes, strata, and protect the interests of the ruling class (in this case, the law is part of politics), but also can go beyond politics to coordinate people's interests in all areas of social life. Therefore, compared with politics, legal interest coordination is broader in scope.

The basic character of the law is the stipulation of rights and obligations of the people, which are verified and guaranteed by the state. When their legal rights are compromised or threatened, people can request the state to provide protection to ensure the realization of their interests; if a person refuses to fulfill his obligation, the relevant authorities of the state can compel him to do so. Some thinkers during the Warring States Period in China had recognized that the law can play the role of "stopping disputes or quarrels" and "stopping disputes and chaos. " That is, by stipulating rights and obligations, the law can coordinate the interest relations among the people, maintain social order and avoid confusion caused by interest conflicts. Since the law is formulated and approved by the state, it represents the will of the state. Power holders of the state are also law makers. Therefore, the law will necessarily reflect the common will of the ruling class. This determines that, this kind of common will is not the will of individuals, nor mixture of the wills of all members of the ruling class, but the concentrated and unified will of the ruling class that is formed on the basis of the fundamental interests of the class by the representatives of the class after coordinating the various interest demands within themselves. It is produced in the process of interaction between all strata, groups and individuals of the ruling class, and the concentrated expressions of the representatives and is fixed in the form of law. So the essence of the law is to establish and maintain the interest trend conducive to the common interests of the ruling class, and through the coordination of interest relations, to maintain social order in favor of the ruling class in governing the society, to ensure that, the society develop toward the direction conducive to the interest and will of the ruling class. On the other hand, seeing from the development of human society, the role played by the law in coordinating social interests and maintaining social order is a necessary condition for the advancement of human society. The basic functions of the law are reflected mainly in the following aspects:

First, in a class society, the law verifies and coordinates the interest relations between the ruling class and the ruled class, and puts down and even suppresses the revolt of the ruled classes. The ruling class always uses the law to ensure and protect their dominant position in the economy and politics and compel the ruled class to succumb to the social order conducive to ruling class, and control the activities of various social classes, strata within the limits allowed by the fundamental interests of the ruling class. Otherwise, they will be banned or even suppressed by the law. But, under the strong pressure and rebellion of the ruled class, the ruling class may also make some concessions, including punishing the elements from within the ruling class or criminals who have overtly infringed on the interests of the working people, in order to ease the contradictions between the two classes. However, these concessions are made with the precondition of having no prejudice to the fundamental interests of the ruling class

Second, in a class society, the law plays the role of verifying and coordinating the interest relations between the ruling class and its allies. In order to obtain the support of allies and maintain their dominant position and fundamental interests, the ruling class must pay proper attention to the interest demands of its allies, including giving them appropriate rights, maintaining their certain interests, easing interest contradictions between them. The reform of Solon in ancient Greece and that of Gracchus in ancient Rome were actually aimed at coordinating the interests of slave owners and commoners so as to get the commoners or plebian supports for the civil or external wars and for suppressing slave rebellions.

Third, in a class society, the law confirms and coordinates the interest relations within the ranks of the ruling class. Although the fundamental interests within the ranks of the ruling class are identical, the complexity of its internal structure and private nature of their interests determine that, within the ruling class, there are inevitably various interest contradictions and conflicts, which sometimes may be very acute and fierce, among its different strata, among its individuals and the whole class. Therefore, the law is needed to represent the common will and fundamental interests of the ruling class, to coordinate their internal interest relations and to punish the members or groups who have conducted activities detrimental to the common interests of the ruling class. For example, the reform of Wang Anshi in the Song Dynasty of the Chinese feudal society aimed to ease the interest contradictions between the government as the representative of the feudal landlord class and the big landowners and merchants, to ease domestic class contradictions, and ultimately to safeguard the fundamental interests of the feudal ruling class.

Fourth, it plays the function of safeguarding the common interests of the society, including supervision over the handling of social and public affairs, the protection of the basic rights and interests of social members. For example, it protects the security of citizens' personal, life, household, property, etc. , and freedom of will and religion. At the same time, it also ensures the necessary conditions for normal life of every social member; supervises the implementation of environmental protection, social management, etc. , so as to ensure natural and social conditions for the normal life of the citizens. These functions of the law are conducive to all social members.

Fifth, under the socialist social system in which class antagonism no longer exists, the law plays a major function of identifying and coordinate the interest relations among different interest subjects within the ranks of the people. Different social and state systems determine the different nature and forms of the law. The law of a socialist country is totally different from that of the exploiting society. Socialist laws are the expressions of the will of whole people with the working class as the leading class, and the unity of class nature and people-oriented nature. In a socialist country, with the elimination of the exploiting system and class, although there are still class differences, all people form a community of common interests with some differences but not antagonism. In terms of interests, only a handful of the remnants of the exploiting classes and anti-socialist elements are antagonistic to it. As an advanced class, the working class does not have its own special interests, except interests completely identical with the masses supporting socialist revolution and construction. The law of a socialist society is also the unity of class and social nature, which truly reflects the interests of whole society. So socialist laws can truly coordinate the interest relations among the people and ensure fulfillment of their interests. It is a powerful instrument for protecting the socialist system, safeguarding the order of the socialist revolution and construction, promoting socialist economic and cultural civilizations and fighting against anti-socialist elements. Only by continuously improving socialist legal system and governance based on law, and ensuring that everyone is equal before the law, can the common will of the entire people be fully represented, the special interests and interest groups above the control of the law be gotten rid of and the interest relations among different interest subjects be truly coordinated.

4. Ethical coordination

Man as a social being, all his words and deeds as well as that of his groups will have some relations with other persons or groups. If these words or deeds do not violate the law, the law can do nothing about it. This is the limitations of the law. So social codes of conduct in a broader sense than the law are needed, so that people's words and actions are more in line with certain norms and with social order, and their interest relations are in good harmony. The system of such codes is morality.

Morality and the law are closely linked. Moral codes came into being earlier than the law in the primitive society. After entering the class society, sharp interest antagonism led to the state and the law. Some provisions of the law were direct recognition of traditional morals and customs, but morality is independent of and different from the law in terms of functions and forms. The main differences between them are as follows:

First, morality appeared earlier than the law. Second, the law is formulated, approved and enforced or enacted by the state, whereas morality is upheld mainly through public opinion, beliefs, customs, traditions and education. That is, people's behaviors are evaluated and guided through moral codes such as good and evil, justice and injustice, fairness and favoritism, honesty and dishonesty, so that interest relations between people are coordinated. Third, the range of influence covered by morality is much broader than by the law. It can be said the every word and deed of people is subject to moral evaluation and moral codes. But morality and the law have something in common, that is, they both belong to the superstructure of society and play the role of regulating, restricting, encouraging or guiding people's behaviors, and thus coordinate their interest relations. Only that the law is compulsory while morality is not. So morality and the law complement and enhance each other.

What is morality and what is the essence of it? Answers ofmany Eastern and Western thinkers to these questions are either too mysterious to reveal the essence of morality, failing in realizing the underlying relations between morality and people's material life, or take personal interests as the basis of morality. Marxists hold that, morality, as a part of ideology, is also the manifestation or reflection of interest relations of human beings in material life. Engels pointed out that "... we can only draw the one conclusion: that men, consciously or unconsciously, derive their ethical ideas in the last resort from the practical relations on which their class position is based — from the economic relations in which they carry on production and exchange. "① In the primitive society, in the long practice of production and life, people got to know what kinds of behaviors were good for their long-term and common interests, and what were otherwise. They might have no clear-cut understanding in this regard, but practice taught them what principles they should keep to, by this they corrected their behaviors. Behaviors violating these principles would be denounced by public opinion or conscience. Although there was no literary record of these principles, they passed down from generation to generation. So, in the primitive society, morality was the manifestation of long-term and common interests of the people and behavioral standards established based on it.

Needs and interests appeared since the formation of human society, along with it interest contradictions and mechanism for their coordination. At the very beginning, morality played the dominant role. After entering the stage of acute interest opposition, political and legal means of coordination became more important. In the primitive society, the basic social organizations were communities, clans, tribes and federacy of tribes, which were all interest groups based on kinship ties. Clans were the basic social and economic units in the primitive society. Due to the extremely low productive forces, individual interests could be met only by collective cooperation. Collective or clan interests constituted the prerequisite for the fulfillment of individual interests that were basically identical with clan interests, because people had to work together and shared in the fruits of labor. During this process, morality and customs were formed, whose main content was centered on safeguarding the common interests of the clan and tribe; people worked together, cared for each other, maintaining freedom and equality within the tribe, among others. In addition, tribe affairs were handled by tribal council, a democratic organization in which every adult man and woman had the right to express his opinion. Because there was no fundamental interest contradiction among tribal members, the long passed-down traditions,

---

① *Selected Works of Marx and Engels*, vol. 3, People's Publishing House, 1965, p. 434.

moral codes and customs were enough for settling any possible contradictions appeared in the tribe. Engels marveled at the tribal institution of the Iroquoian people by writing: "And a wonderful constitution it is, this gentile constitution, in all its childlike simplicity! ... All quarrels and disputes are settled by the whole of the community affected, by the gens or the tribe, or by the gentes among themselves. "① In these circumstances, traditional morality became the most important means for regulating interest relations in the primitive society. And customs were also institutions mainly maintained by moral forces.

With the replacement of matriarchal by patriarchal society, private family appeared. "But this tore a breach in the old gentile order; the single family became a power, and its rise was a menace to the gens. "② And private family of monogamy became the most basic economic units and the interest subjects independent of tribes. Property, slaves and land were privately owned and people had new needs and new interests. Private property was considered the biggest interest, and the differences between rich and poor widened, which gave birth to classes. Since then, human society entered the period of sharp interest conflicts and opposition. Traditional morality and custom could no longer meet the demands from different interest subjects, nor the contradictions between the exploiting rich people and the exploited poor people. That led to the new mechanism and institutions for resolving interest contradictions, that is, the state and relevant political and legal mechanism of regulation. Traditional customs and morality were incapable of handling the opposition of interests and interest conflicts brought about by private ownership. Only the political system of state could do this. Entering the class society, unified interests disappeared, along with the unified morality followed by the whole society. But morality still played a role, although lower than before, of interest coordination in a certain range. Because of their differences of position in relations of production and other social relations, classes were bound to have different interests. These differences, reflected in people's minds, would inevitably lead to different, even completely opposite moral ideas, moral

---

① *Selected Works of Marx and Engels*, vol. 4, People's Publishing House, 1995, p. 95.

② *Ibid*, 162—163.

emotions, moral principles and moral standards. So morality in a class society naturally has a class nature. For example, in the slave society, the basic principles of morality were the slaves' absolute obedience to and personal dependence on the slave owners, with its moral standards including absolute loyalty to the state. In a feudal society, the basic moral codes were aimed to maintain the patriarchal and hierarchical relations, and loyalty to the rules and filial piety were the basic moral standards. Entering into a capitalist society, individualism and egoism become basic moral principles and money worship, individualism, egoism, etc. are bourgeois moral standards. On the other hand, the ruled classes in all social formations had their own moral principles and standards contrary to those of the ruling classes. Slaves took the struggle against the slaughter of slave owners and for human status and dignity as their basic moral principles, and formed in these struggles, such sublime virtues as brave, resilience, solidarity, mutual assistance, etc. In a feudal society, farmers took the struggle against the feudal patriarchal system and morality and demands for social equality as basic moral principles, and industry, frugality, mutual assistance between the poor, etc. , are their moral standards. The morality of the working class is the noblest one in human society till now, which takes collectivism as its basic moral principle. Under its guidance, selfishness, bravery, solidarity, honesty, high discipline, etc. , are its moral standards. Morality is a historical category and there is no eternal morality. Despite the opposing moralities in a class society, there are also some commonly recognized moral standards, because the antagonistic classes live in the same society after all. Therefore, such standards as " do not steal ", " support parents ", " respect for the elderly ", " be honest and trustworthy ", etc. , become basic moral standards in human public life. In a class society, the morality of the ruling class is always dominant. Despite its own high level, morals of the working class, highly influenced by the morality of the ruling class, have their great limitations. Take China's feudal society for example. Farmers were heavily shackled by feudal Confucian morality. The character in the well-known Chinese writer Luxun's short story " Blessings ", Xianglin's wife, is an vivid illustration of it. She was hard-working, simple and good-hearted, but she followed feudal morals and finally came down to begging.

The morality of the ruling class maintains the common interests of its class, which is but an invisible killing weapon. Therefore, in a society of private ownership, morality, as a supplement to political and legal system, although having the role of coordinating interest relations to a certain degree, aims mainly to protect the interests of the ruling class, so it cannot fundamentally coordinate the antagonistic interest relations between classes. Only the socialist society, where private ownership is eliminated and personal interests and the interests of society are truly unified, the moral principles of collectivism and socialist moral standards can really coordinate the interest relations among all the people. And it is by this time that morality can be given full rein to its function in coordinating interest relations between individuals, between individuals and groups, between groups, between individuals and society, and in mitigating the relevant interest contradictions. The improvement of socialist morality has an extremely important position and role in the socialist economic construction.

Through interest coordination, human society can avoid being doomed by violent interest contradictions, and conflicts and interests can be distributed in a relatively balanced way. Due to the complexity of interests, interest coordination is sure to be multi-level and multi-dimensional, with economic, political, legal and moral coordination as the main approaches, plus some administrative and other ways. Politics, taking the given level of economic development as its basis and the maintenance of certain economic relations as its main task, is sure to serve certain interests. The law and morality, as part of the superstructure, serve politics, which are both the enhancement and expansion of politics and have a broader range of function than politics; while administrative and other means play the role of supplement. Interest coordination can create a better social environment for people's existence and development, of which economic coordination is the fundamental means whereas overall economic and social development is the fundamental way. So, the purpose of interest coordination is not for coordination sake but for creating conditions for the overall development of society. In a private ownership society, the purpose of interest coordination is to safeguard the fundamental interests of the ruling class, which therefore, is impossible to get rid of brutal interest struggle and conflict. In a socialist society that has gotten rid of interest opposition, the purpose of interest coordination is to safeguard the interests of all the people instead of maintaining the self-interests of the ruling class. So, regulating the interest relations of various interest subjects, greatly mobilizing the enthusiasm of the people, promoting economic development and constantly meeting the people's growing interest needs are the ultimate purposes of its interest coordination.

Chapter Ten

Principles of and Views on Interests

The purpose of our study on social interests is to establish a correct view on interests and to analyze, understand, handle and resolve issues concerning social interests by taking the basic position of historical materialism, applying Marxist theory of interests and adhering to the correct principles of and views on interests. In the previous chapters, we have discussed the categories, essence, functions and classifications of interests. In this chapter, the author tries to make a review of Marxist ideas, standards and views in this respect

I. Interest Ideas and Interest Principles

Interest theory is an important part in Marxist theories. It is a basic principle of Marxism to look at and do things from the perspective of Marxist view on interests. Marxists believe that: "The mode of production of material life conditions the general process of social, political and intellectual life. "[1] Mode of production is the unity of productive forces and relations of production, which conditions and influences the totality of human social life and constitutes the economic structure of it. Social economic relations first of all are manifested themselves as material and economic interests. Therefore, social interests, as an important manifestation of social relations, also constitute the foundation of entire human social life. Economic, material and social interests are the fundamental needs of human beings and also fundamental motives and constraint factors underlying human social life. Different material, economic and social relations manifest themselves as different material, economic and social interests. Interest differences exist in all societies. In a

---

[1] *Selected Works of Marx and Engels*, vol. 2, People's Publishing House, 1995, p. 32.

class society, class contradictions and conflicts essentially are antagonistic among different interest groups, and all class conflicts are conflicts of material interests.

Relations of production must conform to the requirements of the development of productive forces as the fundamental motivation of all societies. The purpose of humansocial production is for survival, life and development and the related material means for these. So, human needs and interests are impetus behind the development of social production, and therefore are also impetus behind development of productive forces. Of the components of social productive forces, laborers are the most dynamic andmost active part, whereas the fulfillment of interests is the internal driving forces mobilizing and stimulating the enthusiasm of laborers. Therefore, social interests have the important historical role as impetus and motivation for social development.

It is one of the important distinctions between historical materialism and historical idealism whether or not admitting that material, economic and social interests are the fundamental driving forces and motivations for the development of historical development of human society, the foundation and causes of the entire social life, and roots of all class struggles, social differences, contradictions and conflicts. Engels pointed out, ". . . the old idealist conception of history, which was not yet dislodged, knew nothing of class struggles based upon economic interests, knew nothing of economic interests; production and all economic relations appeared in it only as incidental, subordinate elements in the ' history of civilization. ' "[①] In the process of establishing historical materialism, it was their change in the understanding of material interests that Marx and Engels recognized that, the material conditions of production are the premise and foundation of allsocial life, and the basic needs of human life constitute the fundamental motive for human production and social activities, and the ultimate causes of all social differences, conflicts and changes, as well as the emergence and changes of all social phenomena. Marx andEngels, by making breakthroughs in their research onmaterial interests, analyzed in an anatomic way the economic relations and facts of human societyand discovered thelaw governing the developmentof human society and revealed its characteristics and mystery. In fact, historical materialism refers to explaining all historical

---

① *Selected Works of Marx and Engels*, vol. 3, People's Publishing House, 1965, p. 365.

· 225 ·

events and ideas, andpolitical, philosophical and religiousand other phenomena based on the given material and economic conditions of the times. In a sense, to explain all social and historical phenomena and ideas from the point of view of human material needs is the worldview and methodology of historical materialism in observing, analyzing and dealing with social issues.

Marxist theory of material, economic and social interests is an important part of the basic principles of Marxism, so is Marxist interest principle. To understand, analyze and solve problems from the viewpoint of the interests is a basic stand, viewpoint and method of Marxism. This is just what Lenin, Mao Zedong and Deng Xiaoping did in this respect. Lenin said that "... economic interests and the economic position of the classes which rule our state lie at the root of both our home and foreign policy. These propositions. . . constitute the basis of the Marxist world view. " [1] Comrade Mao said that "In a word, every comrade must be brought to understand that the supreme test of the words and deeds of a Communist is whether they conform with the highest interests and enjoy the support of the overwhelming majority of the people. " [2] Adhering to Marxist views and principles of interests is the starting point and stand of Marxists in observing and handling problems, and also a basic standard for judging the nature and features of all social phenomena, as well as a standard for evaluating words and deeds of all persons. Whether or not acting in the interests of the people is a basic Marxist principle and standard for judging things. Ideas, principles and standards of interests constitute an important part of Marxist theory of interests.

In the early practice of Russian socialist construction, Lenin paid special attention to Marxist view on interests. When summarizing the political experience of the October Revolution and experience and lessons in the early period of socialist construction in Russia in the article "Fourth Anniversary of the October Revolution", he clearly point out, "Borne along on the crest of the wave of enthusiasm, rousing first the political enthusiasm and then the military enthusiasm of the people, we expected to accomplish economic tasks just as great as the political and military tasks we had accomplished by relying on this enthusiasm. . . . Experience has proved

---

① *Collected works of Lenin*, vol. 34, People's Publishing House, 1985, p. 306.

② *Selected Works of Mao Zedong*, vol. 3, People's Publishing House, 1995, p. 1096.

that we were wrong. "① What was the mistake? He then continued that, in the effort to recover the economy and make construction, we could not directly rely on the enthusiasm, but aided by the enthusiasm engendered by the great revolution, and on the basis of personal interest, personal incentive and business principles. The principle of material interests is an important principle that we must rely on in socialist construction. The preliminary practice of socialist construction in Russia told Lenin that, socialist construction could not last long by relying only on political enthusiasm while ignoring the immediate interests of the masses and without considering the incentive role of material interests. So Lenin concluded: "It appears that a number of transitional stages were necessary—state capitalism and socialism—in order to prepare—to prepare for many years of effort—for the transition to communism. Not directly relying on enthusiasm, but aided by the enthusiasm engendered by the great revolution, and on the basis of personal interest, personal incentive and business principles, we must first set to work in this small peasant country to build solid gangways to socialism by way of state capitalism. Otherwise we shall never get to communism, we shall never bring scores of millions of people to communism. "② Here Lenin explicitly pointed out that we must stick to the principle of concerning with personal interests. From here we can see that, the success of socialist construction cannot be achieved without proper attention to reasonable interests of the masses.

Early since the period of revolutionary wars, Comrade Mao Zedong had always adhered to Marxist ideas and principles in this respect. In the article entitle" Be Concerned with the Well-Being of the Masses, Pay Attention to Methods of Work" published in 1934, he pointed out that "our central task at present is to mobilize the broad masses to take part in the revolutionary war, overthrow imperialism and the Kuomintang by means of such war, spread the revolution throughout the country. " We should understand that to accomplish this central task, we should "in no way neglect or underestimate the question of the immediate interests, the well-being, of the broad masses. For the revolutionary war is a war of the masses, it can be waged only by mobilizing the masses and relying on them" "all the practical problems in the masses' everyday life should claim our attention. " "We should convince the masses that we represent

① Collected Works of Lenin, vol. 34, People's Publishing House, 1985, p. 305.
② *Collected Works of Lenin*, vol. 4, People's Publishing House, 1995, pp. 569—582.

their interests, that our lives are intimately bound up with theirs. We should help them to proceed from these things to an understanding of the higher tasks which we have put forward. . . fight to the end for victory in the revolution". ①The purpose of our launching revolutionary wars was for the fundamental interests of the people. On the other hand, to mobilize the masses to join in the war, we must also concern with the immediate interests of the people, so that they can see the purpose as well as the future of the revolution. Only by doing so, could we convince the masses and won the war. So he said: "All empty words were useless, we must let the people see physicalwell-being. "② In the period of socialist construction, Comrade Mao put forward the important principle of "take the interests of the state, the collective and the individual into account. "

Under the new historical condition of socialist reform and opening up, Comrade Deng Xiaoping repeatedly stressed that the principle of personal material interests is an important principle of socialism and also an important principle of Marxism. Early before the Third Plenum of Eleventh Central Committee of the CPC, he explicitly raised the issue concerning with the material interests of the masses. "As far as the relatively small number of advanced people is concerned, it won't matter too much if we neglect the principle of more pay for more work and fail to stress individual material benefits. But when it comes to the masses, that approach can only be used for a short time—it won't work in the long run. "③ ". . . revolution takes place on the basis of the need for material benefit. It would be idealism to emphasize the spirit of sacrifice to the neglect of material benefit. " He also believed that the fundamental task of socialism is to develop the productive forces, so we should meet the material and cultural needs of the people to the maximum extent. He said: "In the final analysis, to take advantage of the superiority of socialism means to substantially develop the productive forces and gradually improve the people's material and cultural life,"④ and respect the needs of personal interests. He stressed that we must bring tangible material benefits to the

---

① *Selected Works of Mao Zedong*, vol. 1, People's Publishing House, 1991, pp. 136—139

② Mao Zedong. "Economic Problems and Financial Problems", Northeast Book Store, 1946, p. 118

③ *Selected Works of Deng Xiaoping*, vol. 2, People's Publishing House, 1994, p. 146.

④ *Ibid.* , p. 251.

people, and formulated the relevant policy on the basis of developing socialist productive forces. He put forth the important idea that some people and some regions get rich first and then common prosperity of the entire population be gradually achieved. He advanced the principle of "three favorables" (whether it is favorable to the growth of the productive forces in a socialist society, whether it is favorable to the increase ofthe overall national strength of the socialist state and whether it is favorable to the improvement of the people's living standards), among which, meeting the interest needs of the people is the starting point and goal. He said that "In short, our work in all fields shouldhelp to build socialism with Chinese characteristics, and it should be judged by thecriterion of whether it contributes to the welfare and happiness of the people and tonational prosperity."① The interests of the people come before everything else is Comrade Deng's Marxist Interest view. He took "whether the people support", "whether the people agree", "whether the people are happy" and "whether the people accept" as the starting point and goal of our every policy and guideline and the basic reference when considering everything.

At present, China is in a great age of dramatic change. During this period, it has become an irresistible trend of history to reform all structures, systems and institutions in economic, political, cultural and ideological realms that are not suitable for the development of social productive forces in this stage and to establish a socialist market economy and other systems. The reform will have influence on all areas and aspects of our social life and will bring about changes in human relations. With the transition from the old social structure to the new one and adjustment of social relations, interest relations in the entire society are bound to change accordingly, with the old interest structure and distribution relations gradually replaced by the new ones. Socialist reform will inevitably have a bearing on the interests of everyone and change the interest relations among the people. The complex changes in the interest relations will often strengthen or shake people's attitude toward reform to some extent, so do the interest adjustments to their motivation for participating the reform. In the process of socialist reform, one of the vital issues related to the success or failure of the reform is how to correctly understand and deal with the interest relations of all sides, to rationally adjust the interest structure so

---

① *Selected Works of Deng Xiaoping*, vol. 3, People's Publishing House, 1993, p. 23.

that through reform to meet people's interest needs to the maximum. In this important historical juncture, it is extremely important and necessary to study Marxist interest views, to adhere to Marxist interest principles and to use Marxist criteria for interest evaluation.

II. Interest Analysis and Criterion for Interest Evaluation

Lenin said that "If you do not show the interests of which classes and which particular interests are dominant at the moment in determining the nature of the various parties and their politics, you are not really applying Marxism. "[1] Interests dominate people's social and historical activities— this is an important principle of historical materialism, which indicates the objective law governing historical movement of human society. Applying the interest principle to analyze complex economic, political, cultural and social and other life is an important method for having an insightful view of the mysteries of society and history. Interest analysis refers to revealing, based on the lawsof historical development and interest principles, interest motives behind people's social activities, and the further explanation of various social relations of human society and historical phenomena. In this sense, interest theory is an important method for observing historical phenomena. Observing interest under the guidance of historical materialism provides a thread to people's understanding of complex social phenomena.

The method of interest analysis is wide used in studies of sociology, political science, international relations and other fields. For example, in the 1930s to 1950s, an academic school of political realism emerged. It put forward the theory of political realism, believing that in international relations, national interests are the basic motivation behind a country's external behaviors; each country is dominated by and always pursuesits national interests and power. From this we can see that political realism analyzes volatile international situations from the perspective of national interests. On the other hand, if the interest analysis of social problems is made from abstract human nature instead of historical materialism, the true natures and features of many complex social problems cannot be correctly understand and thereforeis impossible to be explained.

The reform going on in China is a grand social transformation, during

---

[1] *Collected Works of Lenin*, vol. 15, People's Publishing House, 1988, p. 375.

which, parts of the economic and political systems that do not conform with the development of social productive forces, or that not conducive to mobilizing the enthusiasm of the people will be fundamentally changed. As a result, interest relations of the society will inevitably be profoundly changed. Under these circumstances, correct interest analysis is the prerequisite to correctly assessing reform situation and formulating reform policies and measures. This because, firstly, a few people will lose their unreasonable vested interest in the reform, but most people will get more benefits. Unsuitable structures or systems hinder the full mobilization of people's enthusiasm in a wide scope, so those people who have gotten vested interests and unreasonable power from these structures or systems willsuffer loss in the process. For example, in the early stage of implementation of contracted responsibility system in rural areas, some peoples opposed it. In addition to inadequate understanding, it was also related to interests. In other words, the responsibility system was bound to make some of the officials divorcing from labor lose theirinterests based on their positions. Likewise, the decentralization in reform toward the market economy in urban areas met the obstacle of centralization, which also had relations with interest distribution.

Also, one of the issues in reform is to break the egalitarian system. As a consequence, much complaint would inevitably come from those who were lazy and got used to "eating from the same big pot", or neglected work disciplines, or made poor performance either in quality or quantity of production, or those who worked in enterprises losing money for years. But the new system received the support from the majority of the people, because it can take into account the return to individual and collective labor to the maximum, can reasonably adjust interest relations among the individual, the collective and the state, and can fully mobilize the enthusiasm of the people. Therefore, fundamentally speaking, with the gradual improvement of the new system, most people will get more benefits from the reform. Benefit gained by farmers from rural reform is a good example. Secondly, reform in ownership structure and toward the market economy will bring changes in distribution structure and system, during which, it is impossible for each to receive equal benefit in terms of time, amount and space. Socialist reform is an unbalanced, spiral and wave-like process. This is especially true for a big and backward agricultural country like China with under-developed market economy. So the reform in some localities, departments and industries are faster than others; mistakes and setbacks may occur; and old system or practice may even turn back partially or temporarily. Consequently, some people may get benefits sooner in time and bigger in share; in contrast, some may lose the benefits they have just gained, and others may gain less than what they got before reform. The unreasonably too much and too fast increase of wealth of some people will temporarily lead to unusually wide gap of income. Although this kind of complex changes in interests is inevitable in the process of reform, if we do not have a clear understanding of them, it may cause errors in policy-making, resulting in changes in interests developing toward undesirable direction so that normal process of reform be affected or even ruined. Despite the fact that most people will get benefit from reform, if the interest relations and distribution remain unreasonable for a long time, people's enthusiasm for reform will be dampened, which may change into passive, negative or resentful emotions toward reform.

Therefore, it is an important chain in socialist reform to clearly recognize changes in interests in the process of reform and take timely and effective measures to gradually adjust interest relations. To ensure that the interest analysis is correct, a criterion must be followed. From the point of view of benefit, the core of acriterion is whether and how it is beneficial. But Marxist criterion for interest analysis, which isfundamentally different from others, focus mainly on whether it is beneficial to the majority of the people, and whether or not it can mobilize the enthusiasm and is supported by the majority of the people. This is a key element determining that Communists take people's interests as their starting point and goal of all their work. In leading our party in the democratic revolution, Comrade Mao Zedong always took upholding the interests of the people as the criterion for judging whether our lines, principles and policies were correct. He said: "... the supreme test of the words and deeds of a Communist is whether they conform to the highest interests and enjoy the support of the overwhelming majority of the people."[1] Comrade Deng Xiaoping always advocated that the interests of the people come before everything else, which is also the criterion of interest judgment.

In terms of criterion for interest judgment, there are two fundamental criteria for testing good or bad of reform: first, whether it is the majority

---

[1] *Selected Works of Mao Zedong*, vol. 3, People's Publishing House, 1991, p. 1096.

of the people or a few people get benefits from it, and a successful reform must benefit the majority of the people; secondly, whether the enthusiasm of the majority of people has been fully mobilized through the reform. Interests are the motive behind people's social activities, so a reform benefiting the majority of the people will inevitably arouse people's huge labor enthusiasm. Only after these two results have been achieved, can the reform be understood and supported by the people and achieve its success. In the course of reform, we must unswervingly adhere to the two criteria, so as to clearly understand various interest relations, properly handle profit-making activities of various interest groups, and reduce unreasonable interest pursuits to the minimum. Analyzing interest changes and interest relations, improving socialist consciousness of reform andreducingits blindnessis what Lenin said "apply Marxism".

III. Interest Views and Main Schools of Interest View

The basic tasks of an interest theory is to determine the social substance of interests, emphasizes their historical roles, adhere to their principles, clarify interest criteria, divide interest groups and put forward measures for interest coordination. Interest theory is the rational summary of interests. Marxist theory of interests is a scientific theory founded by Marx and Engels by applying historical materialism to analyze interest phenomena. People can use this theory to observe, analyze and deal with issues concerning social interests. Interest view refers to values, attitudes, ways of thinking, rules, criteria and idea of looking at and dealing with issues concerning interests under the guidance of views on the world and life. A person's view on interests in general, on personal interests, on the relationship between personal interests and overall interests, etc. , is closely associated with his worldview. Views on the world and life determine views on interests and values. For example, the working class' views on the world and lifedeterminetheir views on interests and values, so do the exploiting class. The broad mind and noble and selfless characters of the working class who put the emancipation of mankind before the emancipation of themselves determine that they have the interest view of collectivism that put the interests of the people above their personal interests; on the contrary, the mercenary and narrow vision of exploiting classes determines that they have only egoistic and individualistic view on interests.

In the history of thought of human beings, the representative interest views include: mercenary, anti-interest; pragmatism, individualism, egoism, factionalism, hedonism, money worship; utilitarianism; collectivism, altruism. They can be divided into three categories, that is: mercenary interest view, non-mercenary interest view and utilitarian interest view.

Mercenary interest view is the view that seeks only interests to the neglect of righteousness, and seeks only private interests to the neglect of collective interests. In human social life, interests, without doubt, constitute the basis and premise, and everybody concerns about interests. But besides interests, there are also spiritual pursuits, noble ideas, good morals, positive emotions, righteousness, etc. Mercenary means focusing only on interests but not righteousness, on individualism but not collectivism. The essence of being mercenary is seeking only private interests to the neglect of public interests, which will make a person become wicked, one that seeks only personal or factional interests and money worship, even to extent of satisfying self-interests at the expense of the interests of other people, the collective, the state as well as the long-term and fundamental interests of the people. Individualism, factionalism and utilitarianism are all manifestations of mercenary view; while egoism, hedonism and money worship are the extremes of it. The doctrine such as "human beings die in pursuit of wealth just as birds die in pursuit of food," "money is above anything else", are extreme mercenary creeds. Anti-interest view is opposite of mercenary view. It takes the negation of interests as its value orientation and standards and way of thinking, stresses only on morals, ideas and ethics with complete denial of the role of interests and people's pursuit for and satisfaction of interests. Some Confucian schools of philosophy advocate typical anti-interest view. Confucius said, "The gentleman knows what is right; the small man knows what is profitable." [1] Mencius said, "Why should we mention interests? What count is benevolence and righteousness" . [2] Dong Zhongshu in the Han dynasty advocated "upholding righteousness instead of interests, elucidating the Way with all-out efforts" . [3] And the neo-Confucians from the Song and the Ming dynasties explicitly proposed

----

[1] *Analects of Confucius*, Chapter Liren.

[2] *Mencius*, Chapter "King Hui of Liang (Part A)"

[3] "Biography of Dong Zhongsu" in *Book of Han*,

"eradicating human desires and maintaining the heavenly principles".
These are all typical anti-interest points of view. In the long history of
Chinese feudal society, the ruling class held high asceticism of
Confucianism with the intention of maintaining their feudal system and
rule, which in fact was an obscurant policy to help their appropriation of
the interests and political control over the exploited classes.

The essence of anti-interest view is not against pursuing interests, but to
prevent the people or others from pursuing interests. During the Cultural
Revolution, the Gang of Four advocated the "omnipotence of spirit,"
which is nothing but amodern variant of the feudal anti-interest
view. According to historical materialism, human beings cannot survive
without material desires like eating, drinking and sex. Only after their
reasonable interests are met, can the enthusiasm of human beings be
mobilized and development of societybe promoted. Therefore, the anti-
interest view is of idealist nature that does not accord with objective facts.

In the debate over the relationship between righteousness and interest in
ancient China, some thinkers advocated emphasis both on righteousness
and interests, and convincingly refuted Confucian asceticism. In the
history of thought in ancient China, "righteousness" refers to people's
motives and deeds being complying withcertain ethical standards, while
"interests" to material interests and utility. Against Confucian view that
"righteousness is the most important principle, Mohists, believed that
interests concerned the loss or gain of the people and state, so they
proposed that "Righteousness is interests". [1]They argued that the
interests of the people and country should be taken as the criterion in
judging good or bad, right or wrong. The greatest thinker of the Legalist
school Han Fei based his interest view on the gain or loss of the ruler. He
believed that any ethical theory divorced from practical things such as
agriculture, war, was only hypocrisy of self-deception. Opponents of New
Confucianism in ancient China such as Ye Shi, Chen Liang, Wang
Fuzhi, Yan Yuan all advocated balancing righteousness and interests and
opposed Confucian view that interests were necessarily related to personal
gain and had nothing to do with righteousness. For example, Yan Yuan
diametrically proposed the utilitarian view on interests by saying that
"upholding righteousness while seeking interests, and elucidating the Way
while considering results." Utilitarian concept of interests takes actual

---

① *Mozi*, "The Canon I".

outcomes and interests as value orientation, way of thinking and behavior, ethical norms, standards and view. Utilitarianism was first put forward by some 19th century bourgeois thinkers. To meet the bourgeois needs for opposing the feudal system and morals of the church, and for promoting bourgeois individualism and bourgeois revolution, they thinkers put forth utilitarianism. It is an interest view based on the theory of human nature, which believes that, personal interests are the basis of human acts, and public interests should subject to personal interests. Only in this way can it accord with the selfish nature of human being and its requirements. The earliest proponent of utilitarianism is the 18th century French materialists Helvetius. He believed that the pursuit of individual interests was human nature, and egoism should be the norms of human behavior. The representative of utilitarianism is British philosopher Jeremy Bentham, who believed that personal interests were the only real interests and the abstract and the sum total of individual interests. John Mill developed Bentham's principle and put forth the concept of utilitarianism and published a book of the same title. But he rejected the utilitarianism in the narrow sense. He argued that, in addition to the principle of self-interests, altruism should also be included into the scope of utilitarianism and he advocated intellectual pleasures.

In China's feudal society, some progressive thinkers also promoted the principle of utility, a utilitarianism of Chinese version, in opposition to Confucian arguments denying interests. Ye Shi, the most famous figure of theYongjia School, and Chen Liang, the founder of the Yong Kang school believed that, utility and effect should be stressed in learning and righteousness and interests should be integrated. They both opposed the Neo-Confucian views on righteousness and interests that deny utility and interest and indulge in empty talk about benevolence and righteousness. Chen Liang criticized that "The pedants indulge only in empty talk about righteousness but know nothing about utility. "[1] Ye Shi also criticized Neo-Confucianism and stress utility. He said: "Without utility, righteousness is totally empty. "[2]

Mao Zedong said, "Materialists do not oppose utilitarianism in general but the utilitarianism of the feudal, bourgeois and petty-bourgeois classes; they oppose those hypocrites who attack utilitarianism in words but in deeds

---

[1] "A Memorial to Emperor Xiao Zong in the Year Wushen (戊申并上孝宗书)".

[2] *Notes of Studies* (习学记言), vol. 23

embrace the most selfish and short-sighted utilitarianism. There is no 'ism' in the world that transcends utilitarian considerations; in class society there can be only the utilitarianism of this or that class. We are proletarian revolutionary utilitarians and take as our point of departure the unity of the present and future interests of the broadest masses, who constitute over 90 per cent of the population; hence we are revolutionary utilitarians aiming for the broadest and the most long-range objectives, not narrow utilitarians concerned only with the partial and the immediate. "① Marxist theory of interests is not opposed to utilitarianism in general, but stresses that the people's material needs are the primary thing, the premise of and motivation behind all social life. It resolutely opposesextreme utilitarianism such as the feudal, bourgeois and petty-bourgeois selfishness, and it advocates concerning about the material interests of the people; raising the people's living standards on the basis of the development of the productive forces; taking the people as the starting point in correctly handling the relationships between the immediate and long-term interests of the people, between partial and overall interests and between individual and public interests. Marxists adhere to proletarian utilitarianism embodied in altruism and collectivism.

IV. Firmly Establishing the Working Class's View on Interests

What interest principles should we promote and adhere to? The answer is: We should insist on and advocate, under the guidance of historical materialism and Marxist theory of interests, proletarian view on interests determined by proletarian view on the world and life. The proletarian view on interests is essentially a utilitarian concept of collectivism.

Marx said: "Everything for which man struggles is a matter of his interest. "② As to how to face the issue of interests in the real life of China's reform toward socialist market economy, there are three different kinds of people with different attitudes and behaviors: The first kind is those advanced elements like Kong Fansen, who, in the impact of the

---

① *Selected Works of Mao Zedong*, vol. 3, People's Publishing House, 1991, p. 864.

② *Collected Works of Marx and Engels*, vol. 1, People's Publishing House, 1956, p. 82.

market economy, can stand the test and always put the interests of the people first, and they can sacrifice their personal interests even their lives for the interests of the people. The second kind are those who, under the condition of the market economy, basically can stand the test and observe Party disciplines and laws and serve the people, and in general can the properly handle the relationship between personal interests and the interests of the people. The third kind is those who are defeated in the test of the market economy test so thatthey have degenerated into criminals. In the ranks of Party members, there are a few people, some are even senior officials, putting the interests of the Party and the people behind and deviated the Party's purpose and principles, abused power and became corrupt and degenerate to the extent that they became criminals. Although the number of the third kind is not large, if unchecked, they will destroy our social morals in general and ruin our cause in particular. People belonging to the second category, although the majority of them are good, some of them could also be misled by wrong interest views to make some wrong words and deeds. Presently, regarding how to face the issue of interests, there are some incorrect understanding and ideas, which will affect the behaviors of Party members and the people. We must correct them and uphold correct working class'view on interests through ideological and education.

Under the conditions of the market economy, what are the main points of the working class'view on interests?

First, the fundamental principle of the proletarian view on interests is that the interests of thepeople is supreme.

The interests of the people are the starting point and purpose of all our work. We should adhere to and uphold the people's interests above all else, personal interests unconditionally subordinate to people's interests, which is the interest view of the working class that should be upheld and advocated. Chairman Mao said: "Our point of departure is to serve the people whole-heartedly and never for a moment divorce ourselves from the masses, to proceed in all cases from the interests of the people and not from one's self-interest or from the interests of a small group, and to identify our responsibility to the people with our responsibility to the leading organs of the Party. "① The interests of the people is supreme,

---

① *Selected Works of Mao Zedong*, vol. 3, People's Publishing House, 1991, pp. 1094—1095.

this is the fundamental principle of the interest view of the working class. The Communist Party of China is the representative of the fundamental interests of Chinese proletariat and the people. It had represented the interests of the broadest masses of the people in all periods of the Chinese revolution, and it will continue to do so without any changeunderthe new environment and conditions of the market economy. Today, under the new historical conditions, Deng Xiaoping always concerned about the interests and wishes of the masses and took "whether the people support or not," "whether the people agree or not," "whether the people are happy or not" and "whether the people accept or not" as the criteria for making all our policies. The aim of theories, line, principles and policies of socialism with Chinese characteristics advocated by Comrade Deng is to develop socialist productive forces and make Chinese people realize common prosperity so that it embodies the fundamental interests of the people. The purpose of people's revolution led by the Party is to release the social productive forces and bring happy life to the people. After coming to power, the Party should concentrate more attention on the development of the productive forces to better address the issue of making the people happier.

Therefore, the fundamental task of socialism is to develop the productive forces and this is where the fundamental interests of the people lie in. The rigid planned economy in the past severely hindered the development of the socialist productive forces so that people's interests could not be met. Reform and opening up and developing socialist market economy are in line with the fundamental interests of the people. This is because: Firstly, it is for the people. The tortuous path of our socialist construction shows that a highly centralized planned economy hampers the development of the productive forces so that the superiority of socialism could not be demonstrated, as a result, the people's interests could not be fully realized. Developing the market economy can improve our efficiency of production, increase social wealth and develop the productive forces, which will ultimately make the people enjoy common prosperity. This has been proved by the practice of China's reform and opening up. Secondly, in the socialist market economy, the enthusiasm of production of the people can be better mobilized. The people can ensure their status as masters of the country through socialist public ownership, and at the same time, they are relatively independent and autonomous producers and operators at the micro level, which fully confirms the main position of the people in the socialist economic life and safeguard their interests. Thirdly, the market economy canfully invigorate socialist economic life. As the independent producers, operators and consumers, the people can directly make their choices based on the variety, quality and services of commodities, which is a mechanism irreplaceable by the macro-control of the state. This also fully reflects the interests of the people.

But there are also some negative sides in the market economy. Among which, the spread of individualism, money worship, hedonism, mentality of small group, even corrupt and degenerate phenomena, etc. , has the risk of harming the fundamental interests of the people. What our Party members asthe advanced elements of the working class should do under this new conditions? The answer is as follows:

(1) Putting the interests of the people above everything else, this is the supreme principle for the advanced elements of the working class in making their words and deeds. The CPC is composed of the advanced elements of the working class, so the principle that people's interests are above everything else must be strictly observed bythe Party and its members. It is more so facing the challenges from the market economy.

(2) Serving the people's interests wholeheartedly is the fundamental starting point and ultimate goal of all the words and deeds of the advanced elements of the working class. Working in the interests of the majority of the people rather than a section or a small group's interests is a fundamental symbol distinguishing working class parties from other parties, and the starting point and purpose of all the work they do and all their activities and policies in all periods. Since the Third Plenary Session of the Eleventh Central Committee of the CPC, the policy of reform and opening up has fully embodied this purpose. In practice, the Party requires that every word and deed of its members should conform to the interests of the majority of the people and play an exemplary role.

(3) Not self-serving is the basic principle for the advanced elements of the working class in facing the issue of interests. Apart from the interests of the overwhelming majority of the people, the Party does not have or pursue any special interests of its own. The Party demands that all its members, starting from the moment theyjoin the Party, must take working in the interests of the people the criterion of their actions, and have no selfish ideas and interests.

(4) Subordinating personal interests to the interests of the people is the requirement of Party spirit. The CPC never denies personal interests,

personal ambitions or personal pursuits, but the personal interests of its Party members must subordinate to the people's interests, and personal ideals and aspirations must conform to the common pursuit of the Party's political ideals. For every Party member, how to properly deal with personal interests is an outstanding issue. The purpose of reform and opening up is to develop the economy and meet the needs of the people's increasing interests, which of course includes the reasonable interests of individual Party members. The Party is in favor of, rather than in opposition of, meeting the reasonable interests of its members under the premise of satisfying the interests of the people. However, Party members are more advanced than ordinary people just because they consciously put the interests of the people first in everything they do.

(5) Whether it conforms to the interests of the people or not, whether it meets the interests of the people or not, and whether it brings about happiness to the people or not: these are the fundamental standards for judging the success or failure of our work. We must always make sure that the aim and outcome of all words and deeds and all lines, principles, policies and methods of the Party is to realize the fundamental interests of the people. During the revolutionary wartime, our Party fought bravely and feared no sacrifice in leading the people to seize the power and liberate the productive forces, which satisfied the people and got their support; during the socialist construction period, we made some mistakes, so that people were not satisfied; during the new era, we have carried out reform and opening up, which have emancipated and developed the productive forces and the people have gained intangible benefits so they are satisfied and support us. All Party members should set these as their standards. Presently, the people strongly resent corruption in the ranks of the Party, so we must strive to get rid of it.

Second, working wholeheartedly in the interests of the people is the concentrated expression of interest view of the working class.

The working class is the most selfless class in history and working wholeheartedly in the interests of the people is the concentrated expression of the interest view of them. Ina class society, all political parties represent the interests ofsomeclasses or strata. The CPC represents the fundamental interests of the working class and the broad masses. It is in this sense that the spirit of the Partyisa concentrated expression of its class interests and people's interests. To safeguard the advanced nature of the working class, we must adhere to the principle of keeping the Party spirit, for which the principlethat the people's interests are above everything else must be strictly kept to. Although this is not a new requirement, it is not easy thing but an important and strict test for the all Party members in the new era ofreform and opening up.

To enhance Party spirit, the Party members mustfirmly uphold the interest view of theworking class. Only by doing so can communists completely break the mental shackle of pursuing private interests to dedicate themselves, even sacrifice their lives, for the interests of the people. Otherwise, they could not stand the test of life and death in wartime and various material temptations in peaceful time. Today, under the conditions ofreform and opening up, some Party members failed in the test ofthe market economy, who, inducedby wrong interest view, put money above everything else and become degenerate. This fundamentally deviates from the Party's spirit and principles.

Third, serving the interests of the people is the core of the interest view of all Party members and their value system.

The question of "for whom?" involves both world view and view on life, and the core of interest view and view on values. Values are guided by world view and determined by interest view, the essence of which is the evaluation of interests. The interest view of the working class determines the proletarian view on values and determines that the core of it is working in the interests of the working class and the people. An important reason for the corruption, degeneration and evil deeds within the ranks of the Partyis that, the views on interests and values of these evil doers are deviant, confused or completely wrong.

Communists uphold the values of the working class and socialism, the fundamental principle of which is wholeheartedly working for the interests of the people. Although view on values as part of ideology and ideaschange along with social and economic development, the fundamental principle of communists remains unchanged either in the revolutionary war years or under the conditions ofthe market economy. The core of these values is the collectivist interest view that puts the interests of the people above everything else, in contrast to the capitalist interest view of individualism that put personal interests above everything else. The CPC keeps to the collectivist values and takes working in the interests of the people as its absolute principle in value evaluation. Comrade Mao Zedong said: "As we Chinese Communists, who base all our actions on the highest interests of the broadest masses of the Chinese people and who are fully convinced of the justice of our cause, never balk at any personal sacrifice and are ready at all times to give our lives for the cause, can we be reluctant to discard any idea, viewpoint, opinion or method which is not suited to the needs of the people?" ① Comrade Deng Xiaoping said: "If what the Party members mean to do or their tasks are put in a nutshell, there are just two: serve the people whole-heartedly and put the interests of the people first in doing everything. " ②

To foster a correct view on values, it is important to establish lofty criteria for their assessment. World outlook is key to a person's words and deeds, so does the person's view on values. The core of value assessment concerns about interests, that is, "whether is there any interests in it?" and "In whose interests is it?" A Party member must be judged with and guided by these value standards. On this basis, in face of interest issue, a Party member must properly deal with the following relations:

(1) Correctly handling the relations between personal interests and the interests of the people, putting people's interests first and firmly opposing ultra-individualism. Communists put people's interest above everything else, but this does not mean that they have no personal interests; only that they have reasonable personal interests, and they subordinate personal interests to the people's interests. As to how to deal with personal interests, there are two completely different attitudes: one is ultra-individualism that takes the satisfaction of personal interests as the starting point and the purpose of life. Individualism is a doctrine centered on personal interests, a doctrine that considers individual interests as above everything else and believes that the realization of individual values is the supreme in social life, by hook or by crook. In real life, there are some communists seek only their personal interests, who conduct "interest exchange" even within the Party. Another attitude is just the opposite, which integrates personal interests with and subordinates them to people's interests. Marx and Engels believed that "If correctly understood interest is the principle of all moral, man's private interest must be made to coincide with the interest of humanity" . ③Comrade Mao said: "At no

---

① *Selected Works of Mao Zedong*, vol. 3, People's Publishing House, 1991, pp. 109—1097.

② *Selected Works of Deng Xiaoping*, vol. 1, People's Publishing House, 1994, p. 257

③ *Collected Works of Marx and Engels*, vol. 2, People's Publishing House, 1957, p. 167.

time and in no circumstances should a Communist place his personal interests first; he should subordinate them to the interests of the nation and of the masses". ①According to communist interest outlook, personal interests are always associated with and should be integrated into people's interests. The interests of the people are the basis and precondition of personal interests, without which personal interests will have no guarantee.

(2) Correctly handling the relations between the realization of personal valuesand that of social values and advocating that the realization of man's social value is the most important. Man's value includes personal value and social value. Man's social value refers to man's contribution to society. The greater is his contribution to society, the fuller the realization of his social values, and vice versa. Personal value refers to the extent of personal material and intellectual satisfaction given by a society to a person. The greater the satisfaction is given, the fuller the realization of personal value. We communists advocate the unity of personal value and social value, and believe that personal value can only be realized after social value has been realized. Communists should maximize the realization of their personal value in the realization of social value, that is, taking the realization of people's interests as the highest standard. Based on this standard, communists are required: Their words and deeds are guided by collectivist value and people's interests are placed above everything else at all times and on all occasions; working in the interests of the people is considered as the highest form of realization of personal value; correctly handling relations between personal interests and collective interests, that means, individualism must be overcome, collectivism must be held high and personal interests must be subordinated to the fundamental interests of the people while reasonable personal interests are allowed for.

(3) Correctly handling the relations between observing the standards of a Party memberand implementing the Party's current policies, so as to set a good example in leading the masses to get rich. At the current stage, the Party not only adheres to its ultimate goal, but also has formulated lines and policies for the present time. The goals and basic lines of the Party require that, all Party members should play an exemplary role in implementing these lines and policies, and can never lower the standards

---

① *Selected Works of Mao Zedong*, vol. 2, People's Publishing House, 1991, p. 522

at the excuse of implementing the current policies. The government policies encourage both Party members and ordinary people to get rich through honest labor, but Party members must firstlead the masses in realizing common prosperity rather than concerning themselves only with personal wealth, let alone desperately seeking personal fortune. The Constitution of the Party stipulates that communist party members must not seek personal gain or privileges, although the relevant laws and policies provide them with personal benefits and job-related functions and powers. Under the conditions of the market economy, Party members are allowed to gain personal interests through their own labor and by observing the principles of the market economy. But they are not allowed to act against regulations and policies, or abuse power for personal gains. A Party member is different from an ordinary people, therefore, he does not measure up to standards who concerns only about self-interests or prosperity instead of leading the masses in attaining common prosperity.

(4) Correctly handling the relationship between giving and taking, advocatingthe spirit of devotion and oppose money worship. Should we still advocate the spirit of devotion under the conditions of the market economy that follows the principle of exchange at equal value? Some people think that under these new circumstances, the spirit of devotion is out of date; communists are also human beings, who, in the market economy, can maximize their benefits at minimal costs. Some people even put money above everything else. There are three relationships between taking and giving: the first is more taking than giving, the second is taking equals giving and the third is less taking than giving. The first case will threaten the survival of a society; in the second case, the society can only maintain its simple production; only in the third case can a society develop and advance forward. The Communist Party as the promoter of social progress should advocate more giving than taking and take it as its value principle and oppose money worship.

(5) Correctly handling the relationship between power and interests. Party members must use the power entrusted by the people to work in the people's interests. We should advocate keeping close ties with the masses, hardworking and combating bureaucracy. The power of the CPC as a governing party is entrusted by the people, so it must take good use it in working in the interests of the people. Power for people's interests instead of personal interests is the characteristic distinguishing the CPC

from other parties. Bureaucracy is a kind of power corruption, and is incompatible with the purpose of the Party and interests of the people as fire and water, so we must firmly oppose it.

Part 3

The Practice of the Interests Theory

Chapter Eleven

Basic Economic Relations and Interest Relations in the Primary Stage of Socialism

Interest relations in a society, in the final analysis, are economic relations. Therefore, to study interest relations in the primary stage of socialism, we must first of all study its economic relations, and in light of the existence of the market economy in this stage, must begin from examining its basic economic relations in the market economy.

I. The Starting Point for Understanding the Basic Economic Relations in the Primary Stageof Socialism

To study interest relations in the primary stage of socialism, we must analyze the economic ground on which the interest relations of the primary stage of socialism rely. Facing the extremely complicated economic realities in this stage, our starting point of analysis should be: First, sorting out the basic economic categories from the complex social and economic phenomena, because it is economic relations that finally determine people's economic behavior; Second, finding out the most basic logical order of the economic relations as the determinants of interest relations and find out the approaches for revealing these relations.

Marx's research on capitalist economy provides us with a way of thinking in our analysis. In capitalist production, commodity is the most universal presence and commodity exchange is the most basic economic relations. Commodity, the smallest economic cell, embodies the most basic economic relations of capitalism, thus contains the budding of all capitalist interest relations. It was from the bearer of all social relations of capitalist society, that is, commodity, that Marx ultimately revealed the basic social, economic and interest relations of capitalist society. Specifically,

Marx, proceeding from the intrinsic contradictions of the two factors, value and value in use, of commodity production, extending to the analysis of the duality of labor of commodity production, finally revealed the basic economic relations of commodity production in capitalist market economy. Based on this and the theory of surplus value, he further revealed the specific expression of the basic economic and interest relations of capitalist mode of production.

Marx's research method gives up an inspiration that, to have a deep understanding of the issue of interest relations in the primary stage of socialism, we must first recognize the fundamental economic characteristics in this stage and grasp its most primary and most basic economic relations. The ownership pattern that public ownership is the mainstay and diverse sectors of the economy develop side by side constitutes the basic economic relations of the socialist market economy in the primary stage of socialism. To analyze the interest relations, we must start from analyzing these relations. The reasons are as follows:

First, the development of human society is a natural historical process, during which, commodity (market) economy is an insurmountable stage. For a new-born socialist country that is economically backward to arrive the future society predicted by Marx, its commodity (market) economy must first become fully developed. That human society is a natural historical process is an important view of historical materialism. It indicates that, human society is a part of the natural world; the development of society is a material, objective natural historical process independent of man's will, and in general the law of social development is subject to the law of historical development of nature. In *Grundrisse*, Marx draws a picture of the third great stage of human society as a natural historical course: "Relations of personal dependence (entirely spontaneous at the outset) are the first social forms, in which human productive capacity develops only to a slight extent and at isolated points. Personal independence founded on objective [sachlicher] dependence is the second great form, in which a system of general social metabolism, of universal relations, of all-round needs and universal capacities is formed for the first time. Free individuality, based on the universal development of individuals and on their subordination of their communal, social productivity as their social wealth, is the third stage. The second stage creates the conditions for the third. "① From this statement we can see that, the first form, "Relations of personal dependence" is actually the character of natural economic society. The second form, "Personal independence founded on objective dependence" is actually the character of commodity (market) economic society. And the third stage, "free individuality" is the character of the society where commodity (market) economy disappear, also known as product economic society. The development of human society from natural economy to fully developed commodity (market) economy and finally to the society without commodity (market), is a real, objective natural historical process independent of man's will.

According to Marxist five formations of social development, i. e. , primitive society, slave society, feudal society, capitalist society and communist society, the period of natural economy exist in pre-capitalist societies, including primitive society, slave society and feudal society. Commodity (market) economy stage is a capitalist society, after it is communist society. Marx initially predicted that socialism would be built up on the basis of highly developed capitalist commodity (market), and therefore, as the first stage of communism, there would be no commodity, market and currency. But in reality, the socialist societies were all established in countries with underdeveloped commodity economy and productive forces. Since social development is a natural historical process, the second stage of the second social formation of human society is also an inevitable natural historical stage, which must go through full development of commodity (market) economy. Commodity (market) economy is a natural historical process that cannot be skipped over in socialist development in reality.

Second, labor is the most basic human material practice, so relation of labor exchange occurred in this process is the most basic material practice. In a commodity (market) society, the relation of commodity (market) economy itself represents the most important relation of labor exchange, i. e. , the most basic social economic relation. In a developed commodity (market) economy, the exchange of social labor has to be carried out through the form of abstract and indirect socially necessary labor, that is, value. Only after the labor of different natures has been

---

① *Collected Works of Marx and Engels*, vol. 46a, People's Publishing House, 1979, p. 104.

transformed into socially necessary labor that is abstract and changeable in quantity in the market, can the relations among all social labor be realized. With the development of commodity (market) economy, this indirect relation of labor exchange gradually extends to all areas of social and economic life, and permeates through, covers and influences all economic relations and phenomena in the society as a whole, forming a huge and all-penetrating network of commodity (market) economic relations. Commodity (market) economic relations reflect the most important and basic economic relations in the society of commodity (market) economy. The commodity (market) economy in the primary stage of socialism under the condition of public ownership as the mainstay reflects the most basic exchange form of labor activities in this stage, and therefore constitutes its most basic and important economic relations. So the research of interest relations in the primary stage of socialism should start from the analysis of its economic relations.

From where then, should we start to understand the relations of commodity (market) economic relations in the primary stage of socialism? In other words, where is the logical starting point of the relations of socialist market economy in this stage? The answer is the category of labor. This is because: First of all, labor is the beginning of the history of human society and the relation of labor activities is the starting point and core of other human social relations, and the category of labor is the logical starting point of the theoretical system of historical materialism. For social organism, the practice of human labor is not only the decisive force promoting its generation, but also the foundation for its existence and development. In labor, the most initial and most basic social practice, and all the buds of future development of social organisms were conceived. The social form of labor and their social relations formed in labor are the starting point and core that determines people's other social activities. Labor combines with means of production through certain social forms, which gives rise to the basic economic relations of society. Human relations formed in labor are the most basic social relations that directly determine the interest relations and contradiction of humankind. Engels pointed out that Marx's brand new worldview finds that " key to the understanding of the whole history of society lies in the history of the development of labor. "①

Secondly, the understanding of the nature and characteristics of labor in the primary stage of socialism is the key and entry to the understanding of basic economic and interest relations in this stage. It is usually believed that the oldsocial division of labor is the precondition and private ownership is the direct reason for commodity production. Under certain economic conditions, the emergence of old social division of labor naturally caused the separation of total social labor into individual labor and social labor, along with it the economic differences and contradictions among producers, as well as their economic independence to a certain degree. This provided the most basic prerequisite for the generation of commodity (market) economy. Marx points out explicitly that commodity production is not direct social production, nor the outcome of the unity in which within itself division of labor is made that "transforming individual products or activities into exchange value. "② And he also said that the private nature of individual production for value of exchange itself is the outcome of history. In other words, this individual isolation and his independence in a single point, is constrained by division of labor.

It is apparent that the individualization and independence of production caused by the old social division of labor is the most general premise for commodity production and the market economy. Social division of labor is necessarily associated with certain forms of ownership, and the consequent separation of total social labor is necessarily to obtain a certain economic form of ownership relation. Private ownership is but a form of ownership adopted by the old social division of labor that is manifested as the opposing separation of labor and takes the form of private labor, and thus cuts its direct links with total social labor. As a result, opposing private producers have to integrate their private labor into total social labor through the form of commodity. From this we can see that, commodity production, even market economy, is not unique to the society of private ownership, because the existence of old social division of labor is an important prerequisite for commodity production. China has established an economic pattern with public ownership as the mainstay and the coexistence of

---

① *Selected Works of Marx and Engels*, vol. 4. People's Publishing House, 1995, p. 258.

② *Collected Works of Marx and Engels*, vol. 46a, People's Publishing House, 1979, p. 105

various forms of ownership. Under this specific historical condition, the examination of the particularity of the economic relations and interest relations of the commodity (market) economy in the primary stage of socialism, it is necessary to begin with examining the changes in labor and labor division in this stage that distinguish them from those in the class exploiting society. In other words, we must, in the first place, examine the particularity of labor and division of labor in the primary stage of socialism, which is the prerequisite for the analysis of its particularity of socialist commodity (market) economy.

Thirdly, the twofold character of labor is root cause for the development and change of basic commodity (market) relations, so the understanding of twofold character of labor in the primary stage of socialism is the hub for understanding the basic economic and interest relations in the primary stage of socialism. Marx said: that the two-fold character of the labor "is the pivot on which a clear comprehension of Political Economy turns. "[1] In a sense, the twofold character of labor is also the key to understanding the inherent contradictions of commodity economy. Therefore, to analyze the basic economic relations and then to understand the interest relations in the primary stage of socialism, we must begin with the understanding of the particularity of the twofold character in the primary stage of socialism.

Fourthly, in a society of commodity (market) economy, on the basis of certain relations of production, the differences in quality and quantity of labor determine the interest differences among the people in the commodity (market) economic relations, and the social form of labor determines the distribution form and interest relations in the primary stage of socialism. In the commodity (market) economy, labor of different natures must be quantized with the same standard, and then through market relations and market competition mechanism to achieve equal quantity exchange of labor. That means, for people's labor activities to be exchanged and their economic interests to be realized through commodity exchange, it must form the relations of equal quantity through market competition and the measurement of the common social standard of socially necessary labor time. In a society of commodity (market) economy, the interest relations among the people are directly determined by the differences in the quality and quantity of labor under the condition of certain relations of

---

[1] *Collected Works of Marx and Engels*, vol. 23, People's Publishing House, 1972, p. 55.

production. The difference in quality of labor refer to the specific differences of labor forms, such as mental labor and manual labor; while the difference in quantity refers to the difference of socially necessary labor time in the production of the same kind of products. In the commodity (market) economic relations, only after they have been translated into the labor of different quantity through the form of value (socially necessary labor time) can labor of different qualities be exchanged and compared in the market and show the differences of people's economic interests. In short, the differences of quality and quantity of labor determine people's income differences and thus the interest differences in the commodity (market) economy, which constitute the basic social and economic relations Interest relations mean interest differences, so the discussion of interest relations means the discussion of interest differences. When examining the differences of interests and their causes, we cannot limit ourselves in the study of the qualitative and quantitative differences of labor, but must take into account the form of implementation of labor activities combined with certain means of production, that is, the decisive influence of the social forms of labor on the interest differences and interest relations. For example, in the labor form of the primitive community, the means of production were commonly owned and people worked together. This kind of social labor determines that the fundamental interests among the people are identical, and people consumed together and there was no class difference. In form of social labor of slave or employment nature, the distribution of economic interests is according to the real differences in quality or quantity of labor, but to the differences of ownership of means of production, which determines that people's interest relations are fundamentally opposed to each other. In the primary stage of socialism, the establishment of ownership relation with public ownership as the mainstay and new form of labor has provided conditions for the equal exchange of labor on the basis of real differences of quality and quantity; and the commodity (market) economy provides the necessary economic environments for the translation, comparison and equal exchange of labor of different quantity in the market. From this we can see that, the differences of labor in quality and quantity and the realization form of labor activities constitute a set of decisive factors causing interest differences; and the labor exchange activities in the commodity (market) economy in the primary stage of socialism constitute the most important economic relation of interest distribution in this stage. To examine the economic and interest relations in the primary stage of socialism, we must begin with the discussion of its differences in labor and its social realization form.

Labor is a basic category of historical materialism and also a category with it we begin the study ofthe relations of commodity (market) economy in the primary stage of socialism. But this doesn't mean that labor is not influenced by other social factors. In fact, there are two basic relations in human labor activities, one is the relation of division of labor between men, i. e. , social division of labor; the other is the combined relations between labor and labor conditions, i. e. , relations of ownership. In addition to the determinant factor of development of productive forces, we should also understand the nature of labor and its development from the perspective of relations between division of labor and ownership relations, because social division of labor determines ownership relations that in turn influence and condition the development of social division; and social division of labor and the ownership relations are important factors influencing the nature and development of labor. Now we have found a good entry into the analysis and understanding of the interest relations in the primary stage of socialism: the economic relations of commodity (market) economy in the primary stage of socialism is the realistic starting point of analyzing the interest relations in this stage; the category of its labor is a category with it we begin the study of its commodity (market) economic relations; And its labor, social division of labor and ownership relations is the most basic economic categories on which we base our study of the market economy along with its basic relations and its interest relations as well.

II. The Social Division of Labor and the Inherent Separation of Labor in the Primary Stage of Socialism

To study labor in the primary stage of socialism, we must first of all study its social division of labor and the inherent separation of labor. In the past, people wrongly believed that, since public ownership and planned economy were the main characters of socialism, and people "commonly possess" the means of production, worked together and made distribution according to work, social labor is naturally direct labor without inherent separation. This understanding misguided people's correct analysis of interest relations among the people in the primary stage of socialism. Therefore, we should have a correct understanding of not only socialist labor, but more importantly, of the labor in the primary stage of socialism. For, only after recognizing the nature and characteristics of the labor in this stage, can we have an in-depth understanding of its relations of the commodity (market) economy and then a correct analysis of its interest relations. Generally speaking, four basic conditions determine the specific nature and characteristics of labor: (1) forms of social division of labor; (2) form of combination between labor and production; (3) form of exchange of labor activities, namely, form of realization of labor products; and (4) material conditions upon which labor is conducted. Among which, on the premise of social and material conditions under which labor can be made, social division of labor is the most direct and fundamental factor affecting social labor and its characteristics. So, the understanding of the labor in the primary stage of socialism concerns first of all its social division of labor.

1. The nature and characteristics of social division of labor in the primary stage of socialism

Social division of labor is a social activity. It is the most basic form of organization of labor activities, which makes social activities, labor activities in particular, become distinctive and relatively independent to each other. So, social division refers, first of all, the division of labor, next to which are the social division in forms of other social activities based on labor, including all economic, political, cultural activities. In its course of development, social division of labor takes the following four forms: (1) The natural division of labor in the primitive society based on geographical and physiological conditions; (2) The natural or old division of labor that emerged in the late stage of primitive society and gradually developed and matured in the slave society, feudal society and capitalist society; (3) The transitional division of labor from the old to the new mode that formed with the establishment of the socialist system; (4) The conscious division of labor in communist society in the future, that is, the new division of labor.

So far, the greatest impact on the development of human civilization isthe old natural division of labor. It is a social activity that has produced and will continue to have extremely profound influence on all areas of social life of human society, including economic life, political life, spiritual life. It contains two aspects: First, the division of labor itself, that is, the total social labor is divided into relatively independent sectors and professions; Second, the division of laborers, that is, all laborers are separately fixed in different sectors and professions of labor. The nature of the old natural division of labor division is the fixation of labor division forcing individuals into a long-term fixed labor or work and not to shit to other works. Naturalness of division of labor, fixation of career and coercion upon laborers that make laborers to succumb to labor and things: these are the characteristics of old social division of labor.

Marx saw the old division of labor as the basic cause of existing social relations and social contradictions. He wrote in *The German Ideology*: "The division of labor implies from the outset the division of the conditions of labor, of tools and materials, and thus the splitting-up of accumulated capital among different owners, and thus, also, the division between capital and labor, and the different forms of property itself. "① "With the division of labor... all these contradictions are implicit. "② When analyzing relations among consciousness, state of society and the productive forces, he pointed out: "The only possibility of their not coming into contradiction lies in the negation in its turn of the division of labor. " The old natural division of labor is an important condition for the inherent separation and contradictions, the basic cause for the appearance of diametrically opposed economic interest groups and class antagonisms, and the fundamental cause for interest differences and contradictions in class society. It is clear that, to study social interest relations, we must study the social division of labor.

However, the old natural division of labor isjust one stage and one historical form of the development of social division of labor, rather than an eternal or absolute form. With the development of social productive forces, this old form is sure to be replaced by new one. Capitalist industrial production on the one hand has created the highest form of the old division of labor, on the other has provided material and technological precondition and basis for the elimination of it. The new division of labor is the communist voluntary division of labor repeatedly mentioned by Marx and Engels. It will eliminate the fixation, naturalness and coercion upon laborers and will certainly contribute to the overall development of man and society. It is a long transition process from the old to the new division of labor, and

---

① *Selected Works of Marx and Engels*, vol. 1, People's Publishing House, 1995, p. 127

② *Ibid*, p. 83

socialism is just the process. The primary stage of socialism is a period in which the old natural social division of labor has just begun to transit but still has its life while the new one is in the shaping. So the social division of labor in the stage has both the characteristics of the old one and new one, with the characteristics of the old one more distinctive. China today is just in this stage, where the new division of labor began to form but the influence of the old division has a role and influence in a rather broad scope. This is manifested in the following aspects:

(1) The nature of fixation of profession of the old social division of labor still remains in the primary stage of socialism. Due to the limitations in technological development, individuals in this stage are not yet all-round developed, and are relatively fixed to their different spheres, occupations or positions, with their freedom in choice of profession being greatly restricted.

(2) The social division of labor in the primary stage of socialism still has a considerable degree of naturalness. The highly voluntary division of labor in communist society is a division voluntarily made and regulated in a planned way through community of free individuals, which is impossible to achieve in the present stage.

(3) Social division in the primary stage of socialism still has some coercive nature. This is because its productive forces are not yet fully developed, the needs of the people cannot be fully met; labor essentially is still the means of living for the people; and the fixation and naturalness of social division cannot allow laborers to choose their profession according to their preference or strong points.

(4) The social division of labor in the primary stage of socialism retains not only some nature but also some specific content and forms of the old one, such as differences between urban and rural areas, between workers and farmers, between mental and manual labor, etc.

It isin this sense we say that the social division of labor is a division with the birthmark of the old society. But it is not a complete old division, because it contains many new elements and new features of the new division as follows:

(1) Fundamentally speaking, the social division of labor bases itself on the economic relation with public ownership as the mainstay and other sectors of the economy developing side by side. This basic economic system endows the social division with features different from the old one. The old social division of labor is the historical premise of the emergence of private

ownership, which in turn strengths the naturalness, fixation and coercion on laborers. The division of labor in the primary stage of socialism, by contrast, is associated with the basic social system of public ownership, and its features come from this system. Under the condition in the primary stage of socialism with public ownership as the mainstay, whether it is state-owned economy, collective economy, or other sectors of the economy containing certain elements public ownership, the workers commonly own means of production in a certain degree, and make reasonable distribution in line with the principle of distribution according to his work, in addition to some relations of joint labor between different sectors of production and different professions. Under these circumstances, the social division of labor in this stage begins to obtain some characteristics of voluntary nature of joint-labor. At the same time, thanks to the restraints of the fundamental system of socialism, the role of public ownership as the mainstay, the division of labor of the workers in the non-public sectors of the economy is not completely the same as the old division of labor.

(2) The division of labor in the primary stage of socialism already has some characteristics of planned distribution, conscious regulation and voluntary subordination. The division of labor in this stage to some degree and in certain scope is related to public ownership, so workers in this sector have begun to become masters of production; meanwhile, the mainstay of public ownership make it possible for the state to regulate the social division of labor in other sectors of the economy. So the society as a whole can consciously grasp the laws of social division, restrict its naturalness and coercion to a certain degree while enhance its consciousness and voluntariness, and therefore combine the requirements of society with personal willingness. This in a certain scope can make social division in a more planned and reasonable way, so as to provide possibility for giving full play to individual strengths and mobilizing everyone's enthusiasm and creativity.

(3) In general, the social division of labor in the primary stage of socialism doesn't have the nature of social antagonism featuring the old one. Private ownership makes the individuals from different sectors and spheres be in interest contradictions. By contrast, the ownership relations in the primary stage of socialism with public ownership as the mainstay makes the different kinds of social division of labor form an integrated whole; although there are differences and contradictions between different

kinds of labor and subjects, in the whole they are contradictions on the basis of identical interests rather than class antagonism that has been eliminated in this stage. Even the division of labor in the non-public sectors, on the whole, doesn't have the class antagonism caused by the old one.

(4) In the primary stage of socialism, there are two forms of division of labor: on the one hand there is the new emerging division of socialist nature, on the other there is the natural division of labor left by the old society; on the one hand it begins to have the characteristics of consciousness, voluntariness and planned nature, on the other it retains the deep birthmark of the naturalness, coercion and blindness of the old one.

2. The influence of social division of labor in the primary stage of socialism on its labor

Engels believed that "The basic form of all production hitherto has been the division of labor."[1] Division of labor is actually the basic form of human labor activities, the development of which has a fundamental influence on the characteristics of labor. In the following part, we'll first examine historically the influence of division of labor on labor in general, and then its influence on labor in the primary stage of socialism in particular.

The earliest natural division of labor in the primitive society was in accordance with the natural primitive economy, which determines that the labor of each member was directly social labor, and labor itself was not necessary to be divided into individual labor and social labor, or concrete labor and abstract labor. In the late primitive society, the natural division of labor began and went through three major changes, which promoted the development of social production and the emergence of private economy and commodity exchange, and therefore caused the profound and huge change of social structure. This brought about the internal separation of labor and the appearance of private labor of commodity producers who obtained value through exchange. Therefore, social labor with single and direct social nature began to split into concrete labor and abstract labor with a characteristic of separation. The old division of labor caused further

---

① *Selected Works of Marx and Engels*, vol. 3, People's Publishing House, 1995, p. 640

specialization, independence and separation of labor, and strengthened the independence of the private laborers, so that laborers and means of production further separated and laborers began to become the slaves of labor, and the total social labor of society increasingly separated into private labor opposed to each other. The development of productive forces and the private ownership brought about by the old division of labor made the characteristics of internal separation and antagonism of labor gain a fully mature form, which finally took the form of external public antagonism: the antagonism between private labor and social labor, between laborers and exploiters and between "dead" labor and "living" labor, meaning the separation and antagonism of labor took the form of class antagonism. With the development of social production, especially in the period of socialized production in the highly developed capitalist market economy, the division of social labor further developed, causing the constant change of nature and characteristics of labor.

Next, we'll analyze the change of nature and characteristics brought by the division of labor in the primary stage of socialism in a comparative way by combining the analysis of changes in social division of labor brought about by the development of capitalist market economy.

(1) *The differentiation and contradiction of labor within society and within productive establishment*

Engels pointed out, " . . . the division of labor has been, on the one hand, within society as a whole, and on the other, within each separate productive establishment. " [1] In other words, social labor was divided into numerous relatively independent individual labors and concrete labors, each producing different products and independent producers necessarily carrying out exchange of labor activities. In private ownership society, division within society is a natural and blind division of labor within society. The division of social labor in a productive establishment " is division of labor in the manufacture of a commodity, hence not division of labor in society but social division of labor within one and the same workshop, " [2] meaning the division of labor is at the micro-level in different organizations and sectors of industry. This kind of division didn't

---

[1] *Selected Works of Marx and Engels*, vol. 3, People's Publishing House, 1995, p. 640.

[2] *Collected Works of Marx and Engels*, vol. 47, People's Publishing House, 1979, p. 305.

appear until the period of capitalist manual workshop. It is a conscious division of labor, which incorporates every specific production process into a planned and scientific way, organically gathering different laborers into one productive establishment as a total labor to use. Within the productive establishment, the exchange of labor activities takes a direct form, and the division of labor is a conscious, scientific and planned one, directly manifesting itself as total social labor. Division of labor within society is the premise of the division within the productive establishment, and the two are consistent. But in the condition of private ownership, they are separated: division of labor within society makes labor have the characteristics of separation and antagonism, while division of labor within the productive establishment makes division of labor have the characteristics of consistence and directness. This kind of contradictions and conflicts reflect the different development trend of the nature of labor.

Capitalist industrial productionhas created the material and technological conditions that negate the separation of labor. The conscious division of labor within the productive establishment is a kind of negative force against the blind and natural division of labor in society. Under private ownership, the contradiction between the division of labor within society and that within the productive establishment is insurmountable, so is the separation caused by it. On the other hand, the division of labor within the productive establishment in capitalist society continuously gives birth to elements negating the blindness of division of labor and that eliminate antagonism of labor.

Specifically in China, with the establishment of the socialist system and economic base with public ownership as the mainstay, it is possible to raise the conscious division of labor within the productive establishment to the equal level of division of the whole society and make it develop gradually toward a conscious one, thus creating conditions for the eventual elimination of labor separation. But due to the limitations productive force level in the primary stage of socialism, the not fully mature of public ownership and the existence of other forms of ownership, the conscious division of labor within productive establishment cannot replace the natural division of labor in society; at the same time, the division of labor within the productive establishment is not yet perfect or fully developed, it cannot reach the level of conscious division of the total labor of the whole society. This nature and state of division of labor in the primary stage of socialism determines that, although it has gotten rid of the inherent antagonistic nature of labor, it still has the nature of inherent separation to a certain degree, and the relative independence of individual labor must be recognized.

(2) *The Separation and contradiction between division of laborers and labor*

The division of laborers refers to the specialty and fixation of the occupation of laborers; while division of labor refers to the differentiation and independence of labor itself, that is, labor is divided into different sectors and varieties. Before the appearanceof capitalist industrial machines, the division of laborers was consistent with the division of labor, with the division of laborers being subject to labor itself and labor of man subject to the domination of things. So to laborers, labor was strongly coercive. With the emergence of the capitalist large-scale machine industry, the division of laborers and division of labor showed a trend of separating from and opposing to each other. In the handicraft labor, division of labor was surely consistent with the division of laborers and laborers and labor activity firmly fixed together. But after the emergence of large-scale machine industry, the division of labor is not necessarily accompanied by a division of laborers. With the development of production technology, more and more laborers break free from the fixed division of labor. In other words, the more developed the division of labor, the more possible for laborers to free themselves from fixed division to continuously improve their labor consciousness and autonomy, thus to reduce and eventually eliminate the coercive nature of labor. When social division of labor develop into a higher form, people will be consciously rather than coercively subject to the division of labor, and the division of laborers will no longer be subject to the division of labor. The development of separation between division of labor and division of laborers is conducive to the emancipation of labor and the new change of the nature of labor. The great development of capitalist production has provided the material premise for the liberation of laborers from the fixation of occupation. However, the capitalist employment system coercively ties the laborers who want to break the shackles firmly to chain of wage-labor, giving birth to the division of labor and division of laborers, thus hindering the trend and speed of the separation between the division of labor and division of laborers.

Socialist system provides the decisive conditions for the liberation of laborers from fixed division of labor. However, because China's socialist system was established on the basis of relatively backward productive forces, laborers are to some extent still fixed on professional occupations. In the primary stage of socialism in China, the separation between the division of labor and division of laborers is not developed yet; so, although labor in this stage begins to gain the characteristics of self-labor, it is not completely independent labor with a characteristics of fixation and means of living.

(3) *Differences and contradictions between old and new division of labor*

The above mentioned two inherent contradictions in division of labor gradually led to the change in the nature of the division of labor itself, which results in the differences and contradictions between the old natural division of labor and the elements of the new voluntary division of labor. The new division of labor makes the planned and conscious division of labor within a establishment gradually improved and upgrade to the level of scientific and conscious division of the whole society. New division of labor makes laborers do not necessarily attach to the division of labor itself, but rather break free from it. As a result, the inherent separation and confrontation of labor is eliminated, making labor becoming direct social labor and free activities of the subject that dominate all natural forces. ①Capitalist socialized production, though providing affluent material conditions for a wide range of new division of labor, the capitalist system restricts and hinders the development of new division of labor and maintains its inherent separation.

The establishment ofsocialist system has paved the way for the development of new division of labor, and to some extent, made the rational, scientific and conscious division of labor within the establishments begin to expand to the whole society and rise to a rational level, so that laborers have begun to get rid of the restraints of the old fixed division of labor, which have improved the directness of social labor and eliminated the fundamental antagonistic nature of inherent separation. However, the primary stage of socialism is a special stage, during which new elements of division of labor constantly grow up while the elements of the old division of labor gradually are transforming. That is to say, on one hand the old division of labor will gradually be replaced by

---

① *Collected Works of Marx and Engels*, vol. 46b, People's Publishing House, 1980, p. 113.

the new one, but on the other, the old one is still extremely powerful and stubbornly playing a role in many aspects of social life. So the division of labor in the primary stage of socialism is still a transitional one from the natural to the voluntary, therefore is not the new division in the true sense. This division, although with some elements of the new one, still bears with it a lot of influence of the old one which will remain for a long time. Development of social division of labor determines the nature and characteristics of labor, and thus determines the nature and characteristics of economic relations and interest relations. Likewise, the division of labor in the primary stage of socialism that still maintains the characteristics of the old one fundamentally determines the existence of its inherent separation and contradictions: Between concrete labor and abstract labor, between individual (private) labor and social labor, and between labor for oneself and labor for the society. Under some conditions, it is possible that this separation and contradictions may develop into antagonism. On the other hand, the elements of new division of labor in this stage make it possible, under ordinary conditions, to get rid of the antagonistic nature of the labor while maintain some characteristics of non-antagonistic separation.

3. Other factors affecting labor in the primary stage of socialism

After discussing theinfluence of the division of labor, next we will examine the influence of other factors on labor in the primary stage of socialism.

(1) *The influence of way of combination between laborers and means of production on labor.*

The combination between laborers and working conditions such as instruments, materials, objects, etc. , is the most basic premise for labor to be conducted. The way of combination between labor and means of production further determines the nature of labor. The establishment of economic system in the primary stage of socialism with public ownership as the mainstay has fundamentally changed the phenomenon in the capitalist private ownershipthat social labor and production are separated, making labor no longer has the nature of wage labor. In state-owned enterprises, workers are no longer isolated individuals but are members of a joint labor integrated with means of production of public ownership, with the purposes of individual laborers are consistent fundamentally with the purpose of production and needs of the whole society. But the diversity of forms of ownership leads to the diverse forms of combination between laborers and means of production. Within the state-owned enterprises, labor manifests itself in three levels: First, the state owns the means of production in behalf of the people, which determines that the united workers have a certain degree of directness of labor; Second, each enterprise is a relatively independent entity of operation and production, reflecting the relative separation between right of ownership and operation, which determines that joint labor in the enterprises has a nature of local labor; Third, individual laborers in the enterprises are both joint laborers and individual laborers for the state, the purpose of whose labor is both for the state and the collectives, and first of all is for the living of individuals. Therefore, the labor of the laborers in state-owned enterprises is also individual labor with a certain degree of individual labor nature. It is more so with the laborers in other forms of public-owned enterprises and other enterprises, especially private enterprises.

(2) *The exchange form of labor activity, including the exchange and distribution ways of labor products, has important influence on labor.*

Exchange of labor activity is a direct manifestation of the social division of labor and any labor must include the exchange of labor activity. Labor exchange activity comprises the exchange of labor activity itself and the exchange of the results of labor. The exchange of labor activity itself determines the exchange of labor products, which in turn determines its distribution. Labor exchange has two basic forms. One is direct exchange. For example, in a society of product economy, labor has a direct social nature with individual concrete labor directly combined into the social labor in the joint labor. Another is indirect labor exchange. For example, the labor in commodity (market) economy, individual and concrete labor still doesn't have the nature of direct social nature, which must be transformed into socially necessary labor and then shows the nature and level of social labor through exchange. Commodity exchange is only one form of the exchanges of labor activity, during which, labor activity must takes an intermediary form of transition, that is, the form of value, so the activity of labor exchange is carried out indirectly. Thus, in the commodity (market) economy, the exchange form of the result of human labor activities, namely, the exchange of labor product, must also takes the form of commodity exchange. The results of the exchange of labor activity determines the distribution of labor products. The distribution form of labor products also has two basic forms: First is direct distribution, namely, the products directly enter into distribution without the transition of commodity exchange; Second is indirect distribution, that is, individual labor products can only be consumed after they gain value and social nature. The indirectness of the exchange of labor activity and distribution of labor products in turn influence the nature of labor, so that individual labor can only gain social nature through exchange, which also makes labor be further dualized into concrete labor and abstract labor that deepens the inherent separation of labor. Under the conditions in the primary stage of socialism, due to the existence of different forms of ownership and relatively independent economic entities within the public sector, labor products still cannot directly enter into distribution, which must be realized through commodity exchange; this indirect labor activity and labor products in turn determines the duality of the social nature and individual nature of labor in this stage.

(3) *The nature and characteristics of labor, in the final analysis, is determined by social material conditions.*

Under the specific conditions in the primary stage of socialism, the productive forces are still not fully developed, nor can the products fully meet people's needs, in addition to the limitations of their moral level, people still take their labor ability as their natural privilege and means of living, so labor in this stage still has the nature of individual means of living.

The above analysis of socialist division of labor and its nature show that: labor in the primary stage of socialism is labor of non-class antagonistic nature without class exploitation, so it already has some characteristics of joint labor, voluntary labor and direct social labor. But on the other hand, labor in this stage still has the nature of individual (private) labor, labor for individual living and indirect labor, and separation of non-antagonism and inherent contradictions, which in certain conditions may lead to confrontation.

The correct understanding of these basic characteristics of labor in the primary stage of socialism is the starting point to recognize the basic economic and interest relations. Its inherent separation and contradictions determines the inherent differences and contradictions of its basic economic and interest relations.

III. The Inherent Contradictions of Ownership of Means of Production in the Primary Stage of Socialism

The nature and characteristics of social division of labor, the diverse forms of ownership of means of production and products, namely, the nature and forms of ownership relations, are the most important preconditions that determine the existence and development of economy, therefore, are the most important conditions determining the economic and interest relations in this stage. We can start from analyzing the influence of inherent separation of its labor on its ownership relations to further analyze the influence of these relations on its economic and interest relations.

1. The ownership relations in the primary stage of socialism

Public ownership as the mainstay with diverse forms of ownership developing side by side is the basic economic system in the primary stage of socialism in China. The nature of socialism and China's specific national conditions determines that, there are not only state-owned and collectively owned economies but also the state-owned and collective elements in the mixed economy. Non-public sectors of the economy, including individual economy, private economy and the individual and private components in the mixed economy, is an important part of China's socialist market economy. This complex pattern of diverse forms of ownership determines the diversity and complexity of its basic economic and interest relations in this stage.

The relationship ofpublic ownership in the primary stage of socialism is an ownership in which means of production does not belong to private individuals, but to the public that combining laborers with means of production. It essentially is a kind of social ownership. The state-owned form of means of production is a form of realizing public ownership and the most important and most concentrated manifestation of public ownership in the primary stage of socialism. It embodies the dominant relations in the market economy in this stage. According to the classical writers of scientific socialism, socialist ownership relations, first of all, is a relation of the joint laborers' possession of means of production on the basis of capitalist large-scale socialized production; and secondly, the most important characteristics of socialist ownership relations is that means of production in the society are possessed by all the working people rather than by the individuals, and the fruits of production are shared by all workers based on the principle of distribution each according to his work. As Marx saw it, the standard identifying economic system in human history is the way of combination between the workers and means of production, that is, the social form of labor. ①The relation of combination between laborers and means of production is capitalist society is wage labor relation, namely, the capitalists own the means of production, therefore, also own the labor of the laborers. In socialist public ownership, especially under the condition of state-owned economy, the means of production are owned by all workers, and the fruits of labor are equally shared by them; so the relation of wage labor is replaced by joint labor. ②It is based on the above analysis that Marx and Engels argued that the basic form of socialist ownership should be the ownership in which the means of production "is converted into common property, into the property of all members of society."③ About the transitional form of socialist ownership, Marx and Engels argued that a socialist country can build its socialist ownership through forms of state ownership and cooperative ownership. ④From this we can see that, public ownership, common property, joint labor and the combination of laborers and means of production on the basis of large-scale socialized production are seen by Marx and Engels as constituting the essence of ownership in future society. The public ownership in the primary stage of socialism represents the essential trend of socialist ownership and nature of fundamental socialist economic system.

But the realities of ownership in socialist countries are very different from that described by the founders of scientific socialism. Marx and Engels, based on the developed capitalist economy in the era of free competition, thought that the only way for socialist mode of production to replace capitalist mode of production is the ownership of means of production by all social members. However, the backward productive forces in China in the primary stage of socialism, the nature of its social

---

① See *Collected Works of Marx and Engels*, vol. 24, People's Publishing House, 1972, p. 44

② See *Collected Works of Marx and Engels*, vol. 16, People's Publishing House, 1964, p. 12.

③ *Selected Works of Marx and Engels*, vol. 1, People's Publishing House, 1995, p. 287.

④ See *Selected Works of Marx and Engels*, vol. 4. People's Publishing House, 1995, p. 499

division of labor and basic characters of its separation of labor, fundamentally determine that, in reality the ownership in China at the present stage cannot reach the level of complete public ownership, common property and joint labor. Our socialist system was established on the basis of backward social productive forces, which makes the backward of social division and labor separation more prominent, and determines the economic base with public ownership being the mainstay and diverse forms of ownership coexisting. Marx and Engels based their concept of socialist ownership on the conditions of highly developed productive forces and high socialization. In fact, when discussing socialist ownership, they just talked about it in a generic way, without distinguishing socialist ownership from communist ownership. In "Critique of the Gotha Program", Marx divides communism into two stages and points out that, in the first stage, "... in every respect, economically, morally, and intellectually, still stamped with the birthmarks of the old society from whose womb it emerges." Applying this idea of Marx in understanding the ownership in the primary stage of socialism, we can make a conclusion that the ownership in this stage is stamped with the birthmarks of the old society. And furthermore, we can conclude as follows:

(1) Communist ownership is a public ownership established on the basis of large-scale socialized production and associated with new mode of division of labor and joint labor. In contrast, socialist ownership in the primary stage of socialism is an ownership established on the basis of relatively socialized productive forces and has the characteristics of division and separation of labor in this stage, and therefore is not fully mature.

(2) Communist ownership is a single ownership publicly possessed by the whole society, that is to say, public ownership is the only form of ownership. In contrast, the pattern of ownership in the primary stage of socialism shows a characteristics of complexity and diversity, in which public ownership is the mainstay and diverse forms of ownership coexist and develop side by side, and the public ownership itself has a multiple forms of realization, including state-owned, collective owned and mixed-owned, and the non-public sectors of the economy are important components.

(3) Within the ownership relations of communism, the four aspects of possession, ownership, access and use of means of production by all members of society are for the interests of all members, which are basically identical in terms of either the four aspects or the relations

between the interests of whole society and the interests of individuals and special groups. Things are different within the ownership relations in the primary stage of socialism. In the public sector of the economy in this stage, on the one hand, the means of production owned and dominated by and serve the interests of all workers, and the rights to ownership and operation derived from them also belong to the workers, so their fundamental interests are the identical. On the other hand, however, due to the separation of labor in this stage, different laborers and work units are relatively independent, which fundamentally determines that the work units that to some extent have the rights of control and use to the means of production own some part of labor products, which further determines the enterprises (collectives) have a certain degree of autonomy in operation, shoulder some responsibilities while sharing certain economic interests. All this gives birth to the certain degree of separation of ownership rights from management rights. That means that in the primary stage of socialism, there are certain right sharing and interest sharing in the ownership and management of means of production, as well as certain contradictions and separation between private interests on the one side and social interests and collective interests on the other side that is determined by the particularity of labor in this stage.

All the characters mentioned above determine the basic economic relations and interest relations in the primary stage of socialism.

2. The inherent contradictions within socialist public ownership

In the primary stage of socialism in China, public ownership of means of production determines that the fundamental interests of the people are identical, which thereby gets rid of class contradiction in its economic relations. Can we say that there is no contradiction within the public ownership in the primary stage of socialism? The answer is no.

Seeing from the historical causes for the formation of the private ownership of means of production, we can find that, in addition to the ultimate decisive condition of productive forces, social division of labor and the nature of labor determined by it is the fundamental cause of the formation of private ownership. Essentially speaking, it is the social division of labor, and the character determined by this division, i. e. , labor is separated into independent private labor, that determines the nature and form of private ownership. To some extent, social division of labor in the primary stage of socialism still has the marks of old division of labor; meanwhile there are also a lot of remnants of the old division of labor in this stage. These determine that labor in the primary stage of socialism has the characteristics of double separations of both individual labor and social labor, which inevitably determines that there are some inherent contradictions within its public ownership. Division of labor in the primary stage of socialism, along with the separation determined by it, is the key to understanding the inherent contradiction within its public ownership. On the one hand, old social division of labor makes production units in the different sectors, and the different departments and laborers in the same production unit form comprehensive social relationships, constituting the total social labor; on the other hand, it divides the total social labor into independent units and individual laborers, leading to the one-sidedness of their activity forms, the narrowness of their activity scope and fixation, singularity and specialty of their profession. The separated and independent units and individuals can only establish connections through intermediaries such as market exchange. Hence come out the inherent contradictions in the commodity production in general, that is, contradiction between the socialization of commodity production and the independency and specialty of specific producers (units) . Essentially, socialist public ownership requires that all social members form a whole or collective joint labor body to control and regulate social or collective production in a planned way, in order to eliminate the separation or opposition caused by individual production in private ownership. That means that all social members can take part in the control and regulation of production through joint labor. In others words, every individual can get the status as one of the owners of public owned means of production. This is in accord with the requirements of overall and social nature of social development. However, there are still remnants and marks of the old division of labor in the primary stage of socialism, for laborers to participate in productive labor by using means of production, they must first of all become specialized shoulders of specific productive functions and form collaborative production bodies, such as enterprises, workshops, work sections, etc. So, although the public ownership in the primary stage of socialism overcomes the inherent contradictions in capitalist private ownership, it cannot completely overcome contradiction between the tendency of socialized production and the independence of specific production units, which is brought about by the marks and remnants of the old division of labor. In the joint labor relations of the public ownership in the primary stage of socialism where means of production are publicly owned, on the one hand, different collaborative production bodies and laborers are equal owners of means of production with the social nature of owners of public means of production; on the other hand, they have a relatively independent special social nature as different bodies and laborers. So the laborers (units) have both the status of public owners of means of production and relatively independent special laborers (units).

This duality of labor in the primary stage of socialism will inevitably find its expression in the state-owned sector of the public ownership. The social nature, autonomy and collaboration of labor in the primary stage of socialism are directly identical with the nature of the public ownership. This determines that, the laborers are masters in economic life and other social lives, labor itself has gotten rid of the wage labor and other form of slave labor, and the purpose and distribution of labor products are first of all in the interests of the people. On the other hand, labor in the primary stage of socialism is still people's means of living. The remuneration of a laborer depends on how much work he paid in the total social labor. This determines that in the primary stage of socialism a laborer has also the character of working for his own living. The duality of labor in this stage determines that, on the one hand, laborers have the status of masters and owners of means of production; on the other, they are also ordinary laborers who work for themselves. Therefore, in the state-owned sector of the public ownership in this stage, all workers have the dual status as co-owners of means of production and as laborers for their own living. This fully demonstrate it that the means of production is owned by all laborers and that the specific producers (units) are relative independent. This kind of inherent duality and contradictions, which also exist in the collectively owned sector of the public economy, is the pivot to understanding basic economic relations and interest relations. The duality of the public sector of the economy in the primary stage of socialism manifests itself as a series of contradictory poles: the laborers are both owners of the means of production and as workers for their own living; means of production and products owned by the working people or part of the working people, but not directly owned by any individual unconditionally in personal capacity; the division of labor leads to socialized production requiring joint labor of social members for production control and regulation that contribute to nature of public property to means of production, but on the other hand, it makes the relatively independent producers (units) can specifically control the means of production thus having the nature of relative independence. Therefore, a profound inherent contradiction exists in socialist public ownership, that is, contradiction between laborers and their combination with means of production. In other words, there is a contradiction between the public nature of laborers ' possession of means of production and the independence of different laborers and production units in the production and use of means of production.

In the level of productive forces in the primary stage of socialism, this contradiction is an objective and inevitable reality. This contradiction in fact reflects contradictions in the public ownership between the interests of the state (and the people) as a whole in the one side and the partial interests of the collective economy, the enterprises and the laborers in the other side, and the contradictions among the collectives, the enterprises and the individual laborers.

This is also true with the collective economy. State-owned economy is a manifestation of social joint labor, whereas the collective economy is the joint labor of a part of laborers. There are contradictions between the joint labor of all laborers and the joint labor of partial joint labor of the collective economy, contradictions among the partial labors in the collective economy themselves, contradictions between the partial joint labor and the labor of individual laborers, as well as the contradictions between the labors of individuals in the collective economy. All these contradictions reflect the interest relations between and among them.

3. Manifestations of the inherent contradictions in the public ownership in the primary stage of socialism

What are the manifestations of the internal contradictions in the public ownership in the primary stage of socialism? Marx and Engels believed that the proletariat, after having seized political power, cannot turn the means of production in the first instance into state property. [1]The establishment of state-owned economy as the form of public ownership is an inevitable road toward social ownership. Practice has proved that, on the one hand, state-owned economy is necessary in the initial period of

---

① See *Selected Works of Marx and Engels*, vol. 3. People's Publishing House, 1995, p. 630.

socialism; on the other hand, if there is no proper system, the state ownership of state sector of the economy will deepen, externalize even sharpen the internal contradictions of socialist ownership, reducing its role in facilitating the productive forces. So do the collective economy. The manifestations of the internal contradictions in the public ownership in the primary stage of socialism in reality are as follows:

First, it manifests themselves as separation and contradiction between the public ownership of means of production and individual ownership of means of consumption. In the state-owned sector of the state economy, all means of production take the state-owned form. In other words, an individual canonly own the means of production as a member in the joint labor and he has no right to own them by himself. But the livelihood nature of labor in the primary stage of socialism determines that he has to participate in product distribution with his natural privilege of "labor capability", manifesting in private ownership of means of consumption. Likewise, in collectively-owned sector of the public ownership, all means of production are collectively-owned, while an individual as one of the co-owners of the means of production owns only his means of consumption. This is similar to other forms of public ownership.

Second, they manifest themselves as the separation and contradiction between the status as common (or partially common) masters of means of production and the actual rights to production and management. In state-owned economy, the state as the representative of all the workers, exercises the rights and takes on the obligations of overall production management on behalf of the owners of the means of production; whereas the direct producers as the co-owners of means of production do not directly take part in the overall management but rather in a position of producers that are under the management of government officials and managerial personnel in the enterprises, who are not direct producers but managers. This gives rise to the contradictory relationship between the direct producers who are only owners of individual means of consumption in the one side, and the government officials and managerial personnel of the enterprises, who both are de facto "agents" and functionaries of the owners of the means of production. This contradictory relationships consist of two contradictions in it: One is the contradiction between state interests and collective interests in the one side and individual interests in the other side; The other contradiction is that between officials and managers as the agents of state or collective interests in the one side and the workers as subjects of individual interests on the other. Of course, the agents of state or collective interests also have their own private interests and demands, which is both consistent and in conflict with state interests; so do their personal interests and demands with the workers' interests. It is undeniable that, although government functionaries and managers of enterprises are exercisers of power and agents of the co-owners of the means of production representing the common interests of all working people, there are also contradictions between these agents and the co-owners. Behind these contradictions, there is the possibility of producing bureaucracy and corruptive elements. The rigid structures of ownership characterized by highly concentrated and administrative means of management established in many socialist countries in the past made the internal contradictions in state-owned economy sharpen to a severe level, seriously affecting enthusiasm of the laborers and hindering the development of productive forces.

Third, they manifest themselves as differences and contradictions between "big public" and "small public" and those among the "big publics and among the "small publics" . ①As to the specific structures of state ownership, Marx and Engels put forward many inspiring ideas in summarizing the experience of the Paris Commune. They believed that state owned enterprises have their particular characteristics and should be the association of workers' joint labor, which can operate independently under the leadership of the state. They also proposed specific ideas of rental and cooperative forms of operation for public ownership. ②Later on, Stalin clearly put forth point the view of collective ownership. Since in the primary stage of socialism the division of labor still has the residue and remnants of the old division of labor and labor itself has the characteristics of livelihood, we must recognize state-owned enterprises as relatively independent economic entities rather than taking it as the only public ownership. In fact, within the ownership system in this stage, there exist contradictions between state-owned sector of the economy in the one side and collectively-owned sector and public part of the mixed sector of the economy in the other side, that is, differences and contradictions between

①　See *Collected Works of Marx and Engels*, vol. 36, People's Publishing House, 1979, pp. 416—417.

②　See *Selected Works of Marx and Engels*, vol. 3. People's Publishing House, 1995, p. 217.

different forms of public ownership such as the "big public" of the whole society and "small public" of collectives; differences and contradictions within the public ownership between "big public" of the state and "small public" of the enterprises; and differences and contradictions among the "small publics" of enterprises within the state-owned economy and among "small publics" within the collectively-owned economy and that among the units within each "small public".

Fourth, they manifest themselves as separation and contradiction between ownership and management within public ownership and those between the state and enterprises as well as entrepreneurs. The inherent contradictions in the ownership in the primary stage of socialism is: the people cannot own or partially own the means of production in a direct way, but rather has to do it through the state and collectives as its representatives; while the state cannot either directly own or control the means of production belonging to the people, but rather entrust them to the enterprises through administrative organizations at all regions, departments or levels, so that the state-owned enterprises do not necessarily be directly managed by the state, but take a variety of operation forms.

4. Manifestations of contradictions between non-public sectors and public sector of the economy and contradictions within the non-public sectors of the economy

The non-public economy is an important part of the economy in the primary stage of socialism. It is different in nature from the public sector of the economy. In terms of ownership, it is mainly characterized by private or individual ownership, including the private sector, individual sector, as well as private and individual elements in the mixed economy, and foreign (private capital) ownership. In terms of distribution, it takes distribution according to capital or operation as the main forms. The nature and characteristics of ownership of the non-public sectors of the economy determine the complexity of the basic economic and interest relations in the primary stage of socialism, which is shown concretely as follows:

First, it is manifested as the contradiction between public and non-public sectors of the economy. Inthe present stage of socialism, our economic system takes public sector of the economy as the mainstay with diverse forms of non-public sectors developing side by side, and the non-public sectors being an important part. There must be some differences and contradictions between the non-public sectors and public sector of the economy, so do between their owners, operators and laborers.

Second, it is manifested as the contradiction within the non-public sectors of the economy. Non-public sectors include individual sector, private sector, individual and private components of the mixed economy. There are certain economic and interest relations among the non-public sectors of the economy.

Third, it is manifested as the differences and contradictions among the owners, managers and laborers in the non-public sectors of the economy.

IV. Contradictions in the Market Economy in the Primary Stage of Socialism

The above analyses of the division of labor and its inherent separation in the primary stage of socialism and contradictions of ownership in this stage have demonstrated the objective necessity of socialist market economy, and at the same time have provided the theoretical premise for the analysis of relations of the market economy and its interest relations. The relations of the market economy in the primary stage of socialism constitute the basic economic relations in this stage.

1. The historical position and essential characteristics of socialist market economy

Human history is bound to experience threesocial economic formations, i. e. , natural economy, commodity economy and product economy, in which commodity economy is only one stage of them. In the primitive community of the natural economy, the low level of productive forces determined that there was only spontaneous natural social division of labor rather than purposeful one. The corresponding relations of production were characterized by personal dependence. Primitive community was directly formed on basis of blood lineage, every members of the community to some extent is the property of the community and organ or limb subordinating to it. [1] All members of the community directly bonded and thus owned together social productive forces, that is, public ownership was

---

[1]   *Collected Works of Marx and Engels*, vol. 46a, People's Publishing House, 1979, p. 496.

adopted. Therefore, the specific labor made by individuals was also social labor. The purpose of production was to make things to meet the needs of the whole community, so intermediary between social production and social needs, and between labor exchange and labor distribution of laborers were unnecessary, and therefore, there was no separation or opposition between concrete labor and abstract labor, or between value and value in use. Marx regarded this natural economic formation characterized by personal dependence as primitive social formation.

With the development of productive forces within the natural economy, the old division of labor spontaneously appeared, along with it also the exchange and distribution of labor. As a result, unequal possession of labor and labor products emerged, which was manifestedin the relations of production as the private ownership of means of production. Therefore, labor was divided into relatively independent and dispersed commodity producers having their special private interests. Exchange of goods came into being, and the original direct social labor split into separate and mutually opposite labor of private labor and social labor, and concrete labor and abstract labor; consequently, the original direct social product became commodity with a contradictory nature of value and value in use; and the original social relations of direct interdependence between persons changed into material relations between persons and " social relations between things" . [1]Marx called this form of " personal independence based on objective dependence" of commodity economy the "second great form" of the development of human history. [2]

Money appeared with the development of commodity production and more extensive relationships were established between men. Against this background, commodity economy came into being. Capitalist mode of production is the highest and also last form of private ownership of commodity production. This makes separation between individuals and society that is characteristic of commodity production take a special historical manifestations, that is, the antagonistic relationships between the capitalists as individuals and the entire capitalist society, and between bourgeoisie and proletariat. This separation, on the one hand, makes the

---

[1] *Collected Works of Marx and Engels*, vol. 23, People's Publishing House, 1957, p. 89

[2] *Collected Works of Marx and Engels*, vol. 46a, People's Publishing House, 1979, p. 104.

interdependent commodity producers split into more independent producers, which further expands the separation of the individual and society; on the other hand, the individual capitalists, striving for profit, expand their accumulation, which objectively promotes the socialization of production and a more extensive social connections between persons and therefore has created necessary material conditions for the elimination of separation between individuals and society. The full development of productive forces in the separation of the individual and society provides sufficient conditions.

This will enable the elimination of the olddivision of labor, the materialized social relations, the integration of the separated individuals and society and the establishment of " community of free individuality" that commonly possess and control the socialized production, in which " the labor-power of all the different individuals is consciously applied as the combined labor-power of the community" . ①he separated labor will become direct social labor, and the antagonism between the private labor and social labor, between concrete labor and abstract labor, and between value in use and value will disappear. As a result, the commodity production will be gotten rid of, and commodity economy will be replaced by product economy. Marx calls this society as the " third stage" of human history. ②

For the emergence of commodity production and market economy, two conditions are closely integrated: social division of labor is the general premise while private ownership is the direct cause. In essence, the relations of ownership must keep in step with the stage and development of social division of labor, otherwise the conclusion will inevitably be one-sided. Marx believed that " The division of labor converts the product of labor into a commodity, and thereby makes necessary its further conversion into money. " The appearance of social division of labor will necessarily lead to commodity production and become the foundation and prerequisite of commodity production and market economy. " The various stages of development in the division of labor are just so many different forms of ownership. "

---

① *Collected Works of Marx and Engels*, vol. 23, People's Publishing House, 1979, p. 95.

② *Collected Works of Marx and Engels*, vol. 46a, People's Publishing House, 1979, p. 104.

Private ownership as a form of social division of labor pushes the separation of labor caused by social division of labor to the extent of opposition, which contributes to and facilitate the formation and development of commodity exchange. Fundamentally speaking, the existence of commodity production and the market economy is not just come from the nature and specific historical forms of ownership relations, but ultimately from the forms of the social division of labor determined by the existence of the relatively independent subjects of economic interests that constitute the most important internal factors for the existence of commodity exchange and the market economy. So the characteristics of division and separation of labor in the primary stage of socialism separation fundamentally determines the inherent contradictions in the ownership in this stage, that is, it must go through the stage of commodity production and the market economy. As long as the remnant of the old division and separation of labor remain in this stage, the separation of labor and differences between or among the different forms of ownership characteristic of this stage, including differences between the "big public" and the "small public," among the "big publics", among the "small publics," between the public and non-public, and among the non-publics, etc. The necessary existence of the market economy determines the necessary existence of interest differences and contradictions among the people.

2. Basic contradictions of the market economy in the primary stage of socialism

In analyzing commodity production in the private ownership of means of production, Marx discovered the basic contradictions between private labor and social labor in commodity economy. Our question is: in the socialist market economy in the primary stage of socialism with public sector of the economy as the mainstay and diverse forms of ownership developing side by side, is there still the contradiction between private labor and social work? The clarification of this issue is of great importance for the understanding of the basic economic and interest relations in this stage.

Marx's general and abstract examination of commodity production discovered a series of inherent contradictions in it, mainly including contradiction between valueand value in use, between concrete labor and abstract labor, and between private labor and social labor. The two aspects of each of these contradictions unified in commodity production and constitute the sources of social commodity economy. Marxist political economy tells us that the inherent two-fold character of labor determines its duality of value and value in use, whose evolution is necessarily manifested as the external opposition between commodity and money. In the above contradictions of commodity production, the contradiction between concrete labor and abstract labor is the basis. In the context of private ownership, this contradiction manifests itself as the contradiction between private labor and social labor and thus is the basic contradiction in commodity production. Under the condition of private ownership, because commodity production is of private nature, so are the commodity and commodity producers, which determines that its value and value in use, commodity and money, and the separation between concrete labor and abstract labor are irreconcilably opposed to each other, which are necessarily manifested as the antagonistic relations between private interests, and thus constitute the main lines of economic and interest relations of capitalist society.

Then, whether we can consider that, the basic contradictions in commodity production and interest relations exist also in the market economy in the primary stage of socialism? To answer this question, we must first of all analyze the conditions on which the socialist market economy depends. By comparing these conditions with those in commodity production in the capitalist societies to find out their differences, we can grasp the manifestations and characteristics of the basic economic relations and interest relations in the market economy in the primary stage of socialism. In fact, the commodity production analyzed by Marx is the most general and most typical form of commodity production with the longest history—private products. What he talked about and analyzed were private labor, products of private producers, and commodity production on the basis of private ownership. Therefore, the contradiction between private labor and social labor and contradictions among private interests revealed by Marx are the basic economic relations and interest relations of commodity production under conditions of private ownership.

It is without doubt that, as long as labor still has certain separation, and the characteristics of the old social division of labor remain, activities of commodity exchange are likely to remain. The establishment of socialist system in the primary stage of socialism did not get rid of the basic premise of commodity production and the market economy, therefore, it is impossible to eliminate the basic economic relations and interest relations inour commodity production and the market economy. As a form of social division of labor, the economic system in the primary stage of socialism in reality only changed some of the nature and characteristics of the commodity economy and its interest relations, rather than eliminated its economic and interest relations, or the basic social conditions for their existence. Next, we will analyze the basic characteristics of labor, the particularity of economic and interest relations in the market economy in the primary stage of socialism. We will proceed from the social division of labor and its social forms in the primary stage of socialism and combine it with the analysis of the characteristics of relations of ownership in the primary stage of socialism.

The analysis of division of labor and labor in the primary stage of socialism has shown the social form of labor, different from those in the societies of private ownership, has the following new features:

First, it begins to take the nature of joint labor. The laborers in public ownership in the primary stage of socialism, joining as a whole or part of a whole as the common (on partially common) masters, possess commonly (or commonly in part) the means of production. So the concrete labor of each individual is part of the joint total economic-social labor, with the means production and laborers joining together in the form of joint labor (in collective economy, it is partial joint labor) .

Second, it begins to have the nature of spontaneous labor. Because the labor in this stage is joint labor (including partial joint labor) with a common purpose and common economic interests, laborers have the rights to the use of means of production, the management of the production process and the possession of the products of their labor, so they begin to become masters of their labor.

Third, it begins to have some of the characteristics of direct social labor. Although its commodity production is socialized labor, it is different from the joint labor. Since social labor or socialized labor is determined by commodity production and the socialization of production, so long as production is socialized, the labor of the laborers is necessarily part of the socialized labor; so long as commodity production exists, labor of commodity production is sure to have a socialized property. Social or socialized work demonstrates the socialized nature of labor. Socialization of labor can exist in different social systems and be associated both with private ownership and public ownership. The joint (and partially joint) labor in the primary stage of socialism under public ownership is also socialized labor to a certain degree. Socialized labor can be divided into direct social labor and indirect social labor. Direct social labor means that the labor has a direct social nature. Marx pointed out, if there is no commodity production in society, then the natural form and the particularity of labor is the direct form of labor, rather than what in commodity production, where the commonness of labor is the essence of labor. According the Marx's presumption, socialism should get rid of commodity economy and along with it the individual and indirect nature of labor. From this we can see that the direct social nature of labor is associated with commodity economy. The direct social nature of labor has the following characteristics: (1) direct social labor is labor directly put in products of use to society, thus having the nature both in terms of quality and quantity of socially necessary labor. (2) In the process of production, from the outset is not special labor, but general labor, and before the exchange should be the general labor. (3) Direct Social work direct regulates the allocation of labor time in various production sectors according to people's needs. (4) in the context that labor has a social nature, individual workers directly participate in product distribution, rather than through the medium of labor exchange. (5) Direct social labor takes the elimination of differences between individual labor and socially necessary labor as its preconditions, so individual labor from the outset have the nature of general social labor. (6) The old division ceases to exist, so do the characteristics of the separation of labor, which is replaced by "free individuality" with common share of productive forces, joint labor and common consumption. ①From the above characteristics we can see that public ownership is the basic condition for the existence of direct social labor. As long as the public ownership is still at a low level, and there are other forms of ownership, the old division of labor, the separation of labor, commodity production, and the market economy, a direct social labor will not come into being.

On the contrary, indirect social labor emerged along with commodity production and market economy, which has the following characteristics: (1) In the condition of commodity production and the market economy, it is through exchange, that is, the medium of value, that specific individual labor become general labor and make individual labor get the nature of or become general social labor; in other words, the social nature

---

① *Collected Works of Marx and Engels*, vol. 46a, People's Publishing House, 1979, pp. 118—120.

of labor is indirect and determined afterwards. (2) For separated individual labor to have the nature of socially necessary labor, the mechanism of the market and economy and economic lever are necessary. (3) Products of indirect social labor must be exchanged through the intermediary of exchange to enter the process of distribution. (4) Laborers of indirect labor have the relative independence brought about by its economic form. (5) Indirect social labor takes individual ability to work as the natural privilege, so it has the feature of simply earning a living.

From this we can see that commodity production under private ownership in the market economy, labor has only the indirect rather than direct social nature, and it is contradictions between indirect social labor and private labor that constitutes the basic contradiction of private ownership in the commodity economy.

Although the basic nature oflabor in the primary stage of socialism has profoundly changed, the vestige of the old division remains, and its public ownership is not complete yet, in which the public ownership coexists with diverse forms of ownership. All this determines that, in the primary stage of socialism, labor still has the characteristics of a certain separation, simply earning of living and duality, which are manifested as follows:

First, labor in the primary stage of socialism is a joint labor with the primary form. Firstly, it is objectively consisted of the following three levels that are closely related yet mutually independent and contradictory: The highest level is the social union with public ownership as the basis and state-owned economy as the representative; Second, the middle level, that is the partial union of laborers with right of management of enterprise as the basis and collective ownership economic entities such as enterprises (state-owned or collectively owned) and collective ownership as the representatives; The lowest level is the labor of the individual laborers as part of the joint labor. Secondly, each of the three levels of joint labor also has a dual nature: on the one hand, the social joint labor and collective joint labor are part of the whole society and partial joint labor; on the other, any level of joint labor in turn is composed of individual labors. Take the partial union of laborers for example. On the one hand, the joint labor of each enterprise is a component of social joint labor, so it is a direct social labor; on the other, because the joint labors of the enterprises or collectives are composed of individual labors with different structures and different qualities, and there is some separation and contradictions between each partial labor, they are special local labor that has the duality of both social and individual natures. This demonstrates that the joint labor in the primary stage of socialism under the public ownership has contradictions among the three levels of the overall, the partial and the individuals, and also the duality of sociality and individuality.

Second, labor in the primary stage of socialism has the nature of incomplete direct sociality. Due to the limitations of the division of labor in the primary stage of socialism, the incompletion and diversity of its ownership and multi-level of its joint labor, the combination of the laborers with the means of production must depend on various intermediate levels, with laborers at each level are only combining themselves with part of the production, so the partial joint labor must be reduced to abstract human labor to become an organic part of the overall joint labor. This is the case of enterprise (collective) joint labor. So labor in the primary stage of socialism has the nature of incomplete direct sociality, or the nature of both indirect labor and direct labor.

Third, labor in the primary stage of socialism is not completely autonomous. In this stage, the passive nature a hire labor eliminated in the public ownership, the laborers work both for themselves and for the society and the two are basically identical, which therefore has some nature of autonomous labor. But on the other hand, this labor has the nature of for their living and natural privilege, but not the first human needs of life, so people still have to look upon labor and labor fruit from the perspective of self-interests. Laborers are both joint laborers for the common interests and individual laborers that take labor as means of livelihood. The former reflect certain characters of autonomous labor while the latter shows that labor is still a means of living in this stage, which means that labor in the primary stage of socialism is not completely autonomous yet.

From this we can see that labor in the primary stage of socialism under the public ownership has the nature of incomplete direct sociality and is still individual labor, so the contradiction between individual labor and social labor is still one of the basic contradictions in the market economy in this stage.

However, individual laborin the primary stage of socialism under public ownership is neither private labor of small commodity production, nor is it the private labor under capitalist market economy, so it no longer have private nature. The joint labor under public ownership, whether social joint labor or enterprise of collective labor, or individual labor in joint labor, no longer takes private ownership but socialist public ownership as the conditions. In this circumstances, in terms both labor purposes, labor activities or the distribution of labor products, labor is no longer private labor, but individual labor. But on the other hand, although the socialist public ownership enable the union of laborers in the ownership of means of production, the process of direct labor go through not in the community of society, but separated as partial and individual labor in different collectives. The direct manifestation of joint labor in this stage are the individual labor in enterprises, collectives and individuals, showing the differences of them in labor tools, technology, management and cost. The products of these individual labor enter commodity exchange to complete the socialization of the labor. Therefore, the contradictory relations between the different types of labor determine relations of interest contradiction between and among the state, the collective (enterprises), and individuals.

The above analysis is just about the labor and interest relations in the public sector of the economy in the primary stage of socialism. As for that in other sectors of the economy, they are very much different from that in the public sector that have certain degree of joint, autonomous and social nature. This is because, although not private labor or wage labor under private ownership, labors under the individual sector and private sector in this stage is different from both that under exploiting class society and that under public sector in the primary stage of socialism. The private labor in the non-public sector of the economy in the primary stage of socialism has obvious contradictions with the overall social labor and the individual labor under public sector of the economy; so is the case with the private labors. All this determines that there are obvious interest contradictions between the public and non-public sectors of the economy, as well as within the non-public sector of the economy. But, in general, the basic relationship in the socialist market economy only express itself as the contradictions between individual labor and social labor, rather than the contradictions between private labor and social labor.

3. The unfolding and manifestations of the basic contradictory and interest relations of the socialist market economy

The characteristics of labor under the public ownership in the primary stage of socialism discussed above cause the unfolding of economic contradictions between concrete labor and abstract labor, between value and value in use, and between money and commodity, which are manifested as the basic economic relations and interest relations of the market economy in the primary stage of socialism as follows:

First, the contradictions between value and value in use. Because the contradiction between social needs and social production intermingle with contradictions between commodity production and the market, the social demands for commodities are very important in settling the contradiction between use and value in use. A commodity can become value in use only after it meets the demands of society, otherwise it can't. In the primary stage of socialism, commodities as the outcomes of social labor, can basically be produced according to the needs of society in a planned way, so their value in use has begun to have a direct social usefulness, or direct social value in use. However, labor in this stage is at the same time individual labor and concrete labor, which determines that, under the conditions in the primary stage of socialism, commodities must receive the test of consumers (consumers in life and production) to see whether and to what extent they suit the needs of society; and the market as the intermediate link is needed to release the value in use of the commodities, and the labor consumption must be measured with value to make the labor get its compensation. Therefore, under the conditions in the primary stage of socialism, commodities have only begun to have some of the direct use value, but not full direct value in use, so it must take the form of value. Thus, the internal contradictions in the commodities in the primary stage of socialism still manifest themselves as the value and value in use. Under the conditions of private ownership, these contradictions are antagonistic, as distinct from that in public ownership, though it has some negative sides. For example, the quality and quantity of commodities in this stage cannot yet meet the needs of the society, so means of value is still needed to settle the contradictions between social supply and demand. Thus, both in terms of time and space, commodity supply and demand may separate from each other with some commodities in short supply while some others oversupply. Because commodity producers and operators are relatively independent, their special interests will make them relatively independent in deciding their production conditions, process and sale, so commodity production also shows a certain degree of spontaneity. The market mechanisms will stimulate commodity producers to make short-term to ensure better returns rather than make long-term plan, let alone considering the overall interests. As a result, contradictions between market and plan, and between special interests and the overall interests will emerge. And the contradiction between value and value in use is sure to take the form of external antagonism between commodities and money, which will result in inflation, commercial speculation, polarization, money worship, etc. These changes may give rise to complex interest relations between and among commodity producers, owners, sellers, consumers, the state, immediate interests, overall interests, local interests, etc.

Second, the contradictions among the social (overall) labor union, partial joint labor (state-owned enterprises and collectively owned enterprises), the individual labor of the members of the joint labor, and contradictions between partial joint labor and individual labor. Here, the three kinds of labor constitute interconnected relations of contradictions. Among which, the relations between social joint labor and partial labor is more important, whose movement and development, combining with social production and needs, will bring the following economic consequences:

In the first place, as long as there is commodity production, there must be differences between individual labor and socially necessary labor. Thus, there comes the issue of whether the labor of enterprises and individuals be recognized by society. Before the value of the commodity is realized, labor consumed in the products cannot be recognized by society and is relatively in the state of "individual labor". If the commodity of enterprises or individuals cannot be sold, or their individual consumption of labor is higher than socially necessary labor, the labor of the enterprises or individuals cannot be transformed into social labor, nor labor consumption cannot be fully compensated or manifested as compensations for socially necessary labor consumption directly. Because of the contradiction between the socially necessary labor consumption and its compensation, enterprises will compete with each other, resulting in the bankruptcy of some of them and the imbalance of social production, overstock or unsalable products, and the inevitable waste of labor.

In the second place, due to the duality of labor in primary stage of socialism, there is the contradiction between the individual value (depended on the labor productivity of the relatively independent economic entities) and social values (depended on the abstract labor consumed by the whole society in producing this commodity) of a commodity. This contradiction can be intensified or become acute because of their thinking of nothing but pursuit of interests of the individuals or enterprises without paying attention to social needs. Enterprises as independent economic entities are of course unable to accurately predict the needs of the society, nor can they turn their labor into direct socially necessary labor. This will cause a certain degree of blindness in production and temporary loss of control, which will have a bearing on the plan, resulting in the disproportion or gap between total production and demands, and even the difficulties of coordinated development of national economy. This may make the relations between and among the state, the collective (enterprises), and the individuals more complex.

Third, the dual purpose of production, the dual forms of economic movement and dual relations in social distribution. From the point of view of labor of public ownership, the ultimate purpose of social production is to meet the needs of the people. But enterprise and individual labor, although subject to the overall purpose of social production, have their special purpose determined by the inherent contradictions of public ownership and separation of labor. So commodity production in the primary stage of socialism has a dual nature. From the point of view of the whole society, the purpose of social production is the pursuit of value in use, which determines that the total social production process takes value in use as its starting point, and more production of wealth of value in use as its goal. Because the society does not directly involved in the specific production process, it must combine the process of direct production and circulation of each enterprise into total social labor in the form of value, so the economic movement of social production manifest themselves as W—G—W'. From the perspective of enterprise labor and individual labor, any enterprise labor are individual labor. That means, for any enterprise to meet the necessary needs of its employees, it must first of all to put their products into the market to realize their value form through exchange, and then use the value to buy the consumer goods needed in individual life. So the purpose of enterprise labor and individual labor is to get more value by creating value in use. In this process, the economic activities of enterprises is G—W—G', and the running process of economic movement show a nature of duality, which fundamentally determines the contradictions between the state, the collective and the individual. In the process of distribution, the relations of the market economy further unfolds as the dual relations of distribution, which are expanded and realized in the interest levels of the state, the collective and the individual. The overall purpose of social production and economic movement represents the interests of the society while special purpose and special form of movement represents the difference between individual interests, which are embodied respectively by the three interest subjects of the state, the collective and the individual and their interest distribution proportions. In the overall distribution in the primary stage of socialism, the contradiction between individual interests and the interests of society and contradictions among individual interests must be properly handled.

Fourth, the contradiction between the planning and blindness in the primary stage of socialism. In the market economy of private ownership, the contradiction between planning and blindness of the economy manifests itself as the planning of the individual commodity producers and the blindness of the whole society. This duality often express itself as fierce social conflicts that can undermine the social and economic development and lead to the antagonistic contradictions between social production and social needs. In the market economy in primary stage of socialism, there is also the duality of planning and blindness, but its nature and manifestations are different. This is because: First of all, the social system with public ownership as the mainstay ensures that the society in general can control the macro economy to meet the needs of the people, so that the consistence between the overall plan of the market economy and plans of the enterprises is possible. The plan of the state can possibly correct the blindness of the enterprises and basically maintain the balance between social production and needs to achieve a sound circle of the economic activities. Secondly, the existence of commodity production make it impossible to completely eliminate its blindness and spontaneity. But if properly controlled, this blindness cannot develop into the degree of damaging the normal order of the socialist market economy; and vice versa.

In the economic life in primary stage of socialism, the contradiction between the planning and blindness of the market economy finds its expressions specifically in the contradictions between the state and the enterprises, between the macro economic planning of the society and the autonomy of the micro production units, between planned control and market regulations, between vertical management control and horizontal economic integration, between centralization and decentralization, etc. The duality in this stage is also dual nature: generally speaking, the market economy can promote the social, economic, political, cultural and moral development of the society and thus can play an active role in historical progress; but the blindness of the market economy will have some negative impacts and stimulate the growth of some negative factors, such as money worship, egoism, etc. These factors will affect, even trigger complex interest contradictions.

Generally speaking, in the market economy in the primary stage of socialism with public ownership as the mainstay, the basic contradiction of commodity production will not develop into antagonistic conflicts or substantial disproportion between social production and social needs. In other words, it will not lead to the economic crisis like that in the capitalist society. However, we should also see that in this stage, although the basic contradictions in the commodity production in this stage do not express themselves as blind production but have a certain degree of overall planning, blindness, spontaneity and unplanned nature still exist. This on the one hand will not lead to the crisis of overproduction or inflation like that in the capitalist society, on the other is possible to cause a certain degree of imbalance, disproportion, inflation, big gap between social production and needs, even serious economic difficulty; and it will not lead to the fundamental conflicts among producers, but on the other it may lead to the interest contradictions among different interest subjects, which, if improperly handled, may trigger temporary, local antagonistic interest conflicts or crisis.

Fifth, the contradiction between individual labor and social labor in the commodity (market) economy in the primary stage of socialism will surely unfold as interest contradictions among the people on the basis of fundamental interest identity. In his *Das Kapital* and relevant manuscripts, Marx, starting from the internal contradictions of commodity, analyzes all the contradictions in the capitalist mode of production, and reveals the antagonistic interest contradictions among human beings. Marx's analysis consists of two aspects. Firstly, he points out that there are contradictions in the general commodity exchange. In the commodity exchange in the private ownership, the two parties of the exchange are all for the sake of their own interests, and private interests are the starting points of their exchange actions. The general interests of the exchanger are demonstrated through their exchange value as the general interest of the whole content of the exchange actions. These interests exist only "behind the back of these self-reflected particular interests". ①Therefore, the commodity production in the private ownership manifest themselves as the antagonism between private interests and general interests. Secondly, he points out that in the capitalist production, because commodity production on the one hand reflects the broader socialization of labor and the expansion of general interests in a larger scope; on the other hand, commodity production is private and commodity producers are separated into opposing private interests, therefore, in the acts of exchange, the mutually exclusive personal interests, which, thanks to the private ownership, transform into private interests. In a class society, there are various interest groups, so private interests will become class interests, resulting in the antagonistic interest contradictions among classes. In a capitalist society, this class antagonism is manifested as the opposition between class interests of the working class and the laboring people on the one side and the so-called state interests of the capitalist country on the other. Of course, in the social structure of capitalism, interest contradictions are very complex. In the commodity exchange, there are contradictions between buyers and sellers, between producers and consumers and between the exchangers themselves; there is also the employment contradiction among the workers, and contradictions among capitalists, etc. Of which, contradictions between the working class and the bourgeoisie play a dominant role.

In theoperation of the market economy in the primary stage of socialism, the public sector of the economy is owned by all the people or members of the collective. This determines that products of labor are also owned them, thereby the exploitation of the surplus value of the workers by the capitalist class is basically eliminated, along with class antagonism. In the labor process, the working people work directly for their own sake and the fundamental interests of the working people are basically identical rather than in opposition. However, there is still commodity production in this stage, which means, on the one hand the state as the bearer of the whole common interests need to meet the requirements of the socialization of commodity production; on the other hand, it must also recognize the relative independence of commodity producers. This determines that there are interest contradictions among the operation entities, among the commodity producers, between the operation entities and the commodity

---

① *Collected Works of Marx and Engels*, vol. 46a, People's Publishing House, 1979, p. 196.

producers on the one side and the whole interests of the society or the interest of the state on the other. These demonstrate that, in the economic operation in the primary stage of socialism, there are differences and contradictions among individual interests, between individual interests and partial interests, between overall interests and individual and partial interests, which belong to non-antagonistic interest contradictions among the people.

To sum up, because of the variety of economic sectors in the primary stage of socialism, there are still private economy and related commodity production. So in this stage, there are not only the contradictions between individual labor and social labor, between private labor and social labor, but also contradictions between public and non-public economic sectors, as well as contradictions within the public sector and within the non-public sector. Due to its private nature, the production of the non-public sector of the economy, through the market as the intermediate, will have greater blindness and spontaneity. If not properly guided and regulated, their evil consequences will become more serious, potentially causing partial or temporary difficulties, even economic crisis and severe interest contradictions. But these contradictions are different from the fundamental contradictions in capitalist commodity economy, because the mainstay of the public sector of the economy in the economic system in the primary stage of socialism can counter and constrain the negative impact and factors of them, so that it cannot cause large crisis that harms the sound development of socialist production. Essentially speaking, facing the interest contradictions or confrontations that is basically impossible to trigger class antagonism, if we lose our vigilance, or handle them improperly, intense and antagonistic interest contradictions, conflicts or unrests are possible to occur.

Chapter Twelve

Interest Differences and Interest Contradictions in the Primary Stage of Socialism

Economic relations will find their expressions in interest relations. On the basis of research of the basic economic relations and interest relations in the primary stage of socialism, we should further study the interest differences and interest contradictions in this stage. In people's production activities of pursuing interests and meeting their needs, there must be certain economic relations among them, which will manifest themselves as interest relations. Lenin said that it is "to seek for the roots of social phenomena in production relations (and) obliged to reduce them to the *interests* of definite classes. "① Interest differences and interest contradictions are important social phenomena. Economic relations are the most profound root causes for the existence and development of interest relations and interest contradictions, while social interest relations are the manifestations of social economic relations. The commodity (market) economic relations in socialist society manifest themselves as interest differences and interest contradictionsamong market entities.

In a class society, interest relations among the people are manifested as serious class confrontations. Under socialist system in China, the exploiting class as a whole has been eliminated, and antagonistic class contradictions, conflicts and struggles havegradually receded to a secondary position with their role of range being narrowing and moving toward ultimate disappearance. In these circumstances, what are the interest differences and contradictions in the primary stage of socialism? How should we analyze further the classes, strata and groups, in particular, the non-antagonistic interest differences and contradictions in

---

① *Collected Works of Lenin*, vol. 1, People's Publishing House, 1984, p. 464.

this stage? This isan important theoretical and practical issue.

I. The Basic Law Governing the Development of Interest Differences and Interest Contradictions in the Primary Stage of Socialism

To understand the interest differences and interest contradictions in the primary stage of socialism, we should first reveal its basic law of development and characteristics. This requires us to explain the basic issues of them, such as reasons for their existence, their fundamental nature, main types, manifestations and important characteristics.

1. The objective necessity of interest differences and contradictions in the primary stage of socialism

To reveal the interest differences and contradictions in the primary stage of socialism, we must first explain why there are still interest differences and interest contradictions in this stage. The reasons are as follows:

First, the relatively backward productive forces are the most fundamental material roots for the interest differences and contradictions in the primary stage of socialism.

Development of the socialist productive forces in China is relatively backward, so its material wealth cannot fully meet the needs of the people: This is the most fundamental reason for the interest differences and contradictions in the primary stage of socialism. In specific, they are: firstly, the production has not fully developed so that people's reasonableand payable needs cannot be satisfied, which inevitably leads to people interest differences and contradictions in distribution. Interests are always related to needs, but not any need is associated with needs; only the unsatisfied needs lead to people's strong impulse for interests and therefore interest differences and contradictions. If the material needs of the people could be met by reasonably planned and organized production, as the endless air in nature can meet the breath need of people, then material needswould not cause interest differences and contradictions. There is no doubt that, our current social production cannot fully satisfy people's material needs yet, that will give rise to vigorous pursuit of and violent competition over interests. The gap between the limited material supply and constant increaseof people's needs will certainly lead to competition, differences and contradictions. Secondly, people's needs are constantly developing and growing: after the old needs are met, new needs will emerge; after the basic needs are met, higher level needs will emerge. That means that, when the production in the primary stage of socialism meet the needs of the people's ability to pay, higher level needs will appear, so that social production again lags behind to a certain degree. Therefore, as long as the society cannot provide the material basis for distribution each according to his needs, a certain degree of differences and contradictions in distribution is inevitable. Thirdly, in the primary stage of socialism, the development of the productive forces is not highly developed and well balanced, which determines the existence of differences in natural conditions and level of equipment in each unit, resulting in the differences in the incomes of producers and further in interest differences and contradictions. Take the differences in natural conditions for example. They exist mainly in the following aspects: (1) Difference in location. In the market economy, producers in urban, coastal or economically developed areas enjoy better natural conditions and communications facilities than those in rural, mountains and inland areas that are economically backward, poor in natural conditions and communications, therefore can get more economic information, technological support, access to market and export with less costs. (2) Difference in land conditions. From the point of view of agricultural production, the output of production is much higher in areas with fertile land, favorable climate and better irrigation than areas with barren land, cold climate or water shortage. (3) Differences in resources. People in areas with rich resources get much higher income than those in areas with poor resources. In the condition of not fully developed productive forces, these differences cannot be eliminated, and they will remain for a considerably long time. In the socialist market economy, with the principle of exchange of equal labor value being dominant, producers in areas with better natural conditions will get higher profits and differential income, which determines the existence of interest differences and contradictions. Another differential income is caused by technological facilities. In the primary stage of socialism, even within the public sector of the economy, due to various factors, there are differences between production entities in the level of technological facilities, which is sure to bring about income differences. For example, with other factor excluded, a factory with modern equipment and technology is certain to have higher productivity and economic efficiency than a factory withold-fashioned equipment and backward technology. Although the income differences can be narrowed by appropriate economic levers, given the level of productive forces in the primary stage of socialism, theirexistence is inevitable, as are the objective existence of interest differences and contradictions.

Second, the nature of social division of labor and the social form of labor determined by it in the primary stage of socialism are the basic factors leading to interest differences and contradictions in this stage.

Since there still exist the separation and duality of labor in the primary stage of socialism, and there are still residue and vestige of the old division of labor, social differences and inequity will necessarily exist. For example, the division of labor between managers and the employees, between manual and mental workers, and between leading officialsand ordinary people determines the existence of social differences between them and therefore their differences in sharing interests. The differences in division of labor and in conditions of possession and distribution will lead to the difference in income of labor. As a result, relatively independent interest subjects will inevitably come into being, resulting in their interest frictionsand conflicts. For example, in the primary stage of socialism, in addition to differences in distribution of labor fruit due to the differences of positions and roles of different classes, strata and social groups in the relations of means of production, the social differences caused by the residue of old social division of labor, such as differences between rural and urban, between manual and mental labor, between workers and farmers, are also basic causes for the existence of interest differences and contradictions.

Third, the diverse forms of ownership and distribution, as well as the incomplete and immature systems of public ownership and distribution according to work are the reason in economic base for the existence of interest differences and contradictions in the primary stage of socialism.

The existence of diverse forms of ownership and distribution determines the existence of interest differences and contradictions in economic base. Even within the public sector, because it is still incomplete and immature, there are still differences between the state-owned economy and the collective economy; within the same type of public ownership, there are relatively independent economic entities. The system of distribution according to work, the different forms of public ownership and their different ways of realization, and differences in distribution: all these will further cause differences and contradictions in distribution of products of labor, and thus will result in interest differences and contradictions.

If we say that the difference in possession of means of production is the main cause for the interest differences and contradictions, then whether we can say that there are no interest differences and contradictions among the people within the public ownership, especially state-owned sector of the economy? The answer is no. Actually, public ownership only determines that the interest differences are non-antagonistic rather than eliminatesinterest differences. Meanwhile, seeing from a longer span of time, that is, from a historical trend of social development, public ownership is notequal to the elimination of personal ownership but is at higher level than it. In *Das Capital*, Marx wrote: " But capitalist production begets, with the inexorability of a law of Nature, its own negation. It is the negation of negation. This does not re-establish private property for the producer, but gives him individual property based on the acquisition of the capitalist era: i. e. , on cooperation and the possession in common of the land and of the means of production. "[1] Private ownership is the negation of the ownership of the primitive communism, while capitalist socialized production is the negation of private ownership itself, which is not to re-establish private ownership, nor to recover primitive communism, but a private ownership on the basis of new possession in common. About the meaning of private ownership, there are two different understandings among scholars. One holds that it means each person as a member of the joint labor really possesses means of production and the total sum of the productive forces. Marx believed that, in communist society, "a mass of instruments of production must be made subject to each individual. "[2] It is the " appropriation of the total productive forces through united individuals. "[3] In the primitive society, dominated by the forces of nature, man cannot truly become master of the productive forces as in the society of public ownership with highly developed social productive forces. Another understanding regards that it refers to individual ownership and domination of means of living. In the advanced stages of public ownership, with the productive forces highly

---

[1] *Collected Works of Marx and Engels*, vol. 23, People's Publishing House, 1972, p. 832.

[2] *Collected Works of Marx and Engels*, vol. 3, People's Publishing House, 1960, p. 76.

[3] *Ibid* , p. 77.

developed, everyone can fully get means of living for his overall development. Therefore, public ownership will not abolish but develop individuality; not limit but fully meet individual needs; not deny but acknowledge private interests, which are not manifested in the economic relations of the producers' ownership of means of production in common but in the distribution of private consumer goods. The author thinks that both these two understandings are reasonable. We can take them as the two levels of private ownership, and the second level precisely explains the inevitability of interest differences in socialist system. If there are private interests in a highly developed society of public ownership, then in the socialist stage when public ownership is not perfect yet and there are diverse forms of ownership, there are not only private interests, but also certain interest differences and contradictions among individuals, among groups, and between individual interests and overall interests.

Fourth, the market economy in the primary stage of socialism is the reason of system for the interest differences and contradictions

The contradiction between social labor and individual labor is the basic contradiction in the commodity (market) economy in the primary stage of socialism, which specifically manifests itself as the interest differences and contradictions between social interests and individual interests and as that among different interest subjects on the basis of fundamental identity of interests. Contradictions in the market economy under private ownership reflect the fundamental interest antagonism among private producers. In the market economy in the primary stage of socialism, in the context of different forms of realization in different sectors of public ownership, each of the public enterprises and each individual can only consider their products from the point of views of operation entity, operation rights and separation of labor, so commodity exchange reflect only changes in rights to product possession and operation, thus does not show fundamental interest conflicts. Enterprises and individuals look at their particular interests from a relatively independent status and distinguish themselves from social interests rather than make them fundamentally opposite to each other. In the condition of socialist market economy in the primary stage of socialism, there are also other forms of ownership. Important differences and contradictions exist among these economic relations between different forms of ownership. The economic relations in socialist market reflect the differences between social interests and individual interests, differences among different individual interests, and differences and contradictions, on the basis of fundamental identity of interests, among the state, the collectives and individuals, and that among different interest subjects.

Fifth, the qualities and labor ability of the laborers are the subjective reasons for the interest differences and contradictions in the primary stage of socialism.

Under the condition of distribution according to work in the primary stage of socialism, the level of living standards of individual workers depends mainly on the individual's labor remuneration, whose most important determinant are the qualities and abilities of the laborers themselves. In this stage, economic and other social conditions will bring about differences among laborers in national education, science and technological training, as well as specialized labor skills training. Even in the same level of training, there are also differences of natural endowment of individual laborers, such as physical strength, nimbleness, receptive ability. Under the conditions in theprimary stage of socialism, laborers have to get means of living through their qualities and abilities. So the objective differences of personal qualities and work ability determine the existence of interest differences and contradictions among individual laborers and among collectives.

Sixth, the political status and the political consciousness of laborers in the primary stage of socialism are the political and ideological reasons for the generation and change of interest differences and contradiction.

The primary stage of socialism was born out of the old society, so it has the birthmarks of the old society not only economically, but also politically, ideologically and morally. In this stage, both its material civilization andcultural civilization have not reached the advanced degree or level. There is much residue left behind by the old society. For example, socialist democracy is not perfect yet, and there are defects in the systems. These things have negative influences on the movement of interest differences and contradictions in terms of politics and superstructure. The political consciousness and moral standards of the laborers have not completely gotten rid of the limitations of history. For instance, the old ideas, old morality and old customs; and the attitudes of the laborers toward labor are still simply from the point of view of livelihood, etc. All these affect the existence, change and development of the interest differences and contradictions.

From the above analysis we can see the existence of interest differences and contradictions is an objective fact independent of man's will.

2. The basic nature and main types of interest differences and contradictions in the primary stage of socialism

The interest difference and contradictions till now can be divided into two major types: one is interest contradictions of antagonistic nature, which manifests itself in two forms, i. e. , those in the society of private ownership such as slave society, feudal society, capitalist society, and those in the society of public ownership such as interest opposition and conflicts between tribes in the primitive society; the other type is interest differences and contradictions of non-antagonistic nature, which manifests itself as the interest differences and contradictions on the basis of fundamental identity of member's interests in a society with a social and economic base where class antagonism no longer exists but old residue of old division of labor still exists. In the primary stage of socialism, although the economic base withpublic ownershipas the mainstay has been established and the interest differences and contradictions of antagonistic nature has been abolished, the residue of the old division of labor still remains, so do some class differences and social differences. Therefore, there are still interest differences and contradictions of non-antagonistic nature, which, in terms of human relations, manifests themselves as interest differences and contradictions among the people. Of course, there are some exceptions of individual or local antagonistic cases.

The interest differences and contradictions in the primary stage of socialism consist of those of non-antagonistic nature determined by thedivision of labor and its nature and by socialist ownership, as well as those determined by the residue of private ownership and olddivision of labor, among which, some antagonistic, some are not. For example, the interest contradiction between the existing hostile elements and a variety of anti-socialist elements in the one side and the people in the other side are antagonistic. The interest differences and contradictions, in terms of human relations, manifest themselves as interest contradictions among the people. In theprimary stage of socialism, interest differences and contradictions are considered from the point of view of their objective causes and social nature, whereas interest contradictions among the people are looked at from the point of view of manifestation of the contradictions in human relations and nature. In this stage, interest differences and contradictions are the fundamental root of the existence, development, intensification and resolution of all contradictions.

3. The concentrated manifestations and features of movement of all interest differences and contradictions in the primary stage of socialism.

The inherent separation of labor, the ownership relations and basic relations of the market economy in the primary stage of socialism determine that the interest differences and contradictions in this stage are in a concentrated way manifest themselves as the contradiction between common interests and particular interests.

From the point of view of the past, the present and the future of human history, the development of social interests will go through three historical stages: the stage of fundamental identity of interests, the stage of fundamental antagonistic of interests and again the stage of fundamental identity of interests. So far, the development of social interests has undergone the first two stages. During the society of primitive communism, means of production were publicly owned, and people worked together and consumed together, so interests within a social group were identical among all members of the group, therefore there was no fundamental interest conflict among them. The collective interests of the primitive community were manifested as the decisive interests and individual interests were included into the social interests, and so did almost all individual independence, because common interests were supreme. Within a tribe, the fundamental interests ofits members were identical. After the emergence of private ownership, society dividedinto classes, and gave rise to fundamentally antagonistic interest groups and individual special interest independent of common interests. From then on, fundamentally antagonistic interest contradictions emerged among private interests, between private interests and group interests, and among group interests, which further gave birth to interest contradictions among the people. The ruling class generalized and ameliorated the interests of their own class as the common interests of society against the reasonable interests ofthe working people; as a result, common interests and individual interests were split into fundamentally opposing interests. With the establishmentof the socialist system and the elimination of exploitation and oppression between people, the interests ofthe working massesare fundamentally identical. But on the other hand, there still differences and contradictions between common interests and particular interests in the primary stage of socialism in China as well as certain interest differences and contradictions among the people. But these differences and contradictions are different in nature from those in the society of private ownership, with the former being on the basis of fundamental identical while the later fundamentally antagonistic. Engels said: "In the communist society, where the interests of individuals are not opposed to each other, but on the contrary, are united,"① "in which community of interests has become the basic principle."② Only after entering the communist society, where there is only public ownership, will all interest differences be settled and reconciled into the stage of fundamentally identity. In the social formation of socialism, especially in the primary stage of it, the fundamental identity of interests like that in the communist society has not been achieved, so it is in a transitional state.

All interest differences and contradictions, whether they are those among the individuals or groups, whether they are vertical or horizontal, always center onthe main contradiction between social common interests and particular interests, in which interest contradictions among individuals and among groups are subject to the interest contradictions between social common interests and particular interests. This is because: (1) Social common interests is the result of interaction between social particular interests, therefore they constitute the backbone of social interest system. (2) Any individual or particular interest is a part of the entire common interests and the function mechanism of the former is subject to and influenced by the latter. For example, when the whole nation faces crisis, the contradictions among the particular interests within the nation, being subject to the common interests of the entire nation, will become relatively mitigated. (3) The existence, development and solution of individual, particular interest contradictions are subject to the existence, development and solution of contradictions between particular and common interests. For example, in capitalist countries, the interest contradictions among capitalists as individualsare subordinated to the interest contradiction between the particular interests of the capitalists and the common interests of the state as the community of them. (4) The contradiction between common interests and particular interests can exist at all levels of interest realization. There are contradictions between particular interests and

---

① *Collected Works of Marx and Engels*, vol. 2, People's Publishing House, 1957, p. 605.

② *Ibid* , p. 609.

common interests within the factory, so do within a group company at higher level. In short, as a universal form of interest contradiction, the interest contradiction between particular interests and common interests exist at all levels and in all fields of social interest relations.

Under China's socialist system, with the elimination of antagonistic private interests of class nature, objectively, social common interests have become the common goals of most individual social interest subjects, and social development is precisely achieved through the creative activities of every social member. The establishment of socialist public ownership as the mainstay of the economy makes the state be able to leverage interests to mobilize the enthusiasm of the laborers. Under the circumstances, the most outstanding issues are how to distribute social common interests among the working people, how to subordinate individual interests to overall interests and how the state takes into account the needs of particular interests. Therefore, in the primary stage of socialism, the non-antagonistic interest contradiction between particular interests and the common interestsbecome more prominent and concentrated among all the interest differences and interest contradictions, which are manifested in the following contradictions:

First, the contradiction between long-term interests and immediate interests. An example is the contradiction between production and needs. Their relationship is unity of opposites: the purpose of production is to meet the needs of the people; to meet the growing needs of the people requires the development of production, which, in turn requires that, rather than eating and dividing everything up, we must proportionately restrict the immediate needs of the people, in order to appropriately expand reproduction. This will give rise to the contradiction between developing production and meeting the needs of the people, which is highlighted in the ratio between accumulation and consumption. Overemphasis on consumption will only lead to the impediment of expansion of reproduction and exhaustion of resources; on the other hand, if stress is placed only on accumulation, the interests and enthusiasm of the consumers will be damaged, which in turn will affect accumulation in the long run. Only by appropriately balancing the relationship between accumulation and consumption can the contradiction between production and needs be properly resolved. For by expanding production through proper accumulation, the needs of the people can be better met, and the expansion of consumption will promote the development of production. If we consume everything up without restraint in a short-sighted manner, the long-term interests of the people will be jeopardized. On the other side, if we focus only on production and accumulation by neglecting the needs of the people and consumption, the enthusiasm of the people will be affected. Relative to collectives and individuals, the interests of the state represent the common and long-term interests. So the state should both uphold the fundamental interests and pay attention to the immediate interests of the people, so that they can consider the long-term interests while enjoying the immediate ones. The contradiction between the common interests and particular interests in socialist countries is inevitably expressed as the contradiction between long-term interests and immediate interests.

Second, the contradiction between local interests and overall interests. Common interests refer to the overall or entire interests of all the members in a social community (enterprise, ethnic group, stratum, class, state, etc.); the interests of any part or member in a community fall into the category of local or individual interests of specific individuals or collectives. Relative to collectives and individuals, the state represents the overall interests; while relative to individuals, the collectives represent the overall interests. The contradiction between local interests and overall interests is mainly reflected on the relationship among the individuals, the collectives and the state. In the economic life of socialist countries, the relationship between the state and the enterprises constitute the main line of the contradictory relationship between the overall interests and the local interests. In a socialist country, the state represents the fundamental interests of the people and entire society, while enterprises, as the elementary cells of economic life of the state, are subordinate to the state. Enterprises as a part of the state must take the overall interests of the state into consideration and fulfill the tasks assigned by the state. At the same time, as relatively independent economic entities, they should have their own independence to fully display their own initiatives. The overall situation cannot be active without the initiatives of the locals. Thus the contradiction between the common interests and particular interests in a socialist country finds their expression in the contradictions between the overall interests and the local (or particular) interests.

Third, the contradiction between the gained interests and future interests. A gained interest refers to any interest that has been obtained or realized; any interest that needs yet to be obtained or realized after certain efforts is future interest. These two kinds of interests are both united and contradictory. The unity of them lies in the fact that, the gained interests are the premise and basis for the realization and accomplishment of future interests, and there will be no future interests without the gained interests. In a class society, gained interests and future interests arecompletely separated from and antagonistic to each other, whose contradiction is demonstrated as class contradictions. Under socialist conditions, productive forces basically conform to relations of production and the interests of the people are fundamentally identical. This determines that the gained and future interests of the people are identical. But because of the differences of interests and the interest groups, there are also some discrepancy and contradictions between them, which are specifically manifested in the following: some people abandon the future interests of the society for their gained interest; some leaders seek special interests by abusing power. Both are in conflicted with the fundamental and long-term interests of the people. The contradiction between socialist common interests and special interests will inevitably find their expressions mostly in the contradiction of gained interests and future interests.

In the primary stage of socialism, interest relations mainly manifest themselves in the contradictions between common interests and special interests. So, what are the basic characteristics of interest relations in this stage? Firstly, their interests are fundamentally identical. The basic system of socialism determines that the fundamental purpose of social production is to meet the people's growing material and cultural needs, although there are some interest differences and contradictions among the people, their fundamental interests are identical. Secondly, the interest contradictions are generally non-antagonistic. Thirdly, the interest differences and contradictions will exist for a long time. Throughout the primary stage of socialism, social division of labor and the social differences caused by the social form will exist for a long time, so do the interest differences and contradictions. And lastly, interest differences and interest contradictions can be resolved through coordination. Since the interest differencesand interestcontradictions in the primary stage of socialism are non-antagonistic on the basis of fundamental identity of interests, their solution can be completely achieved through coordinated approach, rather than approach of one side eliminating the other.

II. The Differences and Contradictions of Interest Subjects in the Economic Life in the Primary Stage of Socialism

To study the interest differences and contradictions in the primary stage of socialism, we should focus our study on the interest subjectsin economic life and their differences and contradictions.

First, we should examine the status and role of interest subjects in interest relations and analyze their relationship to find its rules. The relationships between different forms, different contents, different functions and different natures are bound to be linked through interest subjects and manifest themselves as interest differences and contradictions among them. To study interest differences and contradictions, we must analyze the motives of interest pursuits and seeking activities of different interest subjects and their competition.

Second, since interest subjects are composed of interest individuals and interest groups, to further examine the status and role of interest groups in interest differences and contradictions, we should analyze the differences and contradictions between different interest groups to find out laws governing them. Different interest groups have different and even conflicting interest demands, and their differences and contradictions constitute the main line of social interest differences and contradictions. In the primary stage of socialism, since exploiting class as such no longer exists, and class contradiction has receded into a secondary position, therefore, it is extremely important as for how to understand the differences and contradictions among different interest groups in society, the analysis of which will be made in the next chapter.

Third, we should focus on the examination of interest difference and contradictions of interest subjects, especially interest groups, in the economic life in the primary stage of socialism. Economic life is the foundation of all social life, economic relations is the prerequisite of all social relations, and economic interests are the interests of decisive significance in the system of social interests; therefore, to study interest differences and contradictions in this stage, the focus should be put on the study of interest differences and contradictions among different interest subjects, especially interest groups in economic life. We can examine the differences and contradictions among interest subjects specifically from economic relations (static aspects) and economic operations (dynamic aspects).

1. Differences and contradictions among interest subjects in economic life in the primary stage of socialism

We can analyze the interest differences and contradictions among different interest subjects in the economic life in the primary stage of socialism both vertically and horizontally. Interest is a category involves multi-level, multi-field, multi-purpose and multi-type social fields. Various social interest subjects have not only horizontal but also vertical relations, and they mutually interact, influence and restraint, forming a complex interest network with their differences and contradictions, among which, relations among individuals, groups and the state being the vertical and relations among different interest subjects being the horizontal.

(1) Vertical differences and contradictions among interest subjects

Under socialist system, the interest relations among the individual, the collective and the state as the interest subjects are vertically linked. Individuals are the subjects of individual interests that can be divided from different angles: from the angle of ownership, they can be divided into individual interests of workers in state-owned economy, farmers in collective economy, workers in mixed economy, workers in individual economy, workers in private sector of the economy, etc.; from the angle of division of labor or occupation, they can be divided into individual interests of the manual workers, mental workers, teachers, civil servants etc.; from the angle of employment, they can be divided into individual interests of the employed workers, the unemployed, the retirees, etc. A collective is a community of the common interests of its members. Households, enterprises, government and public bodies, regions, social groups, social strata, classes, ethnic groups, etc., are all communities of certain interests. In social life, households are not only consumption but also production and other business units (such as individual commercial households, specialized households, contract households, etc., in rural areas), and the interests of households as the main undertakers of economic and consumption interests have direct bearing on the individual interests of their members. In addition, in social life, households are also linked to interest relations arising from their unique needs such as marriage and heritance. In socialist economic activities, enterprises are links as well as intermediaries between the interests of the individual and the state. The economic interests of the collectives of enterprises in a socialist country can also be divided from different angles such as those of the state-owned enterprises, collectively owned enterprises, limited liability companies, as well as the interests of different sectors of production in state-owned enterprises. In a socialist country, each government department, each public institution and each region also has its own relatively independent common interests. So do different social groups, strata, ethnic groups, such as the common interests of the intelligentsia, the farmer class, the working class, etc. In socialist economic life, enterprises (including state-owned, collective-owned, mixed-owned and private-owned enterprises), as the economic subjects and the elementary cells with relatively independent status in socialist market economy, are collectives with most salient economic significance. They are at a higher place in terms of economic interests relative to individuals or households, and have clearer economic interests relative to units, regions, classes, strata and ethnic groups in a socialist country.

So, when analyzing interest groups in the vertical interest relations, we focus our research on the interest subjects of enterprises. The state is the pursuer, bearer, representative and embody of the common interests of all citizens of the society, which represents not only partial and temporary interests of the individuals and the collectives, but also the overall interests and long-term interests of all members of the society. Seeing from the vertical interest relations in the economic life in the primary stage of socialism, three economic interest subjects, that is, the individual, the collective and the state, formthe relations of economic interest differences and contradictions on the basis of the fundamental identity of interests.

(2) *The horizontal contradictions among interest subjects*

Due to various social and historical causes, under the conditions of the socialist market economy, there exist differences, economic differences in particular, among individuals and collectives (ethnic groups, classes, strata, regions, enterprises, departments and units), which will necessarily give rise to horizontal interest differences and contradictions among them. For instance, because of differences of income and economic status and treatment, there exist certain economic differences and interest contradictions in public-owned enterprise between the managers and workers, between engineering and technical personnel and manual workers, among engineering and technical personnel themselves, and among manual workers themselves; so do among workers in different working positions (such as between officials and ordinary workers, between intellectuals and manual workers, among soldiers, teachers, artists, sports workers, doctors, nurses, workers in service industries, etc.) Within socialist countries, differences and contradictions will emerge between ethnic groups and between regions due to differences in economic development; so do among the working class, the farmer class, the intelligentsia, the newly emerged social strata, as well as among enterprises, sectors and units of different social division of labor due to economic conditions, environments and benefits.

2. The differences and contradictions among interest subjects in the economic operation in the primary stage of socialism

The dynamic process of economic life in the primary stage of socialism is the operation process of its market economy. The study of the interest subjects in this stage should not be limitedwithin its static aspects, but should cover all levels and all links; not just limited within its micro-, meso-and macro-level or the descriptive study of such links as production, exchange, distribution and consumption, but should be extended to in-depth research of its interest subjects in operation. Only after the problem of operators of production, exchanges, distribution and consumption, and the relations among these operators at all levels and all links in the real economic life, can the complex interest contradictions been understood. In fact, the complex phenomena of the economic relations are precisely the manifestations of the differences and contradictions among the interest subjects of the economic life in the primary stage of socialism.

As to state-owned sector of the public economy, the interest subjects in the micro, meso-and macro-level respectively are: The central and local governments, the sectoral management departments (such as the railway system, telecommunications system, the aviation system) and enterprises (including their employees) . The stateis the main operator and interest entity of macro-levele conomy, who shoulders the important task of macroeconomic regulation and of macroecomic control and represents the overall and fundamental interests of all the people. Local governments and sectoral management departments (in China, sectoral management departments are affiliated both withthe central government and local governments, but they also have certain independence) is both the operators and interest subjects of meso-level economy, who shoulder the task ofmeso-level economic regulation and control and represent the interests of the level. Enterprises are the main operators and also the interest subjects of micro-level economy, representing the partial interest of their own as the cells of socialist market economy. The interest relations among the state, local governments, sectoral management departments and enterprises constitute relations among the interest subjects at the macro-level, meso-level and micro-level in the primary stage of socialism. Among which the enterprises as a micro-economic units constitute the basis. The existence of relatively independent economic interests of enterprises is the most basic premise and the source of vitality of the market economy. Here, the key is to let enterprisestruly have their relatively independent economic interests. To do this, the differences of economic interests among enterprises must be recognized: (1) recognizing the differences of economic interests among enterprises caused by labor skills and labor intensity; (2) recognizing the differences of economic interests among enterprises due to the differences of operation results; (3) recognizing the differences of economic interests among enterprises due to the differences of accumulation capabilities; (4) recognizing the differences of economic interests among enterprises caused by operation in the market economy. Just as the fall of water produces kinetic energy, interest differences will increase the vitality of enterprises. Only when the objective interest differences among enterprises are recognized, can enterprises be invigorated and their enthusiasm mobilized, so that the macro economy be enlivened.

The interest subjects in the dynamic process of the four links of production, exchange, distribution and consumption in the market economy are the state, local governments, sectoral management departments and enterprises and individual workers. The state is the overall organizer, planner, regulator of these four links, which at the overall level represents the interests of the general and determines the reasonable proportions between supply and demands, accumulation and consumption, production and exchange, product and allocation. Local governments and sectoral management depart ments are representatives of local or sectoral interests, which are subject to the general control of the national plan and determine the proportional relations within their localities or sectors. Enterprises are the relatively independent economic entities and basic units in the total production, exchange, distribution and consumption of the whole society, representing the collective interests of their own enterprises. Individuals are the ultimate providers of social labor end consumers in social economic life and they are the subjects of their own interests. In the endless cycle of movement of commodity production and exchange, these interest subjects will alternately or concurrently play the roles as producers, sellers, buyers and and consumers. As long as socialist market economy exists, the law of value will inevitably work, which will bring about interest competition, differences and contradictions among commodity producers, owners, exchangers and consumers, as well as between interest subjects of public sector and non-public sectors, and among interest subjects of non-public sectors in these links.

The interest subjects at all levels in the primary stage of socialist market economy constitute the vertical and horizontal framework and complete structure of interest relations in the economic operation. In this structure, the main relation is the interest differences between different forms of ownership of the economy and their various enterprises, and the competition determined by these differences are the driving forces behind them. Due to their differences of position in the market economy and operation, economic differences inevitably exist among them, so do their different functions and operation purposes. This will lead to their different activities in interest seeking and thus the interest differences and contradictions. Since in these activities, whether individuals or local and sectoral departments, or enterprises, focus mainly on the own interests. If the state's does not properly guide or regulate the operation of the meso-and micro-level of the market economy, the overall production and demand will lose balance and the blindness of production at these levels will make the differences among interest subjects wider and their interest contradictions sharper. On the other hand, however, if the state control is too strict so that the enthusiasm of the various interest subjects is dampened, the contradictions between the state and other interest subjects will deepen.

The contradictions of the different interest subjects in the links of production, exchange, distribution and consumption not only express themselves in vertical way, but also in horizontal way. That is, there also interest contradictions among localities, among sectoral departments, among enterprises (public owned, non-public owned), between state owned economic enterprises and collective owned enterprises and non-public enterprises, and among individual workers. And while taking the roles as producers, sellers, buyers and consumers, there will certainly be complex interest contradictions among them. For example, enterprises producing means of production are consumers and buyers of and therefore have interest relations with enterprises producing raw materials, and at the same time, they are also buyers and consumers of and therefore have interest differences and contradictions with enterprises producing means of livelihood. These differences and relations will lead to contradictions due to the complex social environment and interest differences.

In the market economy in the primary stage of socialism, there are differences and contradictions of economic interests within the public ownership as the mainstay of the economy, so are between enterprises in public and non-public sectors, among various interest groups, among individuals; among enterprises in different forms of ownership of non-public sector of the economy, between these enterprises in the one side and the state, the affiliated enterprises and individual workers in the other side, especially among private enterprises, and between private enterprise and individual workers.

3. The inherent differences and contradictions in the relations of economic interests in the market economy in the primary stage of socialism

The various interest subjects in the economic relations and operation in the market economy in primary stage of socialism constitute a complete interest relation system of the market economy, within which there are differences interest differences and contradictions of fundamentally non-antagonistic nature. Specifically speaking, these differences and contradictions are caused by the differences among interest subjects in terms of conditions, methods, times and levels of realizations of economic interests.

(1) The differences in conditions and methods of interest realization determine the inherent differences and contradictions in the socialist market economy in the primary stage of socialism.

Differences in conditions of interest realization, the big differences caused by division of labor, differences in ownership of means of production, differences in natural, social, scientific and technical conditions, differences in abilities and qualities of individual workers, etc. , all result inthe inherent interest differences and contradictions in the market economy in the primary stage of socialism. Distribution according to work is the dominant form of distribution, in addition to a variety of other forms such as distribution according to production factors, which will naturally leads to differences in forms of realization of economic interests. For example, distribution according to work means that individual economic interests are achieved through individual labor income; distribution according to capital means that individual economic interests are gained by share in investment; distribution according to knowledge means that economic interest is realized through personal knowledge; distribution according to needs means that personal economic interest is realized in the form of social welfare and security; and other forms of distribution according to ways other than work determine that personal interest realization are achieved through non-labor income. The differences of forms of interest realization will inevitably lead to a relationship of "the bigger share of one side means the smaller share of others." And even distribution according to work itself acknowledges de facto inequality and contains a variety of forms such as hourly wages, paid by piecework, bonuses, which also determines that, there are differences and contradictions of interest in form of realization in social and economic interests.

(2) Differences in time and degree of realization determinethe existence of inherent differences and contradictions in the market economy in the primary stage of socialism.

Differences in timeare demonstrated in the fact that "the two kinds of economic interests may not be realized at the same time." For example, although the ultimate goal of socialism is common prosperity of all laborers, in this process, some people are encouraged to get rich first. This time difference, coupled with the changes in socio-economic factors, will inevitably lead to the differences of amount in the realization of economic interests, thus results in certain interest contradictions. Difference in degree of realizationis showed in the fact that "two kinds of economic interests cannot be realized in the same degree." Specifically, it is showed as follows: the realization of one kind of interestis at the expense of that of other kinds of interest as the prerequisite; the bigger the volume of the realization of one kind of interest means the smaller volume of realization of other kind of interest, that is, the increase of realization of one kind of interest is at the decrease of realization of other kinds of interest as the prerequisite. For example, when the total amount of revenue of an enterprise is set, the bigger the amount paid to the state, the smaller the amount the enterprise and its employees will get, vice versa; apart from the amount paid to the state, the bigger the profit retention of the enterprises, the lesser the income of the employees, vice versa; apart from these two parts, the more one employee get, the lesser other employees will have; and so on. These differences of realization degree will certainly lead to interest contradictions.

III. Interest Coordination of Interest Differences and Contradictions in the Primary Stage of Socialism

The establishment of the socialist system provides the possibility for the people to correctly understand and consciously coordinate their interest differences and contradictions. The superiority of socialist system just lies in the fact that it can resolve the problem of social wealth distribution not through brutal class struggle but through coordinating the fundamental interest demands of all classes, strata and groups. It is the socialist political and economic systems that provide the guarantee for the coordination and relevant mechanisms.

First, interest coordination must rely on appropriate system of economic coordination

The fundamental nature of socialist system determines that, the problem of social interest must be resolved by relying on the relevant ownership of means of production and its realization system, and on distribution system and its realization form. Only by establishing the specific structure and form that suitable for the development of productive forces, that is, public ownership is the mainstay and diverse forms of ownership coexist, distribution according to work is the mainstay and diverse forms of distribution co-exist, can the enthusiasm of the laborers be mobilized and the interest differences and contradictions be coordinated. On this basis, we must also take into account the interests of the individual, the collective and the state, make a good balance between individual interests and the interests of society. Besides, various policy and economic method should also be applied.

Second, interest coordination must take political coordination as its guarantee.

Politics is the concentrated expression of economics, and reflects the fundamental interests in economic relations of all classes, groups and individuals. It is one of the main functions of the state apparatus and political system of socialist countries inthe primary stage of socialism to use political system and method to coordinate interest relations among all groups. In this stage, the interests of all groups and individuals and interests of the society are both identical and contradictory, which must be correctly handled. Under the condition that the productive forces are still underdeveloped, making good coordination of interest relations among all classes, strata and interest groups to prevent the intensification of interest contradictions is the prerequisite for building a peaceful and harmonious environment for the smooth development of socialist cause, and also the key to the rapid development of socialist productive forces and the satisfaction of the increasing material and cultural needs of the people. This requires that the socialist country fully promote democracy, so as to take use of its counteraction to coordinate interest relations among all groups and to mobilize their enthusiasm; at the same time it is necessary for the state to fully realize the specific interests of all interest subjects and make overall considerations and correct policies, so that the short-term and long-term interests, specific interests and common interests can be properly balanced. Only in this way can the enthusiasm of all the people be fully mobilized and our socialist drive vigorously developed. In addition, relevant political line, principles, policies and measures are needed to support the political coordination.

Third, the role of the law is also needed in interest coordination.

The interest subjects in the primary stage of socialism are extremely complex, consisting of not only big interest groups such as classes, strata, but also smaller one such as various enterprises and public institutions, as well as private owners and self-employers, whoall have their own special interests and intricate interest relations. These relations, although needpolitical measures or state powerbut cannot completely and directly handled by them. So a diverse and multi-level system of coordination with diverse mechanisms is necessary to maintain social order and avoid unnecessary interest disputes. The law as norms of social behaviors and the fixed and basic rules for adjusting human relations can effectively and directly coordinate interest contradictions among classes, strata, groups and individuals. The law in the primary stage of socialism reflects the will of all the people led by the working class, and therefore really represents the interests of the whole society. So, the law in the primary stage of socialism can effectively coordinate the interest differences and contradictions among the people and ensure the realization of interest of all the people. Besides, administrative measures are also needed in using law as the coordinating means.

Fourth, full play must be given to the role of morals in interest coordination.

The similarities of morals and laws are that that they all belong to social superstructure, are all norms of people's behaviors, and all play the role of constraining, encouraging or guiding, in coordinatingthe interest relations among the people. But law and morals are different in that legal constraints are compulsory while morals are guiding. Therefore, in the primary stage of socialism, they complementto each other in coordinating interest differences and contradictions. In private ownership society, as complement to the law and supplement to politics, morals mainly safeguard the interests of the ruling class, so they cannot really coordinate the antagonistic interest relations. Only after the elimination of private ownership andthe antagonism between individual interests and social interests, can the collective and socialist ethics and principles be full functioned in the coordination of interest relations among individuals, and between individuals and society. Thus, in the primary stage of socialism, moral building is extremely important.

In short, the existence of interest differences and contradictions in the primary stage of socialism is objective. As long as we recognize the diversity of its interest subjects and act in accordance with objective laws, and coordinate and resolve interest differences and contradictions through developing production and establishing appropriate interest coordination system to meet the growing needs of the society, socialism will surely has full vigor and vitality.

Chapter Thirteen

Interest Groups in the Primary Stage of Socialism and Contradictions among Them

Under the condition of the market economy in the primary stage of socialism and the premise of scientific division of classes, the original and new born strata (about their changes, see Chapter Ten), the key to correctly understanding and handling the differences and contradictions among the interest groups is to identify these groups and their differences and contradictions.

I. Interest Groups in the Primary Stage of Socialism and Criteria for their Identification

Theoretically, class contradiction is no long the principal contradiction in the primary stage of socialism. So only by correctly understanding the interest groups and their relations and properly coordinate their differences and contradictions of interests under the condition of adhering to class analysis, can we give full play to the motive forces of interests to mobilize the enthusiasm of all interest groups. Under the new historical conditions and the premise of adhering to the division of working class, the farmer class and the intelligentsia as part of the working class, it is very necessary to identify the interest groups and differences and contradictions between them according to materialistic conception of history, method of class analysis of Marxism and the theory of interest group identification, and on this basis, to make proper policies and strategies, so as to mobilize the enthusiasm of all sides.

What, then, is an interest group in primary stage of socialism? An interest group refers to an interest community formed on the basis of relatively common interests through socio-economic relations. The members of an interest group have relatively identical interest objectives and values while between different interest groups there are certain differences and contradictions. The existence, development, differentiation and combination of interest groups in the primary stage of socialism are subject to the constraints of economic relations and the influence of various complex factors in this stage, such as society, history, ethnicity, mentality, locality, tradition. It is precisely the ownership, division of labor, forms of social labor and other complex social and historical factors that fundamentally determine that there are interest differences and contradictions between interest groups, which, in turn, objectively determine the historical necessity of the existence of interest groups and criteria for their identification.

Given the necessary existence of differences of interest groups in the primary stage of socialism, what criteria should we use to identify them? Basically they are as follows:

First, determining the essential attributes of the interest groups based on their ownership of means of production. In the primary stage of socialism, the Marxist theory of identifying classes by ownership of means of production is still of methodological significance. The differences of status and role of people in the relations of means of production in the primary stage of socialism determine their economic interest groups. In the ownership relationship with the public sector remaining dominant and diverse sectors of the economy developing side by side, great differences exist between different sectors: within the public ownership, there are the differences of state-owned economy and collective economy; within the same economic sector there is the separation between the ownership and management of the enterprises; between the enterprises in the same sector of ownership, there is the differences of degree of independence; and there are also different forms of realization of ownership in the same sector of ownership. All these differences determine that, the social members, who are inevitably integrated with one of the sectors of ownership, will necessarily fall into different interest groups with different interests, and that different production units constitute different relatively independent economic interest groups. So it is a premise to analyze the interest groups starting from the relationship of ownership.

Second, identifying interest groups on the basis of distribution and other relationships in the primary stage of socialism. In this stage, the differences of interests are prominently reflected in distribution: different forms of distribution and different forms of interest realization also determine the existence of different interest groups with certain differences in economic aspect. In the primary stage of socialism the distribution pattern in which distribution according to work is the main form that coexists with other forms of distribution determines the differences of distribution between interest groups. For example, the group that earns their income in accordance with the principle of distribution according to work are different from groups realizing their income according to other forms, such as capital, management, factors of production; even within the same distribution form there are differences of interests. This determines the existence of different interest groups. In addition, relations between people in the production, exchange, consumption and other links also contribute to the existence of different interest groups. For example, in the process of production, there are groups of managerial personnel, technical personnel, salespersons, and so on; in the process of exchange, there are also commodity producers, sellers, buyers and so on.

Third, under the precondition of identifying interest groups on the basis of economic relationships, we can also take into account the differences of social status caused by occupations and other economic and social factors. Same or similar occupations can bring about generally similar economic and political interests, thus contributing to the formation of different interest groups.

In short, in identifying interest groups, we must insist on the criteria of ownerships, possession of products, roles, status of the individuals in social and economic relations, in addition to other social factors. These criteria show that different interest groups have their different demands, interests and contradictions.

II. Causes for the Existence of Different Interest Groups in the Primary Stage of Socialism

Under the conditions of market economy in the primary stage of socialism, the interest relations among the people are composed mainly of the inter-group relations of different interests. In this stage, with the existence of the working class, the farmer class and the intelligentsia as part of the working class, it is an objective existence that there are the differences of interests and values and thus frictions and contradictions within these classes and strata, in addition to their complex interest structure. What, then, are the causes for the existence of these complex and diverse interest groups in the primary stage of socialism?

First, the productive forces in primary stage of socialism are relatively backward, and the material and cultural wealth cannot sufficient meets the growing needs of the people. The considerable gap between the limited wealth and the distribution is the fundamental material reason for the existence of the interest groups.

Second, there remains a lot of residue of the old society, which constitutes extensive social basis for the existence of different interest groups. The primary stage of socialism is just born from the womb of the old society, which, under the complex international and domestic circumstances, still maintains complex social relations with the class exploiting society and its remnants and traces. The great social differences caused by the old division of labor still exist, so do the classes, strata, fixed at relatively independent careers and the old mentality and morality. All these give their contributions to the social and historical basis for the existence of complex interest groups in the primary stage of socialism. For example, the old divisions between urban and rural, workers and farmers, and manual labor and mental labor, determine the existence of the interest groups of urban and rural residents, the working class and the farmer class, the manual and mental workers and so on; the groups of self-employed workers, the private entrepreneurs, etc. , by their very nature, also have the traces of the old society

Even the new criminals, reactionary exploiting class elements and other anti-socialist elements who are gestated from the residue of the old society, under certain conditions, may form interest groups hostile or antagonistic to socialism. The division of labor in the primary stage of socialism place people in relatively fixed occupations, so that people have different status and different material and cultural benefits, thus giving birth to different interest groups. Besides, the quality and physical differences of the laborers also result in different interest groups. For instance, singers, artists and the like are workers having special professional skills. Another instance includes the interest difference between skilled and unskilled workers, and so on.

Third, multiple ownerships and the diversified forms of distribution, as well as the complex relationship in the market economy is the most direct economic roots in the existence of different interest groups in the primary stage of socialism. The relationships in the market economy in the primary stage of socialism determine that relations between interest groups in this stage are complex. The ownership pattern with public ownership playing a dominant role and diverse forms of ownership developing side by side, and the distribution pattern in which distribution according to work is primary and a variety of modes of distribution coexist determine the existence, formation, evolution and development of different interest groups and their complex structure.

There are of course other social causes for the existence of interest groups in the primary stage of socialism, which are not discussed here.

III. The Composition of the Major Interest Groups in the Primary Stage of Socialism

On the premise of recognizing the general division of the working class, the farmer class and the intelligentsia, we can make further divisions of the interest groups in the primary stage of socialism as follows:

By differences of division of social labor, we can divide the social members into urban residents, rural residents; manual laborers, mental laborers (intellectuals), etc.

By class differences caused by fundamental differences of relationship with means of production, our social members can be divided into the interest groups of industrial producers, agricultural producers, intellectuals within the working class, the interest groups of private entrepreneurs, self-employers, etc. in the non-public sectors of the economy.

By forms of ownership and realization, the social members can be divided into interest groups of employees in state-owned, collective-owned units, in township enterprises, in private sectors, in mixed ownership sectors, in joint-stock enterprises, in shareholding enterprises, etc. In addition, there are also interest groups of self-employers, owners or managers of private enterprises and foreign-funded enterprises, etc.

From the prospective of enterprises with relatively independent status in the market economy, there are interest groups of factories, shops, all kinds of companies, etc.

The social members can also be divided on the basis of forms of distribution into the different interest groups, including the civil servants and workers in public institutions, workers based on labor contract system, on leasing management and on the household contract responsibility system, employers and employees in private enterprises, contractors and producers in contracted enterprises, etc.

By occupations and social status in economic activities, they can be divided into interest groups of workers, farmers, individual industrialists and businessmen, engineers and technicians, medical workers, teachers, managers in private sectors, agricultural producers, households involved both in industry and farming, workers in government bodies, managers in public enterprises, etc.

By their economic relations in the socialist market economy, the social members can be divided into interest groups of producers, sellers, consumers, and so on.

By their income and wealth gaps and the tendencies caused by these gaps, the social members can be divided into interest groups of the wealthy, the relatively wealthy, the well-off, those just having adequate food and clothing and the poor. The wealthy group refers to the group of person having assets worthy of millions even hundreds of millions Yuan. According to sampling surveys, surveys of typical cases and related data of the National Bureau of Statistics of China, currently the highest income groups are primarily composed of the outstanding scientific and technological personnel, self-employees, private entrepreneurs, enterprise contractors, managers of leasing operation, as well as popular singers, movie stars, sports stars, etc. The relative wealthy group refers to those who have hundreds of thousands of assets each, live a relatively affluent life, have their own houses, cars, and can afford their children's higher education fee and can enjoy vocations. They include managers in foreign-funded or private enterprises, individual industrialists or businessmen with high incomes, engineers and technicians in advantageous industries, entrepreneurs in public-owned enterprises with good economic returns, etc. Well-off group refers to people who have tens of thousands of assets each and live a relatively comfortable life, including teachers, state officials, ordinary intellectuals, workers of enterprises with good economic returns, and so on. The group with adequate food and clothing refers to the group whose members have just enough income to basically meet their needs for food and clothing, including workers in the city and agricultural laborers in rural areas. The poor group refers to people living below the poverty line and cannot get enough food and clothing.

The above is a broad and extensive division. In general, the components of the interest groups in the primary stage of socialism are as follows:

First is the interest group of material producers within the working class. The working class is composed of three parts, i. e. , the workers of material producers, the managerial personnel in public-owned enterprises, state organs, etc. , and intellectuals engaged in the managerial, cultural, educational, science and technology work. By material producers we mean workers directly engaged in productive labor, including workers in state-owned, collective-owned, mixed-owned economies and in enterprises of joint-stock system, cooperative system, shareholding system, in private enterprises and the self-employee and so on. The group of material producers, based on their occupations, can be further divided into subgroups workers in the fields of industry, transportation, capital construction, commerce, services, agriculture, forestry, animal husbandry and fishery and other. The migrant workers, who derive from the farmer class and enter the urban areas, are also part of the working class.

Second is the interest group of farmer class. Farmers account for the majority of China's population and most of them are agricultural laborers under the household contract responsibility system. Although since 1979 this system has been implemented in rural areas, and the mode of operation has changed with it, the farmers still belong to the interest group of the farmer class in the collective economy. And based on the divisions of labor and occupations, they can be further divided into farmers directly engaged in farming under the household contract responsibility system, farmer-entrepreneurs, farmer-administrators at the community level, farmers engaged both in industry and farming, and so on.

Third is the interest group of intellectuals. In China, intellectuals, as part of the working class, are those engaged in such mental work as management, science and technology, culture, education, ordinary staff in Party and state bodies and so on.

Fourth is the interest group of social leaders and business managers. In the primary stage of socialism, although the leaders of Party and government bodies at all levels and the directors and managers in public enterprises mostly belong to the strata of intellectuals as part of the working class, they still form a special interest group different from ordinary workers, farmers and intellectuals due to the importance of their work, their posts and the political and economic positions as well as the responsibilities they shoulder. The subgroup of social leaders and business managers has dual natures: on the one hand they are representatives of the interests of state or the collective, they should not gain any personal interest from it; on the other hand, as laborers seeking means of livelihood, they have interests and demands of their own. In practice, we should clearly distinguish their capacity as social leaders, managers and representatives of state interests from their capacity as subjects of personal interests.

Fifth is the interest group of the self-employed. In the current stage, the components of this stratum are complex, but their incomes are usually higher than the incomes of those working in public economy or the Party and state organizations.

Sixth is the interest group of owners or managers of the private economy. In the primary stage of socialism, the existence of non-public economy will necessarily give birth to its owners and managers. Along with it, there will be de facto wage-labor relationship between the employers and managers and the employees or workers, and the incomes of the former will inevitably include the surplus value created by the latter.

Seventh is the interest group consisting of managers, agents and operators of foreign-funded enterprises and private enterprises, which has been formed since China's reform and opening up after large amounts of foreign investment were introduced.

IV. Main Features of the Pattern of Interest Groups in the Primary Stage of Socialism

Under the condition of the market economy in the primary stage of socialism, there exist differences and contradictions among interest groups that cannot be ignored on the basis of fundamental identity of interests, which determine their following basic features.

1. Transitional nature

At present, China is in a reform stage of transition from the planned economy to the market economy. With the changes in economic and political structures, the original interest structure is changing accordingly, resulted in the drastic readjustment and reorganization of interest pattern. For instance, the groups of entrepreneurs (managers) and the self-employed have become important components in the interest structure; the group of employers in the private economy has occupied a considerable position in the structure; many intellectuals have taken leading posts at all levels, injecting fresh blood to the groups of social leaders and managers, and so on. The interest structure built on the old system was not conducive neither to the dynamism of interests or to the mobilization of initiatives of all sides. The current differentiation and combination of interest structure will gradually lead to the shaping of an optimized pattern that is going to give full rein to the dynamism of all interest groups.

2. Diversity

Another outstanding feature of the interest pattern under the market economy in the primary stage of socialism is the diversity of interest group awareness and behaviors. Interest group awareness refers to mental reactions of different interest groups to all the aspects of social life in response to the stimulation of group interests. Interest awareness is composed of sense, concern and understanding of an interest group. The complexity of the interest pattern determines the diverse types of awareness of the interest groups: firstly, longing for socialist modernization, support for reform and opening up and for socialism with Chinese characteristics are the common sense of the various interest groups. Secondly, different interest groups have different goals and benefit-seeking behaviors. Finally, comparison mentality and benefit-comparison behaviors between interest groups are commonplace. This kind of comparison comes from the competition for benefits in their pursuit of interests, because every group has the shared mentality to seek greater interests, although they interest motives may vary. There are two types of benefit comparison: one is positive comparison, that is, through proper comparison, higher enthusiasm are triggered; another one is negative comparison, which views the differences of positions of interest groups in the interest structure in a static way, make comparison only with the higher ones instead of lower ones, and concerns only about short-term interests instead of long-term interests, money and so on instead of contribution, so that it mistakenly believes that theirs is the group getting the most unreasonably low income. Different types of interest awareness will inevitably lead to a different type behavior orientation, a human behavior motivated by the sense of profit-seeking. Different interest groups have different types of interest orientation, due to which, interest frictions, conflicts, contradictions occur, along with the complex interest relations among interest groups. Instances include contradictions between workers and farmers because of the scissors gap between the prices of industrial and agricultural products, contradictions between the employers and employees in the private enterprises, contradictions between entrepreneurs and managers and the employees, contradictions between social leaders and the ordinary people.

3. Differences

The contradictions among interest groups frequently and commonly manifest themselves in distribution, specifically in gaps of incomes. It is necessary to allow appropriate interest gaps between groups so as to form a pattern in which reasonable discrepancies of income are recognized so that enthusiasm of different interest groups can be aroused. However, if the discrepancies are widened unreasonably, the differentiation and structure of interest groups will result in the expansion and intensification of interest contradictions. In the process of China's reform, when the traditional economic model has been broken while the new one is still in the shaping, some distorted and complex economic relations have emerged. On the one hand, in the area of distribution, the egalitarian practice of having everyone "eat from the same big pot" still exist in some places; on the other, the problem in which some people get unreasonable non-labor incomes is exacerbating to some extent. For example, some people illegally get high incomes by taking advantage of the defects in our economy and macro-control to take such practices as bribery, abuse of power, fakery, cheating, etc. This has led to many distorted and tense relations, even interest contradictions and conflicts among interest groups. In our effort to develop the socialist market economy, the widening gap between incomes and between rich and poor has become a prominent social problem.

4. Prominence

The backwardness of the productive forces and underdeveloped market economy make the material means of livelihood cannot meet the needs of the people, which, coupled with the not so reasonable distribution policy, causes the interest contradictions among the people extremely prominent and acute.

5. Clear Demarcation

In the primary stage of socialism, the pattern of interest groups are complicated, and boundaries between them are clear-cut, so do the demands of the groups and contradictions between them. For example, Chinese intellectuals have a clear political intention to establish a socialist democracy and strong demands to improve their living and working conditions; whereas the attention of ordinary workers is put more on material interests such as wage, prices and social welfare.

6. Concentration

More often than not, the interest contradictions in the primary stage of socialism manifest themselves in contradictions between the leaders and the masses. When a social interest conflict break, a considerable part of the masses express their discontent to the direct leaders of their work units or places, showing that the contradictions are mainly manifest themselves as those between the leaders and the masses.

7. Acuteness

The tension of interest relations tends to cause some conflicts, which, if not handled properly, may cause unrest. In the primary stage of socialism, intensified interest relationships often develop into face to face conflicts. For example, because of the problems of unemployment, housing, wages, prices, and so on, some people adopt measures of direct confrontation such as strikes, collective petitions, demonstrations, assault on government organizations; fierce disputes and conflicts may also break out within the masses because of property disputes, asset allocation, land use, and the like. If we lax our vigilance against this kind of mass incidents or handle them improperly, they may lead to greater social unrest affecting the political stability and social harmony.

V. Contradictions among Groups in the Primary Stage of Socialism Largely Demonstrate Themselves as Interest Contradictions among the People

The interest contradictionsamong interest groups in the primary stage of socialism will necessarily find their expression in frictions, conflicts and disputes among persons. Apart from antagonistic contradictions among groups, these contradictions largely and frequently demonstrate themselves as interest contradictions among the people. Contradictions of human relations constitute the main part of contradictions among the people at this stage in our society, while interest contradictions are the root cause of all other contradictions among the people.

1. Interest contradictions are the material and economic causes of emergence and change of contradictions among the people

In On the Correct Handling of Contradictions among the People, in addition to analyzing political and ideological contradictions among the people and methods for resolving them, Comrade Mao Zedong also talks about various interest contradictions. But due to the limitations of historical conditions, he didn't pay enough attention to economic causes of contradictions among the people in his analysis. In fact, interest contradictions are the material and the economic causes of and factors affecting the development of various contradictions among the people. Only by making in-depth analysis from material aspect can interest contradictions among the people be correctly understood and handled. And only by profoundly understanding the interest contradictions among the people can contradictions among the people in general be correctly understood and handled.

In the primary stage of socialism, especially in the process of reform toward the socialist market economy, the realistic social and economic conditions determine that there exist various complex interest contradictions within the ranks of the people.

First, in the primary stage of socialism, the less developed market economy and relatively backward productive forces make the relative insufficiency of people's living materials, resulting in further prominence of interest contradictions among the people in distribution. Ours is a primary stage socialist country built on a basis of relatively backward material conditions, whose limited production of material means of life cannot fully meet the needs of the people; on the other hand, the politically and economically liberated working people are in an urgent need of greater improvement of living conditions both in the material and cultural living conditions. In these circumstances, if the distribution is unreasonable, the interest contradictions among the people will become more outstanding.

Second, in the primary stage of socialism, the diverse forms of ownership determine that the interest contradictions among the people are also diverse. In this stage, along with public economic sector, there are also individual or private as well as other forms of economic sectors, such as the mixed ownership, joint ventures, share-holding enterprises. This determines the variety of interest contradictions among the people. For example, contradictions between workers in the public sectors and individual laborers and managers or employers in private sectors, contradictions between employers and employees in private enterprises, contradictions between individual laborers and private managers on the one side and the consumers on the other, etc. Under socialist conditions, the individual laborers are self-employed workers, whose productive activities are not exploitative, and whose existence is an integral part of the economy of primary stage of socialism. In general, interest contradictions between individual producers or traders and workers in public enterprises are non-antagonistic. However, because the means of production and products of labor in the individual sector of the economy are privately owned by individuals, and individual economy represents the personal interests of the individual workers, it in some degree is contradictory to the state interests of socialist country as a whole. In the primary stage of socialism, individual economy is a component of the whole economy, and its existence and development is helpful for economic growth, for creating job opportunities, for invigorating the market, and for better meeting the various needs of the people. But it must be seen that the private economy will inevitably has its negative sides. Firstly, the nature of its employment determines that the relations between the employers and employees are that of wage-labor. Secondly, because of its private nature, it is possible that, driven by profit-seeking, private economy may engage in profiteering activities that can disrupt the market and harm the overall and long-term economic interests of socialism. Within sector of the private economy itself, there are interest contradictions between the employees and employers; interest contradictions among different entities, and interest contradictions between the private economy and the state-owned economy.

Third, the diversity of realization of economic interests in the primary stage of socialism further exacerbates the interest contradictions among the people. The diverse forms of ownership determine the diversity of its distribution forms. In this stage, in addition to distribution according to work as the main form of distribution, there are also other distribution forms. For example, there is distribution according to needs in form of social welfare, distribution according to production factors in form of unearned income, and so on. This determines that, interest contradictions exist among the state, the collective and the individuals; among groups of different incomes; between employers and employees. The diverse forms of distribution determine the complexity of forms of interest realization, and make the interest contradictions among the people more complicated.

Fourth, the complicated economic relations in the primary stage of socialist market economy determine the existence of intricate contradictions of economic interests among the people. For example, in this stage, the public economy as the mainstay coexists with non-public sectors of the economy. This structure determines that there exist interest contradictions reflecting these economic relations. In the relations of market economy in this stage, the intertwined contradictions between the social labor of the public sector of the economy and individual labor, and that between the social labor of the non-public sectors of the economy and individual labor leads to the extreme complexity of contradictions among the people. Other interest contradictions include those in resources allocation, market segmentation, those among commodity producers, those between commodity producers and business operators in the circulation links, and those between the producers and operators on the one side and the direct consumers on the other. All these intricate interest contradictions determine the existence of complexity and development of interest contradictions among the people.

Fifth, in the primary stage of socialism, there are still remnants of the old economic base, old superstructure and old social elements, making the interest contradictions among the people interweave with those between the people and the enemy. This contributes to the acuteness of the interest contradictions in this stage. The existing remnants of old economic base and superstructure and their negative impact on interest contradictions in the primary stage of socialism makes it possible that non-antagonistic interest contradictions become antagonistic. Meanwhile, due to historical, realistic and international and other reasons, there are still hostile elements, new-born hostile elements, secret agents, counter-revolutionaries, etc. , who represent the private interests of a small group of the old exploiting classes and the anti-socialist forces. Their contradictions with the people are of antagonistic nature, which sometimes take the forms of fierce class struggles. The interweaving of these two interest contradictions of different nature is bound to make the interest contradictions among the people more acute, more intricate and more difficult to be correctly handled with.

Sixth, the specific forms of economic base of primary stage of socialism are immature and unsound, so are its specific forms of superstructure. This makes the interest contradictions among the people more outstanding. In this stage, socialist public ownership is not a public ownership in complete sense in that there are differences as well as contradictions between state-owned economy and collective economy, and the relative independence of different economic entities must also be recognized. In this stage, due to the relative low level of market economy and unbalanced development, there are tremendous differences between the state-owned economy and collectively economy in terms of possession of means of production, sale conditions, quality of workers, environment of profitability, etc. , which exacerbate the existing interest contradictions. From the point view of counter reaction of superstructure on economic base, the immatureness of the superstructure, especially the drawbacks and defects in political field in the primary stage of socialism, aggravate the already outstanding interest contradictions. For instance, when the interests of the people are seriously damaged by the bureaucratic style of work, the people cannot effectively stop it immediately due to the unsoundness of the socialist democracy. In this case, contradictions among the people can change into fierce conflicts of interests.

Seventh, the relative low level of cultural and moral standards in the primary stage of socialism aggravates the existing differences of interests and contradictions among the people. In China's primary stage of socialism, people's ideological, moral and cultural standards are not high enough, which adds to the acuteness of interest contradictions among the people.

In summary, after the establishment of the socialist system in China, the deep-seated and complex economic, political, cultural, ethical causes in the primary stage of socialism determine that, in the different classes, strata and interest groups, contradictions exist not only among individuals or specific interests, but also between individuals or specific interests and the common interests of the whole society. Interest contradictions among the people are the root causes of existence and development of contradictions among the people.

2. The position, forms, nature and features of interest contradictions among the people

Contradictions among the people constitute a complex system composed of many contradictions, including contradictions between ethnic groups, contradictions between regions, contradictions among collective units, contradictions between enterprises, contradictions within the ranks of the working class, contradictions within the farmer class, contradictions within the intelligentsia, contradictions within individual labors, contradiction within private economic operators, contradictions between the working class on the one hand and the farmer class and other working classes on the other, contradictions between the governing party and the government on the one hand and the people on the other, contradictions between the leadership and the masses, contradictions between the higher levels and lower levels, contradictions between Party and non-Party, contradictions within the Party, contradictions among the state, the collectives and the individuals, contradictions among individuals, contradictions among social strata, contradiction among interest groups, and so on. These contradictions are manifested in economic, political, ideological and other fields, among which, the interest contradictions among the people are the material and economic roots of the emergence, existence, development and intensification of all other contradictions among the people, and are the dominant type of contradictions constraining the development of other types of contradictions.

In contemporary China, although the social system for the existence of antagonistic interest contradictions among classes is abolished after the establishment of socialist system, the remnants of the old relations of production and the old division of labor remain, and in particular, there are different forms of ownerships. Therefore, there are still interest contradictions of non-class antagonism nature within the ranks of the people. In the primary stage of socialism, the existence of remnants of the old society and anti-socialist elements determines that some the interest contradictions among the people are inevitably antagonistic, but this type of contradictions is not in the dominant position.

Although interest contradictions exist both in societies of class exploitation and socialist society, the interest contradictions among the people in the primary stage of socialism in China are distinctive in features.

First of all, the nature of the interest contradictions is different. The interest contradictions in societies of class exploitation are class antagonism in nature, while those in the primary stage of socialism are non-antagonistic because of fundamental identity of interests of the people. Here "fundamental identity" means that, in the primary stage of socialism, every member of the working people have the same status in possessing the means of production and in realizing their own interests through their own labor. So there is no fundamental antagonistic interest contradiction among them; on the contrary, they have the same interest aspirations and sources, therefore, these contradictions exist only within the ranks of the people. In this stage of socialism, the interest contradictions between the employers and employees within the non-public sectors of the economy are also different from those between the exploiting and the exploited classes in the old society, for they usually are non-antagonistic in nature either because of their subjection to the restrictions of socialist system. The fundamental identity of interests of the people determines that, the interest contradictions among the people are non-antagonistic. Here non-antagonism refers to its nature, in that neither of the two contradictory sides take completely negating or excluding the other side as the necessary conditions for proving or realizing its own interests. That is to say, fundamentally and generally speaking, these contradictions are non-antagonistic, although it does not exclude the possibility of local or temporary conflicts between them.

Secondly, the interest contradictions are manifested in different areas. In a society of class exploitation, interest contradictions are outstanding already in production. In the process of capitalist production, through their ownership of and control over the means of production, the capitalists appropriate or occupy the fruits of labor of the workers, whose amount of labor is in inverse proportion to the amount of material interests their gained, suggesting that in capitalist society, interest contradictions occur already in the process of production. In the socialist society, in contrast, because the social basis of class exploitation and opposition is basically eliminated, workers in the production area are working for themselves, for their own interests and for the overall interests of society that are closely related to their own interests, and there is no interest relations of class opposition among the workers or between the workers and the managers. Therefore, in the primary stage of socialism, the interest contradictions among workers are mainly manifested in distribution. This is because the system of distribution according to work brings about the de facto differences of distribution, which in turn results in the differences of distribution of means of subsistence and production.

Thirdly, the methods of solving interest contradictions are different. In the primary stage of socialism, the non-antagonistic nature of interest contradictions among the people determines that, in resolving these contradictions, as precondition, we can neither change socialist economic or political system nor eliminate or negate any side of the contradictions. In short, these contradictions cannot be solved through social revolution or by force. Instead, they can only be resolved through the self-improvement and self-reform of socialist system, through the establishment of appropriate economic and political structures, and through the development of productive forces, that is say, through socialist system itself, by economic means, political and ideological work, criticism and self-criticism, and by adjustment and coordination of interests.

In real social life, the interest contradictions among the people in human relations in China are manifested as follows:

First, interest contradictions between all workers and a section of workers and those between different sections of workers. State interests represent the interests of all workers, while enterprises and groups represent the interests of some sections of workers. Therefore, contradictions between state interests and group interests are directly manifested as contradictions between all workers and some sections of the workers. Different enterprises and different groups, respectively representing the interests of their own, request the increment of their interests. So the contradictions between the interests groups are directly manifested as interest contradictions among different sections of the workers. Since in the primary stage of socialism, we must recognize and respect the personal interests of the workers, interest contradictions will occur among individual workers due to the differences of their interests.

Second, interest contradictions between leaders, administrators on the one side and the ordinary people on the other. In the primary stage of socialism, Party and government leading cadres and administrative personnel at all levels and all economic units, are the representatives of state or collective interests. They decide the orientation of state or collective interests through exercising administrative or operational power. In this context, the interest contradictions among the people are manifested as contradictions between the leading cadres or administrators at the higher level and those at the lower level, between different levels of leaders and administrators, and between leaders and administrators at different levels on the one side and the workers on the other. The interest contradictions between leaders and administrators at different levels on the one side and the workers on the other has two implications: one is that, the leaders and administrators are not the subject of their own interests but as representatives of the state or collective interests, so their contradictions with the ordinary workers are those among the state, the collectives the individuals; the other is that, the leaders and administrators also have their own individual interests, so the interest contradictions between them as subjects of individual interests and the working people, belong to, in fact, contradictions of individual interests. So if a leader or administrator imposes unreasonable personal interest demands on the overall interests, it will be in contradiction to the interests of the masses and other leaders or administrators who uphold the overall interests.

Third, interest contradictions between operators in non-public sectors of the economy such as private economy and individual economy on the one side and the state leaders, administrators and workers in public economy on the other side; interest contradictions between laborers in non-public economy and workers in state-owned and collective economy; and interest contradictions within the operators of non-public economy. Under socialist conditions, the non-public sectors of the economy and state-owned and collective economy come under different types of ownership, there will certainly exist interest differences between the operators of the former and the leaders, administrators and workers in the latter. And because of the differences of income distribution between the laborers in the former and those in the latter, there will also exist interest contradictions between them. And there will be interest contradictions among the different operators of non-public economy because the law of the market economy. On the other hand, the operators of the non-public economies, including the private economy and individual economy as integral components of the economy of the primary stage of socialism, are also citizens of the country. Therefore, there are certain interest contradictions between them and the state leaders and administrators.

Fourth, the ongoing reform toward the socialist market economy has given rise to some new situations in the contradictions among the people. Firstly, the reform, on the one hand has made the socialist economy more vigorous, on the other, it has made the interest contradictions among the people more outstanding. The reform of state-owned enterprises is a good example of it. By plunging the enterprises to compete in the market, it has mobilized the initiatives of them and made them establish broader horizontal economic links, but at the same time it has made the social and economic relationships more complicated, in which the enterprises may focus only on their own performances and profits so that the contradictions in the production and distribution links become more obvious and intricate. Another example is the market. The gradual emergence of various kinds of market as the mechanism of economic regulators, while invigorating the socialist economy, makes the socialist market relations and contradictions become more complex. Secondly, the socialist economic reform requires the corresponding political reform. As a result, the various relationships and contradictions in political life, including the handling of relationship between the government and the Party, between the government and enterprises, between central and local governments, etc. , become more outstanding than ever before. Thirdly, the market-oriented economic reform has profoundly changed people's ideas as well as the structure of human relations, making relations among the people more complex and multi-leveled. In short, our reform toward socialist market economy has brought about profound changes in our social life and thus given new content and forms to interest contradictions among the people.

Because of the combined interaction between the domestic and foreign factors, interest contradictions among the people often interweave with contradictions between ourselves and the enemy and with class struggle existing in certain limits, making the interest contradictions among the people find intricate expressions.

3. Measures for handling interest contradictions among the people

To correctly handle interest contradictions among the people, we first of all must analyze the nature of the contradictions to distinguish contradictions among the people from contradictions between ourselves and the enemy, and accordingly to properly handle them in different ways. In his *On the Correct Handling of Contradictions* among the People, Comrade Mao Zedong proposed the use of economic measures to address interest contradictions among the people. In 1979, Comrade Deng Xiaoping pointed out: "We must adjust the relations between this various types of interests in accordance with the principle of taking them all into proper consideration. Were we to do the opposite and pursue personal, local or immediate interests at the expense of the others, both sets of interests would inevitably suffer. "[1] Economic approach serves as the major method for solving interest contradictions among the people, and "make overall

---

① *Selected Works of Deng Xiaoping*, vol. 2, People's Publishing House, 1994, pp. 175—176

plans and take all factors into consideration" on the basis of "care for personal interests" are the two fundamental principles in handling interest contradictions among the people.

Not directly relying on enthusiasm, but aided by the enthusiasm engendered by the great revolution, and on the basis of personal interest, personal incentive and business principles, we must first set to work in this small peasant country to build solid gangways to socialism by way of state capitalism. "Care for personal interests" is an important principle in correctly handling interest contradictions among the people. Lenin once explicitly pointed out that "Personal incentives can step up production." And socialist construction cannot "directly relying on enthusiasm," but on the basis of personal interest, personal incentive and business principles. "Otherwise we shall never get to communism, we shall never bring scores of millions of people to communism."[1] "We must not count on going straight to communism. We must build on the basis of peasants' personal incentive." "We say that every important branch of the economy must be built up on the principle of personal incentive. There must be collective discussion, but individual responsibility. At every step we suffer from our inability to apply this principle."[2] After the victory of the socialist revolution, the basic interest contradictions of society are no longer those between the exploiting and the exploited classes, but rather the non-antagonistic ones among the individuals and groups within the ranks of the people. The realistic interest demand of the people is no longer to get rid of their exploited and oppressed social status, but to improve their material and cultural life. Under these new conditions, we should mobilize the enthusiasm of the people by giving full play to their concern about their material interests to build socialism in the process of constantly meet their material interests and demands. In the primary stage of socialism, affirmation of people's concern over their interests means the affirmation of their concern over the outcome of their labor. By doing so, people's pursuit of personal interests can be channeled into the direction of increasing income through work. This can both promote the development of socialist economy and help resolve the interest contradictions among the people.

First, establishing a primary stage socialist political-social system that conforms to the complex interest pattern, can give full play to the impetus

---

①   *Collected Works of Lenin*, vol. 42, People's Publishing House, 1987, p. 176.
②   *Collected Works of Lenin*, vol. 42, People's Publishing House, pp. 190—191.

of interests and can arouse the enthusiasm of different interest groups. Interest relations, in fact, are no other than the relations among the interest subjects. The reasonable and specific interests of each individual laborer and each interest group, which are the motives for their work, should be taken into full account. On the other hand, however, the specific and individual interests of each group and individual must be subordinated to interests of the state as a whole, because specific interests without constraints will have a negative impact on the society. In the primary stage of socialist market economy, we must take into full account of the interests of the individual, the collective and the state. At the same time, we must also take full consideration of the interests of all the subjects of different sectors of the economy, on this basis, to establish a distribution system with diverse forms and correct policies of distribution, and an effective macro regulation system to take full advantage of the market mechanism. The complexity of interest groups in society will inevitably lead to the complexity and diversity in ideological and political fields. This requires that we should further improve socialist democracy at the primary stage of socialism, improve Party leadership, strengthen socialist legal system, expand the scope and channel of all strata of society to participate in political activities, in order to effectively carry out the ideological and intellectual work in all aspects and at all levels. Therefore, we should build an effective social, economic and political system in which the interests of all groups can be properly taken into consideration and all the people can joint hands to give full play to their enthusiasm.

Second, maintaining a good socialist market order so as to create a competitive environment that can provide fair and equal opportunities to all interest groups. In the market activities in the primary stage of socialism, all individuals and groups evaluate their economic performance by the returns the get, they all want to get a maximum income at minimum pay, which requires that the product of labor be distributed through the law of value of the market economy in its normal sense. But in the current economic life in China, the foundation of our market economy is relatively weak and the market is not mature enough and is full of loopholes, which provides opportunities for speculative activities, leading to the unreasonable interest distribution. This requires us to further regulate the economic order, develop a market economy and improve the market system with law as its safeguard, so as to maintain a good market order and provide a fair starting line for different interest groups.

Third, strengthening the study of different interest groups among the people, to base the settling of interest contradictions among the groups on scientific analyses. We must carry out in-depth research and wide survey to get a clear grasp of the interest groups within the ranks of the people, and get a full understanding of the conditions and causes of their formation, their sense of community and demands, the features of relations among the groups and the basic law governing the development of the contradictions, to formulate the correct measures for handling inter-group conflicts.

Fourth, comprehensively using policy, legal, ideological, cultural and moral measures and strengthening our education to properly coordinate and reasonably adjust relations and resolve contradictions among the interest groups. In the primary stage of socialism, there are considerably large interest differences among individuals and among interest groups within the ranks of the people. Some of these differences will produce negative influence on the society and mental imbalance of some groups, which will dampen their spirits, or exacerbate their negative consumption mentality and behavior of comparing with others, eventually leading to complaints, frictions even conflicts between groups. Although some of these phenomena are not unusual in the process of reform, some of the unreasonable differences, if not properly adjusted, will affect people's enthusiasm in the long run. Some reasonable differences should also be adjusted through measures of policy, laws, and intellectual and moral measures. We should develop and adopt proper economic and political policies, use such economic means as taxes and finance, take advantage of the political strength of our party and state and all kinds of administrative disciplinary measures, strengthen ideological and political work and the building of socialist political, material and cultural civilizations, to gradually alleviate and ultimately solve the interest problems, to ensure that our interest structure in the primary stage of socialism is always in the optimum state.

Appendix I

On Social Crises in Socialist Countries[1]

In the social life of socialist countries, due to complex factors, there are the phenomena of conflicts and acuteness of confrontations among the people, and there are also social conflicts, social unrests and even social crises. Correct understanding and handling these problems is of great significance for the social stability and long-term peace and order in our country and for the consolidation and development of socialism.

I. The Antagonistic Side and Intensification of Contradictions among the People

Generally speaking, the contradictions between ourselves and the enemy are antagonistic in nature, while those among the people are not. But if we confuse the two different types of contradictions, lose vigilance against them or handle them improperly, the contradictions among the people can become intensified or transformed, leading to serious confrontations or social conflicts.

First of all, to understand the antagonistic side and intensification of the contradictions among the people, we must make clear what is the antagonistic contradiction and what is non-antagonistic contradiction.

Comrade Mao Zedong pointed out in *On Contradiction* that: "... antagonism is one form, but not the only form, of the struggle of opposites."[2] Based on this statement, we can regard antagonism as the

---

[1] This article is one section of the author's doctoral dissertation written in 1987, part of which was published in the journal of *Reform of China's Political Structure* (中国政治体制改革), no. 3, 1989. Necessary revisions have been made when it is included in this book.

[2] *Selected Works of Mao Zedong*, (bound volume), People's Publishing House, 1968. p. 308.

form of struggle of open conflict between opposites to resolve the contradiction when it develops to a certain stage. Contradiction is universal, while antagonism is a particular form of solution. A contradiction is antagonistic only when opposites are fundamentally opposed to each other and have to resort to open conflict, or, antagonism, as its solution. The non-antagonistic contradiction refers to the contradiction whose opposites are fundamentally identical and its solution is not necessarily in the form of open conflict.

We must, based on the above definitions, make necessary distinctions between the antagonistic nature and antagonistic form or phenomenon of contradictions, between antagonism of whole society and individual, and between class antagonism and non-class antagonism, etc. The antagonistic nature of contradiction refers to the antagonism of opposites of a contradiction because of their fundamental opposition. The antagonistic form of contradiction refers to solution of contradiction in the form of open conflict, which is determined by the specific circumstances. If the opposites of a contradiction are fundamentally antagonistic in nature and it is resolved by open conflict, this contradiction is antagonistic. But if the opposites of the contradiction are not fundamentally antagonistic, although open conflict occur between them, this kind of contradictions are not antagonistic, only that they occasionally or momentarily manifests themselves in the form of conflict, which is only an antagonistic phenomenon of contradiction. Entire antagonism of society refers to the antagonism among major classes or forces of a society, which is originated from the living conditions of the society. Individual antagonism refers to the antagonism among individual elements, individuals or group of society. Since there is no antagonistic contradiction in socialist system, no class antagonism exists between classes except for those between individuals, such as contradictions between working people and the remnants of the old society, occasional contradictions among individuals within the working people, contradictions between the new social elements and those of the old society. Class antagonism originates from the interest contradictions between classes of fundamentally antagonistic, while the interest contradictions originate mainly from the private ownership of production means. Non-class conflicts have no relationship class antagonism. For example, the war between tribes in the primitive society is not class conflict. If we believe that antagonism can only occur between classes, we cannot understand the antagonism in non-class society, nor can we understand non-class antagonism in class society.

Second, to understand the confrontation and intensification of contradictions among the people, we must have a clear understanding of thespecial nature of the two concepts of antagonistic contradiction and non-antagonistic contradictions.

In examining the antagonistic contradictions among the people, the two concepts of antagonistic contradiction and non-antagonistic contradictions in socialist society are necessarily involved. Discussions about these issues have a long history. After the publication of *History of the Communist Party of the Soviet Union (Bolsheviks), Short Course*, around Stalin's proposition "that the relations of production completely correspond to the character of the productive forces," a discussion was made, which involved the discussion on the nature of contradictions in socialist society. Frasov disagreed with Stalin by pointing out that there were contradictions in socialist society, only that these contradictions were non-antagonistic and " it is these contradictions that constitute the driving forces for the development of socialist society. "[1] Since then, the view that "It is the characteristic that there are no antagonistic contradictions in socialist countries" has been widespread, and often seen in the press at home and abroad. In China, in 1957 when the "anti-rightist" movement was widely carried out, the antagonistic contradiction between proletariat and bourgeoisie and between socialism and capitalism were so improperly stressed that it was asserted that life and death fight between the two classes would run throughout the whole socialist stage. Such conclusion clearly regarded antagonistic contradiction as the principal contradiction in socialist countries. The Third Plenary Session of the Eleventh Central Committee of the CPC corrected the error evaluation of the antagonistic contradictions of socialism. It correctly recognized that in a socialist society, non-antagonistic contradictions are large in number, but at the same time there are also certain antagonistic contradictions.

Non-antagonistic contradictions underthe condition of socialism are not inherent to socialist system, so they are non-antagonistic essentially, which are not necessarily been resolved through external conflicts. It cannot be excluded that, under certain conditions, non-antagonistic

---

[1] Tian Guang and Zhang Liangtai (ed.), *The Contradiction between the Productive Forces and Relations of Production under Socialist System*, SDX Publishing House, 1964, p. 13.

contradictions temporarily find expression in antagonistic forms. Antagonistic contradictions under socialism are caused by internal factors and external conditions, so the solution of which, under certain conditions, has to take the form of external conflicts. On the other hand, many antagonistic contradictions of socialist society can be solved by non-antagonistic approach, some even can be converted into non-antagonistic contradictions.

The characteristics of both antagonistic and non-antagonistic contradictions in socialist society are different from those in the old society. Firstly, in the old society, antagonistic contradictions took the dominant position, which directly influenced the change of other non-antagonistic contradictions. After the establishment of socialist system, although antagonistic and non-antagonistic contradictions overlap and mutually influence, the intrinsic antagonistic contradictions in socialist society obviously play a dominant role. Secondly, antagonistic contradictions constituted the main driving forces for social development in the old society, while in socialist society it is the non-antagonistic contradictions that mainly constitute the driving forces for social development. Thirdly, the antagonistic and non-antagonistic contradictions in the old society respectively reflected its inherent antagonistic and non-antagonistic relations between classes. In the socialist society, the antagonistic contradictions reflect the antagonistic relations between socialist forces and a few remnants of forces, elements and factors of the old society; there are no relations of class antagonism in socialist society. Fourthly, there are some new characteristics in the transformation between the antagonistic and non-antagonistic contradictions in socialist society. Mistakes in decision-making or problem-handling are potential to cause temporary or partial antagonism of non-antagonistic contradictions, and can even transform them into antagonistic contradictions. For example, mistakes in distribution policy or serious shortage of consumer goods because of our error will cause dissatisfaction of the masses, which may lead to their direct confrontation with the government. Meanwhile, the antagonistic contradictions in socialist society, under certain circumstances, can be handled as non-antagonistic contradictions. For example, the antagonistic contradiction between socialist ideology and capitalist or feudal ideologies can be handled as contradictions among the people in terms of ideological struggle as long as they are not anti-socialist or anti-Party. Fifthly, in a class society, both antagonistic contradictions and non-antagonistic contradictions, mainly manifest themselves in class relations, with antagonistic class contradictions being dominant. In a socialist society, however, although class contradictions will exist within certain limits for a long time to come, they are no longer the principal contradictions. Antagonistic and non-antagonistic contradictions in socialist society manifest themselves largely as contradictions of non-class and non-antagonistic nature, which have a more and more important positions in the system of socialist system. But on the other hand, there are also non-antagonistic contradictions between classes in socialist society, such as those between the working class and the farmer class; non-class contradictions may also manifest them in opposing forms, such as conflicts within the laboring people.

The existence of antagonistic contradictions among the people is connected with the issue of antagonistic contradictions in socialist society. There are both antagonistic and non-antagonistic contradictions in socialist society, and antagonistic contradictions can transform into a non-antagonistic contradictions. This answers the question whether there are antagonistic contradictions in socialist society, and at the same time explains the reason why contradictions among the people may intensify.

Second, after making the above distinctions, we can now see clearly that, in the primary stage of socialism in our country, there exist conflicts or antagonism among the people and also the possibility of intensification and transformation of these contradictions. The reasons are as follows:

(1) There are isolated phenomena of antagonistic contradictions among the people. In the present stage in China, there are still economic, politic, ideological residue of the old society, in addition to the influence and subversion of external anti-socialist forces in economic, political, ideological and cultural fields, leading to the existence not only contradictions between ourselves and the enemy in a certain scope, but also occasional antagonistic contradictions among the people. Take the relationship between the private and public economy for instance. These are two different economies in nature, and in the primary stage of socialism private economy is permitted to exist. Therefore, under certain conditions, contradictions between private and public economies manifest themselves in non-antagonistic form. So does the relationship between the private owners and their employees, contradictions belonging to the category of contradictions among the people. In political field, the contradictions between the people and elements left over from the old society, such as the feudalists, bourgeois, historical reactionaries, etc. , are antagonistic in nature. However, as long as these elements no longer engage in anti-socialist political activities, honestly submit to socialist transformation and do things beneficial for the people, their contradictions with the people can be regarded and handled as contradictions among the people. Some antagonistic contradictions within the Party also belong to the category of contradictions among the people. Contradictions between the leaders and the masses are non-antagonistic in nature, but those between the severe bureaucrats in the leadership and the masses are antagonistic. In the realm of ideology, contradictions between socialist ideology and feudalist and capitalist ideologies are antagonistic, but the contradictions among the people arising from the influence of these two ideologies come under the category of contradictions among the people in general.

The above analysis shows that individual antagonistic contradictions among the people do exist. By "an individual antagonistic contradictions among the people" we mean: firstly, by saying that the opposites of a contradictions are antagonistic in nature, we refer to its nature, but not the occurrence of antagonistic phenomenon or its necessary resolution through open conflicts. Secondly, a contradiction of antagonistic nature cannot be equated with antagonistic state in reality; it is a latent antagonistic contradiction, which, if handled properly, can become non-antagonistic. And thirdly, an antagonistic contradiction is not equivalent to a contradiction between ourselves and the enemy. Also, in the entire system of contradictions among the people, contradictions of antagonistic nature among the people are few in number and secondary and subordinate in position. With the continuous development of socialism from primary to higher stages, the individual antagonistic contradictions among the people, which are transient in character, will decrease in number. Lastly, the non-antagonistic contradictions among the people, deriving from the basic and principal contradictions of socialist society, are endogenous and the dominant in feature and reflect the essential characteristics of socialism, while the individual antagonistic contradictions among the people are non-endogenous, subordinate ones not reflecting the essential characteristics of socialism.

(2) There are contradictions of class struggle nature among the people in a certain limits. Due to domestic and international factors, class struggle will continue to exist within certain limits in our socialist country, which will inevitably be reflected in the ranks of the people, causing the existence of contradictions with class struggle nature. In China, except for Hong Kong, Macao and Taiwan, class opposition and class struggle between the exploiting and the exploited classes exist only in a limited range, but they do no exist within the ranks of the people. The differences between the working class and peasantry do not manifest themselves as class struggle. And the contradictions prevailing within the ranks of the people are not antagonistic in nature and they do not fall within the category of class struggle. However, this does not exclude the fact that, some of the contradictions among the people have a nature of class struggle. For example, the combating against bourgeois liberalization; the fighting against corrosion of bourgeois ideology; the contradictions between the people and some persons who commit petty crime of endangering public security or social order; these contradictions, although having a nature of class struggle, are still belongs to the contradictions among the people.

(3) In reality, the two types of contradictions differing in nature intertwine, forming a complex situation, in which the class struggle in a limited range and the contradictions of no-class struggle in nature; the limited number of contradictions between ourselves and the enemy and the overwhelming majority of contradictions among the people; the antagonistic contradictions in the non-dominant position and the dominant no-antagonistic contradictions, etc. , are often inextricably intertwined rather than clearly distinguishable from each other, thus forming a complex social situation. This is particularly true in the primary stage of socialism. Take the demonstration of some students, workers, farmers or ordinary citizens for example. Generally speaking, the majority of the masses are patriotic and their demonstration actions belong to the category of contradictions among the people. But the causes are very complex, including instigation of hostile forces, our mistakes in work, and so on. Among them contradictions between us and the evil elements hiding behind and deliberately making incitement and subversion belong to the contradictions between ourselves and the enemy.

(4) Non-antagonistic contradictions among the people can transform into antagonistic ones, and contradictions among the people can transform into contradictions between ourselves and the enemy. Facing complex factors at home and abroad and social contradictions, if we lose vigilance, confuse contradictions, make wrong decisions or handle improperly, a

non-antagonistic contradiction among the people can transform into antagonistic one, and even a contradiction among the people can transform into that between ourselves and the enemy. If our policy is incorrect or our handling is improper, some contradictions among the people can intensify, even result in conflicts. For example, some incidents such as worker strikes, mass violent conflicts or incidents of bloodshed are caused by the improper handling of discontent of the masses over shortage or the increase of prices of consumer goods. In this kind of incidents, except for a few bad elements, the majority of those involved belong to the category of the people. Another example is the quarrel over means of production in rural areas. After the implementation of household contract responsibility system, disputes often happen between farmers over irrigation, land boundary and the like. If not handled timely and effectively, they can develop into violent conflicts. On the other hand, antagonism is only one form of manifestations of contradictions among the people. It is neither the ultimate nor the only resolution. These phenomena, often as the result of insufficient vigilance or improper handling and usually temporary and local, do not represent the essence of contradictions among the people which are non-antagonistic in nature. These antagonistic phenomena do not mean that these contradictions are antagonistic in nature, because they are only temporary and individual form of manifestation of the contradictions.

II. Social Crises in Socialist Countries

The occurrence of periodic crises is unique to capitalist production and the necessary and concentrated manifestation of the inherent contradictions of capitalist system, that is, thecontradiction between its productive forces and relations of production. Although capitalism has not collapsed because of these crises, and even survives one crisis after another, fundamentally it cannot overcome and get rid of them by itself. Marx put forth the theory of capitalist crisis through scientific analysis of capitalist economy. Whether, then, is there any social crisis in socialist countries? This is both a very sensitive and extremely important theoretical question.

1. The raise of the issue

Stalin is among the earliest who discussed this issue. In his Report to the Fourteenth Congress of the C P S U (B.) in 1925, he said: "There, in the capitalist countries, private capital reigns; there, the mistakes committed by individual capitalist trusts, syndicates, or one or other group of capitalists, are corrected by the elemental forces of the market. . . No mistake of any magnitude, no overproduction of any magnitude, or serious discrepancy between production and total demand takes place in capitalist countries without the blunders, mistakes and discrepancies being corrected by some crisis or other. . . There we see economic, commercial and financial crises, which affect individual groups of capitalists. Here, in our country, things are different. Every serious hitch in trade, in production, every serious miscalculation in our economy, results not in some individual crisis or other, but hits the whole of our national economy. In our country, every crisis, whether commercial, financial or industrial, may develop into a general crisis that will hit the whole state. "① While Bukharin, in his article "Notes of An Economist" published in September, 1928, explicitly expounded the economic crisis in the transition toward socialism. He believed that compared with capitalist crisis, the economic crisis occurred then in the Soviet Union was reverse in nature: the former was due to overproduction, over-supply and over-accumulation, while the later was due to shortage of commodity, shortage of supply and shortage of capital. He believed that there were imbalance and unemployment in production area in the Soviet Union. He argued that, economic crisis may occur in the transitional period in a socialist country that was backward and surrounded by enemies and whose citizens were composed of petty bourgeoisie, because its economic production in this period is relatively unplanned. ②It should be noted that, crisis mentioned by Stalin and Bukharin referred to the crisis took place in the country of proletarian dictatorship in a transitional period and was based on the practice prior to the establishment of socialist system. Is there social crisis in a socialist country? After the establishment of socialism, Stalin even didn't admit the existence of basic contradiction in the Soviet Union, let along social crisis. He believed that "economic crises and the destruction of productive forces are unknown" to the USSR. ③

---

① *Collected Works of Stalin*, vol. 7, People's Publishing House, 1958, p. 248.

② See *Selected Works of Bukharin*, Dongfang Publishing House, 1988, pp. 274—276.

③ See *History of the Communist Party of the Soviet Union (Bolsheviks), Short Course*, People's Publishing House, 1975, p. 187

Later, theorists in Yugoslavia were among the earliest who raise the issue of social crisis in socialist countries. This was because Yugoslavia had taken the lead in abandoning the rigid economic model of the Soviet Union to adopt the autonomy system and mechanism market economy, which, to varying degree, gave birth to domestic commercial and financial crises. After that, in the 1960s and 1970s, some theorists in Hungary and other Eastern European countries also put forward their views on the existence of social crisis in socialist countries

It was in 1980 after the Polish Incident that the problem of whether there is social crisis in socialist countries as a major theoretical issue was raised. During that period, an important Polish sociologist Jerzy Józef Wiatr, who was a theoretical authority of Solidarity, in his numerous articles and lectures, discussed the Polish political crisis. This triggered a great debate in socialist theoretical circles over whether there is social crisis in socialist countries, among which, views of the Soviet philosopher Semenov and Anatoly are typical. In their articles published in 1982 and 1984, they believed that, under some specific conditions, there are antagonistic contradictions and crises in socialist countries. But many scholars from former Soviet Union and Eastern European socialist countries, especially those with official capacity, disagreed with or refuted them. Around 1987, some famous Hungarian scholars visiting China on many occasions raised the issue of social crisis in socialist countries. An article published on March 17 in the newspaper Népszabadság read: "It was after painful lessons that we gave up the one-sided view that social crisis exist only in capitalist society. Overall social crisis is indeed a characteristic of capitalist society. But it is possible that in socialist countries there may be temporary or partial crisis in certain historical conditions. " On Nov. 23, 1987, Vice Minister of Central Social and Economic Policy of the Polish United Workers' Party said: "Now there are various conflicts in socialist countries, including the most dangerous risks threatening the existence of socialism. "[1]

Chinese theorists are always careful about this issue. But as a social phenomenon, crises had repeatedly occurred in the development of socialism, including the Polish and Hungarian incidents in 1956, the Prague Spring in 1968, the Solidarity Movement in Poland, the Cultural

---

[1] See *World Economic Herald*, Nov. 23, 1987.

Revolution in China. The core of the problem is how to explain this kind of intensification and antagonistic conflicts within socialist countries.

Second, causes of social crises in socialist countries.

What is a social crisis? Social crisis refers to a social phenomenon in whichthe intensified social contradictions come to a full-scale outbreak because of the accumulation of social conflicts. In other words, social crisis is the result of accumulation, intensification or white heat of social contradictions to the extent of open conflict. Theoretically speaking, the appearance of social crisis in socialist countries is because: first of all, there are antagonistic contradictions in certain limits in socialist countries, which, if not handled properly, are possible to become intensified to the extent of overall outbreak, threatening the survival of the socialist system; Second, the non-antagonistic contradictions in socialist society, if not properly handled, are potential to change into antagonistic contradictions and overall outbreak. In practice, although some of our comrades are reluctant to use the word "crisis", social crisis in socialist countries is an objective phenomenon, whose reasons are as follows:

(1) Since the socialist society will inevitably go through the stages of the commodity economy, it must follow thelaw governing the development of commodity economy. Over-rigid planning or failure in macro-control will lead to losing control or structural imbalance, resulting in overproduction or insufficient production, overstock or short of supply, etc. , which ultimately cause the intensification of contradiction between social production and demand. As a result, there will be inflation or deflation and labor oversupply or shortage. Consequently, there will be a series of problems, such as the decline of economic growth, standstill of production, deficit of budget, deficit of international payment. If these problems lose control further ahead, the inherent contradictions of socialist commodity production will become worse, causing serious economic difficulties.

(2) The remaining of commodity economy of the nature of private ownership in socialist countries is possible to give birth to the local existence of social phenomena of its nature.

(3) Since there are interest contradictions among the people in socialist countries, it is possible that, because of improper handling of these contradictions or insufficient political education of the masses, the erroneous ideas of the masses can temporarily prevail, thus resulting in the intensification, political conflicts, and even nation-wide intensification of contradictions.

（4）In socialist countries, especially at the primary stage of socialism, factors such as remnants of the old society, interference of foreign imperialists, the impact of foreign capitalism, etc. , are all possible to intensify the existing contradictions in socialist countries.

The above four points are objective but not sufficient conditions for the outbreak of social crisis in socialist countries. If the leadership in socialist countries does not make mistakes subjectively and properly handle all kinds of contradictions, social crisis can be avoided. Thus, in a socialist society, if the governing party makes serious mistakes in guiding ideology or guideline of action, the objectively existing contradictions may intensify and social crisis may occur.

Social crisis caused by social unrest in the primary stage of socialism is easier to erupt, because this is a stage when the country is changing from a country with relatively backward productive forces toward developed country, that is, from " adequate food and clothing to moderate prosperity. " During this period, people's demand become even more intense and diverse, in addition to the complex social conditions and social conflicts, conflicts may occur among different interest groups, causing wider social conflicts and social crisis.

Third, features of the intensification of social crisis in socialist countries.

There is the possibility of intensification of antagonistic contradictions in socialist societies, which may lead to social crisis. However, this crisis is only partial and temporary and can be addressed by socialist system itself. Thisis essentially different from the insurmountable overall socio-economic and political crisis in a capitalist society. Social crisis appears as a social phenomenon in socialist countries does not mean that it is the crisis of socialism. Socialism is a new social formation replacing capitalist society in terms of fundamental systems, so it is not in crisis.

The essential differences between crisis in a socialist country and that in a capitalist country are mainly as follows:

（1）The crisis in capitalist society isthe crisis of overall economic, political and cultural crisis caused by its insurmountable and essentially antagonistic basic social contradictions, while social crisis in a socialist society occurs under specific historical conditions and so is temporary. In a capitalist society, the contradiction between private ownership and socialized production makes the entire social production anarchic and people's purchasing power inadequate, resulting in overproduction. At the same time, the inherent contradictions of capitalist private ownership will cause inflation and credit crisis, which will lead to periodic economic crises of capitalism that will further lead to the outbreak of overall crisis in capitalist society. In contrast, social crisis in a socialist society is only the result of intensification and accumulation of some existing social contradictions. Fundamentally speaking, the basic contradiction in socialist society is non-antagonistic nature, and therefore cannot lead to a social crisis of system nature, so it is preventable and can be overcome.

(2) Crises in capitalist countries are inevitable, periodic, structural, and thus insurmountable; therefore they cannot be overcome by capitalism itself, which can only be resolved by social revolution. Social crises in socialist countries are not periodic or inevitable, that is to say, if properly handled, they can be reduced to a minimum extent, or even be eliminated. Socialist system itself can consciously overcome social crises.

(3) If not handled or handled improperly, coupled with the foreign interference of anti-socialism, crisis in a socialist country can become worse, even lead to temporary transmutation of socialism.

III. The Issue of Correct Understanding and Handling of Mass Incidents

In many cases, the intensification of contradictions among the people results in mass incidents, some of which may occur even if there is no social crisis. By a mass incident we mean a mass conflict happens in forms of petition, strike, demonstration and the like, which is triggered by local contradictions, conflicts or confrontations, or temporary economic difficulties, or when the demands of some of the masses have not been met, or when the bureaucratic or corruptive behaviors of some of the personnel in the Party or the government severely violate the interests of the people and have not been timely rectified, or when some of the masses having incorrect ideas are incited, and so on. Mass incidents are objective social phenomena reflecting the intensification of contradictions or conflicts among the people. They are different from the political conspiracies of a handful elements opposing to the Party and socialism, and from the criminal activities of rioting and looting; and the majority of the masses involved in these incidents are also different from those criminals who fish in troubled waters and make looting, rioting or other sabotage. Mass incidents can cause social unrest or instability to varying degrees, disrupt public order and economic development. Social contradictions can become sharper, even become antagonistic by mass incidents, besetting the society and economy of the country and directly endangering the power of the state. How to understand and deal with mass incidents constitutes an important part of the correct handling of the intensification of contradictions among the people.

The direct causes of mass incidents are often serious economic difficulties, especially some wrong economic policies and measures that undermine the people's immediate interests, resulting in the relative decline of their living standards and their demands unsatisfied. These demands, except for a few, mostly are reasonable and resolvable. Among the causes of mass incidents, one factor merits attention, that is, the bureaucracy and corruption of some leaders. Because of bureaucratic style of work some leaders, the reasonable and resolvable demands of the masses are ignored; and no work has been done in rejecting the unreasonable demands of some of the masses. Especially with regard to the malpractices bitterly detested by the people, such as corruption, oppression, nepotism, etc. , the leaders with a bureaucratic style of work take no effective effort to correct them; on the contrary, they sidestep them, even take a protective attitude toward them, so that the discontent of the masses accumulate and eventually erupt into mass incidents. Another cause of mass incidents is that no sufficient efforts are made to educate and persuade the backward section of the masses, so that the masses are possessed by bigotry or erroneous views, resulting in radical words, emotions, behaviors and acts of some people to vent their dissatisfaction to the Party and government, or put forward unreasonable demands, and so on. In these circumstances, the main reason of the insufficient education of the masses is still the bureaucracy of the leaders. Yet another cause of mass incidents is that, the discontent and tendency of riot of the masses are made use by some domestic and external reactionary elements that spread feudal and capitalist ideas, political philosophy and rumors, sow discord and instigate troubles and incidents. The key to preventing the sabotage of a few bad elements lies also in the hands of the leaders. The factors of instability in the complex relations between different ethnic groups are also an important cause of mass incidents. Many socialist countries are multi-ethnic. Complex historical, religious, cultural and other social factors may bring about frictions and conflict between ethnic groups, which can develop into mass incidents. The mass incidents in some socialist countries are more or less associated with the defects in their institutions. After the establishment of socialist system, these countries copied in a different degree, the highly centralized government model of the Soviet Union and in a fairly long period of time ignored improving socialist legal system. Because their democracy and legal systems were not sound, some socialist countries even wrongly carried out inner-party struggles and political movements, which seriously violated democracy and the laws, giving birth to large numbers of unjust, false and wrong cases and strong resentment of the people. Lastly, in the process of socialist reform, the transition of the old system to the new and the adjustment of interest distribution will highlight the social contradictions, which, if not properly handled, will intensify and result in temporary mass incidents.

Some mass incidents actually reflect the contradictions between the bureaucracy of some of the leaders and the masses, in which the main participants are the masses, but their targets are often leading organs of the Party and government.

If we relax our vigilance against mass incidents or handle them incorrectly, the contradictions will further intensify even develop into serious political conflict or turmoil, which is possible to make the contradictions among the people transform into those between ourselves and the enemy, thus directly endanger the fate of the Party and the state. Therefore, in dealing with mass incidents, we must in the first place distinguish between the two different types of contradictions, because, except a handful of evil elements, most of the participants belong to the category of the people. We must resolutely guard against two erroneous tendencies: one is heaping of all the blame on the masses without any discrimination, which will encourage the bureaucracy of the leaders; the other is the failure in seeing the erroneous tendency of the masses, and thus relaxing vigilance against the evil elements. While meeting the reasonable demands of the masses, ideological education given to them must be strengthened. The small number of individuals who flout the public interests andwilfully break the law and commit crimes must receive legal sanction. Lessons must be drawn up to resolutely abolish various malpractices, corruption and bureaucracy; defects and mistakes of the leadership must be corrected in their relationship with the masses and in their properly handling of various contradictions. On the other hand, the fundamental way to resolve mass incidents is to, through socialist reform, promote the development of productive forces, vigorously improve socialist democracy, legal system and the socialist system itself, so as to uproot the latent risk of the social unrest, facilitate the growth and constantly improving people's lives.

IV. Basic Measures for Preventing the Intensification of Contradictions and Occurrence of Social Unrest

Socialist reform is the basic way to correctively handle the contradictions among the people and institutionally and legally prevent the intensification of contradictions, mass incidents and social unrest.

First, we must establish an economic-political system conducive to the development of social productive forces. The various expressions of contradictions among the people at the primary stage of socialism, in the final analysis, are due to the fact that the existing material and cultural level cannot meet the people's growing needs. In China, the root cause of contradictions among the people at the present stage is nothing but the contradiction between the backwardness of our social production and the growing needs of the people. Therefore, the only way to fundamentally solve the contradictions among the people is to unswervingly take the development of social productive forces and economy as our focus of work. So our attention in socialist reform should be paid into the establishment of a economic-political system favoring the development of social productivity and socialist market economy, which is the ultimate approach to resolving the contradictions among the people at the primary stage of socialism.

Second, we must establish a socio-economic-political system that can bring the initiative of the masses into full play. The most profound significance of the correct handling of the contradictions among the people lies in mobilizing the enthusiasm of the people. Suppressing or discouraging the enthusiasm will make the contradictions more acute. Comrade Mao Zedong pointed out in his On the Ten Major Relationships that if we are to promote socialist construction, we must bring the initiative of internal and external factors. The essential idea of making reform of socialist institutions is to better mobilize the enthusiasm of the masses. As a country at the primary stage of socialism, China is relatively in a low level of productive forces. In order to adapt to this reality, we should establish structures compatible with this reality in the systems of ownership, distribution and management, and in the links of production, circulation, exchange and distribution, to better resolve the economic and distributive contradictions among the people and coordinate interpersonal economic relationship. An incompatible economic system that discourages the initiative of enterprises and individuals is unfavorable to the resolution of various contradictions among the people. Stress should also be put on the reform of political structure by centering on the improvement of democracy and legal system, to institutionally guarantee people's right of participation and right to act on one's own in the political and economic life, so as political relations between individuals more rational. The reason why an unsuitable political structure affect the enthusiasm of the people is that it is unfavorable for relieving political contradictions among the people. So, socialist reform must be focused on the correct handling of the contradictions among the people in economic and political life to mobilize their enthusiasm in production and politics.

Third, we must establish a socio-economic system in favorable to the resolution of contradictions of material interests among the people. Within the ranks of the people in socialist countries, there are different subject of interests with different interest demands. To reasonably meet these demands, the incomes representing the rational demands of the subjects of interest must be guaranteed. The differences of the incomes should at once reasonable and not too big. This requires the establishment of an economic-political system that can both effectively distribute incomes among different subjects of interests and reasonably cope with the differences.

Fourth, we must economically and politically establish and improve the socialist legal system, so that contradictions among the people can be handled in an institutionalized way and according to procedure and law. To handle the contradictions among the people by the rule of man will inevitably make the mistake of confusing the two different types of contradictions; only the legal system can provide guarantee for the correct handling of them. Thus, the improvement of socialist legal system to make it as the ordinary way of solving the contradictions among the people is of great significance.

In short, the institutional guarantee and basic measure to correctly handle the contradictions among the people and to prevent the intensification of the contradictions, mass incidents and social unrests is to deepen reform, so as to build an economic and political system that can effectively resolve the various contradictions among the people, and can keep the socialist market economy, democracy and harmonious society all in good order.

Appendix II

Contradictions among the People under the New Situation①

The correct handling of contradictions among the people under the new situation is both a theme of our political life in the market economy in the primary stage of socialism and an important guarantee for maintaining social stability, speeding up reform and opening up, developing socialist market economy and building socialism with Chinese Characteristics. So we should careful study, correctly understand and properly handle contradictions among the people by combining it with the new realities.

I. New Situation, New Problems and New Features

Under the new situation of socialist reform and opening up, in the process of establishing a socialist market economy, the transformation from the old toward the new economic structure and the change in the pattern of distribution of interests: all these have made contradictions among the people very different from the past in terms of manifestations and features, resulting in new situations, new forms, new content, new problems and new features in this respect.

1. New situation of contradictions among the people
Since reform and opening up, various relationships among the people are basic balanced and our society is basically stable. Nevertheless, some

---

① This article is a study made by the author in the 1990s. As the text of his lectures in different occasions, the figures in it have been renewed accordingly. For the coherence of the article, some points that have already been discussed in the previous part of this book are not omitted here.

issues require our vigilance.

First, the gap between rich and poor shows a tendency of widening, resulting in the outstanding contradictions in distribution.

Against the prevalence of egalitarianism in the past decades, in the initial stage of the reform, Comrade Deng Xiaoping put forth the idea of "allowing some people to get rich first," and the policies of encouraging some people to get prosperous through honest labor and lawful business was adopted, which has mobilized the enthusiasm of the public. Consequently, some people and some regions have gotten rich, and the income of most people has considerably increased. But some problems have also arisen along with it, including the widening of income gap and the sharpening of the contradictions of distribution. These are specifically demonstrated as follows:

Firstly, indexes of wealth divide is rising fast, indicating the widening gap between rich and poor. Two systems are often used domestically and internationally to measure the gap between rich and poor, one the Oshima index or quintile method, the other is the Gini coefficient. The quintile method divides the citizens of a country into five equal parts or quintiles: the poorest, the moderate poor, the middle, the moderate rich and the richest. From the shares of these different sections of the citizens in the total income of a country, we can know the inequality of wealth; while Gini coefficient is a number between 0 and 1, where 0 corresponds with perfect equality (where everyone has the same income) and 1 corresponds with perfect inequality (where one person has all the income, and everyone else has zero income). In recent years, some sociologists use these two indexes system to measure the income gap in a multi-level and multiple ways, which show that these indexes in China have risen significantly. According to some statistics, in 1997, the Oshima indexes of China's urban and rural residents' per capita household income were: the 20 percent of the richest population accounted for 50. 4 percent of the total income of all the citizens, the moderate rich 20 percent accounted for 8. 6 percent, while the poorest 20 percent accounted only for 4. 06 percent. The income of the richest was 12. 7 time that of the poorest. According to the estimation of some scholars, China's Gini coefficient was 0. 31 in 1979, 0. 38 in 1988, 0. 434 in 1994, and 0. 455 in 1997. These indexes are lower than some countries in South America, South Asia and Africa, the Oshima indexes of which usually are: the richest 20 percent of the population accounts for 60 percent of the total income, while the 20 percent of the poorest accounts only 0. 6 percent, some even over 10 percent. According to Gini coefficient, the internationally recognized warning line is between 0. 3—0. 4. According to the calculation of the World Bank, in 1978, China's Gini coefficient was only 0. 16, the lowest in the world, indicating that China was in an egalitarian country. But presently, the indexes of gap between rich and poor in China are higher than international warning line, showing a relatively fast widening. The income gap in China are demonstrated in the following aspects:

(1) The widening gap between urban and rural residents. The income ratio between them was 1. 7 : 1 in 1984, 2. 54 : 1 in 1993, 2. 61 : 1 in 1994 and 2. 51 : 1 in 1998.

(2) The widening gap within urban residents. According to the National Bureau of Statistics, in 1984, the income gap between rich and poor households in urban areas was 1. 8 : 1 in 1978, and 3 : 1 in 1994. In 1998, per household annual income of the 20 percent richest households in urban areas was 10926 yuan, while the poorest 20 percent had only 2447 yuan per household. At the same time the growth rate of the 10 percent highest income earners was 5 percent higher than that of the 10 percent lowest income earners.

(3) The widening gap among rural residents. The ratio between the richest and the poorest in rural areas had widened from 29 : 1 in 1978 to 6. 6 : 1 in 1994. The Gini coefficient in rural areas in China reached 0. 34 in 1998.

(4) The widening income gap among regions. In 1980, the per capita annual incomes of the farmers in the eastern, central and western regions were respectively 218 yuan, 181 yuan and 217 yuan; in 1992, the average per capita income of the residents in the three regions were respectively 1263 yuan, 1000 yuan and 983 yuan while the country's average was 1238 yuan; in 1993, the per capita annual incomes of the farmers in the three regions were respectively 1222 yuan, 802 yuan and 670 yuan; these figures became 3098 yuan, 2354 yuan and 1468 yuan in 1998.

(5) The widening income gap between the mental and manual workers.

(6) The widening income gap between employees in different forms of ownership. In 1994, the total amount of salary of the state-owned sector reached 517. 8 billion yuan, an annual growth of 35. 8 percent; that of

the collectively owned sector was 60. 7 billion yuan, an annual growth of 13. 5 percent. In 1998, the total salary of the state-owned sector was 681. 25 billion yuan and the collectively-owned was 102. 16 billion yuan, while that of other sectors was 146. 24 billion yuan.

(7) The widening income gap among employees in different industries. In 1991, the income ratio between the highest and lowest income industries was 1. 24 : 1, the figure rose to more than 2 : 1 in 1997, in which, finance, securities, insurance, real estate, electricity, telecommunications, tourism, gas, water production and supply, comprehensive technology services were among the industries of higher income, while agriculture, forestry, animal husbandry, fisheries, wholesale and retail, food services, manufacturing were among the lowest industries. Among them, the industry having the highest annual income was the air transport industry with the average annual income of 16, 865 yuan, and the average annual income of employees in state-owned was 15, 304 yuan; followed by the post and telecommunications industry, with an average annual wage income of 12, 056 yuan, that of employees in state-owned units was 12, 065 yuan; next was employees in the industry of computer application services with average annual income of 17, 416 yuan, those in state-owned units 10, 528 yuan. The lowest income was forestry industry, with an average annual income of 3, 918 yuan. Besides, the income gap is further widened by gray and illegal incomes.

Secondly, the of high income and poor strata emergend.

In the last decades, the wealth gap has been gradually widened, and a high income stratum has emerged. According to an article published in the journal *Reform*, No 2. (1995), in China's big cities, 16. 1 percent private entrepreneurs had an annual income of more than 500, 000 yuan. There were more than 1000 billionaire, a considerable number of ten-million-household and the number of millionaire was more than three million, and more than 5 million households with an annual income of more than 50, 000 yuan, accounting for more than two percent of the population. According to statistics, the savings deposit of the high income households that take up less than three percent of the whole population reached 290 billion yuan. In urban areas, the ratio of annual income between the highest ten percent income households and the lowest ten percent income households had widened from 2. 9 : 1 in 1990 to 3. 8 : 1 in 1995; the ratio of annual income between the highest ten percent income households and the lowest five percent income households was 4. 95 : 1 in 1998; in rural areas, 5. 57percent of the population had an average annual income of more than 5000 yuan, while those earned an annual income less than 800 yuan accounted for 6. 63 percent of the population.

High-income groups include: private entrepreneurs, with an average annual income of 50, 000 yuan, some as high as several million even thousand million yuan; Chinese senior employees in foreign enterprises or foreign institutions in China, with average income more than $ 6600, some as high as more than $ 10, 000; some individual industrial and commercial households, with an average annual income 3. 5 times as that of the employees in state-owned enterprises, a few of them even with an annual income of up to hundreds of thousand or tens of million yuan; some contracted operators of enterprises with an annual income of up to more than 100 million; some stock brokers, real estate developers with annual income of up to one million even several million yuan; personnel in short supply and specialists in finance as well as some lawyers, accountants, beauticians, senior chef, masseurs, athletes, actors, singers, dancers, famous hosts, fashion models, brokers, designers, art advertising personnel, and so on, with considerable income, ranging from tens of thousands to several hundred thousand yuan annually; some people who engaged in illegal activities such prostitution, drug trafficking, human trafficking.

Standing in stark contrast to the rich groups is the poor group. According to the statistics of State Council Leading Group of Poverty Alleviation and Development, until 1999 there were still 340 people in rural areas who were still inadequately fed and clothed. According to the National Bureau of Statistics (NBS), from 1991 to 1995 the overall situation of poverty in urban areas were: the average annual household poverty rate was 4. 26 percent with a total of 3. 432 million household; average poverty rate of the population was 5. 1 percent with about 13. 3 million people living in poor. In 1995, the situation was improved due to a series measures taken by governments at all levels such as formulation minimum wage standards, subsidy to families below poverty line. As a result, comparing with the previous year, annual household poverty rate decreased from 4. 85 to 3. 84; poverty-stricken households reduced to 3. 33 million, a decrease of 0. 78 million; poverty rate of the population reduced to 4. 4 percent, a 1. 3 percentage decrease; the poverty-stricken population was 12. 42 million, a decrease of 2. 84 million.

In recent years, the imbalanced distribution among industries had become importantfactors widening wealth gap between urban households. In 1995, among the poverty-stricken population in urban areas, 55.5 percent was from state owned and collectively owned units, mainly in large coal, machinery, textile and other industries affected by policy or industrial restructuring factors. At present, the urban poverty-stricken groups mainly consisted of the following seven groups: (1) employees in poorly operated enterprises that fail to pay wages or can only pay part of wages, accounting for about 30 percent of the poverty-stricken population; (2) the unemployed, accounting for about 20 percent; (3) some retired workers, accounting for about 17 percent; (4) residents who long engaged in low-paying jobs, accounting for about 10 percent; (5) relief or special-care recipients, accounting five percent; (6) poverty-stricken population due the rise in prices, accounting for about 10 percent; (7) population living below poverty line due to other factors, accounting for about eight percent. According to survey, the average per capital annual income of the poverty-stricken households in urban areas is 1, 059 yuan, 54.7 percent lower than average. The proportion of food expenses in the total consumption expenses in this household accounts for 59.2 percent, only above the level of subsistence. According to the survey of China Disabled Persons, Federation, there are five million disabled persons living below poverty line, of which three million are in special hard conditions due severe disability.

Thirdly, things have yet to be straightened out in the matter of income distribution, social security system has yet to be improved, and there emerged some unfair social distribution of social wealth.

In the more than one decade of reform and opening up, with the adoption of the policy of distribution according to work playing the dominant role while diverse forms of distribution coexisting, the egalitarian practice of everyone "eat from the same big pot," was abandoned and the enthusiasm of the masses has been greatly and successfully arisen. However, during the transitional period, when old system has been changed while the new system is not well-established yet, there emerged some unfairness in distribution which arose some dissatisfaction of the masses, showing in following aspects: (1) In terms of distribution system, in addition to income gained based on the policy of distribution according to work, there are also incomes from assets, investment, venture investment, dividend, as well as interregional income differentials, differences of resource allocation, and so on. These different forms of distribution are somewhat disorder with many loopholes; so the pattern has yet to be made more reasonable, more open, more transparent, fairer and complementary to each other. (2) Income disparity caused by differences in regions, resource allocation and work positions rather than abilities has aroused considerable dissatisfaction of the masses. For example, for the same university graduate, if he works in the Party and government organs, the income difference is big comparing with that he works in the banking system. (3) Because the market mechanism is not perfect and various regulatory and monitoring systems has yet to be established, some people, by exploiting these defects, get rich through illegal ways such as drug trafficking, tax evasion, manufacturing and selling of counterfeit and fake goods, dominating the market, and so on. (4) A few people get rich by using their power or position, commit corruption such as colluding illegally with businessmen, exchanging money and power. (5) Social security and social relief system have not been established, so that the poverty problem of urban residents mainly rely on their work units to solve, while 74 percent of the poverty-stricken household in rural areas depends mainly on their own in solving the problem. The masses tolerate and accept income gap derived from labor, but detest the phenomena of getting rich through unreasonable ways or illegal activities.

Second, the non-publicsectors of the economy, especially private sector, is developing rapidly, making the objective existence of contradictions between the group of private entrepreneurs and groups of employees or between private owners and employees.

In present stage in China, the economic pattern is that the public ownership is playing the dominant role while other forms of ownership coexist side by side. In other words, the socialist market economy in China now is mainly composed of two parts: the public ownership is the mainstay and the non-public sector is an important of it.

According to the statistics from NBS, some authorities published the change of proportions of China's state-owned, collectively own and non-public sectors of the economy (mainly individual, private, and foreign owned and those from China's Hong Kong, Macao and Taiwan regions), and the estimation of them in 2010 (see table below) .

Proportions of Sectors of the Economy in China's GDP

Year	Stated owned (%)	Collectively owned (%)	Non-public (%)
1978	56	43	1
1993	42.9	44.8	12.3
1995	41.5	43.9	14.6
2000	35.8	41.3	20.2
2010 (estimated)	34.7	34.5	30.8

From the changes in ownership structure we can see:

Currently the pattern in which public ownership as the mainstay and diverse forms of ownership develop side by side has been established; the development of non-public economy is faster than the public economy, with the size of public economy increasing while its proportion in the whole economy declining, which is the expected result of the adjustment of ownership policy. From now on to 2010, the proportion of public economy will continue to decline, but remain the dominant position in the economy, while non-public economy will continue to develop and its the proportion in the economy will increase. After the development of more than ten years, although both the number of private entrepreneurs is small, proportion of output value private enterprises to total social output value is not big, and it is still in the secondary position in terms of assets, technology, management, operation, product quantity and quality, non-public economy, especially the private economy in China has gained certain economic strength and social influence in addressing the problem of surplus labor and promoting economic development, and its proportion in the social economy is increasing rapidly. At the same time, the existence of the private entrepreneurs as an emerging and developing social strata with relatively high income is an objective reality, so do the relations between private employers and employees and the employment relationship. On the other side, due to incomplete of our legal system, such phenomena as poor working conditions and protection measures, wages arrear, overtime work, wage deductions, and even personal humiliation and child labor are not uncommon in private enterprises, resulting in the contradiction between employers and employees.

Third, the structure, composition, position and role of China's working class has changed profoundly, leading to the restructuring of social structure and further complexity of social contradictions in China

Since reform and opening up, the structure, characteristics, role and status of China's working class have undergone profound changes. This is mainly exhibited as follows: (1) The economic pattern with public ownership as the mainstay and diverse forms of ownership developing side by side, especially the development of non-public economy, has a great influence on the status of the working class. There emerge the issues of status of the working class both in the socialist country and in the non-public enterprises. (2) Under the condition of socialist market economy, the market orientation of the state-owned enterprises, the establishment of modern enterprise system making enterprises into relatively independent economic entities and overall responsibility of directors and managers: all these will bring some contradictions between the workers and managers; with the introduction of market mechanism and the progressive implementation of labor contract system, the original "iron bowl" has been broken, and operation of some enterprises is poor, and some workers are unemployed, so that worker feel that their status of as the leading class has lost, along with their sense as masters of the enterprises. (3) With the implementation of the policy with distribution according to labor as the main position and other forms of distribution coexisting, income differences are widening among regions, enterprises, industries, occupations, and so on, which give birth to different income groups within the working class. (4) With the deepening of reform and opening up and the development of society, economy, the productive forces and high-technology, the internal structure of the working class has also changed. The proportion mental workers increased continually, along with their incomes and role in production. For instance, proportions of manual workers in state-owned enterprises, in urban and rural collective enterprises and in non-public economy are different. By the end of 1998, the proportions of manual laborers in state-owned enterprises, in urban collective enterprises, in other forms of ownership and in rural township and village enterprises accounted respectively for 15 percent, five percent, seven percent and 73 percent. The proportion of manual workers in large-scale state-owned enterprises has declined. Manual workers in second and tertiary industries take up respectively 24 percent and 27 percent. The composition of working class become diversified, including those work in state-owned enterprises, collectively owned enterprises and non-public enterprises in different industries and sectors. (5) In non-public sector of the economy, especially the private sector, there are apparent contradictions between the working class and owners.

Fourth, the serious corruption and bureaucracy of some of our leadingofficials has resentment of the people, even acute contradictions in some places and units.

After our Party became the governing party, especially in the new conditions of reform and opening up and socialist market economy, the contradiction between leaders and masses become the mainstay among the contradictions in the new era. Reasons for the tension of the contradictions between the leaders and the masses as follows: First, the small number of leading officials have divorced from the masses by living an extravagant and hedonic life, even committing corruption, which fundamentally infringe immediate interests of the masses. Second, some leading officials far divorced themselves from the masses in way of thinking and style of work by conducting bureaucracy, subjectivism, authoritarianism, making wrong decision, not representing even going against the interests of the masses. Third, there is also the contradiction between the correct leadership and some backward elements of masses. For example, some backward elements of the masses, because of their unmet immediate interests, or ideological problems, may have contradictions with the officials who protect the fundamental interests of the masses and keep to correct views.

Among the three major causes worsening the relations between the officials and the masses, the first two are the chief ones. Its harmful manifestations include the following: abuse power for personal profits, trading power for money, racketeering, embezzlement and corrupt practices, violating the law while in charge of its enforcement, seeking private gains at the expense of public interests, extravagance, cronyism, forming cliques and ganging up, and so on. Although these are the conducts of only a few Party members and officials, they have influence on the image and prestige of the Party and the government and the social conduct. Other malpractice of the a few officials include: standing high above the masses; abusing power; divorcing oneself from reality and the masses; spending a lot of time and effort to put up an impressive front; indulging in empty talk; sticking to a rigid way of thinking; being hidebound by convention; overstaffing administrative organs; being dilatory, inefficient and irresponsible; failing to keep one's word; circulating documents endlessly without solving problems; shifting responsibility to others; and even assuming the airs of a mandarin, reprimanding other people at every turn, vindictively attacking others, suppressing democracy, deceiving superiors and subordinates, being arbitrary and despotic, practising favouritism, offering bribes, participating in corrupt practices in violation of the law, craving official positions, selling or buying posts, and so on. These evil-doings exist both in urban and rural areas, especially in rural areas.

Fifth, because of the tremendous economic, political, cultural and social relations changes caused by the reform toward and establishment of the socialist market economy, and the changes in China's relations of production, superstructure, new combination, generation and differentiation have occur in the structures of classes, strata and interest groups although the framework remains unchanged.

In the current stage of China's society, the working class, the farmer class and the intelligentsia are still the main classes. However, new combination, new generation and new differentiation have occured and many new interest groups have emerged. Reasons for these include: socialist reform and opening up, reform toward socialist market economy, the establishment of the economic pattern with public ownership as the mainstay and diverse forms of ownership coexisting, the distribution according to work as the principal mode and a variety of distribution forms coexisting, as well as the complex social, historical, political, cultural and human factors, the role of factors in relations of production and the superstructure, etc.

Reform itselfmeans the adjustment of interest pattern: the original pattern was broken, new pattern of interests formed, which have led to structural and relation changes among and within the original social classes, strata and interest groups and given birth to the formation of new interest groups and the differentiation and combination of old ones.

Diverse forms of ownership with public ownership as the mainstay and diverse forms of distribution with distribution according to work as the mainstay have gradually widened the income gap have made people's economic status, political status and ideological attitude also more diverse and the objective existence of interest differences and contradictions. As a result, people with identical interests have formed interest communities or different interest groups.

In themarket economy in the primary stage of socialism, the interest relations among the people are consisted of intergroup relations. Within the working class, the farmer class and intelligentsia as part of the working class, there exist different interest groups with interest and value differences, among which there are inevitably differences, contradictions, conflicts and frictions, as well as complex interest structure consisting of different types of interest groups.

2. New problems concerning contradictions among the people

Regarding the new developments of contradictions among the people analyzed above, there are different views and opinions from all walks of life and among theorists and academics as well.

(1) As to the existing widening tendency of income gaps, opinions vary. Some believe that "the income gaps are still within reasonable range"; some believe that "the gap between rich and poor is too big"; some even believe that the income gaps have come to the extent of polarization." The reality is: on the one hand, the egalitarian practice of "each eat from the same big iron pot" has been abandoned and the pattern of distribution according to work as the mainstay and other mode of distribution coexisting side by side, on the other the egalitarian phenomenon remains within a certain range; On the one hand, differences in distribution have appeared that is conducive to arousing the enthusiasm of the workers, on the other, there is also the unfairness of distribution and too big a gap. But in general, income distribution at the present stage is still reasonable and has not come the extent of polarization. Our general principle is to let some people and some regions prosper before others, oppose to polarization, and gradually achieve common prosperity. The goal of common prosperity cannot be changed or doubted. Of course, there is the existence and widening trend of income gaps, which may become latent risk affecting social development that must be paid attention to.

(2) For the rise of the group of private entrepreneurs, some people regard it as the emergence of a new bourgeoisie. This view exaggerates the gap of wealth, because we cannot equal the group of private entrepreneurs as an exploiting class, nor can the relations between entrepreneurs and employees be regarded as polarization of the whole society. On the other hand, high attention should be paid to the development of the private sector and its social impact.

(3) As to the change in the internal structure, composition, status and role of the working class, some people mistakenly think under modern corporate system, the directors or managers in the state-owned enterprises as legal persons have more power and the real masters while the workers

are nobodies, let alone masters. It is more so in the non-public sector where workers are passive employees. Therefore the leadership of the working class is doubted. Under these circumstances, we must have a correct view on and safeguard the leading position and role of the working class. In the cause of building socialism with Chinese characteristics, we must unswervingly rely on the working class and give full play to its leading role.

(4) As to the apparent corruption, bureaucracy and serious divorcement from the masses of a few of leading officials, the masses have a strong resentment. Some people even suspect the existence of the existence of privileged interest groups. About this, our answer is explicit: the history of our Party in China's revolutionary struggle, socialist construction and reform and opening up has proved that our Party is a correct, glorious and great party and the vast majority of our Party members and officials can stand the test and work wholeheartedly in the people's interests. Communists do not have selfish interests, nor are they the so-called privileged interest groups. The corruption of few Party members does not represent the Party as a whole, nor the majority of Party officials.

(5) As to the interest groups in the primary stage of socialism, one view holds that the original classes and strata no longer exist and have been replaced by new interest groups, therefore Marxist class analysis method is no longer applicable to the situation today and the analytical methods of Western bourgeois theorists should be adopted. Another opinion, ignoring the changes and differentiation of classes and strata under the new historical conditions of socialist reform and opening up, sticks to the old view and methods of class struggle in analyzing and handling today's interest groups and intergroup conflict. These two views are both biased and deviated from the basic principles of historical materialism and the reality in the primary stage of socialism in China. We should, on the premise of recognizing that the working class, the farmer class and the intelligentsia as part of the working class are still the main classes in the current stage of China, adhere to and use Marxist class theory and analytical method to make a scientific classification of the interest groups in the primary stage of socialism, to correctly understand and deal with contradictions among different interest groups within the people, so as to mobilize the enthusiasm of them. It can be said that in the initial stage of socialism, the exploiting classes and class exploitation society as a whole no longer exist,

nor is class struggle as an overall social phenomenon or the principal contradiction, but class differences still exist, so does class struggle. Meanwhile, due to the socio-economic and political factors, many new interest groups have emerged. It is a major practical issue as how to apply the theory of historical materialism and its theories of class and class struggle to correctly analyze and understand the classes, strata and interest groups and to properly handle their relations in the primary stage of socialism.

In short, we should use the position, viewpoints and methods of Deng Xiaoping Theory to carefully study, analyze and demonstrate these issues and have a clear understanding and ensuring explanation of and the correct answer to them with convincing evidence and reasons. Only by doing so, and effectively address them in practice, pay full attention to them, and resolve the problems in the bud, instead of over-or underestimating them or failing in seeing the mainstream, can we really address the contradictions among the people in the new situation.

3. New features of contradictions among the people

Currently, contradictions among the people show the following new features:

First, the widespread of material interest contradictions.

In the past under the highly centralized planned economy, there was also the contradiction of the material interests among the people, only that it was overshadowed by egalitarian distribution and over-tense atmosphere of class struggle as the key link. Since reform and opening up, especially since the introduction of the policy of allowing some people and some regions to become prosperous before others and the egalitarian practice in distribution was abandoned, the competitiveness and vigor of various interest entities were triggered and along with it the income gap among urban residents gradually become wider, making the contradiction of material interests among the people more widely spread and increased. Fundamentally speaking, the backwardness of the productive forces and underdeveloped market economy make the material means of livelihood cannot meet the needs of the people, which, coupled with the not so reasonable distribution policy, causes the interest contradictions among the people extremely prominent and acute.

In general, contradictions of the material interests among the people largely and frequently occur indistribution, especially in income gaps. Since China's reform and opening up, new social differentiation and combination occurred in distribution pattern. On the one hand, the egalitarian distribution has not been completely broken away and new rational pattern has not been fully established; on the other hand, there is the too large income gap and unfair distribution. Therefore, in spite of the overall increase in income, many people mentally feel unbalanced and unsatisfied, which intensifies the frictions and contradictions of the material interests among the people.

Second, contradictions among interest groups are obvious.

In the primary stage of socialism, due to existence of diverse forms of ownership and modes of distribution, income gaps appear among the people, resulting in the clear distinction between various interest groups among the people. For example, within the working class there are interest groups of employees in state-owned, in collective-owned units, in township enterprises, in private sectors, in mixed ownership sectors, in joint-stock enterprises, in shareholding enterprises, etc. ; within the same group, there are the subgroups of mental workers and manual workers, the operators, managers and material producers; within a private enterprise, there are the subgroups of owners, employees; there also the groups of senior agents and senior managers of foreign enterprises, self-employed group, and so on. The interest patterns become diverse, and the distinction, demands and contradictions among the interest groups become more obvious.

Third, the contradiction between

Under the conditions that the CPC become the governing party, especially under the new situation of reform and opening up and developing the socialist market economy, the contradiction between the leadership and the masses. shows many new features both in terms of content and form. For example, the corruption of a small number ofofficials and the widespread of bureaucracy have aroused strong resentment among the people and intensified the contradiction between the leaders and the masses. It is now clear that, contradictions among the people often find their expression in the relations between officials and the masses, which are in a concentrated way showed in the contradictions between the masses and the bureaucracy and corruption of officials. Relations between the party and the masses and relations between officials and the people have become a hot topic among the masses and focus of contradictions among the people.

Fourth, ideological contradictions become diverse.

Contradictions among the people not only exist largely in economic life, but alsoextensively in political, cultural and moral life. Reform toward socialist market economy requires that political reform should be carried out accordingly, which diversifies the various relations and contradictions of political life, such as relations and contradictions between the government and the Party, between the governing party the democratic parties, between the central government and local governments, and relations and contradictions within the Party, and so on.

In the primary stage of socialism, contradictions in ideological field mainly manifest themselves as contradictions between enemy and ourselves and contradictions among the people. The former are antagonistic while the later are non-antagonistic and constitute the principal kind of contradictions in our society in the ideological field in the current stage, which express as two types: one is that with a class struggle nature, the other is non-class struggle nature but ideological competition and plays a dominant role in the ideological contradictions among the people at the present stage.

In the primary stage of socialism, there are still many ideological remnants of the exploiting classes, as are the stubborn feudalist and capitalist ideas. Thus, in the primary stage of socialism, contradictions between socialist ideology and the ideological remnants of the exploiting class, especially the feudal ideology and decadent bourgeois ideology are still very sharp. In this stage, these contradictions are very complex, because they intertwined with and penetrate into the contradictions between right and wrong, backward and advanced, innovative and conservative, scientific and superstitious and so on, and account for a large proportion. This determines that, in this stage, the contradictions between right and wrong among the people, in many ways, have an antagonistic and class struggle nature. If not properly handled, they turn antagonistic.

At present, China is in a transitional stage of deepening reform and opening up and speeding up transformation from old to the new system, so is in superstructure and ideological fields, which make people's ideas very complex. In particular, with the ideas of the market economy taking root, conflicts and contradictions have occurred in people's ideological thinking, value orientation, way of life, and so on contradictions in lifestyle, such as contradictions between egoism and money worship, etc. , on the one side and collectivist and socialist values on the other; hedonism and other decadent ideas on the one side and spirit of hard work, etc. , on the other. And many other new problems will appear in the process of reform and opening up, which will have influence on everybody's attitudes toward interests, and will be reflected on their immediate interests, resulting in their ideolgocial, mental or emotional fluctuation, imbalance and even conflicts.

Fifth, ethnic and religious contradictions become more complex.

Ethnic and religious contradictions in the present stage of our socialism belong to the contradictions among the people. However, in recent years, after they succeeded in implementing their "peaceful evolution" strategy in former Soviet Union and Eastern Europe, the Western hostile forces have shifted their focus of filtration, separation, sabotage and subversion into China. They attempt to make big troubles of China's ethnic and religious issues; in the meantime, the tendency of ultra-nationalism and ethnic separatism widespread internationally, which colludes with ethnic separatists at home, coupled with our mistakes in these fields, resulting in complexity of these problems, the intertwine of contradictions of antagonistic and non-antagonistic nature, and even the frequent occurrences of incidents that have seriously affected the stability of our country and the border areas inhabited by ethnic minorities. The majority of the people involved in all types of these incidents belong to the category of the people.

Sixth, economic contradictions become sharper.

The ongoing reform toward the socialist market economy constitutes a profound revolution, so it is bound to have influence on interests of the people at all levels and in all aspects, break the old balance and cause the adjustment and changes of interest pattern. During this process, the various economic contradictions among the people will be highlighted and become sharper, along with the constantly emerging economic contradictions. That is to say, the reform, while bringing prosperity to the socialist economy, also makes the contradictions of economic interests among the people more widespread and outstanding. For example, changes will occur and new interest patterns and contradictions will form between central and local governments, between local governments and enterprises, among enterprises of different forms of ownership, among employees in different forms of ownership, within employees in the same enterprises.

Another example is the urban economic reform with the establishment of modern enterprise system and enhancement of vitality as its focus. This reform on the one hand has aroused the enthusiasm of enterprises and enhanced the horizontal economic links between enterprises, but on the other hand made the socialist economic relations more complex, so that enterprises may focus more on their own profits, making the contradictions in production and distribution more prominent and more complicated. Again, the development of various markets and market mechanisms of economic regulation, on the one hand have invigorated the socialist economy, on the other hand have made socialist market relations more complex and more multiplied, such as contradictions among producers, sellers and consumers, between the unified market and regional and industrial division, between legal and illegal operation, between fair and unfair competition, and so on. Besides, because our economic reform is carrying out while the national economy is advancing at a high speed, it is required that the restructuring of the economy and its rapid growth be kept. This makes the economy run in a relatively tense environment, which will inevitably bring about contradictions among reform, development and stability, between production and consumption, between accelerating development and improving efficiency, as well as the gaps and contradiction between eastern coastal areas and western regions. But in general, the reform toward the market economy will gradually make the economic interests of all parties more reasonable; but at the same time, due to the pursuit of their own interests, contradictions of economic interests in all aspects will become more obvious, prominent, complex and acute.

Seventh, contradictions and conflicts have intensified.

In the primary stage of socialism, due to complicated international and domestic causes, there still are conflicts, confrontations and contradictions, some of which may become intensified, and if not handled properly, they can become antagonistic. Since reform and opening up, this kind of contradictions are increasing. For example, some people may take way of direct confrontation, such as strike, collective petition, demonstration, assault on government bodies because of dissatisfactions arising from housing, wages, prices, land demolition etc.; fierce disputes, even violent conflicts may also occur among the masses because of property disputes, asset allocation, land use, etc. If they are not properly handled, these problems may lead to greater social unrests, affecting the political stability of socialist society.

The fundamental goal of our reform and open up and

socialistconstruction is in the people's interests, first of all, in the interests of the workers, farmers and intellectuals as the main body of our socialist modernization. But with the deepening of reform, it will have a bearing on the interests of all interest groups among the people, on every region, every aspect and every individual, which will bring about the entanglement, collisions, frictions and contradictions among the people. This requires our officials to have a correct analysis of the situation, keep sober-minded, and grasp the new developments, new problems and new features as well as the rules governing them, to as soon as possible change the negative factors into positive ones.

II. Some Theoretical Issues about Contradictions among the People

Under the new situation, to raise our level of policy and ability in correctly handle contradictions among the people, we must study the new situations, new problems and new features of them by combining the new reality, to further enrich the theory of contradictions among the people.

1. Contradictions among the people is the principal contradiction of interpersonal relations in the current social stage in China

In the present stage in China there exist two different types of social contradictions, one is those among the people, the other is those between ourselves and the enemy.

Contradictions among the people refer to contradictions of non-antagonistic nature that occur among the people and are identical in fundamental interests. Contradictions between ourselves and the enemy refer to antagonistic social contradictions of class nature between these two social forces on the basis of opposing fundamental interests. Due to complex domestic and foreign factors and economic, political, ideological and cultural causes, in the primary stage of socialism in China, the two kinds of contradictions among the people will exist for a long time, and under certain conditions, contradictions among the people may intensify; and there are also the complex situation where the two types of contradictions entangle together. Nevertheless, among all types of contradictions, contradictions among the people are still the most outstanding, most frequent and most ordinary type taking the basic position among social and contradictions in interpersonal relations. Correctly handling contradictions among the people is the theme of our political life under the new situation of reform and opening up.

First, the nature of socialism in China determines the contradiction among the people is the principal contradiction of interpersonal relations among all social contradictions.

In real social life, basic social contradictions will necessarily manifest themselves in interpersonal relations. In other words, basic social contradictions will necessarily manifest themselves as contradictions of interpersonal relations. In a class society, whether it is slave society, feudal society or capitalist society, the contradiction between the private ownership of the means of production and social productivity is antagonistic and irreconcilable. This determines that the existence of fierce contradictions and conflicts of interests among people is inevitable, and that the basic social contradictions manifest themselves largely and mainly in class relations in forms of class contradictions and class struggle. After the establishment of socialist system in China, its relations of production basically conform to the development of its productive forces, so does its superstructure to economic base, except for some aspects and links. On the one hand, because the basic contradictions in socialist society are non-antagonistic, they can be resolved through conscious adjustment and reform. After more than twenty years of reform and opening up, a basic economic system for the primary stage of socialism is established and socialist market economy has come into being, which have greatly released and developed socialist productive forces; and we have timely and accordingly carried out political restructuring, gradually established the basic political institutions of the primary stage of socialism and strengthened the construction of socialist legal system and democracy, which have greatly aroused the enthusiasm of the people. On the other hand, however, China's socialist reform still has long way to go in that the basic socialist economic-political system and its corresponding economic-political system needs to be further improved; at the same time, even if the basic socialist economic-political system and its corresponding economic-political system be in place, with the development of social productivity and society, new inconformity and imperfection will emerge. Therefore, the contradictions of both conformity and inconformity between socialist economic base and superstructure and between the relations of production and productivity will exist for a long time, and the basic contradictions in socialist society are impossible to disappear. In the present stage of our society, the basic social contradictions are manifested as the inconformity of specific form of relations of production, i. e. , the economic structure with the development of productivity, and inconformity of the concrete form of superstructure, i. e. , the political structure with the economic base. In the current stage, the feature of relationship between the productive forces and relations of production and between superstructure and economic base is that conformity and inconformity coexist, and there are certain non-antagonistic contradictions on the premise of basic conformity. This determines that, there are no antagonistic contradictions and conflicts among the people, and the basic contradictions largely and mainly manifest themselves as contradictions among the people.

Second, the nature and characters of basic contradictions at the present stage of socialism in China determines that contradictions among the people take the primary position among all social contradictions.

In real social life, basic social contradictions will necessarily manifest themselves ininterpersonal relations. In other words, basic social contradictions will necessarily manifest themselves as contradictions of interpersonal relations. In a class society, whether it is slave society, feudal society or capitalist society, the contradiction between the private ownership of the means of production and social productivity is antagonistic and irreconcilable. This determines that the existence of fierce contradictions and conflicts of interests among people is inevitable, and that the basic social contradictions manifest themselves largely and mainly in class relations in forms of class contradictions and class struggle. After the establishment of socialist system in China, its relations of production basically conform to the development of its productive forces, so does its superstructure to economic base, except for some aspects and links. On the one hand, because the basic contradictions in socialist society are non-antagonistic, they can be resolved through conscious adjustment and reform. After more than twenty years of reform and opening up, a basic economic system for the primary stage of socialism is established and socialist market economy has come into being, which have greatly released and developed socialist productive forces; and we have timely and accordingly carried out political restructuring, gradually established the basic political institutions of the primary stage of socialism and strengthened the construction of socialist legal system and democracy, which have greatly aroused the enthusiasm of the people. On the other hand, however, China's socialist reform still has long way to go in that the basic socialist economic-political system and its corresponding economic-political system needs to be further improved; at the same time, even if the basic socialist economic-political system and its corresponding economic-political system be in place, with the development of social productivity and society, new inconformity and imperfection will emerge. Therefore, the contradictions of both conformity and inconformity between socialist economic base and superstructure and between the relations of production and productivity will exist for a long time, and the basic contradictions in socialist society are impossible to disappear. In the present stage of our society, the basic social contradictions are manifested as the inconformity of specific form of relations of production, i. e. , the economic structure with the development of productivity, and inconformity of the concrete form of superstructure, i. e. , the political structure with the economic base. In the current stage, the feature of relationship between the productive forces and relations of production and between superstructure and economic base is that conformity and inconformity coexist, and there are certain non-antagonistic contradictions on the premise of basic conformity. This determines that, there are no antagonistic contradictions and conflicts among the people, and the basic contradictions largely and mainly manifest themselves as contradictions among the people.

Third, at the current stage, the principal contradiction determines that largely, frequently and prominently manifest themselves as contradictions among the people.

In the whole system of contradiction in socialist society, basic social contradictions are at the first level, while the principal contradiction is at the second level. Principal contradiction here refers to the contradiction that plays the dominant and leading role in the complex course of social development (not exclusively concerning interpersonal relations) at a certain stage of a certain form of society. It is pointed out in the Report to the Thirteenth National Congress of the CPC that, the principal contradiction in our society is one between the ever-growing material and cultural needs of the people and the backwardness of social production. As to interpersonal relations specifically, at the primary stage of socialism, this principal contradiction mainly manifest themselves as contradictions among the people: on the one hand, the relatively backward social production can only provide a limited material and cultural wealth; on the other, the material and cultural needs of the people are ever growing, which cannot be met by the limited production. This gives rise to the extraordinary prominence of the contradictions in interest distribution. The principal contradiction at the primary stage of socialism determines that contradictions among the people occupy the dominant position in the system of contradictions in interpersonal relations.

Fourth, in the new conditions of socialist reform and opening up and the process of shifting towards socialist market economy, the transformation of the old structures to the new ones and the change of pattern of interest distribution determines that contradictions among the people are extraordinarily complex.

Reform and opening up, while having boosted the economy and improved people'slife, also made the interest contradictions among the people more outstanding and widespread, because the diverse forms of ownership and modes of distributionhave intensified the differences and contradictions among different interest groups. The development of the market economy makes the economic relations become more complicated, patterns of distribution more diversified and social contradictions multi-tiered. Contradictions in economic area in turn give rise to contradictions in political and intellectual areas. And changes in economic, political and intellectual areas all together make interpersonal relations among the people more complicated, which add new forms and content to contradictions among the people.

2. Interest contradictions, especially interest contradictions among different groups are the concentrated expressions of various contradictions among the people

In On the Correct Handling of Contradictions among the People, in addition to analyzing political and ideological contradictions among the people and methods for resolving them, Comrade Mao Zedong also talks about various interest contradictions. But due to the limitations of historical conditions, he didn't pay enough attention to economic causes of contradictions among the people in his analysis. In fact, interest contradictions are the material and the economic causes and factors affecting the development of various contradictions among the people. Only by making in-depth analysis from material aspect can interest contradictions among the people be correctly understood and handled. And only by profoundly understanding the interest contradictions among the people can contradictions among the people in general be correctly understood and handled.

Contradictions among the people constitute a complex system composed of multi-type contradictions, including contradictions between ethnic groups, contradictions between regions, contradictions among collective units, contradictions between enterprises, contradictions within the ranks of the working class, contradictions within the farmer class, contradictions within the intelligentsia, contradictions within individual labors, contradiction within private economic operators, contradictions between the working class on the one hand and the farmer class and other working classes on the other, contradictions between the governing party and the government on the one hand and the people on the other, contradictions between the leadership and the masses, contradictions between the higher levels and lower levels, contradictions between Party and non-Party, contradictions within the Party, contradictions among the state, the collectives and the individuals, contradictions among individuals, contradictions among social strata, contradiction among interest groups, and so on. These contradictions are manifested in economic, political, ideological and other fields, among which, the interest contradictions among the people are the material and economic roots of the emergence, existence, development and intensification of all other contradictions among the people, and are the dominant type of contradictions constraining the development of other types of contradictions. In the system of contradictions among the people, interest contradictions have the characteristics of root-cause, dominance, mass involvement and non-antagonism.

In the primary stage of socialism, various reasons determine that there exist contradictions among the people.

Firstly, the relative backwardness of productive forces in this stage is the material cause of interest contradictions among the people. The underdevelopment of commodity economy results the relative shortage of material means of livelihood, which will lead to relative tension in distribution relations. If it is coupled with unreasonable distribution, interest contradictions among the people will become more acute.

Secondly, the remnants of old division of labor and social differences are the historical causes of interest contradictions among the people in the primary stage of socialism.

Thirdly, the existence of different types of ownership and distribution is the reason of production relations for the existence and change of interest contradictions among the people. In the primary stage of socialism, the different types and ownership and diverse forms of distribution determines that the interest contradictions among the people are complicated. For example, there are not only components of state-owned, collective owned and mixed owned sectors of the economy that is public nature, but also individual sector private sectors of the economy of non-public nature, which makes the interest contradictions among the people manifested themselves in interest contradictions between employees in public sectors of the economy on the one side and the self-employed laborers and the self-employed individuals and private operator and employers on the other side; interest contradictions between employers of private enterprises and their employees; interest contradictions between individual or private operators and the ordinary consumers.

Fourthly, the socialist market economy is the economic reason for the existence and change for the interest contradictions among the people. Behind the complex economic relations among the people lie various complicated economic contradictions.

Fifthly, the immature and imperfect economic and political systems are the reasons for the existence and change of interest contradictions among the people in the primary stage of socialism, which exist both in specific institutions in economic sector and in superstructure, resulting in more complex, more prominent, sometimes even acute interest conflicts among the people. Sixth, the remnants of the old society in ideological, cultural, social and ethical fields are ideological reasons for the existence and interest contradictions among the people. The relative backwardness in these fields in the primary stage of socialism makes the interest contradictions among the people more prominent.

All of these profound historical, economic, political, cultural and other social factors determine that, at the present stage in China, there exist contradictions among various interest subjects, including contradictions between individuals or special groups, contradictions between interest of individuals or special groups and interests of the collective or and society. The interest contradiction among the people is the root cause of the emergence and development of contradictions among the people at large and can influence the direction, development and change of other types of contradictions.

Interest contradictions among the people manifest themselves both vertically and horizontally. Horizontally speaking, they manifest themselves as contradictions between the various interest groups, strata, classes, even ethnic groups, whereas vertically as contradictions or conflicts among individuals, groups and the state, specifically as contradictions or conflicts between individual laborers and managerial personnel of enterprises, or between the masses and officials. For example, contradictions between the decisions and measures made by the officials that represent the long-term interests and the undesired tendency of some of the masses who care only for immediate interest or excessive individual interests; contradictions and conflicts between bureaucratism that is unconcerned about the people's welfare and legitimate and reasonable interest demands; contradictions and conflicts between corruption of some officials and the efforts of the masses to safeguard their own interests; contradictions and conflicts between the damage to the interests of the masses caused by subjective mistakes of officials and discontent of the masses because of it; contradictions and conflicts between officials of government departments and leaders of enterprises, between central and local governments and between authorities at upper level and lower level, etc.

Interest contradictions among the people manifest themselves mainly in contradictions among different interest groups. In a class society, interest groups are usually of class nature. In a socialist country, although antagonism of between exploiting and the exploited classes has been eliminated, there are some differences between classes and between groups, such as the big interest differences between workers and farmers, between with working class and private entrepreneurs. Especially within the classes of workers and farmers, there are various interest groups due to differences of income and economic status. Contradictions among different interest groups are the concentrated expressions of contradictions among the people.

Generally speaking, contradictions among the people are of non-antagonistic nature, but they may transform into antagonistic contradictions if not properly handled. At present, China is in a new period of transition from old to new systems, during which the economic and political systems are reformed to meet the requirements of the development of our productive forces. Along with the change of China's economic and political structures, the original structure of interest groups has also changed accordingly, with its previous unreasonable pattern of interests being broken down. The current rapid change and combination of interest groups inevitably determines that the organizations and behaviors of interest groups are diverse and multileveled. Certain interest awareness will inevitably lead to certain behavior tendencies, which tend to bring about frictions, conflicts and contradictions between groups, some even cause antagonistic contradictions, unbalanced distribution relationship and more complex intergroup relations and conflicts. For example, the interest contradictions between workers and farmers caused by the differences between agricultural and industrial products, the interest contradictions between the employers and employees in private owned enterprises, and so on. In the course of transformation toward and the formation of socialist market economy, interest contradictions among the different interest groups of the people are especially pronounced and complex.

3. The contradiction between the officials and the masses is an important expression of contradictions among the people in the new era

In general, the contradiction between theofficials and the masses is an important expression of contradictions among the people and the main line through the existence, development and change. This is because:

First, in the political life of our socialist country, because our party is the governing party, its officials at all levels are in the leading positions in political, economic, cultural and other social areas. The success or failure of the entire socialist cause is closely related to the officials, so do all the problems and mistakes. As the leaders of the masses, on the one hand, they shoulder the duty of guiding, educating, organizing and mobilizing the people; on the other, they should rely on and subordinate to the masses, receive the supervision of them and avoid divorcing from them. This determines that the relations between the officials and the masses constitute the principal interpersonal relations in our country and the contradictions between them become an important expression of the contradictions among the people.

Second, most of the major social contradictions in our socialist country in many cases find their expression in the contradictory relations between theo fficials and the masses. For example, the basic contradiction of socialism will find its expression in the contradictory relations between the officials as managers and executives of economic and political functions and the masses as factors of the productive forces. In the primary stage of socialism, the contradiction between the relatively backward social production and the increasing material and cultural needs of the people is saliently reflected in the insufficient supply of consumer goods in meeting people's needs. So it is the unshirkable duty of the officials at all levels to solve the shortage of consumer goods. Especially facing severe economic difficulties when consumer goods are scarce, the officials has become the focus of all social contradictions, and the contradiction between them will become a concentrated expression of all social contradictions.

In general, under our socialist system, the contradiction between the officials and the masses is non-antagonistic. However, it can become acute and antagonistic in the following cases, among others: when the major policy or decision mistakes of the officials damage the people's legitimate interests; when the serious bureaucratic style of work of the officials jeopardize the reasonable interests or demands of the people; when the degenerate or corrupt elements among ranks of the officials embezzle people's property or seriously damage people's interests; when some of the masses fail to recognize the necessity of sacrificing the partial or immediate for the whole or long-term interests and therefore show their discontent about it; when the unreasonable requests of some people are rejected and then taken use by some scoundrels to stir up troubles, which are not dealt with timely, resolutely or correctly by the officials.

In the contradiction between the officials and the masses, the primary aspect is the officials. Just as Comrade Liu Shaoqi put it, "The leadership is responsible for every mistake and everything unreasonable in our society. The people will call the officials in the state, the Party or government, including departments in charge of economic affairs, to account, and we are accountable for them."[①] In a contradiction between the officials and the masses, if the officials are in the wrong side while the masses in correct side, then the primary aspect of the contradiction in no doubt officials, and the resolution of it depends whether the officials can correct their mistakes and secure the forgiveness of the masses; On the other hand, if officials are correct and the masses are wrong, the primary aspect of the contradiction is still the officials, for the resolution of the contradiction depends whether the officials can correctly handle it by educating and persuading the masses. For example, when some of the masses ask unreasonable demands in distribution and make troubles, the

① *Selected Works of Liu Shaoqi*, People's Publishing House, 985. p. 303

key to it is whether the officials can make effective efforts to persuade, educate and guide the masses. Therefore, usually the officials constitute the primary aspect and the dominant side in the contradiction between them and the masses. Of course, we cannot blame all the contradictions or problems appeared in the masses on the leadership. When we say that the officials constitute the primary aspect in the contradictions between the officials and the masses, we refer to the responsibility or work of them, not simply about right or wrong. Comrade Liu Shaoqi also pointed out that, contradictions among the people frequently find their expression in the contradiction between the officials and the masses, "more exactly, in the contradiction between the bureaucracy of the leadership and people. "①
Among which, the primary aspect of the contradiction is the leadership, and the contradictions between bureaucracy, corruptions and other malpractices of the leadership and the masses constitute an important manifestation of it. Our party's fundamental purpose is for the people's interests. To solve the contradiction between the officials of the masses, we must improve the Party's work style and build a clean government to ensure that the interests of the main forces of socialist construction, i. e. , workers, farmers and the intelligentsia, be guaranteed, so that the living standards of all the people be raised.

4. The phenomena of antagonism and intensification of contradictions among the people

Generally speaking, contradictions between ourselves and the enemy are antagonistic in nature, while those among the people are not. But if we confuse the two different types of contradiction, lose vigilance or handle them improperly, contradictions among the people can become intensified or transformed, leading to serious confrontation or social conflicts. This is because:

First, there are isolated phenomena of antagonistic contradictions among the people. In the present stage in China, there are still economic, politic, ideological residue of the old society, in addition to the influence and subversion of external anti-socialist forces in economic, political, ideological and cultural fields, leading to the existence not only contradictions between ourselves and the enemy in a certain scope, but also occasional antagonistic contradictions among the people. Take the

---

① *Selected Works of Liu Shaoqi*, People's Publishing House, 985. p. 303

relationship between the private and public economy for instance. These are two different economies in nature, and in the primary stage of socialism private economy is permitted to exist. Therefore, under certain conditions, contradictions between private and public economies manifest themselves in non-antagonistic form. So does the relationship between the private owners and their employees, contradictions belonging to the category of contradictions among the people. In political field, the contradictions between the people and elements left over from the old society, such as the feudalists, bourgeois, historical reactionaries, etc. , are antagonistic in nature. However, as long as these elements no longer engage in anti-socialist political activities, honestly submit to socialist transformation and do things beneficial for the people, their contradictions with the people can be regarded and handled as contradictions among the people. Some antagonistic contradictions within the Party also belong to the category of contradictions among the people. Contradictions between the officials and the masses are non-antagonistic in nature, but those between the severe bureaucrats in the leadership and the masses are antagonistic. In the realm of ideology, contradictions between socialist ideology and feudalist and capitalist ideologies are antagonistic, but the contradictions among the people arising from the influence of these two ideologies come under the category of contradictions among the people in general. The existence of antagonistic contradictions among the people is the necessary condition for the intensification of contradictions among the people.

Second, there are contradictions of class struggle nature among the people in a certain limits. Due to domestic and international factors, class struggle will continue to exist within certain limits in our socialist country, which will inevitably be reflected in the ranks of the people, causing the existence of contradictions with class struggle nature. For example, the combating against bourgeois liberalization; the fighting against corrosion of bourgeois ideology; the contradictions between the people and some persons who commit petty crime of endangering public security or social order: these contradictions, although having a nature of class struggle, are still belongs to the contradictions among the people, which constitute the deeper reason for the intensification of contradictions among the people.

Third, if not properly handled, non-antagonistic contradictions among the people can transform into antagonistic contradictions, so do contradictions among the people with non-class-struggle nature into that of class struggle nature, and contradictions among the people into contradictions between ourselves and the enemy; vice versa. The transformation of contradictions among the people is an important reason for the intensification of contradictions among the people.

Fourth, in reality, the two types of contradictions differing in nature intertwine, forming a complex situation, in which the class struggle in a limited range and the contradictions of no-class struggle in nature; the limited number of contradictions between ourselves and the enemy and the overwhelming majority of contradictions among the people; the antagonistic contradictions in the non-dominant position and the dominant no-antagonistic contradictions, etc. , are often inextricably intertwined rather than clearly distinguishable from each other, thus forming a complex social situation. This is particularly true in the primary stage of socialism. Take the demonstration of some students, workers, farmers or ordinary citizens for example. Generally speaking, the majority of the masses are patriotic and their demonstration actions belong to the category of contradictions among the people. But the causes are very complex, including instigation of hostile forces, our mistakes in work, and so on. Among them contradictions between us and the evil elements hiding behind and deliberately making incitement and subversion belong to the contradictions between ourselves and the enemy. This complexity is the objective reason for the intensification of contradictions among the people.

Fifth, the mistakes of officials in understanding and handling complex social contradictions may lead to their intensification.

Facing complex factors at home and abroad and social contradictions, if we lose vigilance, confuse contradictions, make wrong decisions or handle improperly, a non-antagonistic contradiction among the people can transform into antagonistic one, and even a contradiction among the people can transform into that between ourselves and the enemy. For example, some incidents such as worker strikes, mass violent conflicts or incidents of bloodshed are caused by the improper handling of discontent of the masses over shortage or the increase of prices of consumer goods. In the initial stage of the kind of incidents, the masses usually only express their discontent; improper handling will lead to the accumulation and intensification of contradictions and antagonistic conflicts. Except for a few bad elements, the majority of those involved in belong to the category of the people. Insufficient vigilance, improper handling, wrong decision, nature confusion, etc. , are the subjective reason for the intensification of contradictions among the people. The antagonistic contradictions among the people can cause wider social conflicts, which, coupled with class struggle and contradictions between ourselves and the people, as well as our subjective mistakes, may further intensify even arouse conflict or social unrest, threatening political stability of our socialist society. Therefore, we must keep high vigilance against the possibility of antagonism and intensification of contradictions among the people.

III. Basic Methods for Resolving Contradictions among the People in the New Era

" Qualitatively different contradictions can only be resolved by qualitatively different methods. "① Therefore, methods for resolving contradictions among the people must differ from that for resolving contradictions between ourselves and the enemy. Contradictions among the people in the new situation, in general, are non-antagonistic contradictions on the basis of fundamental identity of the people's interests with building socialism with Chinese characteristics as the common goal. Therefore, these contradictions, in spite of some antagonistic nature and complex situation, can be properly resolved as long we do our work well. So the key lies in our work.

First, economic means should be mainly used to resolve contradictions of loss and gain among the people.

Contradictions of loss and gain areno other than interest contradictions. In discussing interest contradictions among the people, Comrade Mao Zedong proposed the use of economic measures to address them. In 1979, Comrade Deng Xiaoping pointed out: "We must adjust the relations between this various types of interests in accordance with the principle of taking them all into proper consideration. Were we to do the opposite and pursue personal, local or immediate interests at the expense of the others, both sets of interests would inevitably suffer. "② Economic approach serves as the major and fundamental method for solving internal interest (mainly material and economic interests) contradictions among

---

① *Selected Works of Mao Zedong*, vol. 1 People's Publishing House, 1991, p. 311

② *Selected Works of Deng Xiaoping*, vol. 2, People's Publishing House, 1994, pp. 175—176

the people, and "make overall plans and take all factors into consideration" is the fundamental principles in handling interest contradictions among the people.

How, then, can we implement the principle of "making overall plans and taking all factors into consideration" to use economic methods to settle interest contradictions among the people? Firstly, we must establish a primary stage socialist political-social system that conforms to socialist market economy. Only by taking the interest demands of all sides into consideration can the enthusiasm of the people be aroused, which needs the guarantee of a certain system. Currently China is making socialist reform, aiming to establish a socialist market economy, so that interest contradictions can be settled through systems by using the laws and mechanisms of market economy and implementing economic policies and laws. Secondly, we should establish a rational distribution system, which allows some people to get rich first with common prosperity as the goal, so that the interest relations of all sides can be coordinated. Under socialist market economy, consumer goods are distributed in accordance with the laws of market economy. In the primary stage of socialism, there are different interest groups and significant interest differences between them. It requires: We should build a distribution system that both accords with the market economy and are also suitable for different interest groups; We should takes distribution according to work as the main form with the coexistence of other forms of distribution, such as distribution according to needs, distribution according to production factors; We should both oppose egalitarianism to allow some differences of interest and some people get rich first, and also prevent too wide distribution disparities and polarization to realized common prosperity. Thirdly, we take the correct economic policies and economic ways to resolve interest contradictions among the people. The reason why China's rural household contract responsibility system can greatly arouse the enthusiasm of farmers is that, through correct economic policies and measures, it combined well the individual, collective and state interests. Similarly, one of the important objectives of the reform toward the market economy is to properly handle the interest relations between the state, enterprises and workers. If the relatively independent economic interests of enterprises can be guaranteed, various forms of economic responsibility can be established and the reasonable individual income of workers can be safeguarded, the enthusiasm of enterprises and workers is sure to be aroused. Fourthly, political and ideological work is necessary in handling contradictions of material interests among the people. Necessary political and ideological work and correct economic measures are complementary to each other, the premise and basis of which is the introduction of correct economic policies. But, fundamentally speaking, contradictions of material interests among the people can only be resolved by the economic means, that is, by developing productive forces and "making the cake bigger", so that the constantly growing material and cultural needs of the people can be satisfied.

Second, democratic measures must be used to resolve contradictions of right and wrong among the people.

Ideological and political contradictions among the people are indeed contradictions of right and wrong. Comrade Mao Zedong pointed out: The only way to settle questions of an ideological nature or controversial issues among the people is by the democratic method, the method of discussion, criticism, persuasion and education, and not by the method of coercion or repression. He also summarized the democratic method into a formula of "unity-criticism-unity." Comrade Deng Xiaoping also said: "In political life within the Party and among the people we must use democratic means and not resort to coercion or attack." The method of democracy is not only the basic way but also the basic principle to solve the problem of right or wrong and contradictions in the political life within the people. Democratic methods mainly include two aspects, one is the establishment of democratic system based on the rule of law, through which contradictions among the people can be resolved; second is the democratic ways of persuasion and education.

Third, contradictions among the people need to be resolved by multitude and comprehensive methods based on specific conditions.

In the present stage, contradictions among the people are not isolated to each other but rather constitute a complex system, within which external and internal factors are interlinked and interact. Therefore, to resolve these contradictions, there is no fixed formula or prescription for all disease, we cannot use a single method, but rather take different ways according to specific conditions; even for contradictions of the same nature, due to their different manifestations, different but comprehensive methods are also needed.

Leading bodies and officials at all levels should courageously take responsibility, be serious, cautious and conscientious, and good at doing research, so as to resolve all kinds of contradictions in the new situation based on their reality. In real life, contradictions among the people are diverse and complex and not isolated to each other at all. So they must be solved by using comprehensive measures. Firstly, we must vigorously strengthen ideological and political work with an aim to relieve the discontent of the people, enhance mutual understanding and mobilize all positive factors. All kinds of contradictions under the new situation are mostly derived from interest distribution or problems in thinking or understanding. Therefore, much work should be done in persuasion, mediation, coordination or communication, so that all side concerned can understand and accommodate each other, bear in mind the overall interests, seek common ground while reserving differences; We can never wait until the contradictions have been accumulated or become knotty. Secondly, we must pay attention to the methods of work, concern for the livelihood of the masses, help the masses to overcome their difficulties, instead of talking empty or doing formalism. We must spare no efforts to combat corruption and overcome bureaucracy, which are very important for settling the discontent of the masses and solving contradictions among the people. Today, the complexity of all kinds of contradictions among the people need our close attention and cannot afford our slightest slackness. We should mobilize forces of all aspects, including ideological and political work, reform, democracy and laws, to reconcile contradictions among the people and mobilize their enthusiasm for reform and construction to the maximum.

Fourth, deepening reform, developing socialist productive forces and socialist market economy, and improving socialist democracy and legal systemare fundamental ways to solve contradictions among the people.

To resolve the contradictions among the people under the new situation, the fundamental way is deepening reform, developing socialist productive forces and market economy to guide the people gradually into common prosperity. At the same time we must strengthen the building of socialist democracy and the legal system, and promote political restructuring to provide institutions and mechanisms for fundamentally resolve all kinds of contradictions among the people. We must keep promoting our cultural and ethical building to improve the quality of all citizens. Only on this basis, can we, following the principle of taking all sides into consideration, really establish an effective interest adjustment mechanism to balance all kinds of interest relations so that to unify the broadest masses around the Party and fully mobilize their enthusiasm and initiatives by interest coordination.

Appendix III

Facing Up, Attaching Importance to and Striving to Narrowing Regional Gap by Balancing Development Strategy and Accelerating the Development of Central and Western Regions①

By seizing the rare development opportunity provided by reform and opening up, all regions in China in general has achieved great development. But on the other hand, gap between different regions, especially between eastern and western regions has widened, which faces China with a series of new economic and social problems. In this context, having a scientific understanding of the gap, choosing a balanced development strategy and accelerating the development of central and western regions are of great strategic significance for narrowing the gap, further mobilizing the enthusiasm and creativity of the regions and the people of all ethnic groups, to comprehensively promote the construction of China's socialist modernization and common prosperity.

I. The Reality and Inevitability of the Regional Gap and Its Widening

Regional gap in China mainly refers to the gap between China'sthe eastern, central and western economic areas. According to the Seventh-Five-Year Plan, China was divided into three major economic regions: the

① This article is the presentation made by the author on the International Forum on Balanced Regional Development in China's Economic Reform and Social Progress held in Hong Kong in December, 1996. Data and figures have been renewed before it is included into this book.

eastern coastal regions, including Beijing, Tianjin, Hebei, Liaoning, Shanghai, Jiangsu, Zhejiang, Fujian, Shandong, Guangdong (Hainan had not become a province then) and Guangxi; the central region, includes Shanxi, Inner Mongolia, Jilin, Heilongjiang, Anhui, Jiangxi, Henan, Hubei and Hunan; and the western region, includes Sichuan (Chongqing was not a municipality yet), Guizhou, Yunnan, Tibet, Shaanxi, Gansu, Qinghai, Ningxia and Xinjiang. The gap between the eastern, central and western regions can be historically analyzed from their levels of economic development, industrial structure, investment in fixed assets, foreign investment and income, as follows:

1. Gap in GNP

During the period of 15 years from 1980 to 1994, the ratio of average annual growth rates of GNP between the eastern, central and western regions were 19.88 : 16.20 : 15.78, showing an obvious widening, with the eastern region 3.68 percentage points higher than the central region and 4.10 percentage points higher than the western region. In terms of per capita GNP in 1987, they were 1492 yuan, 888 yuan and 715 yuan in eastern, central and western regions respectively with their respectively ratios of 1 : 0.62 : 0.50, showing not too big differences. By 1993, however, the per capita GNP of eastern, central and western regions changed respectively into 4580 yuan, 2075 yuan and 1408 yuan and their ratios into 1 : 0.45 : 0.31, with the per capita GNP of the eastern region is 2.21 times that of the central region and 3.25 timesof the western region. In contrast, during that period, the proportions of their population in national total almost didn't change, but that oftheir GNP changed significantly. That is, in 1980, it was 52.3 : 31.2 : 16.5, and in 1993, it changed into 60.1 : 26.8 : 13.1. Compared with 1980, the proportion of GNP of the eastern region in national total increased by 7.9 percentage points while that of the central and western regions were declined 4.4 and 3.4 percentage points respectively. With an area of 10.7% of national total, eastern region created nearly 5 times per capital GNP that of the western region that covers 69.1 percent of the country's total land area. By the end of 1998, the per capita GNP of the eastern, central and western regions again changed respectively into 9, 403 yuan, 5201 yuan, and 4021 yuan with their proportions in that of national total were respectively 58.1 : 27.9 : 14.0.

At the same time, their absolute differences in GNP growth continued to widen. From 1979 to 1991, the GNP ofthe coastal areas was 173. 8 billion yuan higher than or 10. 1 times that of the previous difference with the inland; 434. 9 billion yuan higher than or 5. 9 times that of theprevious difference with the central region; and 628. 2 billion yuan higher than or 5. 1 times that of the previous difference with the western region. Changes in absolute difference of per capita GNP were: the coastal area was 768 yuan higher than or 4. 4 times that of the previous difference with the inland; 730 yuan higher than or 4. 7 times that of the previous difference with the central regions; 826 yuan higher than or 4. 9 times that of the previous differences of the western region.

2. Gap in GDP

Statistics for 1993 shows that, 6 of the 9 western provinces or autonomous region shad their per capita GDP below 2000 yuan, falling to low level range, the rest of which fell to the lower-middle range of 2000 to 3000 yuan. Except for Xinjiang, the average per capita GDP of these provinces or autonomous regions was only 1, 232 yuan, 46. 2 percent of 2, 663 yuan of national average. In 1994, the differences of per capita GDP in eastern with that of the central and western regions were respectively 1745 yuan and 2027 yuan, and are expected to rise to 2770 yuan and 3220 yuan in 2000. In the 16 years from 1979 to 1994, the growth rate of GDP of Yunnan Province was 1. 5 percent lower than that of the eastern region.

3. Gap in the industrial growth and productivity

From 1985 to 1990, the ratios of industrial growth rate of China's eastern, central and western regions were 1 : 1. 05 : 1, decreasing progressively from eastern to western regions. In 1991, the national average all-personnel labor productivity was 33, 161 yuan/person year, among which, Shanghai was the highest, reaching 58, 555 yuan, 1. 6 times of national average; Beijing, Tianjin, Jiangsu, Zhejiang and Guangdong were all above 40, 000 yuan/person year; Shanxi, Jiangxi, Guizhou, Shaanxi, Gansu, Qinghai, etc. were all below 30, 000 yuan/ person year. The lowest was Inner Mongolia with 21, 956 yuan/person year, equivalent to 66 percent of the national average.

4. Gap in industrial structure

Thegap in industrial structure between eastern, central and western regions isalso very obvious. In 1993, in the total national industrial structure, the proportion of the primary (agriculture) industry accounted only for 21. 2 percent, with the secondary and tertiary industries accounting respectively for 27 percentand51. 8 percent. In 1998, the figures changed into 18. 4 percent, 48. 7 percent and 32. 9 percent. Of the increase of value-added of the secondary industry, about 90 percent was from industrial manufacturing. From this we can see that the growth of industry is of vital importance tothe overall economic development. The gap in industrial growth between the eastern, central and western regions was significant. During the decade of 1985—1994, the ratios of average annual industrial growth between these three regions were 1. 42 : 1. 06 : 1, which made the proportion of industrial output of the eastern region in that of national total rise from 46. 3 percent in 1985 to 66. 47 percent in 1994 while that of the western region reducing from 12. 75 percent to 11. 33 percent. In 1998, the proportions of eastern, central and western industrial output in that of national total were respectively 67. 0 percent, 23. 8 percent and 9. 2 percent. At the same time, in terms of proportion of the output of the primary industry in the total industrial output, the western regions are higher than the eastern region, and reverse is the case when it comes to the secondary and tertiary industries. The proportion of industrial output of the primary industry in the western region was 12. 8 percentage points higher than that of the eastern region, whereas the proportions of the secondary and tertiary industries were 10. 4 and 2. 4 percentage points lower. Similar gap exists inthe development of township enterprises between them: In 1993 the national output value of township enterprises reached more than 2. 9 trillion yuan, of which, that of the eastern region accounted for 65. 8 percent while the western region only 7. 6 percent; in 1998, the national value-added of township enterprises was about 2. 22 trillion yuan, of which that of the eastern region accounted for 60. 4 percent while the western region only 8. 6 percent. In terms of growth rate of township enterprises, gap between the eastern, central and western regions is also very large. In the five years from 1990 to 1994, the average annual growth rates were respectively 48 percent, 29. 2 percent and 16. 5 percent in the eastern, central and western regions. Take Shaanxi Province for example: The total investment of township enterprises of it accounts for only 0. 7 percent of national total, while those of Jiangsu and Shandong account for 4. 5 percentand 5. 4 percent respectively.

5. Gap in Investment

Gap in investment between the eastern and western region is also widening. During the 1982-1992 period, the average annual growth rates of fixed asset investment in eastern, central and western regions were respectively 21. 7 percent, 16. 10 percent and 18. 28 percent. Of the increase of its national investment, in 1992, about 62. 1 percent are from the eastern region. In 1998, the proportions of investment of the eastern, central and western regions rose respectively from 62. 2 percent, 23. 1 percent and 14. 7 percent in the previous year into 61. 3 percent, 22. 4 percent and 16. 3 percent. In 1985, the per capital investment of Qinghai Province in 1985 was 420 yuan, equivalent to 75. 1 of national average; but that figure changed into 990 yuan in 1994, equivalent to 72. 5 percent of national average, fell 102. 6 percent in nine years. In 1998, it rose to 2144. 7 yuan, equivalent to 94 percent of national average of 2248. 6 yuan. In 1994, the per capita investment of Shanghai, the highest in the whole country was 8031 yuan, 21. 2 times that of Guizhou, which was 379 yuan, the lowest in the whole country. In 1998, the figures were 13, 344 yuan for Shanghai and 759 yuan for Guizhou.

6. Gap in utilization of foreign capital

Compared with the eastern region, the central and western regions much lag behindin the utilization of foreign capital. The utilization rate of foreign capital Guangdong Province is as high as 26 percent. By the end of 1998, the national cumulative amount of contracted foreign capital was $608. 425 billion, and the paid-in foreign investment was $317. 169 billion. Nearly 89 percent of which was in the eastern region, while the central and western regions got only 11 percent. By the end of 1994, the cumulative amount of contracted foreign capital in the eastern region was $262. 682 billion, 7. 8 times that of the central and western regions, which was $33. 64 billion. The paid-in foreign investment in that year was $33. 165 billion, accounting for 17. 9 percent of national gross investment in fixed assets, while that in the central and western regions accounted only for 2. 2 percent, 13 percentage lower than that in the eastern region. In 1998, the proportions of foreign investment in eastern, central and western regions were 87. 3 percent, 9. 7 percent and 3 percent respectively.

7. Gap in Income Level

Income gap between residents in eastern and western regions is also widening. In 1980, the national per-capita annual net income of rural residents averaged 191. 33 yuan, with ratios between eastern, central, western regions being 1. 39: 1. 11 : 1. In 1993, the national per-capita annual net income of rural residents averaged 921 yuan while that in the eastern, central and western regions were 1, 380 yuan, 786 yuan and 604 yuan respectively, with their ratios being 2. 25 : 1. 75 : 1. The income gap between urban residents in the eastern, central and western regions was also significant. In 1993, the national average per capita annual income of urban residents used for living expenses were 2, 878 yuan, 1886. 8 yuan and 2045. 1 yuan in the eastern, central and western regions respectively, with their ratios changed from 1 : 0. 69 : 0. 77 in 1992 into 1 : 0. 65 : 0. 71. In 1998, in the province (municipality) with the highest per capita annual income, it was 11, 021. 49 yuan, in the lowest, 2505. 02 yuan, with the former 4. 4 times of the later. In addition, of the country's poverty-stricken counties, 90 percent are in the central and western regions; so does more than 80 percent of the poverty-stricken population, including most of the poorest parts. Of the population with a per capita annual income below 500 yuan, 54 percent is in the western regions. But the overall price level in the western region is rising to the extent of approaching that in the eastern region, which gives birth to the phenomenon of "low-income, high prices". As a result, the income level of residents in the western region is relatively declining.

The figures above show that, in the last ten more years, the historical and objective gap between the eastern and western regions has not narrowed, but on the contrary, it has been widened, both relatively and absolutely. This gap is mainly manifested in two aspects. First, the economic development. Since reform and opening up, China's economic development has gained great progress in general, but paces differ in different regions: The eastern coastal areas is developing rapidly while the central, particularly the west region and their poverty-stricken areas, are slow in development, resulting in a continuing widening gap. Take the comparison between Shanghai and Guizhou for example. In 1998, the per capita GNP of Shanghai was 22738 yuan, which was 10. 9 times that of Guizhou. Second is the income gap. In 1998, the average per capita annual income of the residents in eastern, central and western regions respectively were 6, 574 yuan, 4, 492 yuan, 4, 754 yuan, increasing respectively 4. 7 percent, 4 percent and 6 percent over the previous year, with their income ratios rising to1. 45 : 1 : 1. 04 comparing with1. 46 : 1 : 1. 06in the previous year. This disparity was more distinctive if we compare Shanghai and Guizhou. In 1998, the annual per capita consumption expenditure in rural areas in Shanghai was 4206. 89 yuan, while in Guizhouit was 1049. 39 yuan; in urban areas, it was 6866. 41 yuanin Shanghai and 3799. 38 yuan in Guizhou. At present, more than 80 percent of China's poverty-stricken population is in the western regionand 90 percent poverty-stricken counties are in the central and western regions. Gaps in economic development and income have brought abouta series of social gaps between them.

In such a large country like China, unevenregional development at certain historical stage is not unusual, and is inevitable to a certain degree. Disparities, especially economic disparity, are caused by many factors, including natural geographical factors, historical factors, system factors, policy factors, cultural and human factors, factor of distribution of productive forces, among others.

First, natural geographical factors.

Regional gap is the outcome of economic development at a certain stage based on the differences in natural geographical conditions and environments. Natural conditions underwhich people live and work in many areas in China's central and western regionsare very harsh with a low agricultural production. This, combined with their limited market, backward transportation infrastructure and poor informationand communications access, leads to their long-term low economic development. Meanwhile, in the market economy, the most important factor determining the flow of resources is the return on capital factor. Where there is a high profit, there capital, talents, technology, means of production, etc. flow into. Since reform and opening up, the geographical advantages of the eastern coastal area shave brought higher return on investment factors, resulting in the flow of production factors from west to east. Take the natural resources for instance. This is one of the advantages and also backbone industry of the western regions. But their markets are mainly in the eastern region. To sell these primary products, long distance transportation lines from west to east are needed, causing the high shipping costs and prices, and thus low profits or even no profitat all. In such an environment, few foreign capitals are interested in the regions. This difference in return on capital investment has further worsened the gap.

Second, historical factors.

Before the founding of New China, China was a semi-feudal and semi-colonial country and many ethnic groups inhibited in the central and western regions where most of the poverty-stricken and backward areas located. For a long timein the old society, discriminative and suppressive policies against ethnic minorities adopted by the feudalists, imperialists and bureaucratic-capitalists had plundered the naturalresources of these regions, which further exacerbated their poverty. At the same time, in order to grab high profits, imperialists built their factories in the eastern coastal areas, which worsened the backwardness of the central and western regions.

Third, policy factors.

The level of economic development in regions is closely related to and greatly influenced by national macroeconomic policies. Since reform and opening up, the country introduced a series of preferential policies and measures of open door inthe eastern coastal areas, including opening sixteen coastal cities, setting up special economic zones, development zones and bonded areas. By fully taking use of their geographical advantages and the preferential policies, the eastern coastal areas flexibly used the market mechanisms to attract foreign investment and firstly developed industries with high returns. Many investment and development hotspots thus formed and rapidly developed. Although these special policies have also gradually been adopted in the west along with the deepening of reform and opening up, it is undeniable that, compared with the the eastern coastal areasthat first got benefits from the policies, the central and western regions are relatively slow and still lag behind.

Fourth, institutional factors.

Under the old planned economy, determined by its own laws and reasons, the economy was bound to widen regional disparities. Under the old system, the central and western regions that have an absolute advantage innatural resources, including hydro-electricity, coal, oil, rare metals and other mineral resources, took primary industries such as raw materials, energy, heavy industry as their backbone and mainly sold primary products. These products that need huge input of raw materials were low in prices, and sometimes even unpaid appropriation were made, which inevitably causes serious price distortions. Since reform and opening up, the practice of planned economy still ran in certain limits and to a certain extent, so that the pricing system has not completely straightened out yet. The eastern coastal areas, by using low-price raw materials from the west, have accelerated their high value-added and high-tech industries, which doubled the value loss of the central and western regions.

Fifth, cultural and human factors.

In terms of cultural and human factors, including people's quality and cultural and educational levels, the differences between the eastern and western regions are rather large. The eastern coastal areas In general are more developed in education and higher in population quality, so that people are more open to foreign cultures and more enterprising and competitive; in contrast, the westerners are weaker in these aspects.

Sixth, factor of distribution of productive forces.

Due to historical and system reasons and the layout of national division of regional industries, processing-oriented industries are mainly concentrated in coastal areas while resources development enterprises are mostly in the west. Joint-venture enterprises, township enterprises and private enterprises have developed rapidly in the eastern region, forming a sharp contrast to the situation in the central and western regions. These phenomena, in addition to the long-standing variance of price from value of primary products, low return on capital and low input, make both capital and talents constantly flow to the eastern areas like rivers flow into the oceans.

The above analysis demonstrates that to some extent, the gap and their widening in certain periods between the eastern, central and western regions are inevitable. For a large country like China with big regional geographical differences and variousother factors, an unevenregional growth is normal, in which the eastern coastal areas develop faster than the central and western regions, and this has been widened by the high speed progress of the eastern region since reform and opening up.

II. Regional Economic Gap Can be Positively Taken Use

Based on the China's special national reality of uneven regional development of productive forces and objective conditions, Comrade Deng Xiaoping proposed the strategy of allowing some regions and some people to become prosperous before others to enable all of them to prosper eventually. According this strategy, China formulated the eastern coastal development strategy, policies and measures of reform and opening up, leading to its high speed development. It turns out that this strategy is very suitable to China's condition. Recognizing this condition is very conducive to mobilizing the enthusiasm of all sides, especially to encouraging the regions with favorable conditions to grow first and faster, and to the overall sound and healthy development of China's economy.

The theories of socialism with Chinese characteristics initiated by Comrade Deng Xiaoping emphasize the ultimate goal of common prosperity. To this end, we must first of all recognize the reality of our uneven regional development and gaps, to allow and encourage areas with favorable conditions, such as the eastern coastal areas, to develop faster and better, so that our overall national strength can be enhanced and the relatively backward central and western regions can be supported and brought along. China is a country with a large population, vast area, backward in economy and technology and uneven in regional development. Any policy, however excellent it is, cannot benefit all areas. From a strategic point of view, whichever area that has the quality, opportunity or advantages, it should develop first. This is important for the general interests. On the other hand, at some stage, those who have become prosperous must support the poor ones to achieve common prosperity, and this is also important for the general interests. Compared with the "common poverty" in the old system, allowing some people and some regions to become prosperous before others is a huge progress. The practice of reform and opening up has proved that, as long as the policies and measures are correct, the rapid development of the eastern coastal areas that have become prosperous first will not hinder the development of the central and western regions. But there is always priority and limit in doing things. Although it is no good denying the gap, too huge a gap is no good, either. We must admit and face up instead of turning a blind eye to the gaps; and we should take overall situation into account to historically, dialectically and correctly look at and pay attention to the gaps. We should see that the regional gapis formed in the process of development and can also be gradually narrowed through development. The emergence and temporary widening of the gapis inevitable to some degree, and the recognition of which is of positive significance.

In discussing the regional gap, some people tendto exaggerate its negativeside without recognizing its inevitability, thus fail to see the positive and beneficial elements contained in it. Fairly speaking, it is somewhat unfair or unjust that citizens of the same country have different lives just because of the difference of areas they live. But if we consider it historically and dialectically from an overall point, we will admit, in the situation when the resources of the entire country are limited and the market economy has not well-developed, imbalance and certain differences in economic, political and cultural development of regions are unavoidable, even its temporary widening is not entirely negative. Today, advocating "eliminating gap" in an indiscriminative way is not necessarily a wise or reasonable choice.

There are three kinds of attitude toward regional gap, The first one holds that regional gap isharmful, so it should be eliminated as soon as possible; The second one believes that regional gap is beneficial, because the bigger the gap, the stronger the impetus to catch up; and the third one argues that regional gapat a certain stage within reasonable limits can be allowed, because at the present stage it cannot be eliminated, and the idea that the whole regional gap can be done away with at one stroke is in direct contravention of and will be punished by objective laws. We should encourage the prospered areas to support the backward areas so as to gradually narrow the gap and finally achieve the goal of common prosperity. Our purposeis not to "eliminate regional gap" but rather to develop production and improve people's living standards. How, then, can we eliminate the gap? One way is to take from the prosperous areas and give it to the backward areas, an absolute egalitarian practice of indiscriminate and unpaid transfer of resourcesprevailed before and during the "Cultural Revolution, which is very harmful. Another approach is to face up the gap and adopt appropriate policies and measures to encourage the prosperous areas to support the backward areas and to gradually eliminate the gap. It is obvious that the second approach is advisable.

The gap is objective and keep it within reasonable limits is allowable. But on the other hand, if the gap exceeds a certain limit, it will affect the social stability and development, which is not conducive to mobilizing the enthusiasm of all sides. We should controlit within a reasonable rangeto neither indefinitely widen it nor indiscriminately eliminate it, but rather take a positive attitude toward it, so as to accelerate the development of the central and western regions to achieve common prosperity.

What does it mean by "reasonable range"? I thinkit involves three aspects: First isto make the allocation of resources, layout of the productive forces and price adjustment as reasonable as we can. For example, we should make reasonable fund allocation between eastern region and central and western regions, and straighten out the distorted prices left by the old system. The second aspect is to make favorable policies and measures for the development of the central and western regions; and third is to take effective methods to increase the people's income to prevent the gap from further widening.

In the final analysis, regional gap is an objective reality indicating income inequality, too large a gap of which is not what we desire, and its widening must be controlled within certain limits; otherwise, the negative effects will come out. First, if the gap or income disparity is too wide, the masses in the poorer areas will show their discontent, which will affect their initiative, the development of productive forces and social stability. Second, if the gap is too wide, the socialist goal of common prosperity is difficult to achieve. Third, too wide of a gap or the low income of the residents in central and western regions is not conducive to the development of the market and the economy in general. Fourth, if the gap is too wide, the investment in their basic industries will be affected so that the development of the regions in particular and whole economic development of our country in general will be unsustainable. Fifth, if the gap is too wide, talents, capital and resources will flow to the eastern coastal areas, resulting in the widening of the gap and imbalance. From the viewpoint of our national reality, without the development of the central and western regions, China's stability and the rapid growth of the eastern coastal areas are difficult to maintain.

III. Speeding up the Development of the Central and Western Regions to Narrow the Regional Gap and Achieve Common Prosperity

The gap between the east and west is a reality, which is an economic issue on the surface but a political issue actually. If it is not handled properly, our political stability will be affected, so high attention must be paid to it. Without the development of the central and western regions, there would be no prosperity of the whole country. To solve this problem, we can no longer use the old egalitarian way of unpaid appropriation, nor can we inhibit or slow down thedevelopment of the eastern region, nor can we act in a Procrustean manner. At the same time, it cannot be allowed to widen unchecked. We should take effective measures topreventits wideningand control it within reasonable range. To this end, we should strategically encourage some people and some regions to become prosperous before others while promoting balanced regional economic development. In addition to national macro regulation and control and support from others, the central and western regions themselves should strive to gradually narrow the gap and achieve prosperity by methods of promoting growth through opening up and promoting development mainly on their own.

Gradually narrowing the gap between east and west, solving the issue of inequitable distribution and promoting balanced development of regional economy constitute important conditions for maintaining social stability and important aspects embodying the essence of socialism. In the Ninth Five-Year Plan on National Economy and Social Development and Long-Range Objectives to the Year 2010, six important policy measures were proposed to narrow the gap between east and west, which was followed by the western development strategy. The Fifth Plenary Session of the Fifteenth Central Committee of the CPC also adopted the Proposal of the Central Committee of the Communist Party of China for Formulating the 10th Five-Year Program for China's Economic and Social Development. It stressed that the principal contradiction in our economic life was the structural problem. It proposed that the distribution of productiveforces should be rationally readjusted for the benefit of the strategy of developing China's western regions; steady efforts should be made to promote urbanization and balanced regional, urban and rural development. This requires both the eastern region and the central and western regions to concert their efforts to ensure that all measures are implemented thoroughly so that the ambitious goal of common prosperity is achieved.

1. Strengthening the macro regulation and control of the central government

The central government should play the role of interest regulator of thewhole society to make effective macro regulation on unreasonable regional disparities. First, the central and western regions should be treated equally in terms of policy, or even be allowed to enjoy some preference. For example, in the coastal areas, the policy of reducing tax on enterprises and allowing them to retain more profits should be replaced by the policy of act in compliance withlaws of the market economy; on the other hand, the central and western regions will be difficult to attract investment if they do not adopt tax reduction. Besides, preferential policies should also be adopted in pricing, transportation, land, credit, etc. , including providing price subsidies on raw materials and energy, adopting exemptions, levying resources tax, tax relief, interest-free, low-interest loans or interest subsidies, and so on. Second, the central government should increase its support of finance and credit to the poverty-stricken areas, revolutionary base areas and ethnic autonomous areas through financial transfer payment, priority of investment, policy-based loans etc. , Third, capital input should be enhanced, which is introduced mainly through four channels: Firstly is direct introduction of foreign capital; secondly is to seek aid projects of the United Nations; thirdly is the support from the eastern region and fourthly is the direct investment of the central government. A western region development fund should be set up and various financial measures should be adopted and policy-based subsidies be provided.

2. Gradually adjusting the unreasonable distribution of the productive forces and rationalize the unfair price relationships to provide a fair market environment for the development of the central and western development.

The central government should take the necessary measures to make the industries in the eastern region more global market oriented, so that to avoid competing with central and western regions in raw materials, labor forces and marketto facilitate the industrial development in the west. Measures should be taken to change the distribution of theproductive forces in the central and western regions step by step through transformation of their energy, raw materials and other basic industrial projects into deep processing, high value-added industries. The prices of their primary products should be gradually raised to the level of average profit, so that the unreasonable product parities be corrected and be set on the basis of equality.

3. Actively promoting the support of developed areas to backward areas in the central and western regions and accelerating their cooperation

The central government should mobilize administrative power of the state encourage the eastern region to provide the central and western regions with necessary demonstration, support and help in education, human resources, capital, technology, management, projects, etc. The eastern regions should be encouraged to carry out "go west" strategy and engage in counterpart aid projects. Of course, the more important thing is that, the assistance is conducted in form of cooperation on the basis of mutual benefit and complement, benefit-sharing, such as joint project, joint venture.

4. Accelerating the economic development of the central and western regions on their own

The advantage of the central and western regions is in their natural resources, which in not necessarily equal to economic advantage. The central and western regions should: First, focus their development on resources that are of strong market demands and high prices, such as oil, water, gas, gold, non-ferrous metals, so as to accumulate capital; Second, develop their deeper processing industries in energy and other sectors to raise their efficiency; Third, speed up the improvement of their infrastructure such as transportation, energy, telecommunications and other conditions to provide a better investment environment; And finally, take advantage of all opportunities to accumulate capital, increase investment and solidify foundation for development.

5. Further emancipating mind, renewing ideas, improvingscience and technology and education, and intensifying reform

Among the many factors contributing to the economic lag of the central and western regions, insufficient mind emancipation of the officials and masses, and low steps in reform and opening up are import ant ones. Some officialsand masses have not yet broken the mental shackles of planned economy. They still have a strong conservative and isolated sense of small peasants and production, which cannot catch up with the development of the socialist market economy, so that they commonly have the attitude of "waiting for, relying on and asking for" . Therefore, the central and western regions should increase their intensity of mental emancipation, focus on the major task of economic development, and spare no efforts in promoting development, buildingup awareness of all-round opening and opening door wider to introduce capital, technology, talents and advanced management skills. They should drive reform and opening up by mental emancipation to resolve deep-seated system contradictions restraining development; meanwhile, they should also give full play to education and science and technology in invigorating the economy and development.

Appendix IV

Correctly Handling Contradictions among the People and Properly Coordinating Interest Relations of All Sides to Building a Harmonious Socialist Society①

Around the theme of "Building a Harmonious Socialist Society" and the topic of "Correct Handling Contradictions among the People and Properly Coordinating Interest Relations of All Sides," my lecture consists of three sections: First, raising the problems, that is, to fully lay out the contradictions among the people and outstanding new situations and problems currently facing the country in our endeavor of building of harmonious socialist society; Second, analyzing the problems, that is, to theoretically analyze these contradictions and problems from the philosophical viewpoint of Marxist world outlook and methodology; And third, solving the problems, that is, to propose some suggestions on solving these contradictions and problems.

---

① This article was written on the bases of a series of lectures, including lectures under the same title made by the author on the provincial-level leading officials' Special Seminar on Strengthening the Capability of Building a Harmonious Society held on February 19—25, 2005 at the Central Party School, and lectures made in the Class One-A and Class Two-A of Advanced Course 2005—2007 at the Central Party School, as well as lectures made in Beijing, Shanghai, Zhejiang, Heilongjiang, Shaanxi and some units of the ministries and armed forces. It was first published in the book *A Collection of Wang Weiguang's Lectures* (王伟光讲习录) published by the Central Party School Press, November 2008. Some necessary deletions were made before it was included into this book.

I. Some Notable New Contradictions among the People and Problems in Our Social Reality and Practice of Building Harmonious Socialist Society

The overall situation of contradictions among the people and other social problems in our country is: various relationships are basically coordinated, the political situation is basically stable and the society is basically harmonious. However, we should also be soberly aware that, there are somenotable new contradictions among the people and problems in our social reality and our practice of building harmonious socialist society. To put it simple, these problems include: although the economy have developed steadily, the people have their living standards greatly improved and they have got substantial benefits, various contradictions among the people become more acute and complex. There are also some potential risks that may seriously affect our social stability and harmony, undermine the sound operation and healthy development of the society. Specificallythey include the following nine problems or issues: problem of social gap, gap between rich and poor and the problem of poverty, differentiation and mobility of social strata, problem of employment, problem of mass incidents, problem of corruption and bureaucracy of a small number of leading officials, problems arising from the operation of the market economy, conflicts in ideological and cultural fields, and problem of ethnic groups and religion. These problems are both the manifestations of and causes for the complex and intense contradictions among the people and our social disharmony.

1. The problem of Social Gap
The income gaps between some social members, as well as gaps between urban and rural areas and between regions continue to widen, which are both the manifestations of and causes for the complex and intense contradictions among the people andour social disharmony.

First, the income gap between some social members keeps widening.

From a long-term perspective, to ensure the progress and harmony of a society, we must combine two principles: one is thewealthmaximization; the other is the fairness of distribution. Only by doing so can we promote social progress and harmony at the same time. Reform and opening up has discarded the practice of the egalitarianism with the practice of having everyone "eat from the same big pot" and has tremendously aroused the enthusiasm of the people, which has given rise to differences of distribution that boosted people's motivation for work and competition. As a result, our economy gets a rapid growth. It is doubtlessly not good to eliminate differences or to make unpaid appropriation. But on the other hand, a new problem has emerged in our society, that is, the continued widening gap of distribution between social members, especially between urban and rural residents.

The income ratios between urban and rural residents in 1978 and 1984 were 2 : 0. 4721 and 1. 83 : 1 respectively. ①The reason for the narrowing in 1984 is the implementation of the household contract responsibility system, which increased the farmers' incomes. Since 1984, especially the 1990s, the gap had been widening constantly. The ratio reached 3. 22 : 1 in 2003. Experts believe that, if social welfare, costs of production, physicalassets and other factors were counted in, the income gap between urban and rural residents would reach as high as 5—6 times. The causes for the widening are: in contrast to the relatively rapid increase of urban residents' income, farmers in some areas have too heavy burden and too slow income growth. From 1997 to 2003, the per capita net income of the farmers were less than 5 percent for seven years in a row, with the highest in 2002 by 4. 8 percent and lowest in 2000 by only 2. 1 percent. Although a series of measures have been taken in 2003 aiming at increasing farmers' income, which made the income growth of farmers in 2004 reach 6. 8 percent, the highest since 1997, the widening trend of income gap between urban and rural residents has not been reversed, with the increase and actual growth rate still lower than those of urban residents, whose income grew 7. 7 percent in 2004. ②

Apart from the widening of income disparities between rural and urban residents, those among urban residents, among rural residents, between residents in different regions, between labor and mental workers, between employees in different forms of ownership, between employees in different industries are also widening.

Second, differences between regions, between urban and rural areas, between manual and mental labor and between industries are widening, especially between regions and between urban and rural areas.

---

① See Ma Conghui, *A Study of Resident Income Distribution under Conditions of Open Economy*, China Financial and Economic Publishing House, 2004. p. 277.

② Ibid. .

One of the important goals of we communists is to eliminate the three major differences: difference between urban and rural, between manual labor and mental labor and between workers and farmers. This goal cannot be achieved in a strike; but on the contrary, a fairly long historical period is needed. Nevertheless, as a goal we strive for, we should actively create conditions and take measures tonarrow, instead of widening them. Although a series ofmeasures have been taken by the central government to supportthe development ofrural andbackward areas and tonarrowthe differences betweenurban and rural areas, and greatprogress has been registered, the contradictionof imbalanced development between urban and rural areas and regions remains outstanding, and the task is still arduous.

First is the difference between regions. In 1980, the proportions of the economic size of the eastern, central and western regions to China's national total were respectively 50 percent, 30 percent and 20 percent. These proportions changed into 58.5 percent, 24.7 percent and 16.8 percent in 2004, indicating an increasing rather than a decreasing of development gap. So do the ratios of per capita GDP between the eastern regions and the central and western regions, which increased from 1 : 1.92 to 1 : 259, and between the central region and the eastern region from 1 : 1.53 to 1 : 203. [1]

Regional differences, in the final analysis, involve the difference between urban and rural areas, because 60 percent of China's rural poverty-stricken populationis in the west, and about 20 million people have not yet solved the problem of food and clothing.

Urban-rural difference is mainly reflected in two aspects. First is the widening income gap between urban and rural residents as well as the widening gap of their economic sizes. In 2002, the prefecture-level cities (counties under their jurisdiction excluded) whose population accounted for only 25 percent of the country national total achieved 63 percent of the country's total GDP, while the agricultural value-added by rural areas with a population of 60 percent of national total accounted only for 15 percent of the country's GDP. The rapid expansion of the urban areas and real estate has made some farmers lose their means of subsistence. Abandoned arable land, exhaustion of cropland, ecological degradation, decline in labor quality, etc. , are common in rural areas, so that wealth flows into urban

---

[1] See Lu Dadaoet al. , *Report on China's Regional Development* (2000), The Commercial Press, 2001, p. 6

areas. Second, the urban-rural dual structure is more obvious. The "urban-rural dual structure" refers to an asymmetric social organization existence formed in our development, in which the relatively backward mode of production and way of life stand in stark contrast to that in urban areas. This structure is a big problem in China: Rural residents enjoy far less public welfare, undertakings and infrastructures than urban residents, includingin employment, social security, education, health care, culture, environmental protection and so on. More than 70 percent of our funds of education, health care and medical services were invested in urban areas; more than 80 percent of farmers are unable to get access to subsistence allowances and health care. Before the end of the "Cultural Revolution," more than 90 percent of farmers were covered by medical care, but it was abolished in the process of reform.

The different degrees of widening of distribution gaps between some social members and the differences between urban and rural areas and between regions have become a major issue affecting our overall development. Therefore, it is imperative to properly narrow these gaps and reconcile the differences, so as to correctly handle contradictions among the people for the building a socialist harmonious society.

2. Gap between rich and poor and the problem of poverty

The gap between rich and poor among some of our some members is widening, highlighting the issue of poverty, which isboth a manifestations of and a cause for the complex and intense contradictions among the people and our social disharmony.

Social equality is one of the important symbols of social progress and harmony. In addition to wealth maximization, equality, fairness, justice, etc. , are also standards in measuring social progress. Reasonable distribution is an important part of social justice, whereas polarization between rich and poor is the biggest injustice. In certain historical stage, to control the disparity between rich and poor within reasonable limits is crucial for the stable and harmonious development of a country. If the gap is too large to the extent of polarization, a series of problems will emerge, social unrest will occur, and the ruling party is bound to lose support of the people and thus its power. On the other hand, it is unrealistic for a society to completely eliminate differences between rich and poor in certain historical stage of development. The key lies in limiting it within a reasonable range. .

There are three systems measuring income equality.

The first is the Gini coefficient. According to the National Bureau of Statistics (NBS) of China, China's Gini coefficient rose from 0. 341 in 1988 to 0. 417 in 2000, which were below the warning line. According to scholars from China Renmin University, Chinese Academy of Social Sciences, etc. , China's Gini coefficients in 1997 was 0. 455 and more than 0. 5 in 2003. (Some estimated it as high as 0. 552) . That means, as early as in 2000, China's Gini coefficient has reached the warning line. According to World Bank, China saw a high speed of widening gap between rich and poor in the last one and a half decades, faster than Western developed countries.

The second measuring system is Oshima index, or quintile method. Some sampling surveys show that, in China, the poorest 20 percent of the population accounted only for 4. 27 percent of the total income of all the citizens, while the 20 percent of the richest accounted for 50. 13 percent. This indicates that the country's wealth gap is widening.

The third system is income ratio between the high income level and low income level. According to NBS, the income of the 10 percent of the highest households sampled in urban areas was 3. 9 times of that of the 10 percent of the lowest income households in 1998, and 5. 02 times in 2000; in the rural area, the figures were 4. 8 in 1998 and 6. 5 in 2000. In 2002, the findings of a research team from the Ministry of Labor and Social Security of China showed that, most Chinese households did not belong to the middle income group but rather to the low and moderate low groups, which respectively accounted for 31. 9 percent and 32. 36 percent of all households, meaning that 64. 25 percent of Chinese households belonged to the low and moderate low income categories.

The direct consequence of the widening gap between rich and poor find their expressions in two problems: First, the outstanding problem of social poverty. Since reform and opening up, China's impoverished population has shrunk substantially and the impoverishment rate decreased from 30 percent to 3. 1 percent. Since the total number of impoverished population has decreased, why does the problem of poverty become highlighted? This is because the gap between rich and poor has been widened, so that the rich get richer while the poor poorer. So, although the poor population is not large, the problem of poverty is strikingly evident. The objective existence of the poverty-stricken group presents a stark contrast to the high income stratum. There is still a population of 12 million livesin relative poverty in urban areas with per capita annual income 1059 yuan. In the rural areas, according to the poverty line of per capita annual net income 882yuan in 2003, the poverty population in rural areas is 56. 17 million, accounting for 6 percent of the rural population.

Another prominent issue issocial inequality. A survey conducted among students in Central Party School of the CPC shows that, according to the participants, the three most serious problems in 2004 in order of seriousness were: (1) income gap (43. 9 percent), (2) public security (24. 3 percent), and (3) corruption (8. 4 percent). Regarding the reforms in 2005, 72. 9 percent of the participants concerned about reform of income distribution. From this we can see that the issue of social inequality should be listed into our work agenda. Resolving the problems of wealth gap and poverty are urgent issues in correctly handling contradictions among the people.

3. The Differentiation and Mobility of Social Strata

As the result of differentiation among classes, strata and interest groups, some new strata and interest groups emerged, and the social mobility become faster and the pattern of interests among the people become diverse: all these are both the expressions of and deep causes for the complexity and intensification of contradictions among the people and factors affecting our social harmony. Because changes have occurred in the ownership structure, mode of distribution, industrial structure, employment pattern, etc. , although the general situation remains unchanged, new combination and differentiation appeared within the classes and strata in our society, with the emergence of new social strata and interest groups. These are mainly demonstrated in the following aspects:

(1) The structure and composition of the working class as the leading class has changed greatly and relationships within it become more diverse. Within the ranks of the working class, due to differences of forms of ownership, distribution and treatment in economic, political, cultural and other social sectors, as well as the faster mobility of workers between regions, enterprises, industries, positions, income gaps between them have widened, leading to their differentiation into different strata and groups. The production and living conditions of some industrial workers, in particular, merit our close attention.

(2) New differentiation, combination and changes within the ranks of

the farmer class make the contradictions within rural residents become more complicated. In present-day China, the farmers have changed from original collective agricultural workers whose distribution was based on their work-points into agricultural workers contracting land. At the same time a huge group of migrant workers, whose number is estimated to be more than 100 million, have joined and become fresh blood of the ranks of the working class and an important force in our socialist modernization drive. In the industries of construction, mining, textile and so on, 80 percent of the employees are migrant workers. But on the other hand, they belong to the lower strata in urban life whose living conditions merit our high attention.

(3) Within the non-public sectors of the economy, especially the private sector, a rich stratum of non-public or private entrepreneurs has come into being. There exist objective contradictions between these entrepreneurs as employers and workers as employees and the contradictions between the managers and the employees. In some non-public or private enterprises, the working conditions are poor, labor protection measures are insufficient, and wage arrears or deductions, overtime work, indignation of workers, child labor and so on are common, so that the relations between the owners of enterprises and ordinary workers are acute.

(4) There emerged new strata and interest groups such as entrepreneurs and technical personnel employed by non-public scientific and technological enterprises, managerial and technical staff employed by overseas-funded enterprises, the self-employed, private entrepreneurs, employees in intermediaries, free-lance professionals and so on. They mostly belong to the middle and upper social levels are builders of socialism, but there are also contradictions between these new social strata and interest groups on one side and the working class, farmer class, intelligentsia, and officials and the officers and men of the PLA on the other.

In his "Analysis of the Classes in Chinese Society", Comrade Mao Zedong points out: "Who are our enemies? Who are our friends? This is a question of the first importance for the revolution." Our party correct political line on the Chinese revolution, first of all, was based on the scientific analysis of the classes and their relations in Chinese society. The very first article in the *Selected Works of Mao Zedong* provides the answer to this question. Today, in the period of socialist construction, reform and opening up, it is also a question of the first importance for us to maintain the leading position of the working class, consolidate the alliance of workers and farmers and unite with all the forces that can be united, and correctly handle the relations between and among various classes, strata and interest groups, so as to correctly handle contradictions among the people and build a socialist harmonious society.

4. The problem of employment

The grim situation of employment and large number of employees are both the expressions and causes for the complexity and intensification of contradictions among the people and direct factors affecting our social harmony.

(1) The great stress of employment. Among the population of more than 1. 3 billion, 909 million are 15—64 years of age, the number is 300 million more than all of the working forces of the developed countries putting together. During 10th Five-year Plan, the number of newly added laborers reaches 10 million each year and 13 million get unemployed or laid-off. The employment of demobilized soldiers, college graduates and the disabled are added pressure to this problem. Especially the college graduates, which was 2. 8 million in 2004. Among them, 0. 74 million had not find jobs until September that year. In the short term the oversupply of work forces will remain.

(2) The problem of unemployment. According to the National Bureau of Statistics, the registered unemployment rate in urban area in 2003 was 4. 3 percent, and it was estimated to be 4. 7 in 2004 and was reduce to 4. 2 percent after various efforts were made. In 2005 it is expected to be controlled below 4. 6 percent. There is certain difference between registered unemployment rate and actual unemployment rate. The 2001 China Social Security White Paper published by the Ministry of Civil Affairs of People's Republic of China points out that, the actual urban unemployment rate in 1993 was 5 percent, and rose to 8—9 percent in 2000, close to 10 percent in 2000. Some experts estimated that currently the figure is nearly 12 percent. A survey of unemployment risk made by a professor from China Renmin University using Delphi method shows that, China's unemployment security line is 7. 03 percent and 9. 73 percent is a point marking China's entry into warning line of employment. From this point of view, China is now in a risk period of social development.

(3) It is difficult for the transfer of rural surplus labor. China has a

rural labor force of 490 million, of which the land and township and village enterprises can absorb around 100 million and 130 million respectively, and 100 million are migrant workers. The rest 150 million are surplus laborers. According to plan, up to 2030, as much as 54.5 *mu* of arable land will be expropriated, meaning more than 100 million farmers will lose their land. The employment is a big test for our Party as the governing party. Reducing unemployment and increasing employment is an urgent need for handling contradictions among the people and for building a harmonious socialist society.

5. The problem of mass incidents

The new emerging mass incidents in recent years are both the expression of contradictions among the people and root causes affecting our social society.

Presently, the mass incidents show the following five features:

(1) Complaints in the form of letters and visits and appeal to the central authorities for help increased significantly. China is currently in the period of high incidence of complaints, which indicates that our social contradictions have increasingly accumulated. The total number of complaints increases every year, among which group complaints increased substantially. Another feature of the issue is the upgrading of the complaints. In recent years, more and more people filed their complaints to higher levels (provincial, central), making the central governmental organs become the focuses.

(2) The number of mass incidents increased, so were their scale. More mass incidents happened than before and their scale expanded. During the 10 years from 1994 to 2003, mass incidents and number of people involved rose sharply. Even several relatively large scale mass incidents happened in the same day in the same city. Since 1998, the scale of mass incidents gradually increased, the number of mass incidents involving more than one hundred people increased from one thousand cases to more than several thousands, and there were cases in which as much as ten thousand people involved.

(3) The composition of the participants was more diverse, their activities were more organized and more violent. Among the 2.564 million mass incident participants, workers accounted for the biggest proportion of 37.7 percent, followed by farmers for 28.2 percent, urban residents for 11.8 percent, retirees for 8.2 percent and self-employees for 3.9

percent. We can see that most participants are workers and farmers, and they came from various industries, areas and regions. In some incidents, there were even inter-regional activities, interrelations and organizations as well as leaders behind the scenes and on the stages. Incidents of blocking the roads, railways that paralyzed the traffic have increased. In 2000, it accounted for 6.3 percent and in 2001, it was 6.6 percent. Such serious cases as violent resistance against enforcement of law, armed fighting that caused casualties were not uncommon, and cases of assaulting Party and government bodies increased.

(4) Material and economic interests, especially material benefits, are the main reasons behind the mass incidents. Compared with political issues, material demands constitutethe main part, and participants are mostly ordinary people, including retired workers, retired teachers, retiredofficials, ex-servicemen, students, civil servants and so on. In 2001, for example, mass incidents involving issues of wages, social welfares and social security accounted for 28.1 percent; income reduction due to enterprise restructuring, bankruptcy, 19.5 percent; land requisition and demolition, 13.5 percent; family and neighborhood disputes, 45 percent.

(5) Political factors have increased behind the mass incidents. Domestic and overseas hostile forces and elements have colluded and merged with other forces, including the so-called "pro-democracy activists", the Falun Gong cult, the elements advocating "East Turkistan," "Independence of Tibet," "Independence of Xinjiang," "Independence of Taiwan" and so on, to make use of, to plot and to instigate mass incidents, and take the advantage of these incidents to create "labor movement", "farmer movement." This merits our high vigilance.

In short, mass incidents affecting the stability of our society are increasing and taking momentum, the opportunities and loopholes that can be taken use by domestic and overseas hostile forces are increasing, so are the threats to our social stability. They impose latent risk affecting our social stability and harmony. Actively preventing and properly handling mass incidents have become a serious problem in our handling contradictions among the people and building a harmonious socialist society.

In addition to the above five aspects, the problems of corruption and bureaucracy of a small number of leading officials, problems arising from the operation of the market economy, conflicts in ideological and cultural fields, problems of ethnic groups and religion, etc. , are also expressions and important issue in correctly handling contradictions among the people and building harmonious socialist society.

II. Scientifically Understanding the Contradictions among the People and the Building of a Harmonious Socialist Society from the Perspective of Marxist Theory

Why should we strive to build a harmonious socialist society? This is because there are so many complex contradictions among the people and other social contradictions needing our handling and coordinating. It is precisely the existence of contradictions that we need to pursue harmony, and the pursuit of harmony requires us to handle contradictions. To build a socialist harmonious society, we must effectively coordinate the interests of all sides to resolve contradictions among the people. To this end, it is necessary to have a theoretical grasp of the laws governing their changes and development.

1. Correct handling of contradictions among the people is the necessary requirement for building a harmonious socialist society and socialism with Chinese characteristics

We know that the real world is full of contradictions andd ialectics that exist in everything, including the objective existence and reality of human society. The Marxist world outlook and methodology of materialist dialectics reveal the laws and the objective world in a scientific way. Therefore, we must learn to apply them to analyze and handle the intricate situations, contradictions and other social contradictions. What, then, is the core or essence of Marxist world outlook and methodology of materialist dialectics?

Lenin called this lawas the essence and kernel of dialectics. Unity of opposites, or the law of contradiction, is the fundamental law of the universe; the idea of unity of oppositesis a fundamental view of Marxist materialist dialectics. What is opposite? Opposite means contradiction; what is unity? Unity means harmony. Unity of opposites means the harmony achieved after the contradiction is resolved. The Marxist world outlook of materialist dialectics requires us to observe and analyze the world from the point of view of unity of opposites, and the methodology to resolve contradictions in reality. Comrade Mao Zedong set a good examplein correctly and flexibly applying Marxist world outlook and methodology of materialist dialectics. His two important works, "On Contradiction", a classic of Marxist world outlook of materialist dialectics, and "On the Correct Handling of Contradictions among the People", were respectively written in the revolutionary period and peaceful socialist construction period. In the former, Comrade Mao, at a crucial point of the Chinese revolution and war, analyzed the contradictions in China at the time by using Marxist world outlook and methodology of materialist dialectics, and proposed the correct strategy and tactics of the Chinese revolution, thus masterly resolved the contradictions in the Chinese revolution, leading to the victory of the people's war and the establishment of the New China. With the latter, Comrade Mao provided a theoretical guide for us to observe and analyze problems and to resolve contradictions among the people by applying the idea of unity of opposites. In our effort of building a harmonious society, we must profoundly understand the spirit of these two works and learn to use the Marxist world outlook and methodology of materialist dialectics to resolve contradictions and social problems.

In these two works, Comrade Mao summarizes the law of unity of opposites into three ideas: First, contradiction exists in the process of development of all things and in the process of development of each thing; Second, contradiction is universal and absolute, it is present in the process of development of all things and contradictoriness within a thing is the fundamental cause of its development; And thirdly, the law of contradiction in things, that is, the law of the unity of opposites, must be applied in analyzing and resolving contradictions among the people and other social contradictions. From this point of view, in terms of contradictions in our society today, it is not a question of whether they exist or not, nor of whether they are good or bad, because contradictions exist ever and everywhere, and independent of man's will. It is a good thing for a contradiction to be resolved, verse versa. After old contradictions are resolved, new contradictions will emerge. Things move forward in the process of ceaseless resolution of contradictions. By a harmonious society we do not mean that there is no contradiction at all in the society, but that we must resolve contradictions and that unity and harmony are realized in the process of resolving contradictions. There are both domestic and foreign lessons we should learn from in our endeavors of handling contradictions and building a harmonious society.

First, the lessons and experience from Stalin era show that, the correct handling of the two types of contradictions differing in nature is the premise of building a harmonious socialist society. In 1936, the Soviet Union proclaimed that it had entered the socialist society. It is a practical and theoretical question of extreme significance to whether recognize or not the existence of contradictions in socialist countries, and if any, what is the nature of them and how to handle them. There were two erroneous, though fundamentally opposed, views on this question. The first refused to recognize the existence of contradictions in socialist countries; the second, though acknowledging the existence of contradictions in socialist countries, exaggerated them to such an extent that all contradictions were regarded as contradictions between the people and the enemy, so that class struggle was arbitrarily expanded. Stalin proposed two erroneous ideas, i. e. , first, the "relations of production" "are fully conform to the growth of the productive forces"; second, "the moral and political unity" "forms the motive forces of the Soviet society" . According to the former, reform is not necessary, which ultimately contributed to the rigidity of political system of the Soviet Union; while based on the latter, there would be no contradictions, that is, no motive for the development of its socialist society. These views are metaphysical and run counter to the law of unity in opposites. Since the existence of contradictions in the Soviet Union was denied, how then, the existing numerous contradictions in reality be explained? To this end, Stalin had to theoretically attribute all kinds of contradictions in the Soviet Union to foreign causes and class struggle, and based on it, put forward a "Left" view: The greater progress socialism achieved, the more desperate the remnants of the exploiting class launched their struggle; one frontline of the class struggle was in the Soviet Union, the other in the capitalist countries. All domestic contradictions were contradictions of class struggle nature between the people and the enemy, and whose causes were entirely foreign, i. e. , the encirclement of the capitalism and the activities of hostile classes. Stalin's erroneous views were extremely harmful to the Soviet Union. As a result, the existence of contradictions among the people was denied, the two types of contradictions differing in nature were seriously confused, class struggle was put as the top priority, and from 1936 to 1939 a series of large-scale purge and repression were carried out, aiming to physically wipe out the enemies within the country. Except for a few secret agents and spies, most of people who were purged belonged to the category of the people. This practice severely damaged the normal life of democracy and legal system, leading to the rigidity and stagnation of the economic and political system of theSoviet Union, and become one of the deep roots of the collapse of the Soviet Union.

Second, lessons and experience of China show that, the correct handling of contradictions among the people is the main theme of building a harmonious socialist country. In China, with the basic completion ofthe three great transformations and the general establishment of socialist system, contradictions among the people had become an outstanding issue of overall importance. The problems occurred in the Soviet Union and Eastern European countries made the Party begin to study and consider the contradictions among the people. The criticism of Stalin in the 20th CPSU Congress in 1956 caused great ideological confusion and tumult in the international communist movement; and in Poland and Hungary, nationwide unrests occurred. From the winter of 1956 to the spring of 1957, the influence of these unrests spread to China, causing some ideological confusion. Additionally, numerous problems arose from the newly established socialist system in distribution, living conditions, housing, prices, education, employment, bureaucracy, and so on. As a result, a series of mass incidents occurred, and a total of 10, 000 workers and more than the same number of students launched strikes. The new situations at home and abroad got the Party's great attention of Comrade Mao and the whole Party. Summing up experiences and learning from lessons about the proper handling of contradictions among the people became an urgent task.

The publication of Comrade Mao Zedong's article "On the Correct Handling of Contradictions among the People" in February 1957 marked the final formation of our Party's innovative Marxist theory of correct handling of contradictions among the people. Later on, however, we did not completely keep to this theory. We made a series of mistakes of long-term class struggle nature in ideological realm, including the expansion of the anti-Rightist struggle in 1957, the so-called struggle against Right deviations in 1959, the socialist education movement in the 1960s, and the decade-long Cultural Revolution in particular, which seriously confused the two types of contradictions of different nature, so that the Party gradually sank into the mire of magnifying the scope of the class struggle, which brought about chaos to the whole country and nearly collapse of national economy. It is the Third Plenary Session of Eleventh Party Central Committee with Comrade Deng Xiaoping at the core that the Party decisively set things right, stopped the wrong line of taking class struggle as the key link and reaffirmed and developed the theory of contradictions among the people, making China embark on a new path of stable, harmonious development of socialism with Chinese characteristics.

Third, lessons and experiences from some countries in their risk period of development show that, it is vital important to pay high attention on various social contradictions and to maintain relative harmony and stability of the society. The modernization experience of various countries shows that, when a country is in the transition from agriculturalto industrial society, it enters a high-risk period prone to intensification of social contradictions, because the entanglement of growth and difficulties, development and contradictions will cause dramatic changes in the society. Development will inevitably bring about changes in the interest pattern, in which some people gained interests while others suffered; the rapid economic growth will bring with it some social problems, like unfair distribution, wide disparity between rich and poor, intensified social contradictions, and so on, which, if coupled with economic slowdown and financial crisis, will inevitably cause social unrest and political instability. A good example of it is the so-called "Latin American trap" or "Latin American disease," referring to the social unrests arising from impoverishment and polarization in the process of economic growth. Since the 1980s, many Latin American countries carried out neo-liberal reforms, which in a short-term had achieved some economic success. Argentina gained high growth rates of 10. 6 percent and 9. 6 percent in 1991 and 1992 respectively. In 2001, the per capita GDPs of some Latin American countries respectively were: Brazil, $2957; Mexico, $6, 200; Venezuela, $4, 877; Argentina, $7417 (decreased to $2912 in 2002 due to economic crisis). But some of their growths were achieved with the ignorance of social fairness. As the consequence of it, unemployment rate rose continuously, reaching 9. 6 percent in 2002. Disparity between rich and poor and polarization were serious problems. In 2004, people lived in poverty reached 227 million; in sharp contrast, the increase of number of millionaires ranked first in the world. In Brazil, 10 percent of the richest population possessed 40 percent of the nation's household wealth, while 10 percent of the lowest income residents owned less than three percent of it. This led to the intensified social conflicts, instability and ceaseless movements of mass protest, such as Chiapas farmer uprising in Mexico, landless farmer movement in

Brazil, *Piquetero* Movement and *Cacerolazo* (pot-banging) in Argentina, and the anti-privatization movements in Peru, Guatemala, Bolivia and other countries. What merits special noting is the PartidoRevolucionarioInstitucional (PRI) of Mexico. It had been in power for consecutive 71 years from 1929 to 2000, who led Mexico in transforming from a closed agricultural country into an open industrial country. In 2000, Mexico's GNP reached $ 670 billion, ranking 13th in the world, with a growth rate of 7 percent. In the 1980s, the PRI abandoned its traditional "revolutionary nationalism" to take the Western line of " New Liberalism. " It fully implemented privatization of the economy and opened up the domestic market. In terms of social policies, it reduced public expenditure in education, healthcare, insurance and other sectors, aiming to promote economic growth. But it failed in properly handlingsocial contradictions in the transitional process, leading to the bankruptcy of a large number of small and medium-sized enterprises, giving birth to a large number of unemployed workers and landless peasants, and along with it, the fall of living standards of ordinary people and great disparity between rich and poor, with the increase both of millionaires and poverty-stricken people (which reached 46 million, accounting for 45 percent of its total population, among which, 24 million lived in abject poverty), whereas about 3000 families possess 50 percent of the country's wealth. This aroused strong discontent among thepeople in the lower levels with the ruling party and thus greatly shook its governing foundation. In early 1994, the Indian farmers in the poor southern mountain areas of the country rose in the largest scale rebellion since PRI in power and finally made the party lose its 71 years long governing position in 2000 election.

In short, we must attach extreme importance to the correct understanding and handling of contradictions among the people to the building of a socialist harmonious society. Due to the complex domestic and international factors, two types of contradictions differing in nature will exist for a long time in China, and class struggle will continue to exist within certain limits for a long time to come and may become intensified under certain conditions, but the more common and frequent contradictions are contradictions among the people, which constitute the principal contradiction of human relations in our society and the theme of our political life. Both positive and negative historical experience have repeatedly demonstrate that whenever we adhere to the theme of correct handling of contradictions among the people, and abandon the erroneous line of taking class struggle as the key link, and to give top priority to development in governing and rejuvenating the country, our society will be harmonious and our socialist cause will thriving; otherwise, we social unrest will happen and our socialist modernization drive will suffer setback.

2. The key to correct handling contradictions among the people and building a harmonious socialist society lies in properly coordinating interest relations of all sides

In addition to focusing on the political and ideological contradictions among the people, Comrade Mao Zedong also discussed interest contradictions among the people, stressing properly dealing with interest contradictions from the link of distribution and advocating the analysis and coordination of them from economic viewpoint. If we do well in this respect, it will provide solid material conditions for a harmonious socialist society. Difference ininterest distribution is bound to cause competitions and contradictions, and interest difference means interest contradictions. From a philosophical point of view, the interest contradiction is in itself neither good nor bad, but an objective existence. An improper handling of it will bring a positive impact; vice versa. If interest competitions and contradictions are properly controlled within a certain extent, they can be turned into driving forces of social development, vice versa. Social revolution, social change, etc. , in the final analysis, are the adjustment of social interests; contradictions among the people, in the final analysis, is interest contradictions among the people.

Contradictions among the people constitute a complex system composed of multi-level and multi-type contradictions involving many aspects. Horizontally speaking, they include contradictions between the working class on the one hand and the farmer class and other working classes on the other, contradiction between ethnic groups, contradictions between the governing party and the government on the one hand and other parties and people without party affiliation on the other, contradictions between regions, contradictions between enterprises, contradictions among interest groups, contradictions within the ranks of the working class, contradictions within the farmer class, contradictions within the intelligentsia, contradictions within individual labors, contradiction within private economic operators, contradictions between within the producers, operators, sellers, consumers, etc. in the market economy, contradictions between the working class and farmers on the one side and the operators of non-public sector of the economy on the other, and so on. Vertically speaking, there are contradictions between the governing party and the government on the one side and the people on the other, contradictions between officials and the ordinary masses; contradictions between the higher levels and lower levels authorizes or officials, contradictions among the state, the collectives and the individuals, and so on. These contradictions are manifested in economic, political, ideological and other fields, among which, the interest contradiction among the people isthe root.

There are the following five natures featuring interest contradictions among the people: First, root nature. Interest contradictions among the people constitute the root cause of emergence, existence, development of all other contradictions among the people; Second, dominance nature. The interest contradiction dominates and influences other types of contradictions among the people and plays a leading role among them; Third, mass nature. The interest demands of different classes, strata, and interest groups are usually expressed in form of interest communities; Fourth, non-antagonistic nature. The interest contradiction among the people is non-antagonistic; Fifth, transformative nature. Under certain conditions, non-antagonistic interest contradictions among the people can transform into antagonistic ones.

Interest contradictions of different types and different natures under different historical conditions must be handled in different ways. During the revolutionary wars period, way to solve the problem of the Chinese revolution is to take up the gun totopple the three big mountains of imperialism, feudalism and bureaucrat-capitalism. Today under the socialist conditions, there more and more complex and intricate interest contradictions among social members, between individual and group interests, between individual interests and interests of collectives and the state, between the immediate and long-term interests, between local and overall interests, between the temporary and fundamental interests, and so on. And the constant growing and diverse material and cultural interest demands of the people are more difficult to be fully satisfied due to our relatively lagged social production and development. In such circumstances, it is more difficult intaking the interests of all sides into consideration and resolving interest contradictions. But on the other side, since interest contradictions among the people are non-antagonistic nature, they can only be resolved through the self-improvement and self-reform of socialist system itself, and through only coordination and overall consideration. Therefore, properly coordinatinginterest relations among the peopleis a key link in building a harmonious socialist society. We must learn to use coordinated approach to address interest contradictions among the people.

3. The contradiction between the leadership and the masses is an important aspect of contradictions among the people and the proper coordination of their relations is an important condition for building a harmonious socialist society

Of the diverse contradictions among the people, the contradiction between the leadership and the masses constitutes a focus. Comrade Liu Shaoqi said, " The leadership is responsible for every mistake and everything unreasonable in our society. The people will call the leaders in the state, the Party or government, including departments in charge of economic affairs, to account, and we are accountable for them. " This is because, our party is the governing party, its leaders at all levels are in the leading positions in political, economic, cultural and other social areas. The success or failure of the entire socialist cause, to a sense, is closely related to the leaders, so do all the problems and mistakes.

In the contradiction between the leaders and the masses, the leaders are in the principal aspect. If the leaders are in the wrong side while the masses in correct side, then the principal aspect of the contradiction is no doubt the leaders, and the resolution of it depends whether the leaders can correct their mistakes and secure the forgiveness of the masses. For example, when corruption and bureaucracy of some leaders arouse the discontent of the masses, the leaders must unhesitatingly combat against the corruption and bureaucracy to regain the support of the masses. If, on the other hand, leaders are correct and the masses are wrong, the principal aspect of the contradiction is still the leaders, for the resolution of the contradiction depends on whether the leaders can correctly handle it by educating and persuading the masses and take correct actions. Of course, we cannot blame all the contradictions or problems appeared in the masses on the leadership. When we say that the leaders constitute the principal aspect in the contradictions between the leaders and the masses, we refer to the responsibility or work of them, not simply about right or wrong. Presently, contradictions among the leaders and the masses are outstandingly manifested in the corruption and bureaucracy of some of our leaders.

4. The phenomena of antagonism and intensification of contradictions among the people and the building of harmonious socialist society

(1) Although contradictions among the people are non-antagonistic, the phenomena of antagonism and intensification can also emerge, against whichwe should have high vigilance.

First, historical and realistic experiences demonstrate that contradictions among the people not only exist, they can turn into antagonistic and intensified, even into social unrest.

About the antagonism and intensification of contradictions among the people, our understanding went through a long process of gradual deepening. Lenin believed that "Antagonism and contradiction are not at all one and the same. Under socialism, the first will disappear, the second will remain. " In other words, under socialist conditions, there are still contradictions but no antagonism. Stalin did not recognize the existence of contradictions among the people in socialist society, and if any, he believed, it must be brought about from the external and means class struggle. In his late years he vaguely realized that there were contradictions within the Soviet Union, which was reflected in his book wrote in 1953, *Economic Problems of Socialism in the U S S R*, but he died before clearly recognizing this issue. In 1957, Comrade Mao Zedong, by summarizing the lessons of the Soviet Union and summing up the situation in China, put forward the correct theory of contradictions among the people. The doctrine of contradictions among the people was expectedly not accepted by the rigid Soviet theorists; instead, they criticized it arbitrarilyas anti-Marxist. Theybelieved that it was impossible that there be contradictions among the people in a socialist country. Up until the 1960s—70s, when contradictions intensified in Eastern European socialist countries and the Soviet Union itself, they began to discuss the issues concerning contradictions within a socialist country and their antagonism and intensification, social turmoil and crises and so on, and came to the conclusion that antagonistic contradictions exist not only in capitalist countries but also in socialist countries. After the June 4 political turmoil in China and drastic changes in Eastern Europe and the disintegration of the Soviet Union, Chinese theorists commonly hold that in some cases, contradictions among the people can be antagonistic, be intensified into major social unrest.

The experience and lessons of development of socialism in the world clearly soberly tell us that, in socialist countries, there exist various contradictions among the people, and these contradictions can intensify into confrontations, mass incidents, resulting in extreme political instability and unrest. Take the Soviet Union for example. During the era of Khrushchev, mass demonstrations broke out in March 1956 in Tbilisi, capital of Georgia; in 1956 and 1959, large-scale strikes and demonstrations occurred, which were all suppressed by the authorities using armed forces andbrought about great casualties. According to incomplete statistics of a scholar from former Yugoslavia, from 1958 to August, 1969, there were a total of 1906 workers' strikes Yugoslavia. In the summer of 1956, large-scale worker unrests and clashes between the workers and the army happened in Poznan, Poland, causing serious bloodshed, the political crisis and major changes in the top leadership of Poland in the autumn of the same year. In the autumn of 1956, the Hungarian Incident shocking the whole socialist bloc broke out. At the end of the 1960s, numerous social crises happened in Poland. In August 1968, students took to the streets in Poland and major riots broke out across the country. Eleven years later, in Ddynia and Szczeciaski, two famous industrial cities in Poland, large-scale worker riots and bloodshed incidents took place, leading to the changes of top leaders of the party and government in Poland. In the middle 1970s, a number of large-scale workers' strikes broke out again in Poland. In the early 1980s, the movement of the Solidarity across the country brought the country into turmoil. The Prague Spring of 1968 in Czechoslovakia shocked not only the country but also the socialist movement around the world. In China, the unprecedented Cultural Revolution also fully exposed our domestic contradictions, so that the development of our socialism beset by an extremely dangerous crisis. The political turmoil on June 4, 1989 in China is essentially the result of intensification of various contradictions. The drastic changes in the former Soviet Union and Eastern Europe are the results of breaking out of the unsolved contradictions accumulated over the years coupled with other domestic and international factors.

Second, theoretically perspective of Marxist doctrine of unity of opposites, the antagonism and intensification of contradictions among the people constitute a serious negative impact on harmonious socialist society.

What is antagonism? Comrade Mao said: "antagonism is one form, but not the only form, of the struggle of opposites. " He took the example of bomb to illustrate this view. "Before it explodes, a bomb is a single entity in which opposites coexist in given conditions. The explosion takes place only when a new condition, ignition, is present. An analogous situation arises in all those natural phenomena which finally assume the form of open conflict to resolve old contradictions and produce new things. " Antagonism of contradictions is different from the antagonistic contradictions. Antagonism represents not the nature but one forms of resolving contradictions. Then what is an antagonistic contradiction and what is the antagonistic form of a contradiction? An antagonistic contradiction means that the two sides in the contradiction are fundamentally antagonistic and external conflict is the ultimate form of its resolution. For example, the contradiction between the Chinese nation and the Japanese imperialism was an antagonistic contradiction, and its only resolution is that the Chinese people took weapons to drive the Japanese aggressors out. The antagonistic form of a contradiction means that, the two sides in a contradiction are not antagonistic, only that the two sides of the contradiction take the form of confrontation to resolve it. By saying that contradictions among the people are not antagonistic we do not mean that it is impossible for antagonistic phenomena to occur in them; in some conditions, the form of open conflict may occur.

(2) Causes for the antagonism and intensification of contradictions among the people

First, natural causes. There are some antagonistic contradictions among the people, and some confrontations. Due to the remnants of the old society, and the influence and sabotage of external hostile forces, there are not only some contradictions between the people and the enemy but also a few contradictions among the people with antagonistic nature. The existence of antagonistic contradictions is the natural cause for the intensification of contradictions among the people.

Second, necessary causes. There are some contradictions within the people that are of class struggle nature. Class struggle still exists within certain limits, which will inevitably find their expressions within the people, making some of the contradictions among the people are of class struggle nature. The existence of contradictions with class struggle nature is the necessary cause of possible intensification of contradictions among the people.

Third, important causes. Due to changes in subjective or objective conditions, the nature of contradictions may transform: non-antagonistic contradictions among the people may transform into antagonistic ones, contradictions with no class struggle nature into that of class struggle nature and contradictions among the people into that between the people and the enemy. The transformation of contradictions is an important cause for the intensification of contradictions among the people.

Fourth, objective causes. Contradictions differing in nature may entwine intricately, making the situation more complicated, including: class struggle in certain limits entwines with contradictions among the people that are non-class struggle nature; contradictions between ourselves and the enemy within certain limits entwine with contradictions among the people that are ordinarily and frequently manifested; and antagonistic contradictions that are in a non-dominant position entwine with non-antagonistic contradictions taking the dominant role. For instance, when some of the masses take to the street, generally speaking, the vast majority of them are patriotic, and they belong to the category of the people, but the causes of their demonstration are complex, including sabotage of hostile forces, mistakes in our work that arouse discontent of the masses. Among which, the few hidden scoundrels that deliberately instigate disruption belong to the category of the enemy. The complicated contradictions are the objective cause for the possible intensification of contradictions among the people.

Fifth, subjective causes. In the face of complicated and intricate contradictions triggered by domestic and international factors, the leading officials may make mistakes in understanding and handling them, such as losing vigilance, confusing contradictions, making wrong decisions, improper handling. All these can be the subjective causes for the intensification of contradictions among the people.

(3) Issue of correct understanding and handling of mass incidents.

In On the Correct Handling of Contradictions among the People, Comrade Mao Zedong calls mass incidents and mass unrests as "disturbances by small numbers of people" and makes analysis of them. He pointed out that "In our society, as I have said, disturbances by the masses are bad, and we do not approve of them. But when disturbances do occur, they enable us to learn lessons, to overcome bureaucracy and to educate the officials and the masses." And he also expounded the causes and their handling principles in a scientific and holistic way.

Mass incidents refer to events triggered by contradictions among the people and severely affect, disturb or disrupt public order. Since the mass incident belongs to the category of contradictions among the people, it should be strictly defined, and the majority of the masses and the few bad elements should be strictly distinguished.

The direct causes for mass incidents and mass unrests usually include: serious economic, political and social problems; the damage of people's immediate interests or the fall of their living standards due to some wrong policies or measures; unsatisfied material or other demands; among others. One of the noteworthy causes for mass incidents or unrests is the bureaucracy, corruption and malpractices of our leading officials, which make the reasonable demands of the masses unresolved for a long time, or no effective measures taken. Another reason for mass incidents and mass unrests is the lack of ideological education of the backward masses. Some people, tending to pay attention to immediate, partial or personal interests, make unrealistic demands. In the circumstances, if our ideological and political work lags behind, and the bigotry and erroneous ideas gain the upper hand, the masses may express their discontent toward the Party and government in radical ways. Of course, the fault for lack of education lies also with the officials. Another important reason for mass incidents and unrests is that, during the initial phase of the incidents, some domestic and foreign reactionary forces step in to disseminate decadent feudal and bourgeois ideology and political views, sow discord, spread rumors and create troubles. The key to preventing this is also lies in the leading officials, who should expose these elements hidden behind. Other important causes for the mass incidents and mass unrests include the complicated ethnic relations and the factors of instability in religious life. Because of the complex historical, religious, cultural traditions and other factors, frictions and conflicts occur between ethnic groups, between followers of different religions and between the government and the some of the people. The occurrence of mass incidents or mass unrests is always related to some degree with the defects in the economic and political system. In the reform process, the transition from old to new systems, the adjustment of interest and distribution pattern, etc. , will inevitably highlight social contradictions. During this process, if wrong or improper guidelines, policies or measures are adopted, mass incidents or unrests may happen. They in general belong to contradictions among the people. However, people's reasonable demands often entwine with their illegal forms of expression, so do historical issues with current problems, in addition to the instigation of hostile elements, under these circumstances, improper handling of them will result in mass incidents or unrests.

When dealing with mass incidents, correct principles and methods are necessary. Errors can be turned into fertilizer and bad things into good ones. We cannot declare the matter closed before it is thoroughly settled; instead, we should calmly and prudently distinguish between the two types of contradictions and between mass incidents and mass unrests and should firmly oppose two erroneous attitudes: First, blaming the masses for all the errors, which will encourage bureaucracy of the leading officials; Second, losing vigilance against the bad elements. The correct approach is: do things well and according to the law, meet the reasonable demands of the masses and various contradictions correctly. Those who involved should be guided into the correct track; the few elements that have violated the law are punished according to the law and lessons should be draw, through which we strive to improve our work and educate our officials and masses; and a variety of measures should be taken to fundamentally eliminate the factors of instability. And institutionally, a long-term and effective mechanism for efficiently responding toand handling public demands should be set up and improved.

III. Basic Principles of and Main Methods for Correct Handling of Contradictions among the People and Building a Harmonious Socialist Society

The key to building a harmonious socialist society is to correctly coordinate interest relations and handle contradictions among the people. Comrade Mao Zedong believed that the correct handling of contradictions among the people "is a branch of science worthy of careful study". So correct principles and methods should be adopted to properly coordinate interest relations of all sides and handle contradictions among the people, so as to build a harmonious socialist society.

1. The basic principle of handling contradictions among the people and building harmonious socialist society is to distinguish between the two different types of contradictions (those among the people and those between the people and the enemy) and handle them in different methods

Correct distinction of the two types of contradictions is the premise of correct handling of contradictions among the people. Comrade Mao stressed, " Qualitatively different contradictions can only be resolved by qualitatively different methods. " Generally speaking, the fundamental identity of the people's interests underlies the contradictions among the people, so we should resolutely guard against using the methods for handling contradictions between ourselves and the enemy in the resolution of contradictions among the people.

Firstly, economic methods should mainly be used to resolve contradictions of loss and gain among the people. Loss or gain concerns interests. Economic approach and " overall consideration and proper arrangements" are the main methods for resolving contradictions of loss and gain among the people. Comrade Mao proposed that we should use economic approach to resolve contradictions of loss and gain among the people. Comrade Deng Xiaoping advocated dealing with contradictions of loss and gain among the people in accordance with the principle of overall consideration.

Secondly, democratic methods should mainly be used to resolve contradictions of right or wrong, namely, ideological and political contradictions, among the people. Mao Zedong pointed out that, the only way to settle questions of an ideological nature or controversial issues among the people is by democratic method, method of discussion, criticism, persuasion and education, and not by the method of coercion or repression. And he epitomized the democratic methods into a formula "unity –criticism –unity" . Comrade Deng Xiaoping said that, in political life within the Party and among the people, we must use democratic means and not resort to coercion or attack. Democratic methods comprise mainly: one, democracy and legal system, and two, ideological education.

Thirdly, comprehensive approach should be adopted to resolve various other contradictions among the people. To settle contradictions among the people, there is no fixed formula or a single prescription for all disease; instead, we must take different ways according to specific conditions. This is because sometimes it is difficult to tell whether a contradiction belongs to the contradiction of gain and loss or of right and wrong, or to both, so comprehensive approach should be resorted according to specific conditions of the contradiction. This is just like the divorce of a couple. Sometimes it is difficult to tell whether it is the problem of finance or relationship that causes a divorce. Therefore we should, according to specific contradictions, mobilize all forces, pay attention to the working methods, use integrated measures, keep in mind to build harmonious relations, soothe the discontent of the public, deepen understanding and motivate all positive factors by ways of comprehensive coordination, overall consideration, education and persuasion, set up a regular and systematic mechanism for handling contradictions among the people, so as to timely meet the reasonable demands of public according to the law. By doing this, contradictions among the people and factors affecting our social harmony can be resolved at the sources andvery beginning at the community level.

Fourthly, the fundamental ways are deepening reform, developing productive forces and improve socialist democracy and legal system. We should build socialist material civilization and develop the advanced productive forces, promote the progress of socialist cultural and morality and build socialist political civilization and democracy, so as to lay a firm material foundation, a common ideological and moral foundation and democratic and legal foundation for the resolution of contradictions among the people.

2. Taking the fundamental interests of the people as the starting points and goals in all their words and deeds is the general guideline for all of our party and government bodies to follow in correctly handling contradictions among the people and building a harmonious socialist society

To correctly handle contradictions among the people, the Party and government bodies must always maintain a blood-and-flesh tie with the people, uphold the mass line and take the interests of the people as the basic starting point and ultimate goals of our line, policies and measures. We must focus on and maintain the most immediate and direct interests of the people and their greatest concern, accurately reflect the interests and demands of the masses from different sectors, and resolutely stop any acts that harming people's interests, timely resolve the outstanding problems and difficulties in their lives.

Currently, we should focus on resolving the outstanding problems such as distribution disparities, gaps between regions and between rural and urban areas, problem of unemployment, poverty, issues concerning agriculture, rural areas and farmers, the problems of corruption of some officials. Relevant laws should be adopted to handle and resolve the problems of enterprise restructuring, land requisition and demolition, judicial injustice.

3. Properly balancing the relationship between efficiency and fairness to maintain social fairness on the condition of giving importance to efficiency is a pressing task in our correct handling of contradictions among the people and building harmonious socialist society

Early at the time when he advocated letting some people and some regions prosper before others, Comrade Deng Xiaoping had already attached great importance to the problem of wealth gap and unfair distribution. In the early 1990s, he put forward the suggestion that, at the end of the 20th century when China realized the initial stage of moderately prosperity, all means, methods and program should be focused to resolve problem of unfairness. He pointed out in 1993, "A few people had got so much wealth while the majority of the people didn't, if this situation went on, problems were bound to arise someday. Unfair distribution would lead to polarization and troubles in the future. We should resolve this problem. In the past, we put development first. In retrospect, there are no less problems when we are developed than when we are not. "[1] And "We should use all means, methods and programs to address these problems. "[2] "We should study when to raise this question and how to settle it. I can imagine that the right time might be the end of this century, when our people are living a fairly comfortable life. "[3] Now it is high time to address this problem.

(1) About the relationship between efficiency and fairness, there are many experience and lessons that we can draw on from the long time development of the market economy of capitalism. It is without doubt that, the nature of capitalist system itself determines that it cannot fundamentally solve the relationship between efficiency and fairness, although for a short

---

① See *A Chronicle of Deng Xiaoping*

② *Ibid.*

③ *Selected Works of Deng Xiaoping*, vol. 3, People's Publishing House, 1993, p. 374

period of time it can deal with the issue, because it cannot overcome the inherent contradictions that determine its inevitable destruction.

How to understand the relationship between efficiency and fairness? The answer is: from the nature of the market economy. The market economy is a double-edged sword: On the one hand, it can optimize the allocation of resources and arouse people's enthusiasm, and thus raise efficiency; on the other, it brings about negative things such as unfair distribution and polarization. In its several centuries process of developing the market economy capitalism have enjoyed its benefits and at the same time experienced sufferings from social chaos caused by polarization and contradiction intensification.

The capitalist market economy experienced four major sufferings derived from polarization and intensification of social conflicts: The first happened in the period of capitalist free competition. Focusing only on efficiency and economic growth by neglecting equitable distribution led to the polarization between the working class and the bourgeoisie and the workers' wage decline and absolute poverty. As a result, class contradictions and class struggles intensified. From 1825 on, a major economic crisis broke out every ten years, among which, an unprecedentedly severe global economic crisis broke out in 1873 and lasted for 5 years. Crises often triggered revolution, the turbulent revolutionary workers' movement of the Paris Commune of 1871 was an example. The second one happened in the imperialist period around World War I. Through the war, capitalist countries tried to transfer their domestic contradictions. Capitalism wanted to overcome its inherent contradictions brought about by free competition by way of monopoly, which gave rise to monopoly capitalism, namely, imperialism. Monopoly further exacerbated the polarization and class contradictions of capitalism, the result of which was the outbreak of the October Revolution in Russia. The third one is the global capitalist economic crisis of 1929—1933, a fatal blow to capitalism. It further intensified the class antagonism and conflicts in capitalist countries. Their attempt to shift domestic conflicts led to World War II and the subsequent emergence of many socialist countries. The fourth one is the state monopoly period of capitalism after World War II. Further intensification of the internal contradictions and polarization generated an unprecedented social crisis. Some far-sighted capitalist politicians began to mediate the internal contradictions of capitalism by launching capitalist reform. They paid more attention to equity and took a series of measures to ease class contradictions by cutting a part of the high profits gained by capitalists, including levying on high taxes on progressive income and inheritance, establishing sound social security and social welfare systems. These measures led to the formation of a huge middle class and olive-shaped social structure and made capitalism enter a relatively stable stage of development. As can be seen from this that, in its course of development, although it promoted rapid economic growth, capitalism in its early stage of development put too much emphasis on efficiency in the neglect of fairness, leading to polarization, social conflicts and turbulence. The early labor movements, World War I, World War II and the postwar labor movements, almost put capitalist system to an end. So Marx said that while developing production, capitalismproduces its own grave-diggers. His work *Capital* fully reveals the intrinsic contradictions of capitalist society in the free competition stage. After World War I and World War II and the post-war worker movements, they began to pay attention to the problem of fairness while stressing efficiency; with this, social contradictions in the capitalist society were temporarily eased. But the problem of high welfare in turn highlighted the issue of efficiency. They paid more attention to equity and took a series of measures to ease class contradictions, including cutting a part of the high profits to make secondary distribution, levying high taxes on progressive income and inheritance, establishing sound social security and social welfare systems. These measures led to the formation of a huge middle class and olive-shaped social structure, thus ease the class contradictions and made capitalism enter a relatively stable stage of development. But on the other side, the problem of high welfare in turn highlighted the problem of efficiency. Take the typical welfare-oriented country Sweden for example. It implements the policies of high taxes, high wages and high welfare, so that provides for the country's citizens from the cradle to the grave. But now it encounters the problems of lacking development motivation and too heavy a financial burden.

(2) The issue of efficiency and fairness is of historical, specific and relative nature.

Efficiency and fairness have different content in different historical conditions and different countries. That means, a thing that is fair in one country is not necessarily fair in another, or fair in one period is not necessarily fair in another, because every period has its own outstanding problems. New problems will arise after old ones have been resolved. Efficiency and fairness are contradictory to each other, but can be unified under certain conditions. The expense of certain degree of income equality and fairness is sometimes necessary for efficiency; but efficiency will be affected if unfairness comes to a certain level, which needs to be resolved at this point. Under socialist conditions, efficiency and fairness can be properly balanced, because the pursuit of unity of efficiency and fairness is an inherent requirement for socialism. Paying attention to efficiency and striving to maximize the development of the productive forces with less input is an essential requirement of socialism and is in line with the fundamental and long-term interests of the people, and also the premise and foundation for achieving fairness. Efficiency can ensure the steady economic growth and fairness in the true sense at a higher level. Efficiency will be constrained and affected by unfairness, vice versa.

(3) Giving priority to efficiency with due consideration to fairness is a general principle. The understanding and implementation of this principle should be combined with the realities of different times with the target of optimizing the balance of efficiency and fairness.

As regards the realities in China, at the beginning of our reform and opening up, the priority was to address the issue of efficiency and make the cake bigger without overlooking fairness. But at a certain stage of development, the issue of fairness will stand out. Egalitarianism is a kind of unfairness, so is the large gap of income. Today, egalitarianism and income gap coexist, with the latter more outstanding to a certain degree and scope. Development is the absolute principle and top priority, and efficiency is a necessity for development. But on the other hand, to keep a healthy and sustainable development, we should, under the precondition of maintaining efficiency and growth, fulfill a relative fairness by allowing for a certain degree of income differences. Achieving and maintaining fairness involves not only the economic issue of wealth distribution, but also the political and social issue of the rights of citizens, social status, democratic governance, freedom and equality, public services, judicial justice, etc. Therefore, fairness is generic concept, involving not only the issue of income. Right now we should focus on the addressing of income distribution. It should be said that, in the primary stage of socialism, China has certain conditions to realize a greater fairness.

What do we mean by greater fairness? It refers to a fairness on the basis of fundamental identity of interests of the people, a fairness that is determined by its ownership system in which public ownership is the mainstay, by itsdistribution system that distribution according to work as the main form coexist with other forms of distribution, including distribution according to production factor, and by its political system in which the people are the masters of the country.

Under the premise of greater fairness, we place realize and maintain fairness on a more prominent place, and should regard the issue of fairness from holistic and long-term points of view, to gradually create a social environment of fairness in terms of legal system, policies and institutions and establish a social fairness guarantee system with fairness of rights, opportunities, rules and distribution as it main content. Fairness necessarily involves distribution, which requires that, in the premise of ensuring efficiency, we should never relax our vigilance against the negative side of the market economy, and pay high attention to the basic role fairness of distribution played in promoting social progress, and we should pay attention to fairness of distribution and the establishment of a fair distribution system.

(4) At present, the main problem in our income distribution is that irregular income is out of proportion while social security income is insufficient, which specifically manifested in two points:

First, in the primary distribution, the irregular income gained by some people is out of proportion, leading to income disparity. In the primary distribution, we must adhere to the principle of giving priority to efficiency, and implement the principle of distribution according to work and production factors, so as to arouse the enthusiasm of the people, realize the incentive income distribution, unleash all the vitality contained in work, knowledge, technology, management and capital. Presently, our market order is not standard enough yet, causing in the primary distribution the unfairness in starting line and the out of proportion of monopoly income, which is gained through the monopoly of the non-open markets, and irregular income. In addition, some people gained a large amount of illegal income through smuggling, taking advantage of various loopholes in our policies, especially through corruption, leading togreat gap of income and resentment of masses. Efficiency can only be guaranteed through when the principle of distribution according to work and to factors of production is fully implemented.

Second, in our secondary distribution, social security income is insufficient and long-term mechanism is absent. The fundamental solution to this problem is the establishment of a long-term and institutionalized social security mechanism.

(5) The way to solve this problems is, while adhering to the principle of giving priority to efficiency and unleashing all the vitality contained in work, knowledge, technology, management and capital, we should gradually increase the weight of fairness in distribution to take fairness into more consideration, streamline relations in distribution, regulate distribution order, focus on solving distribution gap caused by irregular income and problems in redistribution, so that a fair income distribution system is established. To this end, the following steps can be taken:

Firstly, we should solve the issue of fairness of distribution in primary distribution to ensure that all social members have equal opportunities. Generally speaking, the existence of differences in primary distribution, which is conducive to the improvement of efficiency, is reasonable. The problem with the primary distribution in our society is, some people have gained a large amount of illegal income by taking advantage of various abnormal factors and unequal competition conditions and opportunities, such as monopoly, corruption, manufacturing and selling counterfeits, smuggling, evading tax by deceit and other means, etc. , causing the widening gap in primary distribution. In these circumstances, the government should take steps to solve them. In the system in which the public sector is dominant, only by ensuring equal conditions of production and economic relations and progressive establishment of a good market order for equal competition, can fairness of conditions and equal opportunities in primary contribution be safeguarded. To fulfill reasonable primary distribution, we must establish a sound market mechanism, coupled with necessary administrative measures, that is, take efficiency as the premise, and implement the principle of distribution according to work and to production factors to make sure that incentive and efficiency distribution are surely in place while checking irrational incomes, controlling incomes gained by monopoly and banning illegal income.

Secondly, we should solve the issue of redistribution to ensure the reasonable distribution of income of social security. Primary distribution, in which efficiency is achieved through market mechanisms, will bring a certain degree of income disparity, which requires to be adjusted by the government through redistribution. At present, the prominent problems in China's redistribution include: unsoundness of system, no guarantee for security income, the increasingly widening gap between high and low income groups. This requires that the government should strengthen adjustment to properly adjust distribution pattern and effectively solve the problems of widening income gap between regions and among social members, so as to realize common prosperity. In this regard, measures can be taken include economic legislation and policies and tax, financial and administrative means, such as tax reforms, taxation adjustment of different incomes; the increase of transfer payment and public spending; the feedback of industry to agriculture and cities to countryside; support to backward and rural areas; efforts to solve urban and rural residents living in poverty; strict enforcement of the minimum wage system; raising the income of low-income level; expanding middle-income group, etc.

Thirdly, we should establish a sound social security system to solve the problem of fairness of distribution. The government should establish a social security system consisting mainly of social insurance, social relief, social welfare and social charity. More attention should be paid to low-income group to ensure their minimum standard of living is ensured; social security coverage, especially those concerning unemployment, healthcare and elderly support, should be strengthened; social relief and social welfare increase should be increased and security income should be guaranteed.

4. The long-term guarantee for correctly handling contradictions among the people is the formation of a relatively balanced interest distribution pattern, reasonable structure of social members and an economic-political system favorable to harmony, stability and development of society

In the primary stage of socialism in our society, a harmonious society should have a reasonable social structure consisting of two levels:

First, a relatively balanced distribution pattern. Both the egalitarian and polarized distribution patterns are unfavorable to social stability, harmony and development. We should form a relatively balanced income distribution pattern in which a certain degree of differences and fairness are kept.

For this purpose, in the first place we should ensure the equality of competition conditions and opportunities. It is necessary to stress the fairness of results, but at the same time we should also concern about the fairness of starting point, environments, conditions and process. We should strive to establish a good market order and distribution pattern to ensure equal opportunity to education and completely solve the problems in compulsory education, provide free skill training for migrant workers and the unemployed in urban areas, and provide an equal starting line and fair environment of competition for all social members. In the second place we should ensure the relative balance of income distribution among social members. To this end, we should build a distribution pattern adaptable to the market economy, in which distribution according to work is dominant and a variety of modes of distribution coexist, incentive-based, efficiency-based and social security-based distributions properly integrated and a sound social security system should be in place.

Second, the formation of a reasonable social structure consistent with the income distribution pattern. A "gourd-shaped" polarized society, in which the poor account for the overwhelm majority and the few rich areincredibly wealthywhile middle income group is small in size, is not conducive to social harmony. In contrast, an "olive-shaped" social structure, in which the middle income group constitutes its largest proportion, is conducive to social stability, harmony and development. We should raise the income of low-income groups and increase the proportion of middle-income group to form an "olive-shaped" social structure and control social differentiation and social gaps within a proper range, so that all social members share in the fruits of reform and opening up.

We should establish an economic-political system that is consistent with the primary stage of socialism, the reasonable distribution pattern and social structure that is conducive to coordinating interest relationship of all parties and mobilizing the enthusiasm of the different members of society, social harmony and stability, in order to ensure the long-term stability of a reasonable social structure in terms of system and institutions.

5. The improvement the capability of the leadingofficials in handling contradictions among the people, building a harmonious society and maintaining social stability is the key link in the correct handling of contradictions among the people and building a harmonious society

The CPC is the governing party in China, so the Party and its leadingofficials play an extremely important role in our political life. This requires that the governing capability of the Party and its leading officials should be improved, in whichthe capability of correct handling contradictions among the people, building a harmonious society and realizing the balanced and all-round development of the society are its important parts. The Party's leading organs and officials at all levels should enhance their investigation and study, make in-depth exploration of the laws and characteristics of contradictions among the people and explore new ideas and new methods for handling contradictions among the people, so as to provide theoretical and practical support for the prevention, response to and resolution of all kinds of conflicts. They should analyze the development and changes of classes, strata and interest groups in a scientific way, have a full knowledge of the conditions and causes of their differentiation and combination, their interest demands and relations, in order to develop effective countermeasures for coordinating all kinds of contradictions; they should be good at social management under the market economy, and build and improve the mechanisms of social consultation and dialogue, the system and mechanism for complaints through letters and visits, and a warning mechanism, pre-plans and a working mechanism that is quick in reaction, effective in directing, orderly in coordination and efficient in operation in dealing with emergences; they should study and grasp the laws and characteristics of mass work in the new era, take the issues that are the most difficult, most practical and most concerned to the people as their focus of work and be good at dealing with them.

Appendix V

Scientifically Understanding the Essence and Causes of the Global Financial Crisis by Using Marxist Stand, Viewpoint and Method: *Capital* and *On Imperialism* Revisit[①]

In August 2007, the subprime mortgage crisis broke out in the United States, resulting in the most serious financial crisis in the country since the Great Depression, which has subsequently led to the most severeglobal financial crisis and the associated economic and social crises since the 1930s. The crisis is still lingering and its further developmentremains to be seen.

Facing this situation, we should re-read Marx's *Capital* and Lenin's *On Imperialism*, so as to use Marxist stand, viewpoint and method to reveal the nature and underlying causes of the crisis in a scientific way, and based on it, to put forward effective countermeasures against it and system guarantee and long-term mechanism to ensure the sound and stable development of socialism with Chinese characteristics.

I. We Must Recognize the Nature and Causes of the Financial Crisis from the Perspective of Nature of Capitalism

With Regard to the causes of the global financial crisis triggered by subprime mortgage crisis of the US, as well as its impact on China and its countermeasures, opinions differ, although some of them are

---

① This article was first published in *Studies on Marxism*, No. 2, 2009, and was appreciated by several leading cadres of the CPC Central Committee.

insightful. Some people believe that the important reasons include the Americans' overconsumption that far exceeds their incomes, the uncontrolled debt, the uncontrolled market, the unlimited derivative financial instruments, the unchecked speculation, the unrestricted high profits and high incomes, and so on. Some others hold that the consumption pattern, financial regulatory policies, operational modalities of financial institutions ofthe US and the economic structures of the US and the world are to blame. Still othersargue that the real estate bubble is the source of the financial crisis troubles; the financial derivatives covered up the huge risk, while the lagging financial regulatory mechanisms made the so-called "financial innovation" lose control like a runaway horse. Some believe that the financial crisis was attributable to the moral degeneration of some financial tycoon. Some think the crisis isessentially the failure of the American market economy governance and operation modes based on neo-liberalism. There are also some people contribute the crisis to the disadvantages of capitalism, the profit-seeking nature of capital and the greed of financial capital, which, to some extent, involves the fundamental system of capitalism. But, generally speaking, most of the explanations touch only on the phenomena or operation level rather than the very essence of the issue. There are far from enough analyses applying Marxist stand, viewpoint and methodsto scientifically reveal the causes of the crisis, to predict its development trends or propose countermeasures.

On the other hand, communists all around the world, taking Marxismas the guide, try to analyze the situation, reveal the nature and causes of the crisis as well as make action plans, expressing their viewson this issue and showing the strength of communists. A research made by Dr. Yu Haiqing from CASS Marxism Academy shows that, some communists from Europe and America have made in-depth analyses of the origin, root causes and essence of the crisis, which trace the root of thecrisis into the nature of capitalism. This merits our consideration. [1]

Most capitalist governments blame "uncontrolled specul ativeactivitiesin financial markets", "unhealthy competition" or "excessive borrowing" for the severe crisis and hope to solve it and restore the economy through government bailout and normalizing existing systems and mechanisms. In

---

[1]   See Yu Haiqing, "Comments on the Current Financial Crisis by Communist Parties of the Developed Countries in Europe and the U. S. ", in *World Studies on Socialism* (《世界社会主义研究动态》), no. 50, 2008.

sharp contrast, some communists in Western capitalist countries believe that, although the immediate causes of the crisis are the absence of regulation, the inappropriate monetary policies, the imbalanced financial development, etc., its root causes cannot be simply found from the problems of financial ecology. They commonly believe that the crisis has its deep-rooted system reason and that it marks the bankruptcy of neo-liberalism and is the inevitable result of the development of the inherent contradictions of capitalism.

French Communist Party believes that the crisis stemmed from the excessive greed of the financial institutions, but in the final analysis it derived from the crisis of the capitalist system. Rather than a bolt from the blue, or just an "out of control" of capitalism, the crisis is the inevitable result of the defects of capitalist system and the mercenary nature of capitalists. The global crisis is not just a financial or economic nature; it is also a political crisis and the crisis of the capitalist mode of production as well. The underlying problems lie in the capitalist system. The Communist Party of the United States believes that the crisis is a product of the neoliberal capital accumulation and governance mode, which seeks to restore the momentum of American capitalism and its dominance in domestic and international affairs. It is also the consequence of the weaknesses and contradictions in American capitalism. The crisis drew the world and American economy into a new downturn. The Communist Party of Germany holds that the financial crisis has a global impact and has brought global economy into recession; and the real sector of the economy is increasingly affected by it. It is not caused by the mistakes of the bankers, nor is it the failure of state supervision over the banking sector. The bankers simply took advantage of the loop holes in the system, resulting in the rampant speculative activities. Speculation has been the constituent elements of capitalist economy, which, in the stage of monopoly capitalism, has become a determinant factor permeated into all aspects of the economic and political lives.

The Communist Party of Britain thinks that the current economic and financial crisis cannot be mainly attributed to the "subprime" crisis. It pointed out that the underlying cause is that, in order to serve the interests of big enterprises and their market system, almost all economic sectors in Britain, including public sector, are under the control of the finance capital. The Portuguese Communist Party believes that the crisis should not be interpreted merely as the burst of the subprime bubble; rather, it is also the result of increasing financialization and rampant speculation of world economy by big capitals. It demonstrates that dogmas of the neo-liberalism such as "non-interventionist state," the "invisible hand of the market," "adjustable market," etc. , are all wrong. Capitalism once again exposed its inherent nature and profound contradictions. Capitalist system failed to solve the problems facing human society; on contrary, it has worsened the inequality, injustice and povertyof society. The Communist Party of Greece believes that the crises are inevitablefor capitalist economy, whose inherent decadence cannot be solved by any governance policy. The financial crisis once again shows that capitalism cannot avoid the outbreak of periodic crises, and that it is inevitable for socialism to replace capitalism.

From this we can see that, in analyzing this crisis, if we take it only from financial perspective or as a financial phenomenon without associating it with the inherent contradiction of duality incommodity and commodity exchange in private system, the profit seeking nature of financial capital and the nature of capitalist system, we can hardly answer the question such as "Why the 'perfect' market system like that in the US failed in preventing the outbreak of the financial crisis?" nor can we seethe essence and underlying causes of the crisis, nor can we recognize that the root cause of this crisis lies in the capitalist system.

China is a socialist country introducing the market economy. If we fail in understanding the causes and essence from the perspective of system, we cannot find a fundamental ways to prevent and overcome the crisis, nor can we build a long-term and institutional crisis prevention system. Therefore, a correct understanding of the essence of the crisis is of profound and practical significance for China in its efforts to build a socialist market system and establish a long-term and institutional crisis prevention system.

II. The Inherent Contradictions of the Two-fold Characters of Commodities Determine the Outbreak of Latent Crisis, the Private Ownership in Capitalist Society Makes the Outbreak of Economic Crisis Unavoidable

It is a scientific way that Marx started from commodity to analyze capitalism. Commodity is the most basic cell and most universal existence in the market economy, and commodity exchange relations are the most basic relations in the market economy. Therefore, the inherent contradictions in commodities and commodity exchanges represent and contain the basic contradictions in the market economy and the social formation in which the market economy takes the dominant role. To understand the characters of the market economy and a society dominated by it, we must start from the inherent contradictions and the substantial relationship between commodities and commodity exchange. Commodities and commodity exchange gradually developed along with the emergence of social divisions of labor and private ownership. Capitalist market economy is the outcome of development of commodity production to a certain stage under the conditions of private ownership. After commodity and commodity exchange developed into the dominant role in the economy, they gave birth to a global market system, a capitalist market economy characterized by the capitalist private ownership.

Marx first revealed the inherent contradictions of two-fold character in commodities. He believes that a commodity is the unity of value and value in use, the two are unified and contradictory: "unified" means that they are interdependent and condition one another; "contradictory" means that they are mutually exclusive and opposite, even mutually antagonistic. The contradictions between value in use and value of commodities are determined by two-fold nature of labor, that is, concrete labor and abstract labor. The value in use of a commodity is determined by the concrete labor, but for it to be exchanged in the market, the concrete labor must be changed into abstract general labor that can be compared, which is the congealed general human labor embodied in commodities. The general human labor can be abstracted as quantitative socially necessary labor time, by which the value of commodities is generated.

Since commodities have duality of value and value in use, it inevitably has two forms, namely, the forms of value and value in use. Value in use of commodities are the concrete commodities while their value forms are manifested as forms of universal equivalent.

At the beginning, commodities were directly exchanged, and their sales and purchases are unified and made at the same time and same place. With the development of commodity economy, commodity exchange evolved into commodity circulation, with sales and purchase not conducted in the same time and space, or separated. Some people did only sales and other purchases. And value and value in use were increasingly separated. The value form of commodities developed from universal equivalent, such as gold, to gradually become currency, such as gold coin; and currency further evolved into paper money, such as the US dollar; and into invisible virtual currency, such as securities, credit cards. With the development of commodity economy, money not only have the function as means of circulation, but also functions of as means of reserve and payment; money cannot appear in trading, that is, delay in payment. Currency gradually evolved into something virtual and far from the reality of commodity exchange. The exchange value of commodities becomes more and more independent, and separation between the value and value in use manifests itself in the independence of currency, and further the independence of paper money, and finally the independence of currency symbols. This separation makes excessive printing of banknotes become possible, so do the independent operation of securities that gradually evolved into a virtual market and virtual economy (virtual economy based on virtual value symbols). When money becomes an important means of commodity circulation, it already makes economic crises become possible; when currency become a means of currency circulation, the possibility of crises become larger. In the circulation of commodities, currency and commodities are separated; in the circulation of currency, paper money, symbols of currency and commodity universal equivalent are separated from the value represented by currency, so are time and space of currency circulation and commodity circulation, which further increased the possibility of economic crises.

Marx made detailed analysis of the inevitability of contradictions of the two-fold character of commodities under the conditions of capitalist private ownership. Under the condition of private ownership, the contradiction between concrete labor and abstract labor is manifested as the contradiction between private labor and social labor, which is the basic contradiction of commodity production. Because commodity production is private nature, so are commodities, which determine that, the separation and antagonism between value and value in use, between commodities and currency, between concrete labor and abstract labor, are irreconcilable. This results in the vicious cycle of periodic economic crises. The contradiction of two-fold character of labor inherent in commodities determines the further evolution of the contradiction between value and value in use, which manifests itself as the opposition between commodities and currency, between real economy and virtual economy. Under certain conditions, private ownership makes this inherent contradiction more intensified so that it becomes more and more antagonistic and insurmountable. In the several hundred years of capitalist development, currency has become more and more separated from commodities, so are virtual economy from real economy, which constitutes the internal cause of financial bubbles, financial crises and economic crises.

Under the condition of capitalist private ownership, currency becomes capital in the hands of capitalists. Any capitalist must have money when he begins with his exploiting acts. To turn money into capital, the money holders must be able to buy the labor of the free laborers. The added value produced through the combination of labor and means of production in the circulation of capital is surplus valuethat capitalists gained by exploiting workers. Capital, essentially speaking, is the value that can bring about surplus value. The only motive behind and immediate purpose of capitalist production is to grab more surplus value, so the capitalist is personified capital. Capital has a two-fold character: on the one hand, it pursues the maximization of profits, so it is profit-oriented and greedy; on the other, it can strongly promote economic development and production.

Capital, in the process of capitalist production, manifests itself as three forms: money capital, production capital and commodity capital. They are identical yet increasingly separated and contradictory. In its development, money capital becomes more and more independent to form loan capital, banking capital, share capital and the credit system, thus giving rise to loan capital market and such marketable securities as stocks, corporate bonds, marketable bonds, government debt, real estate mortgage bonds and regular income to the owners as well. This produces an illusion that money begets money. Credit sales and purchases emerged in currency circulation form extremely intricate relations of interlocking credit. The development of paper money, securities and credit system gradually breed the virtual capital and virtual market. The virtual capital is separated from real capital, so is the quality and quantity of them, in other words, the quantities of virtual capital and real capital are separated from each other. According to statistics of some experts, the virtual wealth (capital) of the United States is as high as $400 trillion, 30 times of its real capital. With the development of capital, the formation of monopoly capital, financial capital and financial oligarchies, "It reproduces a new financial aristocracy, a new kind of parasite in the guise of company promoters, speculators and merely nominal directors; an entire system of swindling and cheating with respect to the promotion of companies, issues of shares and share dealings. It is private production unchecked by private ownership. "[1] Capitalist private ownership is the deep-rooted cause of system for the financial crisis, while the separate, profit-seeking and greedy nature of financial capital is the immediate cause of it.

After entering the age of large-scale machine industry in the 19th century, capitalist society had experienced an economic crisis every few years, the serious of which triggered overall social crises. Economic crises were the expressions of the inherent and insurmountable contradiction of the two-fold character of commodities under capitalist private ownership, in which the former determines the possibility the economic crisis while the later makes it occur.

The fundamental cause of crises in capitalist societies lies in its system of private ownership. On the one hand, development of the productive forces and capital are highly socialized, but on the other hand the means of production and the results of production are increasingly monopolized by a handful of oligarchs. The basic contradiction of socialized production and the private ownership of means of production make the latent crisis in commodity production become inevitable. This proves that, the economic crisis is outcome of the capitalist economic system and the inherent contradiction of capitalist mode of production. To eliminate the crisis, we must destroy the capitalist system.

III. The Financial Crisis Originated in the US Is an Inevitable Crisis of Capitalism Whereas the Combination of the Market Economy and Socialism Is Possible to Prevent Similar Crisis

The subprime crisis broke out in the US unstoppably spread the world and developed into a global economic crisis, which once again proved that Marx's conclusions are truth that periodic economic crisis in capitalist society is inevitable and that capitalist mode of production will doom. Marx believed that capitalism cannot avoid periodic economic crises, " Hence the phenomenon that crises do not come to the surface, do not break out in

---

① *Collected Works of Marx and Engels*, vol. 25, People's Publishing House, 1974, p. 496

the retail business first, which deals with direct consumption, but in the spheres of wholesale trade, and ofbanking, which places the money-capital of society at the disposal of the former. "① As long as the capitalist private ownership has not been changed, the inherent contradictions of commodities and the inherent internal contradictions of capitalism cannot be resolved fundamentally, which will inevitably manifest themselves as periodic worldwide economic crisis.

Economic crises in capitalist societies are periodic, occurring every few years. In 1825, economic crisis for the first broke in Britain; 1836, it broke again in Britain and spread to the United States. In 1847—1848, an economic crisis swept Britain, USA and continental Europe. Then, crises broke again in 1857, 1866, 1873, 1882 and 1890, the most serious of which was that occurred in 1873 that greatly promoted the concentration of capital and production and the formation and development of monopoly organizations, and advanced the transition of capitalist society to monopoly capitalism.

In the early of the 20th century, economic crises occurred in 1900—1903 and 1907, and then in 1920—1921, 1929—1933 and 1937—1938. The most serious one was that occurred in 1929—1933, which lasted for 4 years, resulting in the 44 percent drop of industrial production, 66 percent drop of trade volume in the entire capitalist world and a total of 30 million employees in 1933.

After World War II, periodic economic crises in capitalist society continued, with nine occurring in the US, respectively in 1948, 1953, 1957, 1960, 1969, 1973, 1980, 1990 and 2007, among which, crises in 1957—1958, 1973—1975, 1980—1982, 2007 were the four serious ones that spread to Canada, Japan and the major countries in western Europe.

The economic crises in the course of capitalist development form an endless cycle of crisis –recovery –crisis. Its momentary prosperity is only a sign of its next crisis. Capitalism will come to an end in the periodic crises. When it is in the peak of the cycle, capitalists always trumpet that capitalist will remain "permanent prosperity," "exist for millennia"; but when a crisis comes, this myth will burst like a soap bubble. Economic crises are the periodic outbreaks of the antagonistic contradictions in the

---

① *Collected Works of Marx and Engels*, vol. 25, People's Publishing House, 1974, p. 340

capitalist system, which clearly and unmistakably indicate that, capitalist mode of production has its historical limitations and that the antagonistic contradictions of capitalism will intensify, and sometimes will become sharper.

The global crisis triggered by the financial crisis in the US is a historic event since the advent of the 21st century. It is not only a serious financial crisis, but also a deep economic crisis, an ideological crisis, a social crisis and a crisis of the capitalist system as well. In other words, it is an overall crisis of capitalism, which will bring about profound social changes. Historically, every global crisis of the capitalist society had caused significant changes in world pattern of the time. This financial crisis, in the long run, will bring great adjustment and turmoil to world economy, and its comprehensively devastating, profound and enduring negative impacts will bring significant and sustained devastating effects to world economic and social development for a long time. An all-round global economic recession has begun. As a result, the world situation and structure will undergo major changes and the development course of the world is at an important turning point.

1. The global financial crisis originated from the US is an overall crisis of capitalism

The financial crisis originated from the United States, although broke out first at and concentrated on financial sector, and have brought a destructive effect to financial system, it is not limited to the financial sector, but has spread non-financial sectors, from the virtual economy to real economy, from economic areas to social areas, and from operational level to levels of concepts, models, institutions and systems, affecting all areas, levels and aspects of global capitalism.

2. The global financial crisis originated from the US is a global crisis of capitalism

Capitalist globalization is the globalization of capitalist relations of production. Therefore, the global crisis is the globalization of the crisis of capitalism. Soon after breaking out, it quickly swept the Western countries, developing countries and all over the world. The trouble maker is the US, but it's the whole world that is the sufferer that pays the cost. This demonstrates the negative effect of globalization. The U. S. financial monopoly capitalists as masters in shifting crises have exported the crisis to other capitalist countries and developing countries that have close linked with them, causing global panic and crisis.

3. The global financial crisis originated from the US is a system crisis of capitalism

Financial crisis is not unique to the US but a typical system crisis of capitalism. The social productive forces are highly globalized and socialized, international finance highly monopolize by a handful financial oligarchs in Wall Street: this contradiction of extreme privatization is the expression of the basic contradiction of contemporary capitalism. Wealth created around the world is unprecedentedly abundant and concentrated; meanwhile, polarization between rich and poor is becoming more serious. Fundamentally speaking, this crisis, rooted in intensified inherent and insurmountable contradictions of capitalist system, is a contemporary exhibition of the unstoppable trend toward the defeat of capitalism. The crisis tells us that, the fundamental contradictions of capitalism have not been overcome; on the contrary, they manifest themselves in an intensified way. Some people blame neo-liberalist ideas and model for the crisis, aiming to take it as a counter evidence of the correctness of controlled capitalist ideas and governance. But this argument touches only the institution rather than systemlevel. In fact, both liberalism and conservatism are only remedies that can only temporarily ease instead of fundamentally saving the capitalist system, which has once again be proved as incurable by this crisis.

4. The global financial crisis originated from the US is the ideological crisis ofcapitalism

The crisis makes people rethink the ills of the capitalist system and re-examine the hypocrisy and anti-science nature of capitalist ideology. On the surface, it is a crisis for some capitalist thought such as neo-liberalism, but in factit is a crisis stemming from capitalist core values, universal values, concepts of human rights, democracy, etc. Neo-liberalism, ideologically, is actually an ideology that represents the interests of and fully meets the needs of the super-financial monopoly capitalists to manipulate the monetary market and exploit the world. Some personages of insight in capitalist countries began to re-examine new liberalism as well as the capitalist system. In the meantime, China's socialist reform and market economy trial under public ownership have achieved great success. This makes those stubbornly insist on capitalist system step up their attempts to sell Western ideology to China and their westernization, differentiation and privatization practice inChina. This is a counterevidence of the crisis of capitalist ideology.

5. The global financial crisis originated from the US is a counterevidence that China's socialist market economy is successful

Chinese people have established a socialist market economy with Chinese characteristics that for the first time in human history combines the market economy with public ownership. Prior to it, market economy is associated only with private ownership. The essential difference between socialism and capitalism lies in their ways of possessing means of production, so is the difference between the socialist market economy and capitalist market economy. Capitalist private ownership of the means of production determines that the crisis triggered by the two-fold character contradictions of capitalist commodity economy is incurable. In contrast, in the condition of the socialist market economy, the potential crisis because of the two-fold character contradictionof commodity production can be avoided, and if it happens, can be overcome. This is determined by socialist public ownership. The socialist market economy has the nature of a market economy, so the inherent contradictions in its commodity production are immutable; but the potential crisis arising from it is avoidable. Under the socialist market economy, however, if our vigilance is relaxed or our preventive measures are not effective, they may develop into crises. We should have a clear awareness of the profit-seeking nature of capital, especially financial capital, to prevent them from bringing about disorder or going extreme. Under public ownership, profit-seeking nature of capital can be adjusted or put under control; while under conditions of private ownership, it can evolve from being profit-seeking to greedy, which although can be controlled temporarily, not permanently.

IV. Capitalism and Liberalism: System and Essential Level vs. Institutional and Operation Level

The global financial crisis originated in the US make people have a more sober-minded understanding of the neo-liberalist philosophy of market economy governance and its operation model, which is like a good medicine for those who have blind faith in liberalism and capitalism. It should be noted that, there are some differences between faith in neoliberalism andin capitalism. The former is the faith in a specific philosophy and model of governance of capitalist market economy, while the latter is in the fundamental system of capitalism.

Capitalism and liberalism are identical yet different, with one involving the level of system and essence and other involving institution and operation.

The so-called neo-liberalism, inherited from Adam Smith's theory of free competition, advocates reviving classical liberalism and minimizing government intervention in the economy and society. It is also labeled as market fundamentalism or capital fundamentalism, or "total non-interventionism." Its main conceptions were expressed in the Washington Consensus in the late 1980s and early 1990s. Its popularity was related with the failure of the Keynesian economics in coping with the problem of stagflation in the late 1980s when former US President Ronald Reagan and former British Prime Minister Margaret Thatcher were in power. Therefore, it is also known as the "Reagan doctrine." Neo-liberalists worship the force of capitalist free market. They think that the market under capitalism is of high efficiency, even almighty; all problems ineconomic operation can be solved by self-regulation of the market. They advocate radical privatization, decentralization, further open international and domestic markets, trade liberalization, interest rates; they oppose nationalization and support putting the economic operation of individual countries into the systems of globalization dominated by the World Bank, International Monetary Fund and the World Trade Organization. Neo-liberalists are enthusiastic proponents of the globalization led by superpowers and the global economic, political, and cultural integration, which in fact, is global capitalization. Neo-liberalism is essentially anti-socialist.

Neo-liberalism is regarded by its proponents as a panacea that can cure all diseases. Neo-liberalists believe that the "invisible hand" of the market can solve all the problems. Therefore, they strongly propose the ideas of free market economic model and governance. But practice has proved it is wrong. In terms of governance principles and model, in market economic activities, the roles of "two hands" must be played instead of using only the "invisible hand" and abandoning the "visible hand," although the use of them must be identified in a scientific way. If the "invisible hand" is let unchecked, it will inevitably exacerbate the negative aspects of the market economy, which will lead to crisis when it comes a certain degree. Therefore, the "visible hand" is needed to make adjustment, in order to overcome the inherent flaws of the market and promote its healthy development.

is the mainstream ideology of contemporary capitalism and the core philosophy and values of financial monopolies and international cartels, so we must resolutely oppose them. But on the other hand, on the level of institution and operation, it is an economic theory about how to govern capitalist market. As a method of market economic operation, neo-Neo-liberalism liberalism has some positive effects in this respect, some of its valuable understandings and practices we can learn from. In this sense, itis distinct from capitalism as a fundamental system. As for the relationship between capitalism and neoliberalism, the former is the fundamental system that can have different governance concepts, institutions, models, operation methods, etc. , while the latter is determined by the former and serve the former. Although it created different institutions and models in its development, capitalism has never changed its system and nature.

A social formation is composed of specific economic, political, cultural and social and other systems, which is of course consisted of specific economic, political, cultural, social and other institutions. Social system constitutes the main content and essential symbol of the social formation and is a generic term. Among which, the economic system belongs to the economic basis of the society and the political, cultural, educational, legal and other systems belong to its superstructure. The economic system is the sum total of relations of production of a society and economic basis, the most important part of which is the ownership of its means of production. The economic system of a society determines its basic nature. The political system of a society is the "superstructure of the economic basis" with state power or state system at the core. In other words, it involves the questions of "Who is in power?" and "Over whom the dictatorship is exercised?" Economic and political systems determine the fundamental nature and the main features of a society. Socialism is marked mainly by and refers to its economic and political systems. Once the social system is established, it should be relatively maintain stable in order to create a relatively stable social environment to develop production. When the relations of production can no longer correspond to the development of its productive forces, social change will occur.

Social institution refers to the specific forms of relations of production and superstructure based on a social system, known as " specific institutions ". The economic institutions corresponding with certain economic system are the specific structure and forms of certain economic relations, so is relationship between political institutions and the corresponding political system, that is, the form of government. In other words, it involves the issue of "how the state power is exercised". After the establishment of socialist economic and political society, the major tasks facing the working class party and the people are to build the social institutions that correspond with its development of productive forces.

The relations between social systems and social institutions are dialectically interdependent yet contradictory, unified yet complementary. Social system determines social institutions and social pattern; the formation of social institutions is subject to social system. But on the other hand, social institutions have a certain degree of independence of and counterforce to social system. Good institutions can strengthen social system while a bad system can constrain the functions of the institutions. Institutions can be either consolidating factors or damaging factors to a system. Under an established system, there may be a variety of institutions to choose, and institution may be changed with the development of the existing system; and there may be a variety of institution models coexisting within the same system; new institutions can also absorb some form and function from the old ones. Capitalist political and economic systems are opposed to its socialized production, which is manifested intheir contradictions. But to some degree, capitalist institutions are separated from its system, and under certain conditions they can promote the development of capitalist production. The reverse is true with the relationships between socialist system and its institutions: the former corresponds with the development of its productive forces, but socialist system may also be separated from its social institutions to some degree, and under certain conditions may even hinder the development of socialist productive forces.

Capitalism has had a history of several hundred years from free market capitalism, monopoly capitalism to its present stage, in which, state monopoly, international monopoly, international financial monopoly, etc. have replaced individual monopoly. All these forms of monopoly are the features of modern capitalism. There are different opinions about how to define the present stage of capitalism. Some people think it is the monopoly capitalism described by Lenin, some think that it has begun a new phase.

About the characteristics of free market capitalism and capitalism in general, Marx and Engels had made in-depth analyses and came to the conclusion that capitalism will fail ultimately. They believed that, the inherent contradictions of free market capitalism are insurmountable. The repeated crises will eventually lead to revolution and thus sound the death knell of capitalism. At the turn of the 20th century, with the development of capitalist production, free competition gave way to monopoly, which replaced competition and took the leading and dominant position, but this did not overcome the inherent contradictions of capitalism, let alone its inevitable historical end of failure. Applying Marxist methods, Lenin made a scientific analysis of the monopoly capitalism and revealed that monopoly have not changed the inherent contradictions inherent in capitalism, and came to the conclusion that imperialism is the highest stage of capitalism and monopolistic, parasitic and moribund capitalism.

Lenin's judgments about the general characteristics and development trends of the monopoly capitalism are correct, although his prediction about the time of its doom is a bit shorter. Lenin said: "The complexity of the process and disguising its substance can delay but not avert final collapse. " The subsequent development proved Lenin's views. The outbreak of World War I and World War II were the results of the intensification of the internal contradictions of capitalism, which further worsened after World War II. The rise of socialism, the internal and external troubles of capitalism, the periodic economic and social crises and the development of contemporary capitalism confirmed Marx and Lenin's conclusions. Capitalism as a system, after going through its early progressive and rising period, the period of frequent crises and the period of slow development, is inevitably going toward its final collapse.

After World War II, the development of capitalism was beset with troubles. After institutional reform, coupled with the development of high technology and globalization, it entered a period of relatively stable and rapid development. At the same time, socialism came into a hard time, some countries even fell into dilemma due to ideological mistakes, highly centralized planned economies and complex objective and subjective reasons, particularly the disintegration and system changes of the former Soviet Union and socialist countries in Eastern Europe in the 1980s and 1990s. Some people regard events in former Soviet Union and Eastern Europe as the victory of capitalism and failure of socialism. In fact, those changes do not mean the failure of the socialist system, but rather show that the model or way they chose do not work, and a highly centralized planned economy is not impractical. The further development of the United States and other capitalist countries can only shows that the reform policies and model of the Western developed capitalist countries adopted have temporarily eased the inherent contradictions of capitalism. Capitalism is bound to collapse in the futurebut not in the near future, this is because: First, from perspective of existing system, it still has some space and room for the development of its productive forces; Second, from the perspective of institutions, there are not a few advantages that can maintainits system and promote the development of its productive forces and thus the existence of capitalism. When these two conditions no longer exist, capitalism will come to an end.

Although capitalist private ownership is bound to end, the system of market economy suitable to private ownership has its advantages, relying on which, capitalism, in just a few hundred years, has created a development miracle unmatched in thousands of years in human history. But market economy is a double-edged sword that has both positive and negative sides. As how to make use of the market economy, that is, how to face the market economy and overcome its negative sides, there are two different notions in capitalist development: one advocates state effective control of the market that may be called "regulated market economy," such as Keynesianism or conservatism; another is laissez-faire governance, that is, liberalism. In the process of capitalist development, the two notions and governance models had been adopted alternately depending on the situations.

Liberalism prevailed in the free competition stage of capitalism, during which, the market was entirely unregulated. After World War II, in response to the situation, regulated market governance, such as Keynesianism was adopted and macro-regulation was strengthened, which helped capitalism ride out the storm and entered a development period of "twilight brightness." In this context, when the drastic changes occurred in former Soviet Union and Eastern Europe, some people wrongly regarded it as the failure of the socialist system and planned economy and victory of capitalist system. They further believed that regulated market economy also didn't work and only liberalism was operational. This gave birth to Reaganism and Thatcherism. Liberalism essentially advocates capitalist system and fully privatized market economy. In this sense, it is identical with conservatism in that they take maintaining capitalist system as their purpose; the only difference lies in their means.

Although the immediate cause of the current financial crisis is the free market policy, the underlying causes of it lies in the inherent contradictions of the capitalist system, rather than technical or operational reasons. The crisis proves the failure of liberalist ideas and modes of governance; more importantly, it demonstrates that capitalist system will inevitably fail.

Some people in China also support liberalist thought and the governance model of free market economy, advocating full privatization and the abandonment of macro-regulation. Some even radically hold that socialist system and market economy cannot fit each other so that capitalist system should be introduced. But historical facts have showed that new liberalism had brought waves after waves of disasters to human kind, which has been best shown in some countries in Latin America. Since 1990s, they accepted the Washington Consensus to make liberalization, privatization and financial deregulation, resulting in big setbacks and troubles.

V. It Is Necessary to Treat both the Incidental and Fundamental Aspects of Financial Risks

Marx's analysis of and basic views on the contradictions of capitalism and its nature provide the following important inspirations for us to look into the global financial crisis originated in the US, and to think about how to effectively avoid similar crisis in China.

1. We should understand the insurmountable inherent contradictions of capitalism and the underlying system cause and nature of the crisis from the perspective of internal contradictions of commodity production and exchange under private ownership

The insurmountable inherent contradictions of the capitalist system lies in its commodity production and exchange, and the capitalist private ownership of the means of production determines that these inherent contradictions are antagonistic and insurmountable, and are the root causes of periodic economic crisis of capitalism. They are bound to bring capitalist system from prosperity to decline and to its inevitable final collapse. To scientifically explain the nature and causes of the crisis, we must start from analyzing capitalist system. The crisis is a concentrated reflection of the inherent contradictions of capitalist system and manifestation of the internal contradictions of commodity production under private ownership. It indicates that, although at this stage the crisis can be solved, capitalism is going to its doom in waves after waves of financial crises.

2. We should understand the similarity and differences between socialist and capitalist market economies from system level and nature perspectives, scientifically analyze the possibility of crisis in socialist market economy and effective measures for preventing it

Marx's scientific analysis of the inherent contradictions in commodities and commodity exchange in market economy is applicable to any form of market economy, whether capitalistor socialist. But on the other hand, due to the differences in ownership of means of production, market economy in different social systems will have different properties, characteristics and thus results. The private ownership nature of the capitalist market economy determines the ultimate inevitability of economic crisis, while the nature of public ownership of the socialist market economy determines that economic crisis can be avoided or prevented. The essential difference between socialism and capitalism is the ownership of means of production, which determines the different nature of their systems and their market economies. China's socialist market economy is associated with its public ownership, so it has both the characteristics of commodity production in general and the inherent contradictions in commodity production in particular. Therefore it has the possibility of financial and economic crisis. If we ignore this possibility and do not take any measures to avoid and prevent it, the healthy development of the socialist economy will be affected. On the other hand, the public ownership condition determines that effective measures can be taken to avoid and prevent the potential financial and economic crisis triggered by the contradictions in commodity economy.

3. We must have a full understanding of the dual character of market economy and capital, give full rein to socialist system to prevent negative aspects of market

Market economy has a dual character. Its positive side is that, it can effectively allocate resources and mobilize people's enthusiasm in the most efficient way thus promote economic development; Its negative side is that it is possible to cause economic crisis, because enterprises are seeking profit maximization, which brings about great blindness and overproduction. Under the conditions of capitalist private ownership and market economy, on the one hand, it has playeda powerful role in promoting economic development and obtained huge achievements in its several hundred years of development. However, capitalism and private ownership also allows the negative aspects of the market economy to expand continuously and constantly divorce away from its positive aspect, so that the inherent contradictions in commodity and commodity exchange keeps intensifying, leading to waves of waves of economic crises. Capital bred out by market economy is born with dual character: on the one hand, its profit-seeking nature can have a positive role in regulating the market, allocating resources, mobilizing enthusiasm and promoting economic development; on the other hand, it can lead to economic imbalance and polarization, resulting in a serious crisis posing a negative impact on economic and social development. Under the conditions of capitalist private ownership, the greedy nature of capital cannot be eventually containment. Marx believed that in the capitalist mode of production, "the production of surplus value, or money, is the absolute law of this mode of production. " Capital is the value that can bring surplus value. Therefore, capital with a profit-driven nature will never give up its pursuit of surplus value. "With adequate profit, capital is very bold. A certain 10 percent, will ensure its employment anywhere; 20 percent, certain will produce eagerness; 50 percent, positive audacity; 100 percent, will make it ready to trample on all human laws; 300 percent, and there is not a crime at which it will scruple, nor a risk it will not run, even to the chance of its owner being hanged. " In the history of the development of capitalism, the profit-driven nature of capital has been fully exposed. From primitive accumulation, to colonial deprivation, to war plunder, money "comes into the world with a congenital blood-stain on one cheek, capital comes dripping from head to foot, from every pore, with blood and dirt. " None of the developed capitalist countries in the world was developed by merely relying on its democratic system, but by exploiting the surplus value of the laborers and other working people in their own and other countries. They built their "prosperous country" withthe sweat and blood of the working people. After hundreds of years, the barely veiled exploitation or plunder is difficult to sustain. Capitalism, after coming to the stage of international financial monopoly, has changed their approach of grabbing surplus value and way of exploitation. They monopoly the financial market and global economy under the mask of financial innovation, with a real aim of moving money from other countries to their own pocket. The establishment of the dollar empire is a case in point. It is the avarice of financial capital that gave rise to today's financial crisis.

One of the essential differences between socialism and capitalism and between socialist market economy and capitalist market economy is the ownership of capital. Under capitalist system, the highly concentrated private ownership is currently demonstrated in the high degree of monopoly of international financial capital, which exacerbates the greed and speculative activities of capital and its uncontrolled operation speed. Once they come to the extent of damaging capitalist system, notions and operations would come out from capitalist system itself to control them; otherwise the system would be destroyed. This kind of notions or governance models, such as Keynesianism, supports government intervention, known as conservatism. But once the situation improves, free market governance principles and practices known as liberalism, will gain the upper hand. In the history of capitalism, the alternation of crisis and recovery produced the alternate prevalence of conservatism and liberalism. At present stage, they still can maintain the development of capitalism, but the inherent ills of capitalism will eventually lead its doom.

4. In response to financial risks, we should both treat its symptoms and root cause, which means that we should prevent them both from the institutional level and system level

In response to the current crisis, although more and more strong measures have been taken by many countries, the effects are not obvious yet. This indicates that the measures treated only the symptoms but not the causes and that it is necessary to solve both the immediate and root causes of the crisis; otherwise financial and economic crisis cannot be avoided.

We should have a sober-minded understanding of the dual character of capitalism: On the one hand, it has some advanced nature in promoting human civilization and some of its institutions and mechanisms are reasonable; but on the other hand, its disadvantages are fatal, which will lead to its inevitable doom. The current financial and economic crisis demonstrates the superiority of socialist system. But absolutely pure public ownership is not suitable to the actual situations of productive forces in socialist countries; the socialist market economy with public ownership as the mainstay is a correct road whereas highly centralized planned economy does not accord with to the law of socialist development; in adopting the socialist market economy, the strength of socialist system must be given to full play, which means, we should adopt a macro-regulated rather than a free market economy. In the process of socialist development, the superiority of the socialist system can only be better displayed when public ownership and the market economy are integrated.

In summary, measures for avoiding and preventing financial crisis should be taken at following three levels. First is the system level. We must unswervingly adhere to socialist economic system with public ownership as the mainstay and socialist political system with people as masters of the country, and establish fundamental and standard regulations for the management of the private sector of the economy, the market economy and virtual economy. Second is the institutional level. We should firmly establish and improve the socialist market economic system and its relevant credit system. Third is the level of market regulation. We should establish effective supervision, regulation and prevention measures, especially in the financial sector and monopoly industries. At present, although the measures from operation level taken by the Chinese government in response to the current financial crisis are cautious, fast and effective, from system and institutional levels, more comprehensive, strategic, forward-looking methods and approaches all still needed.

This book is the result of a co-publication agreement between China Social Sciences Press (China) and Paths International Ltd (UK)

Title: On Social Interests and Conflict: A Socialist Analysis of Contemporary China
Author: Wang Weiguang
Translated by Huang Yusheng & Lin Wanping
ISBN: 978-1-84464-268-7
Ebook ISBN: 978-1-84464-390-5
Copyright © 2015 by Paths International Ltd, UK and by China Social Sciences Press, China

Paths International Ltd
PO Box 4083
Reading
United Kingdom
RG8 8ZN
www.pathsinternational.com

Published in United Kingdom

CPSIA information can be obtained at www.ICGtesting.com
Printed in the USA
BVOW03*1117260515

400889BV00004B/4/P